DISCOVERY IN THE JUDEAN DESERT

Discovery in the Judean Desert

GÉZA VERMÈS

Docteur en Théologie
Licencié en Histoire et Langues Orientales

DESCLEE COMPANY

NEW YORK · TOURNAI · PARIS · ROME   1956

ACKNOWLEDGMENTS

Photographs courtesy of M. l'abbé J. Starcky of the Centre National de la Recherche Scientifique, Professor M. Burrows of the American Schools of Oriental Research, M. M. Spitzer of the Foundation Bialik of Jerusalem, Israel and M. N. Avigad, professor at the Université Hébraïque.

The quotations from D. C. Rabin's translation of the Zadokite Documents are reprinted with the permission of Dr. C. Rabin and the Clarendon Press, Oxford, England.

CONTENTS

ILLUSTRATIONS

1. *Judean desert*
2. *The Qumrân Plateau seen from the North-West. The ruins are on the right side of the tents. (Photo Starcky)*
3. *The first Qumrân Cave. (Photo Starcky)*
4. *The ruins of the main building seen from the South-East. On the left, the cliff of the caves. (Photo Starcky)*
5. *The large cistern of Qumrân seen from the North. The foreland of the cliff comes to an end at Ras Feshkha. (Photo Starcky)*
6. *A hall in the main building. (Photo Starcky)*
7. *The Commentary of* Habakkuk *Scroll, column XI. (Cliché American Schools of Oriental Research)*
8. *The* Manual of Discipline *Scroll, column X. (Cliché American Schools of Oiental Reseach)*
9. *The Hymns Scroll, Hymn IV. (Cliché American Schools of Oriental Research)*

first part

DISCOVERY
IN THE
JUDEAN DESERT

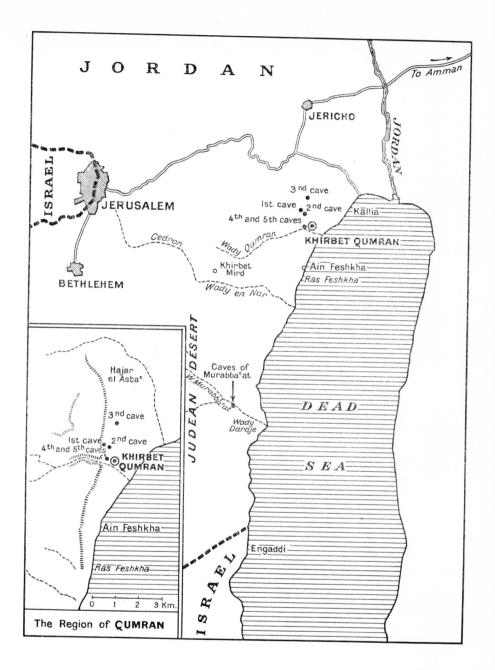

1 - Judean desert

2. — The Qumrân Plateau seen from the North-West. The ruins are on the right side of the tents.

The road from Jerusalem to Jericho covers, for a good part, the ancient Roman road; it descends abruptly, for there is between Jerusalem and Jericho a difference of level of over a thousand meters. The traveler coming from Jerusalem's Old City finds himself at once in the heart of the Judean desert (fig. 1), inhabited here and there by Bedouins and, quite lately, by robbers.

The car leaves the main road to Amman, Jordan's capital, shortly before reaching the city where Christ healed the two blind men and received hospitality in the house of Zacchaeus. It turns down to the Dead Sea, stretching out in gorgeous blue, with the mountains of Moab of a brown-violet tinge providing a background of unparalleled grandeur.

The car progresses now on a cattle-beaten track, leaving on the left Kalia with its Jewish thermal establishment, sacked during the recent Palestinian war. A plot of land stretches out between the steep, chalky cliffs on the right and the Dead Sea, almost totally flat with scarcely any protuberances to break its monotony.

The cliff is seen to meet the beach at a point called Râs Feshḥa, shot through with rifts and natural caves, most of which are very difficult of access. One of those caves will be ever memorable for having yielded ancient Hebrew scrolls, the first to be discovered in modern times. Although many other hiding places have been discovered since, that one will always remain, for those at least who witnessed the startling discoveries from the beginning, the cave, the cave of the manuscripts, the cave of Aïn Feshḥa, the cave of Qumrân.

Aïn Feshḫa and Qumrân are two neighboring sites, and the cave is named impartially after either of them, although they are not of the same importance for us.

Looking down from the top of the cliff, one will discover a kilometer southward a heap of big stones: this is the Ḫirbet (ruin) of Qumrân [1] *(fig. 2).*

Aïn Feshḫa is three kilometers farther south. The land, after the crossing of Wadi-Qumrân, grows less desert-like, and vegetation is found even in the dry season, owing to the presence of springs, the last of which is the magnificent Feshḫa spring, of a faintly chemical flavor, flowing into the Dead Sea. Again to the south, some twenty kilometers off, is Engaddi, but the border between Israel and Jordan is not easily crossed.

The most ancient Hebrew scrolls to be known remained hidden in that vicinity for some two thousand years. Skins and papyri have been preserved owing to the dryness and crushing heat characteristic of a spot which is, as it were, the bottom of the earth, for the Dead Sea is 394 meters below sea-level. Archaeologists, too, left it undisturbed, as the experience of the last hundred years left them convinced that any attempt to find in Palestinian soil a document prior to 70 B.C. would prove futile.

The first documents were discovered by sheer chance. But since then, clandestine diggers and official explorers have been busily at work on the lookout for new treasures: a tireless exploration that has many a surprise yet in store.

---

[1] The Arabs of the region pronounce it *Goomrahn;* it is, according to their tradition, the site of Gomorrah. This was adopted a century ago by F. de Saulcy (*Voyage autour de la Mer Morte*, I, 1853, pp. 165–167).

chapter one

SUCCESSIVE DISCOVERIES

IN THE DESERT OF JUDAH

1. The First Lot of Manuscripts

The first tidings of ancient Hebrew scrolls discovered in Palestine came to Europe from the United States in the spring of 1948, rousing everywhere the keenest interest.

Professor W. F. Albright, the Biblical scholar and world-famous archaeologist, announced with great enthusiasm, in the April number of the *Bulletin of the American Schools of Oriental Research,* "a sensational discovery," nay, "the greatest manuscript find of modern times." [1] Professor G. E. Wright was no less enthusiastic, to judge by the title of his article in *Biblical Archaeologist,* "A Phenomenal Discovery," and asserted that *"the most important find ever made in the field of Old Testament manuscripts* has just been officially announced. . . ." [2]

Those two articles made known to the general public the incredible importance of the new discovery. At first, interest centered on the complete scroll of the Book of Isaiah, which according to Professor Millar Burrows dated from the First, and according to Professor Albright, from the Second century B.C. It was known, moreover, that the Syrian Orthodox monastery of St. Mark had acquired a "Commentary" of the Book of Habakkuk, "a curious manual of rites and discipline" of an unidentified Jewish sect,[3] and a fourth scroll which it was impossible, so far, to unroll.

---

[1] *B.A.S.O.R.,* 110, 1948, p. 2.   [2] *B.A.,* XI, May, 1948, p. 21.
[3] W. H. Brownlee felt convinced from the beginning that it was the Essene community. Cf. *B.A.,* XI, 1948, p. 22.

It was then announced that the Jerusalem Hebrew University also possessed a scroll of Isaiah,[4] a collection of "hymns recalling the Psalms," the story of a war, and the Hebrew original of several Apocrypha known hitherto only in their Greek translation.[5] None of the manuscripts in his possession, Professor Sukenik asserted, was posterior to Jerusalem's storming by the Romans, i.e. 70 A.D.[6]

This piece of information was swiftly spread by the press, rousing the liveliest curiosity. Could it be true, or was it just a hoax? Archaeological fakes are met with all too often, especially where Oriental antiquities are concerned. We were anxious to know more before making up our minds, and our wishes were to be quickly gratified. A few months had scarcely elapsed when the eventful, and somewhat obscure, story was made public.[7]

FROM ST. MARK'S MONASTERY TO THE AMERICAN SCHOOL

On February 19, 1948, Father Butros Sowmy, the librarian of the Syrian convent of St. Mark, rang up the Director of the American School of Oriental Research, asking his help toward identifying some ancient Hebrew scrolls; their catalogue, he said, provided no information about them.

An interview between the monk and Professor John C. Trever, acting for the Director, took place on the same day, and the course of events went on in the best Oriental style. While Dr. Trever was examining the five scrolls which Father Butros submitted to him, the latter decided to reveal the *true* story of the discovery.

The manuscripts, of course, had not emerged out of some dusty spot in St. Mark's library; they had been found in 1947, in a cave close to the northern extremity of the Dead Sea, by Bedouins of the Taamre tribe. These men tried unsuccessfully to sell them to a dealer in antiquities from Bethlehem, who thought the manuscripts were Syriac and of no great value, and finally sold most of their find to Mar Athanasius Yeshue Samuel, Jerusalem's Syrian Metropolitan who was in residence at St. Mark's.

The colorful story has been recounted by Mar Athanasius himself.[8]

As soon as he heard about manuscripts discovered in the spring of 1947 in the vicinity of the Dead Sea, he made up his mind to buy them. That arid and unhealthy spot of the Judean desert had remained uninhabited ever since the beginning of the Christian era; any manuscripts found there must of necessity be very ancient:

---

[4] Some confusion was felt for a time about the scroll. Professor Sukenik having published several chapters of the Saint Mark manuscript, specialists wondered whether the Hebrew University possessed a copy of its own; this proved later to be the case.

[5] Cf. *B.A.S.O.R.*, 110, 1948, p. 3. Those fragments have never been mentioned again.   [6] Cf. *Ibid.*

[7] J. C. TREVER, *The Discovery of the Scrolls*, B.A., XI, 1948, pp. 46–57.

[8] *The Purchase of the Jerusalem Scrolls*, B.A., XII, 1949, pp. 26–31.

the inference might be ingenuous, but not, on the whole, unreasonable.

The three Bedouins arrived at the convent in due time, but the porter slammed the door in their faces: the sight of workmen offering dubious antiquities (the scrolls were dirty and torn) is an everyday occurrence in Jerusalem. The Metropolitan's hope was thus nearly ruined, but he managed to find two of the Bedouins again, who eventually sold him their property; the price he paid was, it may safely be guessed, not an exorbitant one. The third Bedouin, however, ill-pleased with the hospitality of the convent, decided to try his luck elsewhere, thereby causing great joy to Professor Sukenik.

After the purchase of the manuscripts it was necessary to check the sellers' story about their location: a cave close to the Dead Sea, where the documents had been found hidden in jars. This was confirmed by two friends of Mar Athanasius who were brought to the spot. The cave was found still to contain pieces of cloth, pottery débris and an intact jar which they decided to leave where it was, in view of its weight and the heat. Two other intact jars had been found by the Bedouins upon their first visit. Their owner would not hear of selling them; he needed them, he maintained, for keeping water, and all the Metropolitan's efforts and eloquence proved of no avail. He knew why when, sometime later, Professor Sukenik published the photograph of two well-preserved jars he had bought.

Mar Athanasius was not particularly interested in old manuscripts for their own sake. When he acquired the scrolls he took steps to contact competent people in order to ascertain their nature, date and value. He consulted various personalities, a Syrian employee of the Department of Antiquities, Father Marmardji, of the École Biblique, Father van der Ploeg, now Professor at the University of Nijmegen, and a Jewish "specialist" who turned out to be none other than the journalist, T. Wechsler, of whom I shall speak again; the verdict was unanimous and negative: the manuscripts possessed no value whatever.

Here the Metropolitan's story brings us to his consultation with the American School.

Dr. Trever recognized the Book of Isaiah at once in the biggest scroll; a quick paleographic perusal convinced him that the whole lot was of great antiquity. He spared no pains in getting permission for the photographs and the measures. Some photographs he sent at once to Professor Albright, proposing a date with which the latter entirely agreed. "My heartiest congratulations for the greatest manuscript discovery in modern times . . . ! I should choose a date some time about 100 B.C."

Dark clouds had been hovering over Palestine skies for some months. The U.N.O. had decided, in November 1947, on partition of the country, and sanguinary riots broke out at once. The members of the staff of the American School were leaving for the United States. They were permitted to publish the photographs taken by Professor

Trever, and were relieved to learn that the precious manuscripts had been transferred to safety in a neighboring land.[9]

PROFESSOR SUKENIK'S NEGOTIATIONS

The learned archaeologist of the Hebrew University heard the story of ancient manuscripts having been discovered in November, 1947, from a Moslem dealer in antiquities in Bethlehem. Acquiring the document was a delicate matter; he contrived to bring it to a successful conclusion through the help of Moslem and Christian friends on November 27, the very day when the United Nations decided on the creation of the State of Israel. The scrolls which had not been brought to the Syrian convent came to enrich the Museum of Antiquities of the Hebrew University; and now Professor Sukenik set out to acquire the lot purchased by Mar Athanasius as well.

The latter did not hesitate to acknowledge that a businessman sent by him had approached Professor Sukenik and had loaned him the St. Mark's manuscripts for two days.[10]

Determining the exact time when the two men came into touch is not easy. According to Mar Athanasius the Americans had priority, and Professor Sukenik did not see the manuscripts before the end of February. The latter, on the contrary, maintains that he was the first to whom the scrolls had been offered, in the first days of February, and that the Metropolitan's envoy had even pledged him his word that priority would be his for eventual sale.[11]

To carry on the argument would be idle, since the purchase has become an accomplished fact. Anyway, the energetic Israeli Professor succeeded in forestalling his American colleagues; as early as 1948, in spite of war raging in Palestine, he published the first general survey with abundant illustrations of the manuscripts in his possession.[12]

Here the first stage of the Dead Sea discoveries comes to an end. In spite of valuable information, many points remained up to that time obscure.

It is therefore, not surprising that most scholars did not feel inclined to share Professor Albright's optimism concerning the documents' authenticity.

---

[9] The Metropolitan was later to take them to the United States. Quite recently, on February 13, 1955, Israel's Prime Minister announced at a Press conference that Israel had just bought the four Manuscripts of St. Mark's Monastery. Thus all the great scrolls of the first cave of Qumrân are now to be found in Jewish Jerusalem.

[10] Cf. B.A., XII, 1949, p. 31.   [11] M.G., II, pp. 12–15.

[12] Meghillôth genûzôth . . . , Seqîrah ri'šônah (First report), a book beginning with the following dedication: "Let Israel remember her sons and daughters who gave their lives to free their people and their country, among them my younger son Mattithyahu and his comrade David Sprintzak, of the Israeli Air Force, who, having fought the Egyptian fleet come to attack the city of Tel-Aviv on Iyyar 26, 1948, did not come back."

Professor Sukenik himself was to die on February 28, 1953.

Not to mention Professor Solomon Zeitlin, who suspected a "hoax" [13] without waiting to know more about the discoveries, most Biblical specialists were averse to taking a definite position; many were not slow to recall some of the most notorious archaeological frauds, above all the Shapira Deuteronomy.[14]

Any doubts, however, concerning the authenticity of the scrolls, were soon to be dispelled. It was announced that the cave visited by the Bedouins two years previously had been rediscovered and explored by archaeologists.

2.   The Hiding Place of the Manuscripts

No specialist, it has been seen, was able to reach the manuscripts' cave in the course of 1947 and 1948. The only ones to pay it a visit were the Bedouins, Mar Athanasius's emissaries, and, much worse, clandestine diggers. Trever could not risk so dangerous an expedition, and much less could Sukenik. The American scholar confessed with some melancholy that "the last chapter of one of the greatest discoveries remains yet to be written." [15]

M. Philippe Lippens, Belgian U.N.O. observer in Amman, undertook to shed light on the "missing final chapter." [16] He set out to gather information, and with the help of two officers of the Arab Legion, found the cave, arriving there in the last days of January, 1949.

The cave is situated twelve kilometers south of Jericho, four kilometers off the Dead Sea (fig. 3).

Mr. G. L. Harding, Director of the Service of Antiquities in Amman, and Father R. de Vaux, Director of the Ecole Biblique et Archéologique de Jérusalem, arrived at the spot a few days later, and started a methodical exploration of the site. They worked there, helped by three specialized laborers, from February 8 to March 5, 1949.[17]

THE EXCAVATION [18]

Results appeared, at first sight, meager enough; no new scroll was found anywhere. Supposing some important fragments had been

---

[13] *A Commentary on the Book of Habakkuk. Important Discovery or Hoax?* *J.Q.R.*, XXXIX, January, 1949, pp. 235–247.

[14] For instance: G. LAMBERT, *Les manuscrits découverts dans le désert de Juda,* *N.R.Th.*, March 1949, p. 286. — W. BAUMGARTNER, *Der palästinische Handschriftenfund, Theol. Rundschau,* XVII, 1949, p. 344.

[15] *B.A.*, XI, 1948, p. 56.

[16] Cf. G. LAMBERT, *La grotte aux manuscrits du désert de Juda, Revue Générale Belge,* January, 1950, pp. 405–424.

[17] Cf. *Comptes rendus de l'Académie des Inscriptions et Belles-Lettres,* 1949, pp. 96–103.

[18] For more details, see R. DE VAUX, *La cachette des manuscrits hébreux, R.B.*, April, 1949, pp. 234–237 and *La grotte des manuscrits hébreux, ibid.,* October, 1949, pp. 586–609.

left by the first Bedouins, they had all been picked up by clandestine diggers.

That first campaign did not, however, prove fruitless. It led to the discovery of pottery, cloths, and hundreds of tiny manuscript fragments.

Ceramics: there were, according to the archaeologists, two main groups:

a) *Hellenistic shards* of about fifty jars, corresponding lids, and two lamps;

b) a handful of *Roman shards,* including the fragments of two lamps and a pot.

The *cloths* found in the cave were obviously used as envelopes for the scrolls.

Now for the fragments of manuscripts, six hundred of which were found in the hiding place and the rest purchased later from the clandestine diggers: they are, for the most part, very tiny, written on skins and papyri, mostly in square Hebrew characters. Some skin pieces are however covered with archaic, so-called Phoenician characters, and are parts of chapters XIX to XXII of *Leviticus.* Some fragments were part of the scrolls belonging to St. Mark's and the Hebrew University, the *Hymns,* and the *War of the Sons of Light with the Sons of Darkness.*[19]

Those fragments were evidence that the cave had once been a rich library, containing both Biblical books and Hebrew Apocrypha.

The account drawn by Mr. Harding and Fr. de Vaux was read at the Paris Académie des Inscriptions et Belles-Lettres, at the session on the 8th of April, 1949;[20] it proved conclusively that no reasonable doubt about the authenticity of the manuscripts could be entertained any longer.[21] The archaeological surroundings, moreover, argued very earnestly in favor of the scrolls' great antiquity; too earnestly if anything, for subsequent exploration has disproved the opinion that the hiding place was definitively closed at the end of the Second or beginning of the First century B.C. at the latest.[22]

But before proceeding with the story of the discovery, there are two problems that first need elucidation.

THE DEPOSIT

We must find out, to begin with, why such a lot of old manuscripts were put in a place to which access was so difficult.

The cave may have been a cemetery for discarded scrolls, or a library, or a hiding place.

---

19 Cf. G. L. HARDING, *The Dead Sea Scrolls, P.E.Q.,* LXXXI, 1949, p. 113.

20 R. DE VAUX–L. HARDING, *La cachette des anciens manuscrits hébreux, Comptes rendus de l'Académie des Inscriptions et Belles-Lettres,* April-June, 1949, pp. 96–103.

21 Professor Zeitlin, however, who is the most tenacious opponent, has so far remained unshaken.   22 Cf. *R.B.,* October, 1949, p. 596.

The first opinion was advanced by Professor Sukenik: [23] the cave, he asserted, was an Essene *Geniza*.[24] He felt in fact so sure about it that he called his work: "Hidden Scrolls from a *Geniza* found in the Judean desert."

As a matter of fact, since the cave was discovered, Fr. de Vaux' opinion that it was a hiding place is well-nigh universally accepted: "Those scrolls of various age and carefully arranged in jars of the same period, are not some pieces thrown aside, but constitute archives, or a library, taken to safety at some particularly critical moment." [25] The situation of the cave favors such an interpretation: why should anyone choose a spot so difficult of access, unless for the purpose of keeping undesirable visitors at a distance from highly valued documents?

FIRST ROBBERY IN ANTIQUITY

The cave must have contained, to judge by the number of fragments of various manuscripts collected therein, a good many documents besides those discovered by the Bedouins. What, then, of the others?

The explorers, considering a recent plunder on a great scale as unlikely, hold that it probably occurred a very long time ago.[26]

Some Biblical scholars were not slow to remember, even before the hiding place was discovered, a find of which Origen was not unaware: Hebrew and Greek manuscripts were found in the vicinity of Jericho, in A.D. 217, under the reign of Caracalla.[27] The few Roman shards which I have mentioned were considered as the remains of that event in the beginning of the Third century.[28]

Specialists in Jewish traditions remembered the "Jericho Pentateuch," highly valued by the Masoretes, doubtless for its antiquity.[29]

Mr. Harding here observes that the neighboring Qumrân site was still inhabited at the beginning of the Third century. A cursory archaeological survey made by him in 1949 led him to this conclusion.[30]

The explanation appeared quite satisfactory until, one day, Professor O. Eissfeldt drew attention to a letter written about A.D. 800 by the Nestorian Patriarch Timotheus, mentioning the recent discovery of Hebrew manuscripts in a cave near Jericho.[31]

[23] Cf. *M.G.*, I, pp. 10 and 16.
[24] i.e. the place where the Jews put religious manuscripts worn out of use; they may not destroy them, out of reverence for God's name.
[25] *R.B.*, April, 1949, p. 236.   [26] R. DE VAUX, *R.B.*, 1949, pp. 236 and 587.
[27] Cf. P. KAHLE, *The Cairo Geniza*, London, 1947, pp. 161–162.
[28] *R.B.*, April, 1949, p. 236.
[29] E. L. SUKENIK, *M.G.*, I, p. 15. — J. SCHIRMAN, *Les manuscrits hébreux récemment découverts dans le désert de Juda*, Semitica, II, 1949, p. 46.
[30] *Illustrated London News*, 10.1.1949, p. 493.
[31] *Der Anlass zur Entdeckung der Höhle und ihr ähnliche Vorgänge*, Th. L.Z., LXXIV, 1949, col. 597–600. Timotheus' letter was published by O. BRAUN, *Der Katholikos Timotheos I und seine Briefe*, Oriens Christianus, I, 1901, pp. 138–152.

It was then remembered that Jacob al Qirqisânî, the famous Jewish Karaite writer, mentioned a Jewish sect called the "men of the cave," *al-Maghariya* in Arabic, because their books had been found in a cave.[32]

Fr. de Vaux, who at first was in favor of the hypothesis of an early robbery going back to the beginning of the Third century, inclines now to the opinion that the cave was visited and plundered twice, the second time being the occurrence recounted by Qirqisânî or Mar Timotheus.[33] Other authors, above all Professor Kahle, are convinced that the cave was robbed in the Eighth century only.[34]

It is too early yet to decide who deprived us of the library's treasures. We cannot solve the riddle until subsequent discoveries shed more light upon it.

3. Exploration of the Qumrân Ruins

One kilometer south of the cave are ancient ruins, the *ḥirbet* of Qumrân. Explorers often visited them, never undertaking any close investigation.[35]

Mr. Harding and Fr. de Vaux, upon exploring the cave, made a cursory survey of these ruins, so cursory in fact that they found no archaeological data connecting them with the hiding place of the scrolls.[36]

Such, however, was not P. Kahle's opinion; he felt convinced that the scrolls could only have been deposited in the cave by the inhabitants of ancient Qumrân, and that excavations of the ruins, therefore, would not fail to shed light on the whole problem.[37]

An excavation was accordingly decided upon in Jerusalem, and the first campaign was conducted by Mr. Harding and Fr. de Vaux from November 24 to December 12, 1951. A first account of the excavations was communicated to the Académie des Inscriptions et Belles-Lettres on April 4, 1952; it proved to be of the highest interest.[38]

THE QUMRÂN EXCAVATIONS

The main edifice is a rectangular building of thirty meters by thirty-seven meters (fig. 4); it is surrounded on the northeast, west and south by secondary buildings.

Ceramics were plentiful. The smaller articles (pots, pitchers,

---

[32] R. DE VAUX (on Fr. Barthélemy's suggestion), *R.B.*, July, 1950, p. 421. An English translation of Qirqisânî's text can be found in L. NEMOY, *Karaite Anthology*, New Haven, 1952, p. 50.   [33] *R.B.*, July 1950, p. 420.

[34] *Th.L.Z.*, 1950, col. 540. – *V.T.*, 1951, p. 41. – *Die hebräischen Handschriften aus der Höhle*, Stuttgart, 1951, pp. 59–60. J. L. TEICHER, *J.J.S.*, 1951, pp. 79–80, has expressed the same opinion.

[35] Fr. de Vaux mentions de Saulcy, Rey, Clermont-Ganneau, Conder, Masterman, Dalman and Avi-Yonah. Cf. *R.B.*, January, 1953, pp. 88–89.

[36] Cf. *R.B.*, October, 1949, p. 586, n. 2.

[37] *The Age of the Scrolls*, *V.T.*, I, 1951, p. 41.

[38] Cf. R. DE VAUX, *Fouille au Khirbet Qumrân*, *R.B.*, January, 1953, pp. 88–106.

lamps) were rather like those found in Jewish tombs of the Roman period (end of the First century B.C. and First century A.D.), while the shards of the cave of the manuscripts were of exactly the same pattern. More than that, the explorers found in one of the rooms an intact jar thrust into the soil which was identical in every respect with those of the scrolls. Other similar jars were to be found in the various caves about the neighborhood. The close connection of Qumrân with the hiding place was now an established fact.

Pottery pointed to the First century A.D. as the main period when the site was used; this hypothesis was also supported by the discovery of twenty-four Roman coins: the oldest dated from the reigns of Herod and Herod Archelaus [39] and the epoch of the first Roman Procurators, the latest from the second year of the First Revolt (A.D. 67–68).

Fr. de Vaux concluded from this that "the building, such as we have found it, was occupied at the beginning of our era, and probably abandoned at the time of the Jewish War from A.D. 66 to 70." [40] But even in that first campaign some signs pointed to the possibility that the occupation of the site was not limited to the First century A.D.; those remains found at the northeast angle of the central building, in particular, allowed for an occupation prior to our era. The shards of the lowest strata appeared to be the oldest, and the earliest coins were also found there. The same archaeologists, assisted this time by Abbé Milik and Fr. du Buit, again explored the ruins from February 9 to April 24, 1953, gathering complementary information of great importance.[41]

THE BUILDING

The main error found in the preliminary report concerned the confusion of the various occupation levels of the building (fig. 4). Three such levels can be discerned at the present stage, beginning with virgin soil and covering a period of some two hundred and fifty years.

The building at its most ancient level (level I) measured thirty-seven by thirty meters, with about twenty rooms, and inner courtyards. An upper floor is found in at least some parts, particularly in the massive northeast tower, connected with the ground floor by a stair.[42]

The edifice, it would seem, was roughly built, with the exception of the remains of a portico and a colonnade which was re-employed later. There can be no doubt that it was intended for the use of a community. There were, in Fr. de Vaux's opinion, meeting halls or refectories, storerooms, a washroom with a sink, a large kitchen provided with several hearths, etc. . . . The southeast part included

---

[39] Cf. art. cit. and Fouilles au Khirbet Qumrân, R.B., April, 1954, p. 260.
[40] R.B., January, 1953, p. 94.
[41] See R. DE VAUX, Fouilles au Khirbet Qumrân, R.B., April, 1954, pp. 206–236.
[42] Cf. art. cit., pp. 208, 212.

two tanks or piscinae, covered with plaster; a staircase of fourteen stairs led to one of them. Water was supplied from another large cistern situated south of the building and connected through an aqueduct with the Wadi Qumrân. "The magnitude of the water installations," Fr. de Vaux observes, "is characteristic of its first condition." [43]

The building was badly damaged by an earthquake, and it was necessary to strengthen it. The arrangement of some rooms was changed during that restoration, a door walled here, a portion of wall erected there, a new entrance opened. The location of the inner tank, the most seriously damaged, was abandoned altogether; the exterior piscina, on the other hand, remained apparently in use. Another large reservoir was erected some fifteen meters south of the building (fig. 5). A bench twenty centimeters high was fitted against the walls of *Locus* 4, where cupboards in the walls can also be seen (fig. 6). The building was somewhat enlarged at the north.

These transformations, it will be seen, did not affect the use for which the whole establishment had been erected. *Locus* 30, a large hall of thirteen by four meters, was probably used as a meeting place. A *scriptorium* found on the upper floor was probably of the same size, judging by the remnants of two or three brick tables; the largest one has been reconstituted: it is narrow, about five meters long, and fifty centimeters high. One bronze and one terra cotta inkpot were also found in the room. A third, also in terra cotta, was found in the adjoining hall.

That period came to an end when the building was destroyed and burned, obviously in the course of a battle, for arrows have been found in many rooms. Thenceforth communal life in Qumrân ceased.

The remnants of level III testify to a very different use, with its large halls characteristically divided into many small rooms. The individuals who now occupied the building by no means constituted an organized community.

Period III saw the last of the building, the ruins of which were visited only occasionally. Archaeologists did find some fragments of Arab pottery of the Ninth and Tenth centuries, but they are too scarce to constitute a level IV. The three levels being thus clearly defined, it remained to date them as accurately as possible. This Fr. de Vaux was able to do with the help of pottery fragments and coins found in Qumrân.

POTTERY

The ceramics ascribed to period I were found either in the rooms which were no longer used after the earthquake, or came from a trench some thirty meters north of the building which served, in Fr. de Vaux' opinion, to receive the rubble while the repairs after the earthquake were carried on. The shards are of the same pattern as

---

[43] Cf. *ibid.*, p. 210.

those found in Bethsur and in the Jerusalem citadel of the Hasmonean period; they may thus be dated from the end of the Hellenistic period.[44]

The ceramics of level II related to those of the Jewish tombs of the Herodian period. That level is particularly rich both in shards and coins.

In the last level, on the contrary, pottery is very scarce; it cannot be doubted that it dates from the Roman period.

"The examination of the ceramics," so Fr. de Vaux concludes, "and the comparisons it brings to mind, suggest therefore the following dates: level I is from the end of the Hellenistic period, level II from the beginning of the Roman period, level III is only slightly more recent. . . . The use of the caves was contemporary to that of the Ḥirbet at the periods I and II, the material corresponding to period II being preponderant (the heap of jars)." [45]

Besides some iron tools (sickles, ledge-bills, nails, keys, etc.) the explorers were lucky enough to discover some items of inscribed pottery. A jar bearing the name of *Yôḥanan Ḥaṭṭalah* [46] was found at level I. To the same period probably can be ascribed the shard on which a student scribe has clumsily drawn the Hebrew alphabet, leaving out some characters, repeating others unnecessarily. A terra cotta seal with the name ΙΩϹΙΠΟϹ was also found in level II; a pitcher with several Greek characters engraved on its pipe may be ascribed to level II or III. Finally half a dozen ostraka, with some Hebrew characters or words, were found.

COINS

The discovery of about two hundred and fifty coins has been of the greatest help in shedding light on the history of the building. Some seventy have not been identified at all. Fr. de Vaux gives a list numbering one hundred and seventy-nine remaining coins, a good many of which have not yet been satisfactorily identified: [47]

It is a curious fact, as Fr. de Vaux points out, that Herod's long reign is hardly represented. Coins later than the 2nd year of the First Revolt have all been found in level III, or on the surface. The trench into which was thrown the rubble of the works while the restoration of the building was carried on, contained coins from the Hasmonean period only, with the sole exception of a coin from Archelaus. The coins of the Procurators and of the First Revolt are all from level II. The testimony of the ceramics is thus fully confirmed by that of the coins: the earthquake which brought the first period to an end occurred probably during the reign of Herod, while the second period

---

[44] Cf. *ibid.*, pp. 214–216.   [45] *Ibid.*, p. 228.

[46] Fr. de Vaux compares this name to the *Ḥaṭṭil* of *Esdr.*, II,57 and *Neh.*, VII,59. The Nabatean *Ḥṭlw* may also be taken into account. Cf. J. CANTINEAU, *Le nabatéen*, Paris, 1932, vol. II, p. 95.

[47] Cf. *R.B.* April 1954, p. 230. — Apart from the exceptions that are specified, the coins are made of bronze.

Date	Number	Remarks
Antiochus VII, 136, 130, 129, B.C.	3	Silver
John Hyrcanus, 135–104	14	Some are not quite identified
Alexander Janneus, 103–76	38	
Unidentified Hasmoneans	15	
Antigonus Mattathias, 40–37	2	
Herod the Great, 37–4 B.C.	1	The coin mentioned in *R.B.*, 1953, p. 93, is more probably from the time of Archelaus
Tyre, 29 B.C.	1	Silver
Herod Archelaus, 4 B.C. to 6 A.D.	6	One not quite identified
Procurators under August	3	
Procurators under Tiberius	7	
Agrippa I, 37–44	23	
Procurators under Claudius	5	
Procurators under Nero	15	
First Revolt, year II, 67–68	11	
Cesarea under Nero, 67–68	8	
Dora under Nero, 67–68	1	
Dora under Nero, same type	1	Date outside the disk
Vespasianus, 70	1	Silver
Askalon, 72–73	1	
Askalon, same type	1	Date erasures, countermark, with .X. on the reverse
Judea capta, under Titus, after 79	3	
Agrippa II, about 86	1	Outside the building
Second Revolt, 132–135	17	Including a group of ten coins, 5 in bronze and 5 in silver (1 denarius dating from the Revolt, 1 from Vespasianus, 3 from Trajan).
Byzantine	3	Of which 2 on the surface
Arab	2	Of which 1 on the surface

was brought to an end by the Judeo-Roman war from 66 to 70 A.D. The flourishing community did not survive the turmoil of the great revolt; it has, however, left in that solitary spot, not only the stones and bricks shaped and carved by its members, but also, and mainly, the great necropolis where the inhabitants of ancient Qumrân have come to their rest.

THE NECROPOLIS

The necropolis is situated to the east of the building on a plateau and four small hills; its tidily arranged eleven hundred tombs are not artistic monuments, but humble pebble heaps which are, with a few exceptions, directed southward.

Fr. de Vaux explored two tombs in 1949, nine others in 1951, and nine in 1953. The skeletons were lying on their backs, with their heads, in most cases, to the south. Contrary to the Jewish custom at the time, no funeral offerings were found, no jewels and no sign of any garment. The raw bricks and earth trash of the tombs yielded nothing but a few pottery shards, apparently contemporary with the ceramics found in the building. A jar found in one tomb might, however, be dated from the last century B.C.

No general conclusion may so far be drawn from this exploration, since only a fiftieth part of the necropolis is as yet known.

Nine skeletons have been unearthed, and parts of them closely examined. Several skeletons (the exact figure is not given) were found to be of women. Professor H. V. Vallois, the Director of the Paris Musée de l'Homme, proposes the following approximate age: two individuals from twenty to thirty, four of about forty, two over fifty years old. The ninth is not mentioned by Fr. de Vaux in his article. No child's skeleton has so far been traced.

Later when Mr. H. de Contenson directed excavations in 1953, he found in tomb 16 two corpses, and in tombs 17 to 19, situated at the western limit of the cemetery, the debris of three wooden coffins.

It should finally be noted that the necropolis has not yielded a written document of any kind.

A building which could not be a private habitation, a necropolis of over a thousand tombs, both in the inhospitable vicinity of the Dead Sea. . . . It was now left to the explorers to find some explanation.

AN ESSENE MONASTERY

The Essenes have already been mentioned in the present chapter. According to Professor Sukenik, there must have been a link closely connecting the hiding place of the manuscripts with the famous community of Jewish "monks." But foremost of all, it was Professor A. Dupont-Sommer [48] who maintained that the scrolls were of Essene origin. Long before Qumrân was explored, he asserted that Pliny's passage: "Below them (*infra hos*) was the city of Engaddi," [49] could only mean that the city of the Essenes was situated north of Engaddi, precisely in the region of Aïn Feshha.[50] The Roman historian at the same time observes that their abode was sufficiently remote from the Dead Sea for the inhabitants to feel safe from its unhealthy vapors.

The geographical situation of Qumrân fits, it would seem, that description. "It is therefore very likely," Fr. de Vaux concludes, "that the Ḥirbet was the conventual building of a group, perhaps the

---

[48] *Aperçus préliminaires sur les manuscrits de la Mer Morte*, Paris, 1950, pp. 105–117. — *Nouveaux aperçus sur les manuscrits de la Mer Morte*, Paris, 1953, *passim.*   [49] *Hist. Nat.*, V,17.
[50] *Aperçus préliminaires.* . . . p. 106, n. 3.

main one, of Essenes, and that the necropolis was their resting place." [51]

The results of the second excavation have enabled Fr. de Vaux to reconstitute the story of the "monastery." Founded under John Hyrcanus (134–104 B.C.), it was most certainly in use during the reign of Alexander Janneus (103–76 B.C.). The earthquake mentioned above is probably the one related by Josephus as having occurred in 31 B.C.[52] The learned archaeologist infers from the absence of any coin from the time of Herod that the building was not in use under that monarch, and that the Community began its restoration only at the time of Herod Archelaus (4 B.C.–6 A.D.). The conjecture is not unlikely, but it is, I think, premature to judge at the present stage, since one third of the coins have not yet been identified nor is the exploration of the site in any way terminated.[53]

The second year of the First Revolt saw the end of period II. From that time on we find no more Jewish coins (eleven are dated A.D. 67–68) but Roman coins instead, including eight minted in Cesarea where the Tenth *Legio Fretensis* was stationed during the winter of A.D. 67–68. It may therefore be supposed that the Qumrân building was destroyed and set on fire in the summer of A.D. 68. Archaeology thus confirms the opinion I ventured in the first French edition of this book.[54]

The fact that the Roman coins follow on without interruption after the Jewish ones, leads us to believe that the Tenth Legion was garrisoned in the Qumrân ruins for some ten years, inaugurating thereby the beginning of period III. At the end of that period the ruins of the building were for a short time used again by a group of Jewish resistants during Bar Kokhba's war.

Qumrân, however, was not the only place where discoveries were made; the exploration of the Judean desert has recorded other quite as remarkable discoveries.

4.   The Discoveries in the Vicinity of Qumrân

As soon as the archaeological mission had left, the Bedouins resumed their activities in the neighborhood of Qumrân. They hoped for some new and profitable bargain, as the price of manuscript fragments was constantly rising.

They did find in fact another cave, some distance south of the first, containing a few fragments.

Representatives of both institutions and of the American School of Jerusalem were immediately dispatched to the spot. During the four weeks' campaign, the rocky cliff was explored from Hadjar el-Asba' in the north, to the south of Râs Feshha.[55]

Twenty-five caves were explored and remains of pottery were

---

[51] *R.B.*, January, 1953, p. 105.   [52] *B.J.*, I, XIX, 13.
[53] The excavating campaign of the spring of 1954 will not have been the last.
[54] p. 104.   [55] Cf. R. DE VAUX, *R.B.*, January, 1953, pp. 84–86.

found of the same type as the shards of the first cave and of the Qumrân building.

The explorers had the good fortune to discover a third cave, containing fragments of manuscripts and three copper sheets, two of them rolled together, the third constituting a separate scroll. They must have originally formed a strip two meters and forty centimeters long, with a lengthy inscription in Hebrew square characters, probably a notice board setting out some regulation or prohibition.

The texts from caves 2 and 3 included fragments from *Leviticus* in archaic characters, from *Exodus, Deuteronomy, Numbers, Jeremiah*, the *Psalms* and *Ruth*. There were also fragments of the Apocrypha, including a *Commentary on Isaiah*.

The cave exploration, as well as the following 1952 campaigns, were more like mountaineering than archaeological expeditions. Rope ladders had often to be used, and Abbé J. T. Malik, who was the mainstay of the group, can relate many a funny story.

Their work done, the explorers went back to Jerusalem, but the tireless Bedouin diggers remained on the spot. They carried on and found more fragments, including a passage from the *Damascus Document*. The richest and most startling discovery, however, was made close to the ruins of Qumrân. On a terrace of grayish marl west of the plateau, a small hole drew their attention; there where nothing, normally, would have been preserved, they stumbled upon a heap of fragments, large and small, amounting to thousands: Biblical texts including fragments from *Tobias* in Hebrew and Aramaic (only the Greek version of this book was known hitherto), the Apocrypha in Hebrew and Aramaic, Greek fragments from the Bible, books of the Sect, phylacteries. It is Fr. de Vaux' opinion, though it might seem exaggerated, that this cave surpasses in importance the one found in 1947.

An archaeological expedition once more set off hastily to Qumrân. The explorers completed the Bedouins' work and collected all the fragments left over by the latter; they found moreover a neighboring chamber which was intact, yielding nothing however but a handful of badly damaged fragments, some of them entirely covered with marl.

The exploration lasted from the 22nd to the 29th of September, 1952. But the Department of Antiquities went on bargaining with the Bedouins, and even more with go-betweens; one of those, a dealer in antiquities from Bethlehem, became a rich man from the sale of fragments. I witnessed, at the beginning of November, 1952, a bundle of them arriving at the Museum. Some of the fragments were clumsily pasted together, the dealer being well aware that the bigger they were the better they would sell.

No new fragment has apparently been found since then in the Qumrân vicinity. As it is, a clear, intelligible edition of those in our possession will take many years of patient labor. We are all of us, of course, anxious to have access to the texts as soon as possible and are inclined, therefore, to grow impatient. But only one who has seen the heap of fragments scattered about in disorder can have an accurate idea of the puzzle involved in classifying them according to the shade of the skin and the shape of their characters, and then trying to put them together. And I am here speaking of the physical difficulties only, leaving aside the problems of deciphering and correct interpretation. Yet would it be asking too much from those who have the documents in their possession to publish from time to time the nature of the material already identified?

While the Qumrân region looks, for the time being at least, as if it were exhausted, other areas of the Judean desert have been until quite lately the scene of new discoveries.

5. The Discovery of the Murabba'at Caves [56]

Taamre Bedouins and a Bethlehem dealer in antiquities offered in Jerusalem around the end of 1951 new Hebrew and Greek fragments, coming, they asserted, from the Qumrân vicinity. The information was untrue, but the repeated offers pointed to the evidence of clandestine diggers having come upon a new hiding place. It was all-important to find out where.

Fr. de Vaux successfully achieved the difficult feat. But let us listen to his own story, which sounds like an Oriental tale.

"When I proposed to my Bedouin friends that I should go and work with them, they protested that it would be quite impossible; the presence of a stranger in the desert would rouse the police and ruin everything. On their next visit, when I discussed their price and asserted it to be too high, they insisted on the remoteness of the site, the great number of workmen, the difficulty of the task; as I still professed skepticism, they said: 'Well, you just come and see for yourself!' I jumped at the opportunity; might I really come? They reassured me: there was nothing to fear, sentries would watch from the neighboring heights, and if the police appeared in the vicinity they would find a hiding place in some hole, the constabulary being none the wiser! Having thus ascertained that they trusted me I ventured on a further step: what if I obtained from the Department of Antiquities permission to employ them at the excavations, without any fear of being imprisoned? This they applauded. And what if the Director of Antiquities came with me? They again agreed. And would it not be better if I asked for a police escort, not for me, of course, for was I not their brother, but for the purpose of protecting them from the jealousy of their fellow tribesmen? This idea they pronounced to be excellent." [57]

And thus, on January 21, 1952, Mr. Harding and Fr. de Vaux, guided by two Bedouins, and escorted by a Bethlehem police officer

---

[56] Cf. R. DE VAUX, *Les grottes de Murabba'at et leurs documents*, R.B., April, 1953, pp. 245–267.   [57] *Ibid.*, pp. 245–246.

and two soldiers, arrived at Wadi Murabba'at,[58] and made their first discovery: thirty-four clandestine diggers, half of whom were to be engaged as workers.

Conditions of work were difficult in the wild valley, but four large caves were successfully explored. Many finds showed them to have been occupied at various periods, but the occupants of one period often destroyed what remained of a previous occupation; severe damage was also caused by falling stones, and lastly by the Bedouins.[59]

ARCHAEOLOGICAL OBJECTS

The chalcolithic period (Fourth millennium B.C.), is well represented: pottery fragments, silex, carved stones, and what is less common, articles of wood and leather, remains of a fish-net, and several fragments of basketwork.

The Middle Bronze II age (Eighteenth to Seventeenth centuries) has left some shards of pottery, two bronze pins, a small alabaster vase and a Hyksos scarab.

The Iron Age is represented only by some fragments of ceramics (Judean pottery from the Eighth and Seventh centuries).

The Roman period is, on the contrary, very well represented, not only by pottery, similar in many respects to that of Qumrân, but also by weapons, bronze spearheads, iron arrowheads, tools (knives, including one with a wooden handle, nails, a sickle, etc.), wooden objects (plates, spoons, bowls, combs, studs), fabrics, some of them embroidered, remains of sandals and of leather outfits.

The date of occupation could be figured out exactly, owing to some twenty coins found in the cave: three are of the Procurators under Nero (A.D. 58–59), one from Askalon probably under Domitian (A.D. 84 or 85), one from Tiberias under Hadrian (A.D. 119–120), and nine from the Second Revolt. Two worn Roman coins are countermarked with a galley, one of the *Decima Legio Fretensis'* emblems; that Legion was stationed in Judea from Titus' victory on.

Lastly the Arab period left the shards of a bowl, a piece of fabric, and two coins, one from the Omeyyad period.

The caves of Murabba'at, occupied again and again in the course

---

58 *Ibid.*, p. 246. Wadi Murabba'at rarely figures on Palestinian maps. It is the name given to a section of the great Wadi which begins south of Bethlehem, where it is called Wadi Taamre, and falls into the Dead Sea some twelve kilometers south of Engaddi, under the name of Wadi Daraje. The caves are situated 25 kilometers southeast of Jerusalem and 18 kilometers south of Qumrân, a three hours' journey from the Dead Sea.

59 "When men abandoned (the first cave)," Fr. de Vaux writes (*ibid.*, p. 247), "it became the haunt of animals and the refuge of pigeons. The manure heaped up thereby was sold by the Taamre, in the course of the first years of British mandate, in Bethlehem, to Jewish colonists. The Bedouins do not remember having seen manuscripts of any kind, but they may have overlooked them, since their attention was not, at the time, drawn to the newly discovered wealth of their desert; it is, therefore, not impossible that fragments of papyri and skins were used to manure the orange groves."

of four thousand years, from the chalcolithic age down to the end of the Middle Ages, offered an unquestionable archaeological interest. Coming upon fabrics and wooden articles, preserved to our days by the dry desert climate, is a good fortune not often met with in Palestinian excavations.

But that almost inaccessible area, however rich in archaeological documents, is even more remarkable for the variety of Hebrew, Aramaic, Greek, Latin and Arabic texts found there.

THE TEXTS

The most ancient of these documents, a palimpsest papyrus, goes back, it would seem, to the period of the kingdom of Judah (Eighth to Seventh centuries B.C.); both its earlier and later texts are written in archaic characters. The most recent document is a list of proper names, among which Fr. de Vaux mentions that of Shema'yahu.[60] Next, Biblical fragments from the First and Second century A.D. (Genesis, Exodus, Deuteronomy, Isaiah) were found. They are in very poor condition due, probably, to Roman soldiers, then to the wear of centuries and to rats.

A complete phylactery was also found. All the scriptural texts agree on every point with the masoretic recension and spelling, which is not the case with the Biblical texts of Qumrân.

One lot of papyri brings us to the time of the Second Jewish Revolt under Hadrian (A.D. 132-135). Many of them are dated from the years of "the deliverance of Israel by Simeon ben Kosebah, Prince of Israel": the latter is none other than the famous Bar Kokhba, the chief of the second anti-Roman revolt. Two letters addressed by him to Yeshau'ben Gilgola, "the chief of the camp," have been found in Murabba'at; the third letter is addressed to the latter by the administrators of an otherwise unknown locality, Bêth Mashkô. Other texts are mere fragments.

Aramaic is represented by contracts. Some fragments, letters and contracts have not so far been deciphered, owing to the difficulty of their cursive writing.[61] The language used is either Hebrew or Aramaic.

The Greek papyri include two contracts dealing with matrimonial matters: one mentions the reconciliation of husband and wife Eleos

---

[60] The use of the longer form of the divine name (-yahu) in the theophoric names is a sign of their being more ancient. It was common before the Exile (for inst.: Yesha'yahu = Isaiah, Yirmeyahu = Jeremiah, etc.). The shorter form (-yah) was commonly used only after the Exile (for inst.: Zekharyah = Zechariah, Nehemyah = Nehemiah, etc.). E. I. Kutscher (The Language of the Scroll A of Isaiah of the Dead Sea Scrolls, Ha'areṣ from 9.28.1952) has observed that the scribe of the Isaiah scroll of St. Mark's often uses the shorter form of theophoric names instead of the longer one which the Masoretic texts have preserved.

[61] See, for a tentative deciphering, S. A. BIRNBAUM, A fragment in an unknown Script, P.E.Q., 1952, pp. 118–120: An unknown Aramaic Cursive, ibid., 1953, pp. 23–41. Abbé Milik in his article of R.B., April, 1954, p. 189, expresses some doubt regarding the accuracy of Professor Birnbaum's deciphering.

and Salome, in the seventh year of Hadrian (A.D. 124). A debt acknowledgement dates from A.D. 171; another text mentions the Emperor Commodus (A.D. 180–192). There are two literary fragments: one might be a part of some religious text, the other is historical, judging by the names of Salome and Mariamne, possibly the sister and the second or third wife of Herod the Great.

Administrative registers are written on skins or parchments. A long text, almost entirely erased, was even found on the inside of a sack: two inscribed skins had been sewn together.

The only fragment in Latin may be dated from the middle of the Second century A.D.

The list of the Murabba'at documents ends with Arabic texts written on paper, one of which has been preserved intact.

THE MURABBA'AT CAVES AND THE SECOND REVOLT

Both archaeological and epigraphical documents point to the fact of the caves having been a shelter, during the Bar Kokhba war, for a Jewish military post under the command of Yeshua' ben Gilgola. The Romans apparently succeeded in dislodging him, and sacked the place, impregnable though it seemed. The texts and coins later than A.D. 135 show that a Roman post was established in the heart of the desert for controlling the way to Engaddi.

Another important lot dates from the same period, but its original hiding place has not yet been ascertained. It includes Biblical fragments (Genesis, Numbers, Psalms), a complete phylactery, important Greek fragments of the minor Prophets, which are, according to Fr. D. Barthélemy, a missing link in the history of the Septuagint,[62] a letter addressed to Simeon ben Kosebah, and two Aramaic contracts dated "from the third year of the deliverance of Israel, in the name of Simeon ben Kosebah." Greek and Aramaic documents are dated from the era of the Province of Arabia.[63] There is finally an important collection of Nabatean papyri.

6.   The Belgian Expedition to Ḥirbet Mird

During the summer of 1952 the ever alert Bedouins brought to Jerusalem a new bundle of fragments, coming, as they said, from a cave in Wadi-en-Nar, an extension of the Cedron Valley.

The texts included fragments of codices written on both sides, from the Book of Wisdom, the Gospels of Mark and John, and the Acts of the Apostles; they are written in Greek uncial and may be dated from between the Fifth to the Eighth centuries A.D. Biblical fragments range from Joshua to the Gospels of Matthew and Luke,

---

62 Redécouverte d'un chaînon manquant de l'histoire de la Septante, R.B., January, 1953, pp. 18–29.
63 The Roman province of Arabia was erected on the ruins of the Nabatean kingdom of Petra in 106 A.D. Cf. F. M. ABEL, Géographie de la Palestine, II, Paris, 1938, p. 165.

the *Acts*, and the Epistle to the *Colossians*, all of them written in the Syro-Palestinian tongue and script. Greek fragments of non-Biblical works, documents in cursive script, and Arabic and Syriac papyri were also included in the lot.[64]

A Belgian archaeological mission conducted by Professor R. de Langhe, of the University of Louvain, who explored the Judean desert from February to April, 1953, has been able to establish that the documents mentioned above were found not in the Wadi-en-Nar but in Ḥirbet Mird, ancient Hyrcania. Upon the ruins of the citadel built by John Hyrcanus, and later stormed by Herod, St. Sabas was to found, in A.D. 492, the Castellion monastery, which flourished until the Ninth century.

The expedition found Greek fragments in uncial and cursive writing, as well as Syro-Palestinian and Arabic texts.

Deciphering work is only beginning, but a fragment of Euripides' *Andromache* has already been identified. It dates from the Sixth century A.D., i.e. a thousand years older than the most ancient manuscript on parchment hitherto known. The field of classical literature brings us into a world very different from that of Qumrân.

The expedition, however, has brought new, although negative, evidence about Qumrân. A methodical exploration of the coastal cliffs of the Dead Sea, from Râs Feshha to the mouth of Wadi Daraje, convinced the Belgian archaeologists that no fragments of manuscripts are anywhere to be seen. From this we may infer that the Qumrân Community was confined to a not very extensive area. Further exploration will no doubt reveal new literary treasures which are still buried in the desert of Judah. What we do possess is, in itself, invaluable.

It has seemed to me necessary, before embarking on the investigation of our documents, to establish a list of them; the amplitude of these extraordinary discoveries will then be better perceived.

THE DISCOVERED MANUSCRIPTS

It is hardly necessary to observe that the following list cannot be anything but temporary. I will mention only those titles which are found in the various preliminary reports. The place where they were found, the lot to which they belong, the sources of manuscripts already published, will also be mentioned.

In the first column (*title*) f. stands for fragments. In the second (*finding place*), 1Q, 2Q, 3Q, etc. . . . mean the first, second, or third Qumrân cave, Mu = Murabba'at, Mi = Mird, and unc. = origin uncertain. In the third column (*the bundle*), I stands for the documents bought by St. Mark's Convent in 1947, II the documents acquired by Professor Sukenik, III for all the documents and fragments found by the various archaeological expeditions, or bought by Mr. Harding and Fr. de Vaux.

---

[64] Cf. *R.B.*, January, 1953, p. 85.

Texts from the Old Testament

IN HEBREW

Isaiah, complete	1Q	I	*The Dead Sea Scrolls of St. Mark's Monastery*, ed. M. BURROWS, etc. vol. I.
Isaiah, incomplete	1Q	II	E. L. SUKENIK, *Oṣar hamme-gillôth haggenûzôth.*
Genesis, f.	1Q	III	
Genesis, f.	Mu.	III	
Genesis, f.	Unc.	III	
Exodus, f. of two Mss.	2Q	III	
Exodus, f. of two Mss.	Mu.	III	*R.B.*, Apr. 1953, p. 268 and pl. XII a.
Leviticus, f. (Phœnician script)	1Q	III	*R.B.*, Oct. 1949, pp. 597 sq. pl. XVIII.
Leviticus, f. (Phœnician script)	2Q	III	
Numbers, f.	2Q	III	
Numbers, f.	Unc.	III	
Deuteronomy, f.	1Q	III	Photograph in *Ill. London News*, 10.1.1949.
Deuteronomy, f.	2Q	III	
Deuteronomy, f.	4Q	III	*B.A.S.O.R.*, 136, Dec. 1954, pp. 12 sq.
Deuteronomy, f.	Mu.	III	
Judges, f.	1Q	III	
Samuel, f.	1Q	III	*B.A.S.O.R.*, 132, Dec. 1953, pp. 15 sq.
Isaiah, f.	4Q	III	*B.A.S.O.R.*, 135, Oct. 1954, pp. 28 sq.
Isaiah, f.	Mu.	III	
Jeremiah, f.	2Q	III	
Psalms, f.	2Q	III	
Psalms, f.	Unc.	III	
Qoheleth, f.	4Q	III	*B.A.S.O.R.*, 135, Oct. 1954, pp. 20 sq.
Ruth, f. of two Mss.	2Q	III	
Daniel, f.	1Q	I	
Tobias, f.	4Q	III	
Florilegium of Messianic promises	4Q	III	
Phylactery, complete	Mu.	III	Partly published in *R.B.*, Apr. 1953, p. 269 and pl. XII b.
Phylactery, complete	Unc.	III	
Phylacteries, *f.* with the Decalogue	1Q	III	
Phylacteries, *f.* with the Decalogue	4Q	III	

IN ARAMAIC

Daniel, f.	1Q	I	
Tobias, f.	4Q	III	

Texts from the Old Testament (Cont.)

IN GREEK

Minor Prophets, f.	Unc.	III	Partly published in *R.B.*, Jan. 1953, pp. 18 sq. and pl. I.
Undetermined fragments	4Q	III	
Wisdom, f.	Mi.	III	

IN SYRO-PALESTINIAN

Joshua, f.	Mi.	III

Texts from the New Testament

IN GREEK

Mark, f.	Mi.	III
John, f.	Mi.	III
Acts, f.	Mi.	III

IN SYRO-PALESTINIAN

Matthew, f.	Mi.	III
Luke, f.	Mi.	III
Acts, f.	Mi.	III
Colossians, f.	Mi.	III

Non-Canonical Religious Texts

IN HEBREW

Jubilees, f.	1Q	III	*R.B.*, Oct. 1949, pp. 602 sq. and pl. XVI a.
Jubilees, f.	2Q	III	
Enoch, f.	1Q	III	Photograph in *Ill. London News*, 10.1.1949.
An unknown Apocryph, f.	1Q	I	*R.B.*, Oct. 1949; pp. 605 sq. and pl. XVII.
Undetermined fragments	1Q	I	
Undetermined fragments	3Q	III	
Undetermined fragments	4Q	III	

IN ARAMAIC

Commentary of Genesis	1Q	I
Liturgical fragments	2Q	III
Undetermined fragments	4Q	III

Texts of the Qumrân Community

IN HEBREW

Commentary of Habakkuk	1Q	I	*The Dead Sea Scrolls . . . ,* ed. M. BURROWS, vol. I.
Commentary of Micah, f.	1Q	III	*R.B.*, July 1952, pp. 412 sq.
Commentary of Ps., 37, f.	4Q	III	*P.E.Q.*, May-Oct. 1954, pp. 69 sq. and pl. XVIII.
Commentary of Ps., 68, f.	1Q	III	

Texts of the Qumrân Community (Cont.)

IN HEBREW

Commentary of Isaiah, f.	3Q	III	R.B., Oct. 1953, pp. 555 sq. and pl. XXIV b.
Manual of Discipline	1Q	I	The Dead Sea Scrolls . . . , ed. M. BURROWS, vol. II, fasc. 2.
Manual of Discipline, f.	4Q	III	
Two Columns, f.	1Q	III	
Benedictions, f.	1Q	III	
Document of Damascus, f.	4Q	III	
Document of Damascus, f.	6Q	III	
Book of the War	1Q	II	SUKENIK, 'Osar hammegîllôth haggenûzôth.
Book of the War, f.	4Q	III	
Hymns	1Q	II	Ibid.
Hymns, f.	4Q	III	
Undetermined fragments	4Q	III	
Copper leaves	3Q	III	Tentatively and partly deciphered in R.B., Apr. 1954, pp. 193 sq.

Historical and Literary Documents, Contracts, Letters

IN HEBREW

List of proper names (Phœnician script)	Mu.	III	
Incomplete texts from the Second Revolt	Mu.	III	
Letter of Simeon ben Kosebhah	Mu.	III	R.B., Apr. 1953, pp. 276 sq. and pl. XIV.
Letter of Simeon	Mu.	III	
Letter, f.	Mu.	III	
Letter to Simeon	Unc.	III	
Letter to Yeshua' ben Gilgola	Mu.	III	R.B., Apr. 1953, pp. 269 sq. and pl. XIII.
Ostraka	Mu.	III	

IN ARAMAIC

Contracts dating from the Second Revolt (two)	Unc.	III	R.B., Apr. 1954, pp. 182 sq. and pl. IV.
Contract	Mu.	III	
Documents dated from the era of the Province of Arabia (two)	Unc.	III	
Nabatean documents	Unc.	III	R.B., Apr. 1954, pp. 161 sq. and pl. I-III.

Historical and Literary Documents, Contracts, Letters (Cont.)

IN GREEK

Marriage contract, *f.*	Mu.	III
Reconciliation contract between spouses	Mu.	III
Acknowledgment of debt	Mu.	III
Incomplete documents posterior to the Second Revolt	Mu.	III
Registers, *f.*	Mu.	III
Fragments	Mu.	III
Documents dated from the era of the Province of Arabia (two)	Unc.	III
Andromache, f.	Mi.	III

IN SYRO-PALESTINIAN

Letter from a monk	Mi.	III	*R.B.,* Oct. 1953, pp. 526 sq. and pl. XIX.

IN ARABIC

Complete document	Mu.	III
Fragments	Mu.	III
Letters, *f.*	Mi.	III

This impressive list will be much longer when the contents of the fourth Qumrân cave are published.

A lacuna, all too obvious, will have been noticed: the manuscripts are not dated.

It is a complex matter which will be dealt with in the following chapter.

(Photo Starcky)

3. — The first Qumrân Cave.

chapter two

THE DATING PROBLEM

Whatever doubts or hesitations may have been entertained in various quarters concerning the authenticity of the Qumrân discoveries, they have now been dispelled by archaeological work. Professor Zeitlin is the only one who has so far refused to acknowledge defeat, and there is no sign that he is about to change his mind.[1]

The theories presented by Professor Zeitlin appear for the most part so unlikely now, that any discussion of them may be dispensed with.

---

[1] Here is roughly an outline of his thought:

The manuscripts cannot be anterior to the storming of Jerusalem in 70 A.D. because of the Habakkuk Commentary, as Biblical commentary was a *genre* that had not yet come into existence during the period of the Second Temple.

Mr. Tovia Wechsler, a Jewish journalist from Jerusalem, has identified, among the manuscripts of St. Mark's Monastery, a scroll of *haphṭarôth*, (Prophetical pericopae used in Synagogal liturgy). Now this scroll has disappeared, because its testimony disturbed the hypothesis of the manuscripts' antiquity.

The non-Biblical documents offer so many likenesses to Karaite literature, that their Karaite and medieval origin cannot be doubted.

The archaeological discoveries are in no way related to the manuscripts, for the latter do not come from the Judean desert caves. They originate from Egypt, or, according to the latest interpretation, from the Hebron Synagogue which was plundered in the 1929 pogrom.

Neither are the documents of the Second Revolt authentic, because Ben Kozeba (Son of the lie) was not the name of the chief of the rebels: it was a nickname forged by posterior Rabbis. Professor Zeitlin, when he put forward that opinion, did not know that the real spelling of the name is Ben Kosebha ("Coriander" according to J. T. Milik, *R.B.*, 1953, p. 281, a partisan's nickname).

With respect to the *haphṭarôth* scroll, it must be acknowledged that its disappearance has not yet received a satisfactory explanation. I shall come back later to the relationship between our manuscripts and Karaite writings.

For the list of articles by S. Zeitlin and T. Wechsler, see bibliography at the end of the book.

Professor G. R. Driver has also expressed doubts concerning the methods which have been used to date the manuscripts. He questions the value of each argument taken separately (archaeology, paleography, identification of the *Kittim*), and does not pay due consideration to the testimony borne out by the collective evidence. Above all, he appears unaware of the results of the more recent diggings in Qumrân. Cf. *Once again the Judean Scrolls, J.Q.R.* XLIV, July, 1953, pp. 1–20.

We are, at the same time, witnesses to a spectacular reshifting concerning the date to be assigned to the scrolls. Some years ago, the differences of opinion were disconcerting: some scholars assigned the manuscripts to the Second century B.C.; others to the Second or Third centuries A.D., some coming down as far as the Twelfth century A.D.

We must, of course, take care not to confuse the date when a manuscript was hidden with the date when it was written, or the date when a work was transcribed with that when it was actually composed. A work, moreover, may allude to events which happened much earlier.[2]

We will thus look for archaeological evidence in order to determine the date of the hiding place; paleography, i.e. the investigation of the writing, as well as of spelling and grammatical peculiarities, will help to date the manuscript; and lastly, literary criteria alone will guide us in establishing the date on which a work was composed, if it has not been already indicated. Allusions to historical facts will be dealt with in the same way.

Besides, discrimination ought to be clearly made henceforward between the various groups of manuscripts yielded by the Judean desert. We are not concerned of course with the fragments of Mird, most of which are so far unpublished, or of those of Murabba'at, with which we are hardly familiar. And besides, they do not give rise to any problem, since a good many of them are dated. We shall narrow down our research to the finds of Qumrân, which are at once the most important and the most baffling.

1.   Dating the Hiding Place at Qumrân

The previous chapter has described the various stages of archaeological exploration at Qumrân. As long as one cave only was known, archaeologists maintained that the shards fell into two groups, the main part being *Hellenistic* and dating from the First century B.C. and some insignificant fragments of *Roman* pottery, dating from the

---

[2] Characteristic examples of this kind of confusion are periodically expressed even in Biblical reviews.

Third century A.D.[3] They had, however, to confess that for the shape of "Hellenistic" jars parallels were lacking.[4]

Father de Vaux, considering it just possible that the jars were made with the express purpose of hiding those very scrolls in that very cave, arrived at the following conclusion: "No manuscript is posterior to the beginning of the First century B.C., while some of them may be much older."[5] In his estimation the hiding place should be dated from the end of Alexander Janneus' reign (103–76 B.C.).[6]

Such an interpretation of the facts was not, however, universally accepted, notably not by Professor Albright and M. Parrot; the former, whilst preferring the years 50 to 25 B.C., did not exclude the possibility of the manuscripts being hidden some time around A.D. 70.[7] As for M. Parrot he expressly pronounced for that latter date.[8]

Besides the pottery, some cloths found in the cave were also investigated. In addition, one of the latest discoveries of nuclear physics, the decomposition of "Carbon 14" was used.[9] This did not however clinch the evidence, since the date it suggested, A.D. 33, allows for a margin of error of 200 years on either side.[10]

It rested with the Qumrân excavations to bring the dating problem much nearer to solution, by leading the archaeologists to reconsider seriously their positions.[11]

It has thus become highly probable that the documents were hidden during the First century A.D., most probably when the inhabitants of Qumrân, hard pressed by the Roman legions, were preparing to leave the region altogether.

2.   Dating the Qumrân Scrolls

As has already been pointed out, the date of the concealment has no direct bearing on dating the manuscripts. Only their writing charac-

---

[3] Cf. *supra*, p. 10.

[4] Cf. R. DE VAUX, *R.B.*, October, 1949, pp. 587 and 589. — E. L. SUKENIK, *M.G.*, II, p. 17. — J. T. MILIK believes he has found partially convincing parallels two Ptolemaic jars from the Turin Museum dating from the Second century, B.C. (*Bibl.*, pp. 504–508.)

[5] *R.B.*, April, 1949, p. 236.   [6] *Ibid.*, July, 1950, p. 429.

[7] *Postscript to B.A.S.O.R., Supplementary Studies*, 10–12, 1951, p. 58, n. 5.

[8] *Nouvelle Littérature* from 24.2.1949; *Réforme*, from 24.3.1951, p. 5. — Professor Dupont-Sommer has advanced the same hypothesis (*Aperçus préliminaires . . .* p. 105). It was also inferred in my own "*Le Commentaire d'Habacuc*" *et le Nouveau Testament, C.S.*, n. 4, 1951, pp. 347–348.

[9] Every living organism contains carbon 12 (ordinary) and carbon 14 (radioactive). So long as a living body goes on assimilating, the proportion between the two kinds of carbon remains unchanged. But as soon as life has stopped, the quantity of radio-active carbon diminishes progressively owing to eradiation. A chemical decomposition may thus, through establishing the present relationship between the two elements, testify to the time when assimilation of carbon 14 has stopped. Cf. A. BAUCHAU, *N.R.Th.*, 1950, pp. 515–517. — D. COLLIER, *B.A.*, XIV, 1951, pp. 25–28.

[10] Cf. O. R. SELLERS, *B.A.S.O.R.*, 123, 1951, p. 25.   [11] Cf. *supra*, pp. 9–10.

teristics can tell us that, and this, simple as it sounds, is well-nigh impossible.

Paleography is, at its best, an intricate science, for our handwriting is not subject to any mechanical rules. Its progress of course is not haphazard, but always testifies to an evolution towards a given direction; no one could confuse a contemporary manuscript with one written even a hundred years ago. Nevertheless, to trace such an evolution, and further, to estimate the lapse of time between two different handwritings, firmly established landmarks are imperative.

The problem is even more difficult where Hebrew paleography is concerned. We were, for one thing, poorly documented for the period close to the beginning of our era until the discoveries in the desert of Judah. Palestine had provided us with but epigraphic texts, mostly ossuary inscriptions.[12] Egypt had yielded papyri and ostraka from the Ptolemaic period (Third century B.C.).[13] There were some liturgical fragments from Dura-Europos (Third century A.D.). And there was lastly a tiny Biblical fragment, known as the Nash Papyrus, which bears a strong resemblance to our newly found documents, but which is itself very unsatisfactorily dated.[14]

In view of such unfavorable circumstances the paleographers, it must be owned, have made a very good job of it. The conclusions arrived at by Trever,[15] Birnbaum,[16] Albright,[17] for the St. Mark's manuscripts, and by Sukenik,[18] Tournay,[19] and Kanael,[20] for those of the Hebrew University, are, on the whole, acceptable even today, for dates they suggested vary from the Second century B.C. down to the middle of the First century A.D.[21]

---

[12] J. B. FREY, *Corpus Inscriptionum Iudaicarum*, Vatican, 1952, vol. II, pp. 245 and sq.

[13] See the excellent paleographical table in F. ROSENTHAL, *Die aramaistische Forschung seit Th. Nöldeke's Veröffentlichungen*, Leiden, 1939.

[14] The following dates have been proposed for the fragment discovered in Egypt:

Beginning of Second century A.D.: S. A. COOK (*Proceedings of the Soc. of Bibl. Arch.*, 1903, p. 51).

First century A.D.: F. C. BURKITT (*J.Q.R.*, 1903, p. 400); E. L. SUKENIK, *M.G.*, I, p. 14.

50–25 B.C.: J. C. TREVER (*B.A.S.O.R.*, 113, 1949, p. 19).

100–50 B.C.: W. F. ALBRIGHT (*B.A.S.O.R.*, 115, 1949, pp. 10–19).

Second century B.C.: W. F. ALBRIGHT ("early Maccabean": *J.B.L.*, 1937, pp. 145–176).

Beginning of Second century B.C.: S. BIRNBAUM, (*B.A.S.O.R.*, 115, 1949, p. 22).

[15] *B.A.S.O.R.*, 113, 1949, p. 23.

[16] *Ibid.*, 115, 1949, p. 22.

[17] *Ibid.*, 118, 1950, p. 6.

[18] *M.G.*, I, pp. 14–15.

[19] *R.B.*, April, 1949, p. 208.

[20] *Bulletin of the Israel Explor. Soc.*, XVI, 1951, pp. 46–52.

[21] The texts mentioned so far are all in *square* characters (Aramaic writing). But, as I have remarked, fragments of *Leviticus* in Phoenician writing are also found in the lot. S. Birnbaum dates them from the Fifth century B.C.

The method of using the five *final letters* [22] also brings us to the last two centuries of the Second Temple's existence.[23] On the other hand, no conclusive evidence could be drawn from the abundant use of *matres lectionis*,[24] or from the archaic characters employed in writing the Name of God.[25]

No substantiated paleographic study has been published so far. A more thorough investigation will be possible only when the Murabba'at documents are published. Then, and only then, shall we be able to establish not merely a relative chronology,[26] but, approximately at least, an absolute one for the Qumrân manuscripts.

For the time being, then, it would seem better to adopt a more elastic system, and place the Qumrân manuscripts within a period of some 200 years, beginning at about 150 B.C.

(*B.A.S.O.R.*, 118, 1950, p. 27); D. Diringer from the end of the Fourth or beginning of the Third centuries B.C., while not altogether excluding a later date (*B.A.*, XIII, 1950, p. 95); S. Yeivin from the First century B.C. (*B.A.S.O.R.*, 118, 1950, p. 30). It ought to be observed here that another fragment of *Leviticus* in Phoenician characters has been found in a new cave in Qumrân. It would appear that the Community tradition honored at Qumrân required that the cultural code *par excellence* should be written in archaic characters.

[22] Five characters of the Hebrew square alphabet have a special shape at the end of the word (*kaph, mem, nun, pe* and *sade*).

[23] The double shape of *nun* is attested since the beginning of the Fifth century B.C. (Cf. Table II in F. ROSENTHAL, *Die aramaistische Forschung*.) Final *kaph* and final *nun* are found on the *ostraka* of Edfu (Third century B.C. — *Ibid.*, Table IV.) There is a certain fluctuation in the use of the double letters, even in those manuscripts which paleography pronounces to be of a more recent date (thus a final *kaph* in the middle of a word in the *Hymns* scroll: *M.G.*, II, pl. VII, line 3; a medial shape of *sade* and *nun* at the end of the words in the *Habakkuk Commentary*: XII, 15 and XIII, 2). That fluctuation is even more manifest in the *Isaiah A* scrolls and in the *Manual*. Moreover, these two manuscripts do not yet show the final *pe* — with the exception of a later addition in *Isaiah A* (pl. XXVIII, line 19) — while the final *kaph* and *sade* are different from the medial ones only by their size. These scrolls are therefore prior to the invariable use of final characters, which was introduced towards the end of the First century A.D.

[24] i.e. the consonants *Waw, yodh, he* and *aleph*, which help to indicate certain vowels in a purely consonantic text. They were intended to make reading easier. They are more frequent in the writings of Qumrân than in the Biblical masoretic text. Biblical fragments at Murabba'at conform already to the latter. Elimination *en masse* of *matres lectionis* must have happened at the turn of the First century A.D. Nevertheless, that indication, taken alone, is not sufficient to date the manuscripts. A tendency to use *matres lectionis* has been noticed in the Palmyra Biblical inscriptions dating from the Third century A.D. (Cf. J. B. FREY, *Corp. Inscr. Iud.*, n. 821, 822.)

[25] They are always found in the *H.C.* Phoenician characters are also used sometimes for writing "God" ('*el*: *M.G.*, II, pl. VII, and *Illust. London News* of 10.1.49, p. 494, fig. 6). Origen testifies that this manner of writing the tetragram is found in the best Biblical manuscripts (MIGNE, *P.G.* XII, col. 1104). See P. BOCCACCIO, *Bibl.*, 1951, pp. 90–96.

[26] This relative chronology could be established in the following order: Prior to Christian era: *Isaiah A* and *Manual*. First century A.D.: The *Habakkuk Commentary, Isaiah B, War, Hymns*.

chapter three

THE QUMRÂN COMMUNITY

Our investigation has proved that the newly discovered scrolls were hidden about 70 A.D., by the members of a group which was once established in the vicinity of Qumrân. Archaeological exploration has not given us precise information about the identity of the group, or its internal organization and customs. The *Manual of Discipline,* fortunately, is a literary document which provides us with first-class evidence about the laws and customs of the inhabitants of Qumrân.[1]

Nor is that scroll the only literary document in our possession. We have at our disposal the *Damascus Document,* which is closely related to it,[2] as well as Rabbinic texts on communal life in Judaism,[3] and lastly, many passages from various authors, Jewish (Josephus and Philo), classical (Pliny the Elder, Dion Chrysostomus), and Fathers of the Church (Hippolytus of Rome, Jerome, Eusebius), about the most famous Jewish religious groups, the Essenes and the Therapeutes.[4]

The evidence gives rise to a problem of method: should we put together indiscriminately the information gathered from the various

---

[1] Edited by M. Burrows, *The Dead Sea Scrolls of St. Mark's Monastery,* vol. II, fasc. 2, New Haven, 1952.

[2] That document has been edited by S. SCHECHTER, *Documents of Jewish Sectaries,* vol. I, *Fragments of a Zadokite Work,* Cambridge, 1910. There is a new and better edition by L. ROST, *Die Damaskusschrift neu bearbeitet,* Berlin, 1933. The complete manuscript has been published in facsimile by S. ZEITLIN, *The Zadokite Fragments,* Philadelphia, 1952. — The best study is that of Ch. RABIN, *The Zadokite Documents,* I. The Admonition, II. *The Laws,* edited with a translation and notes, Oxford, 1954.

[3] Concerning "companies" or *ḥabhûrôth.* Texts collected in the article *Ḥaber,* in *The Jewish Encyclopedia,* vol. VI, p. 121–124.

[4] For sources, cf. article *Esséniens,* in *Suppl. du Dictionnaire de la Bible,* t. II, cols. 110–111.

sources, or rather treat each group of documents separately, stressing each time the common features as well as the discrepancies? The latter method is perhaps the slower, but was considered to be more instructive, and therefore preferred.

1. The Community as Reflected in the "Manual"

The Qumrân Sect was by no means a common association of devout people, but a real monastic order,[5] organized and provided with a hierarchy of its own, in view of a particular and well-defined aim. It was based on the Covenant of a return to the authentic Law: it differed in its ways from the rest of the people; in fact it was separated from them. The Community was an Israel within Israel, nay, in the eyes of its members it was Israel, the only and true people of God.

THE AIM OF THE COMMUNITY

The ideal which they pursued, was to seek God "according to what He commanded through Moses and all His servants, the Prophets"; [6] practicing in common all the virtues: "truth . . . humility, righteousness and justice, benevolent charity and modesty." [7] Nor were they satisfied with mere personal sanctity, they also wanted "to make atonement for the guilty rebellion and sinful infidelity to obtain mercy for the earth." [8] When, at the end of time, God would come to pass judgment, they, the "members of the party of God," would be called as witnesses of truth to condemn the adepts of Belial. This would be the great day of vengeance they were patiently awaiting. They proposed to prepare for the advent of God by an uninterrupted study of the Law, and having broken off from "the congregation of the men of iniquity," they lived as strangers within Jewish society, and kept jealously to themselves the secret doctrine that God had entrusted to them.[9] That solitary life in the midst of a perverted world was to last down to the end of time, down to the advent of the two Messiahs, that of Aaron and that of Israel.[10]

THE ORGANIZATION OF THE COMMUNITY

The Sect was the people of Israel in a microcosm, its true representative and its true successor, the faithful remnant of which the Prophets spoke.

Just as the elected People, the Community was also divided into Levites, priests, and laymen, into "Aaron and Israel." Likewise, it contained groups of thousands, hundreds, fifties, and tens.[11]

---

[5] An article by F. Nötscher is entitled: *Jüdische Mönchgemeinde* (monks' community) *und Ursprung des Christentums nach dem jüngst am Toten Meer aufgefundenen hebräischen Handschriften, Bibel und Kirche,* 1952, pp. 21–38.

[6] *M.D.*, I, 2–3.   [7] *Ibid.*, V, 3–4.   [8] *Ibid.*, VIII, 3; IX, 4.

[9] *Ibid.*, VIII, 12–16; IX, 17.   [10] *Ibid.*, IX, 11.   [11] *Ibid.*, II, 21–22.

Whether a "thousand" really corresponded to a thousand members or was merely a traditional title, matters little, but it seems fairly certain that local groups did exist. In other words, Qumrân was not the Sectarians' only abode, as clearly appears from the following passage: "In every place where there are ten men of the Council of the Community . . . " a passage out of the paragraph determining their behavior "in the dwellings of their exile." [12]

Nor does this apply to confederate local unities only; every member had his assigned place, his entrance number, within the Community's larger frame, in which he must remain, neither pushing himself forward nor retreating: "Let every man of Israel know the status of his office in God's Community according to the eternal counsel. Let no one step down from the status of his office or rise from his allotted place." [13] Again, the *Manual* mentions annual general assemblies at which all members are required to observe the order of precedence of their respective groups and within each of them. [14]

THE GOVERNMENT OF THE COMMUNITY

The Community, thus strongly organized both on its general and local level, led a peaceful life under the authority of its responsible leaders. These we find at every degree, and they were apparently always priests.

It is clearly stated that every group of "ten" was governed by a priest; [15] we find elsewhere that "only the sons of Aaron shall have the authority in matters of laws and properties, and according to their judgment the lot shall be established for every group of the men of the Community." [16] They took precedence over all their brethren who were the "men of their Covenant," [17] and of that Covenant, they, the "priests, the sons of Zadok," were the established guardians. [18] That last characteristic is significant, and points to the sacerdotal origin of the group. We can safely infer from all this that the "Surveyor" or the "Inspector" who was at the head of the "Great Ones" was also a priest.

Those "Great Ones" who were members with full authority, also had a share in the government of the Community. [19] They were present, together with the priests, at the councils; their vote was required to admit new members; [20] they had their seat in the tribunal which judged various trespasses, and inflicted penalties that could

[12] *Ibid.*, VI, 2–3.   [13] *Ibid.*, II, 22–23.   [14] *Ibid.*, II, 19–23; V, 8.

[15] *Ibid.*, VI, 3–4.   [16] *Ibid.*, IX, 7.   [17] *Ibid.*, V, 9.   [18] *Ibid.*, V, 2, 9.

[19] A. M. Habermann is, I think, quite right in asserting that this name does not apply to all the members of the Sect, but only to those belonging to an upward class. I find more difficult to accept his interpretation opposing the "Great Ones" to the "men of the Community" (*'Edah we-'Eduth*, Jerusalem, 1952, pp. 35–37. — *Sinai*, XXXII, 1953, pp. 141–148). The latter expression is a very general name which includes all the categories (postulants, novices, brethren), while "Great Ones" is a title reserved for the members definitively admitted.   [20] *M.D.*, VI, 8–23.

go to the length of definitive exclusion. They could also pronounce, under given conditions, the reintegration of members previously excluded.[21] The *Manual* does not mention any appointed judges; that office, apparently, was jointly exercised by all the "Great Ones."

Three priests and twelve laymen composed the Supreme Council of the Community, whose task, however, was a doctrinal and spiritual one, rather than judiciary and administrative.[22]

The authority of the superiors could not be disputed; they had the right to be obeyed. Those who revolted against them might be excluded forever; [23] the very fact of refusing obedience involved very serious consequences.[24] It is of course obvious that, had the Sect not practiced true obedience, no communal life would have been possible.

COMMUNAL LIFE

The Community knew no half-measures. Those who "dedicated themselves" had to pledge themselves absolutely and unconditionally; they "shall bring all their knowledge, all their mind, all their property into the Community of God, to clarify their knowledge by the truth of God's ordinances, to regulate (the use of) their mind according to the perfection of His ways, and that of their property according to His righteous Counsel." [25]

Communal life thus involved a common doctrinal basis, communal observances, and common ownership of property. We are here particularly concerned with the last two points.

Every communal life presupposes, on one hand, the practice of some particularly indispensable virtues, such as fraternal love, humility, modesty, docility.[26] On the other hand, defects particularly opposed to the communal spirit are banned, and subject to the strongest sanctions. Thus the arrogant, the irate, the calumniator, those who harbored rancor or would take revenge, incurred a whole year's penance, or exclusion from "purity" for the same period.[27]

Communal observances included communal meals, communal prayers and meetings: "They shall eat communally, bless communally, and take counsel communally." [28]

Only those who had been definitively admitted might have access to the communal meals, to the "banqueting of the Great Ones"; candidates and brethren who had incurred a two years' penance were excluded from them. It cannot therefore be doubted that those meals had a sacred character, which is why only initiates could partake of them.

All the information that can be gathered in the *Manual* about

---

[21] *Ibid.*, VI, 24–VII, 25; VIII, 16–19; VIII, 21–IX, 2.
[22] *Ibid.*, VIII, 1–4.   [23] *Ibid.*, VII, 17.
[24] *Ibid.*, VI, 26: the culprit was excluded from purifications for a year, and his food ration diminished by a fourth.
[25] *Ibid.*, I, 11–13.   [26] Cf. *Ibid.*, V, 3–4, 24–26; X, 25–XI, 2.
[27] Cf. *Ibid.*, VI, 25–26; VII, 2–3, 4–5, 8–9.   [28] *Ibid.*, VI, 2–3.

those ceremonial meals may be put into one single sentence: "When the table is set to eat or the must to drink, the priest shall be the first to stretch out his hand to invoke a blessing upon the first portions of the bread and the must." [29] This, no doubt, refers to the banquet of the "ten," presided over by the priest.[30] The blessing was recited over the bread (*leḥem*) and the must (*tîrôš*). Any mention of wine (*yaïn*), it will be noted, is avoided. It may be supposed that the meal ended with another prayer, according to a custom well attested by the *Mishna*.[31]

Sunrise and sunset were the appointed times for communal prayer.[32] To this was added a vigil of the "Great Ones," a third of every night of the year, which consisted in "reading the Book, studying the Law, and blessing communally." [33] One man out of a "ten" was specially appointed "to study the Law day and night, continually, for the improvement of all." [34] The "Searcher," freed from any other occupation in order to devote himself wholly to the meditation of the Bible, could not fail to discover "things hidden from Israel" which he was to reveal to his brethren.[35]

Was the Community's worship connected with the official cult of Judaism? And what was the Sectarians' opinion of the sacrifices which were offered in the Jerusalem Temple? The *Manual* does not allow us to make any definite statement on the matter. It seems, however, that the connection had been broken. The Community was now the true "sanctuary of Israel," a "foundation of the holy of holies for Aaron." [36] In that eschatological sanctuary, sins would be expiated "without the flesh of burnt offerings and the fat of sacrifice"; prayer, "the offering of the lips," would take the place of the "odor of justice," and "perfect conduct would be considered as an agreeable offering." [37] Sacrificial cult was thus, if not formally condemned, relegated to a secondary plan.

All decisions concerning the life of a group had to be made at the meetings of the Community. Everything was carefully regulated.

Firstly, the order of precedence: "The priests shall sit first, the elders second, and the rest of the people shall sit according to his position." [38] The order of the day had, unless presented by the Surveyor, to be approved by the "Great Ones." No one, not yet entitled to take an active part in the deliberations, could speak without their permission.

Strict order reigned throughout the discussions. Brethren could express their opinions one after the other, according to their respective seniority.[39] It was everyone's duty to listen patiently to a speech, however long and tedious. A ten days' penitence would follow the interruption of a speech, while the poor fellow who succumbed to slumber was punished for a whole month. Nor were they allowed to

---

[29] *Ibid.*, VI, 4–5.   [30] *Ibid.*, VI, 3–4.   [31] *Berakhoth*, VI, 8.
[32] *M.D.*, X, 1–3.   [33] *Ibid.*, VI, 7–8.   [34] *Ibid.*, VI, 6–7.
[35] *Ibid.*, VIII, 11–12.   [36] *Ibid.*, VIII, 5–6.   [37] *Ibid.*, IX, 4–5.
[38] *Ibid.*, VI, 8–9.   [39] *Ibid.*, VI, 9–13.

go out without permission: anyone who left the meeting more than twice had to expiate this by a penitence lasting from ten days to a month.[40] Other regulations concerned good manners, for instance it was forbidden to spit in the presence of the "Great Ones": the culprit had to do penance for a month.[41]

Some prescriptions dealt more particularly with modesty and behavior, not at the meetings only, but at any time. Conspicuous gestures, intemperate laughter, vain speeches, brought respectively ten, thirty, and ninety days of penitence.[42] Modesty rules were very strict: "Whoever stretches out his 'hand'[43] from under his garment and stirs so that his nakedness becomes apparent shall be punished for thirty days."[44] "Whoever walks naked before his fellow without being sick, shall be punished for six months."[45]

It will be seen that chastity was held in high esteem by the members of the Community. They were, in fact, pledged to "follow no more . . . after lustful eyes."[46] Should we infer from that that they were constrained to celibacy and total chastity? Taken alone, the *Manual* does not allow us to give a definite answer to the question. No mention, it is true, is ever made of women and children,[47] and the Sect's communal ways were not easily adaptable to family life. We must not forget, however, that feminine skeletons have been found in the Qumrân cemetery. The pros and cons being thus equal, it is not possible at the present stage to decide one way or another.

Lastly, a most characteristic trait of communal observances, we find common ownership of property. Members definitively accepted into the Community could not possess anything in their own right. Their personal belongings became "Community property"; their salary went to the common fund through the hands of the "treasurer of the Great Ones."[48] Their "pure" property must never be mingled with that of "the men of deception,"[49] from whom they could accept nothing without payment.[50] Everything, in one word, was common among the brethren, but they were altogether severed from the rest of the world.

Scrupulous care had to be taken of articles belonging to the Community; any loss had to be made good and whoever was in no position to do so, incurred a sixty days' penitence.[51] But any conscious

---

[40] *Ibid.*, VII, 9–12.   [41] *Ibid.*, VII, 13.   [42] *Ibid.*, VII, 15, 14, 9.
[43] This is a euphemism: cf. *Is.*, LVII, 8.
[44] *M.D.*, VII, 13–14.   [45] *Ibid.*, VII, 12.   [46] *Ibid.*, I, 6.
[47] W. H. Brownlee, it is true, holds the opposite opinion, but his hypothesis does not carry conviction. Cf. notes to my translation for I, 1 and IV, 2–15. A. M. Habermann thinks that XI, 8 (*sôd mibbenôth qôdeš*: an assembly of the daughters of sanctity) alludes to feminine members of the Community, not mentioning marriage however. His interpretation springs from a faulty reading. Cf. *'Edah we-'Eduth*, p. 86.
[48] *M.D.*, VI, 20.   [49] *Ibid.*, IX, 8.   [50] *Ibid.*, V, 16–17.
[51] *Ibid.*, VII, 6–8. — But then, how could one who has nothing of his own possibly be able to make a restitution? That ruling probably concerned postulants and novices, whose property was still set apart from that of the Community.

fraud could be remitted only after a whole year's penance, during which the culprit was considered as unclean.[52]

To sum up, it will be enough to quote the *Manual:* "The lesser shall obey the greater in regard to labor and wealth. They shall eat communally, bless communally, and take counsel communally."[53] All these rules, however, concerned only the "Great Ones" and the brethren by full right. How one might accede to that dignity now remains to be explained.

THE VARIOUS STAGES OF ADMITTANCE INTO THE COMMUNITY

It has been seen that the Community members were men dedicated to God of their own free will, and pledged to live according to the rules of the *Manual*. A postulant had to present himself to the "Overseer of the Great Ones," and submit to a preliminary investigation as to his intelligence, education and behavior. The candidate who possessed the requisite qualities for bearing the burden of the Community discipline was admitted by the Overseer into the Covenant "to turn to the truth and to turn away from all perversity."[54]

The ceremonial of admittance is described at length in the *Manual*. It must be public, in the presence of all the brethren, and included a sworn pledge, an irrevocable oath "to return to the Law of Moses . . . according to all that is revealed of it to the sons of Zadok, the priests . . . and to the great (assembly) of the men of their Covenant, who communally dedicate themselves to His (God's) truth."[55]

The ritual also included the recital, by the priests, of God's mercies, and the perusal by the Levites of Israel's iniquities. The new candidates then spoke in their turn, confessing their sins. The ceremonial ended with blessings upon the members of the "party of God," and dreadful curses upon the wicked men of the party of Belial, the candidates answering "Amen, amen."[56]

The conversion required by the Community must be sincere and firmly decided upon; the sin of hypocrites was held to be as grave as that of the wicked, and the punishment which awaited them was not less terrible: "May the wrath of God be kindled against him for (his) eternal destruction . . . ! May He place his lot in the midst of the eternally cursed!" And the future members answered: "Amen, amen!"[57]

A period of instruction and purification followed the entrance ceremonial. The Overseer explained to the candidates the laws of the Community, the struggle between the spirit of truth and the spirit of iniquity, the true calendar. It was his task to judge everyone according to his mind, to distinguish and select those who might be presented to the meetings of the "Great Ones." The length of that period is not stated.

The admission of the "postulants" into the "novitiate" depended

52 *Ibid.*, VII, 24–25.   53 *Ibid.*, VI, 2–3.   54 *Ibid.*, VI, 13–15.
55 *Ibid.*, V, 7–10.   56 *Ibid.*, I, 20–II, 10.   57 *Ibid.*, II, 11–18.

on the vote of the assembly, which had the duty of investigating each particular case. The "novitiate" lasted for two years. During the first year, the novice underwent his doctrinal instruction and observed the rules of the Community, but was never allowed to partake in the Community purifications "in pools and rivers," in "any water for washing." [58] He still enjoyed the full ownership of his property, which was separate from that of the Community. Both he and his property, in a word, were still unclean.

That first year over, every novice was again brought before the "Great Ones," who inquired about his instruction and his deeds. If their verdict was favorable, the novice was admitted to the second year of probation. He might henceforth partake of the ritual bathing without soiling thereby the purity of "holy men." His property was handed over to the treasurer, but registered and kept in reserve, as the novice was not yet a full member or united to the Congregation forever. And the door leading to the communal table, the banqueting of the "Great Ones," remained closed to him, for he was not yet entirely clean.

The novice, however, who persevered to the end of the second year, and after a last examination by his teachers, was considered worthy of being admitted into the Community, was received, definitively, provided with an inscription number among his brethren and shared the community of doctrine, right and purity. His property, now entirely clean and spotless, was joined to the common fund and became "Community property." He had become, in other words, a "Great One," counselor and judge in the Community.[59]

But the right to enjoy his privileges from the new brother a total fidelity to the Law of Moses and the rules of the Community. Grave failings (cheating in the matter of property, arrogance, disobedience, angry words addressed to a priest, calumny concerning a brother) were liable to make him unclean for a year.[60] Anyone who, frightened away by the harsh discipline, had left the Community and later asked to be accepted back, had to begin his novitiate all over again; he was excluded from the purifications during the first year, from the banquet in the second. Those two years over, a favorable vote of the "Great Ones" could permit him to be reintegrated and allow him, it seems, to recover the place in the order of precedence which he had formerly occupied.[61]

The same penalty awaited those who transgressed the Law of Moses through inadvertence. They were excluded from the purifications and barred from any active participation in deliberations or judgments. If however, during a two years' probation, they committed no new sin of inadvertence, they could step *ipso facto* into their former place.[62]

But some sins might not be remitted or forgiven, such as uttering

58 *Ibid.*, III, 4–5.   59 *Ibid.*, VI, 13–23.
60 *Ibid.*, VI, 24–27; VII, 2–4, 15–16.   61 *Ibid.*, VII, 18–21.
62 *Ibid.*, VIII, 24–IX, 2.

the Name of God, deliberately transgressing a commandment of the Law, calumniating the "Great Ones," or rebelling against the Community's authority; those were crimes which carried definitive excommunication: "he shall be banished and return no more." [63] Likewise, a member who betrayed the Sect after a ten years' service became something like an *excommunicatus vitandus*. Any contact with him involved definitive exclusion.[64] To cast one's lot with the "sons of light" required, it will be perceived, courage, sanctity and perseverance.

Such was the communal life at Qumrân, as it appears in the *Manual* in our possession.

It was undoubtedly a community of the monastic type, whose members practiced, under the guidance of their superiors, the various rules of communal life.

It was a society governed by priests, and probably of a sacerdotal origin.

It was an esoteric group that had deliberately parted ways with Israel, considering itself as the true successor of the Elected People and its own doctrine as the true and only teaching of God, the sole and acceptable interpretation of the message of Moses and the Prophets.

It was a community of "clean" men, whose purity, however, had to surpass the mere outward requisites of ceremonial purity: "He may not come to the water to share in the purification of the holy men, for they will not be cleansed unless they have turned from their wickedness!" [65]

It was also an eschatological and apocalyptic community whose members had received new divine revelations, and thought that the sufferings of the last days before the universal Judgment were at hand.[66]

We shall now have to compare this evidence with the descriptions provided by other ancient sources concerning communal life within Judaism.

2.   The New Covenant in the Land of Damascus

No sooner had the first texts from the Judean desert been published, than scholars perceived them to be akin to the *Zadokite Fragments* or the *Damascus Document*.[67] There can be no doubt that the document discovered in 1897 in the famous Old-Cairo *Geniza* is closely

---

[63] *Ibid.*, VI, 27–VII, 2; VIII, 21–24; VII, 16–17.

[64] *Ibid.*, VII, 22–25.   [65] *Ibid.*, V, 13–14.

[66] The application of *Is.*, XL, 3 to the Community (cf. VIII, 12–16) testifies to an eschatological outlook. The use of the word *qeṣ* (end) in the sense of "time" is no less revealing: for the brethren, present "time" and the "end" were one. To them, their epoch immediately preceded the Messianic era (cf. IX, 9–11).

[67] Among others E. L. SUKENIK, *M.G.*, I, pp. 21–24. – R. TOURNAY, *R.B.*, 1949, pp. 216–218, etc.

related, from a literary standpoint, to our manuscripts, especially to
the *Manual of Discipline*. Even a cursory perusal of the translation
which is given at the end of this book will convince the reader that
these documents employ expressions not only akin to each other but
entirely identical. Moreover, we now know that fragments of the
Damascus Document were found in the Qumrân caves.

Let us endeavor to find out in which way, and to what extent the
Damascus Document may complete our information about the
Qumrân Sect. To emphasize the likenesses only, and ignore the di-
vergences would be indefensible. That self-evident truth has perhaps been somewhat neglected.

AIM AND ORGANIZATION

The religious ideal of the Damascus Community is identical with
the one that emerges from the investigation of the *Manual*. Both
stress the necessity of a return to the Law of Moses, "for everything
is minutely regulated therein." But that Law was truly understood
by the sons of Zadok only, — Israel had erred — so that many rules
were imposed through opposition to errors current in Israel. Those
who entered the Covenant had to be careful to "act according to
the exact statement of the Law in the epoch of wickedness; to
keep apart from the children of perdition, to refrain from the unclean wealth of wickedness . . . ; to put a distinction between the
clean and the unclean . . . ; to keep the Sabbath day according to
its exact statement, the feasts and the fast days according to the
computation of the members of the New Covenant in the land of
Damascus . . . ; to love each man his brother like himself . . . ;
not to defile the holy spirit within them . . ." [68] The Sect was a
community of penitents [69] who separated from Israel in order to
safeguard the true doctrine within a renewed Covenant.

Its organization did not differ from that which is described in the
Qumrân *Manual*, save on one point only.

We find, in fact, the same division into Aaron and Israel, but the
Damascus Document adds to the priests, Levites, and common people mentioned in the *Manual* a fourth category, that of the proselytes. Division into thousands, hundreds, fifties and tens was also
used.[70] Local groups lived in "camps" [71] where they were numbered
and registered.[72]

THE GOVERNMENT OF THE DAMASCUS SECT

Here again, harmony with the Qumrân documents is consistent in
every point, and the more fully expounded *Damascus Manual* gives
invaluable information about the age and duties of the superiors.

The hegemony of priests is as evident as in Qumrân, if not more
so; they are everywhere the first in the order of precedence,[73] and
must normally govern. Access to power, however, was subject to

[68] *D.D.*, VI, 11–VII, 6.   [69] *Ibid.*, IV, 2.   [70] *Ibid.*, XIII, 1–2.
[71] *Ibid.*, XII, 23; XIV, 3.   [72] *Ibid.*, XIV, 3–4.   [73] *Ibid.*, XIV, 3–6.

two conditions: the priest had to be over thirty years old and under
sixty, and fully acquainted with the fundamental doctrine of the
Sepher hehegi (see note to X, 6 in my translation) or *Book of
Meditation*.[74] Nobody might remain in office after he was sixty, "for
because of the infidelity of man, his days have been lessened and
because of the anger of God against the inhabitants of the earth,
He decided to remove their understanding even before they had
completed their days." [75] If there were but one priest in a group,
and he were ignorant, a Levite could act in his stead, except in the
matter of a leper's internment, which was the priests' inalienable
right.[76]

The local superior, or the "Overseer of the camp," was more than
an administrator; it was his duty to teach the "Great Ones." More
than that, he was to love them "as a father loves his sons," carry
"the burden of their anguish as does the shepherd for his flock" and
take care that "there shall be no oppressed or broken hearts in his
congregation." [77] It was his task too, to accept new candidates, and
his authorization was required for all commercial transactions.[78]

The "Overseers of the camps" were in their turn subordinate to
the "Overseer of all the camps," who was aged from thirty to fifty,
and "had acquired the mastery of every secret of man and every
language," [79] and was the supreme chief of the Community.

Besides the "Overseers," the *Damascus Document* also mentions
"inspectors," whose chief duty, it would seem, was the census of
young men.[80]

While in Qumrân the office of a judge could be filled by anyone
who had the right to vote at the deliberations, we find, in Damascus,
a special tribunal composed of ten judges, four out of the tribe of
Levi and Aaron, six out of Israel, aged from twenty-five to fifty, and
fully cognizant of the community law.[81]

Yet there were pagan courts too, in the region of Damascus; but
anyone who referred to them a culprit who might be condemned to
death, committed an offense involving capital punishment, according to the code of the Sect.[82]

COMMUNAL LIFE

While in matters of organization and government the *Manual of
Damascus* differed but slightly from that of Qumrân, matters were
different where communal life was concerned. Of course, a communal life of a sort did exist in Damascus; there too, communal virtues such as charity and fraternal reproof were insisted upon,[83] revenge and rancor were just as severely banned.[84] The gulf between
Damascus and the monastic structure of Qumrân remains wide,
nevertheless.

---

[74] *Ibid.*, XIII, 2; XIV, 6–8.   [75] *Ibid.*, X, 8–10.   [76] *Ibid.*, XIII, 3–7.
[77] *Ibid.*, XIII, 7–10.   [78] *Ibid.*, XIII, 11–16.   [79] *Ibid.*, XIV, 8–12.
[80] *Ibid.*, XV, 5–6.   [81] *Ibid.*, X, 4–7.   [82] *Ibid.*, IX, 1.
[83] *Ibid.*, VI, 20–21; VII, 2.   [84] *Ibid.*, IX, 2–8.

No mention is found anywhere of the communal meal, the "Banquet of the Great Ones." It is of course possible that they might have been mentioned in some passage that has been lost, but it seems more likely that the banquet was introduced at a later period. As for the cult, although the priests who founded the Damascus Sect had left the Jerusalem Temple because the legal prescriptions were not observed there in the way they deemed fit,[85] they had not for all that entirely severed their connection with the Temple: it was, for instance, prohibited to send to the sanctuary offerings that had been stolen,[86] or food needed in one's own family; [87] the greatest care was prescribed lest any legal impuritiy should pollute the Temple.[88] All this goes to show that prayer had not yet taken the place of sacrifice.

The Damascus Document does not say much about the deliberations of the "Great Ones"; it only mentions that the "Overseer" was to be informed beforehand about any matter a brother wished to discuss, and also that the order of precedence must be strictly observed at the meetings.[89]

The most striking difference between the two communities concerns ownership of property. It was seen that in Qumrân an absolute communism prevailed among brethren, and that the property of those not belonging to the Sect was excluded from the Community.

The Damascus rules also prohibited the acceptance of any present from a "son of perdition"; and in any matter of buying or selling the authorization of the Overseer was required,[90] but the brethren did not renounce their right of ownership, as is borne out by the following prescriptions: "Concerning anything that is lost without it being known who stole it . . . , let its *owner* pronounce a curse . . . Anything unlawfully possessed that ought to be restituted, if there be no *owner*, let the one who returns it confess to the priest, who shall himself become the owner . . ." etc.[91] It is specified that in a suit concerning property matters, two witnesses would suffice; should there be but one available, the accused man would be pronounced unclean.[92]

While remaining masters of the private property they brought to the camp, the brethren kept also the wages they earned through their work. They were, however, obliged to give to the Overseer and the judges the equivalent of two days' salary a month.[93] This money was used for financial transactions, and of course for works of mercy and helping those who were in charge of the Community: the poor, the old, the lepers, the returned prisoners-of-war, the orphans.[94]

Another, and no less characteristic, difference is that the Qumrân *Manual* does not preclude the possibility of a society composed of

[85] *Ibid.*, VI, 11–14.   [86] *Ibid.*, XVI, 13.   [87] *Ibid.*, XVI, 14.
[88] *Ibid.*, XI, 18–XII, 2.   [89] *Ibid.*, XIV, 6, 11–12.   [90] *Ibid.*, XIII, 14–16.
[91] *Ibid.*, IX, 10–16.   [92] *Ibid.*, IX, 22–23.   [93] *Ibid.*, XIV, 12–13.
[94] *Ibid.*, XIV, 14–16. – The text however is anything but clear.

celibates alone. But with the *Damascus Document* no doubt can be entertained; it is certainly concerned with married folk. A good many passages are witness to that: "If they dwell in camps . . . if they marry and beget children, they shall walk according to the Law, according to the rule of the teachings . . ." [95] Laws regarding prohibited marriages are insisted upon, and divorce was not allowed.[96] Prescriptions of legal purity between spouses were most scrupulously observed among the brethren; so much so that conjugal intercourse was prohibited in Jerusalem, lest the Temple should be defiled by entering its precincts in a state of uncleanness.[97] Again, the annulment of an oath taken by a woman was regulated; the husband or father could interfere only with a vow that was liable to transgress the Covenant.[98]

If the celibacy of the Qumrân sectarians should prove to be true, that would suffice to account for the greater strictness of their communal life. Family life, obviously, calls for more freedom and less rigidity.

ADMITTANCE INTO THE DAMASCUS COMMUNITY

In Qumrân, after entrance into the Covenant, there followed a "postulate" of unspecified duration and a "novitiate" lasting two years.

In Damascus, proceedings appear to have been simpler. A man wishing to join the Community had to present himself before the Overseer of the camp, who would investigate "his deeds, his understanding, his ability, his strength, and his property." [99] The "oath of the Covenant" was then imposed upon him,[100] and without any further test or ordeal, he was, it seems, definitely accepted as a member of the Community.[101] That Covenant oath bound the father of the family; his children would take the oath on reaching majority.[102] It was expressly forbidden to bring anyone into the Community without the Overseer's agreement,[103] or to reveal to him the laws of the Sect before he had entered the Covenant, "lest he be led astray while learning them." [104]

A substantial part of the Code has come down to us; among others, prescriptions regarding legal suits,[105] the qualification and age of witnesses,[106] the taking and annulment of oaths,[107] purity and purification by water,[108] strict observance of the Sabbath,[109] and the calendar.[110] Living in a foreign land required precise regulations concerning relations with the pagans.[111]

Capital punishment [112] and exclusion from the Community [113]

---

[95] *Ibid.*, VII, 6–9.   [96] *Ibid.*, VII, 1; V, 7–11; IV, 20–V, 2.
[97] *Ibid.*, V, 6–7; XII, 1–2.   [98] *Ibid.*, XVI, 10–12.   [99] *Ibid.*, XIV, 11.
[100] *Ibid.*, XV, 5–7.   [101] *Ibid.*, XIII, 12.   [102] *Ibid.*, XV, 6–7.
[103] *Ibid.*, XIII, 12–13.   [104] *Ibid.*, XV, 10–11.   [105] *Ibid.*, IX, 1–8.
[106] *Ibid.*, IX, 16–X, 3.   [107] *Ibid.*, IX, 8–13; XV, 1–5; XVI, 6–12.
[108] *Ibid.*, XII, 11–18; X, 10–13.   [109] *Ibid.*, X, 14–XI, 18.
[110] *Ibid.*, XVI, 2–4.   [111] *Ibid.*, XII, 6–11.
[112] *Ibid.*, IX, 1, 6–7; XII, 2–4.   [113] *Ibid.*, XX, 1–10; XV, 12–13.

could be pronounced by the Community tribunal. If the number of witnesses was inferior to that requested by the Law, the culprit was merely considered impure.[114]

It is seen that in Qumrân, a fault committed through inadvertence was liable to a two years' probation; in Damascus, a man who unwittingly violated the Sabbath, could not be reinstated before seven years of probation.[115]

The close comparison of the two documents makes it evident that both communities had a common origin, and that, up to a point, each of them can help to shed some light upon the other. But it is necessary to stress the differences, especially in matters of ownership, and, perhaps, of marriage.

We have the choice between two theories to account for those differences:

a) We are dealing with two separate and autonomous groups within the body of a larger confederation, in which case they might be contemporary with each other;

b) Both documents are concerned with the one and same sect, but at different stages of its existence; this would imply an evolution in its laws and observances.

If, as I think, the second theory should be preferred, we shall have to admit that the *Damascus Document*, still fresh from the doctrinal and political crisis at the origin of the Sect, takes us back, contrarily to what is commonly thought, to a stage anterior to that of Qumrân, as it is attested by the *Manual*.

The evolution of the Sect would, in that case, point to an ever-growing chasm between it and the body of Judaism. This will appear even more striking when we compare the Sect of Qumrân and Damascus to particularistic circles which contrived to remain within the frame of the official Jewish religion.

3.   The "Companies" or Habhûrôth According to Rabbinic Literature

The eminent Rabbinic scholar, Saul Lieberman, who is also a distinguished Hellenist,[116] deserves thanks for having drawn our attention to a Jewish communal life of a kind which has so far been overlooked, that of the "companies" or *Habhûrôth*.[117] Professor Lieberman did not dwell at length on the likeness which those groups offer to the Qumrân Sect; it deserves, I think, to be more systematically expounded. The task, it is true, is not an easy one, for the information at our disposal is scattered throughout Rabbinic literature, the *Mishna*, the *Tosephta*, and the two *Talmuds*. It is only by gleaning here and there that we may find the necessary

---

114 *Ibid.*, IX, 20–21, 23.   115 *Ibid.*, XII, 3–6.
116 His best-known works are *Greek in Jewish Palestine* and *Hellenism in Jewish Palestine*, New York, 1942 and 1950.
117 *The Discipline in the so-called Dead Sea Manual of Discipline*, J.B.L., December 1952, pp. 199–206.

4. — The ruins of the main building seen from the South-East   On the left, the cliff of the caves.

(Photo Starcky)

material for reconstituting as best we can the communal ideal of the "companions" or *Ḥabherîm*.

Jewish religious life was, and is to this day, an essentially communal one; no liturgical prayer can be said unless the minimum congregation, the *minyan* of ten, just as in Qumrân and Damascus, is attained. This is common knowledge; but it is less well known that, at times, smaller circles formed within the Israel Community. The *ḥabhûrah* was in fact an *ecclesiola in ecclesia*.

But what was the *ḥabhûrah*? What was the aim the "companions" pursued? Let us look into the matter more closely.

THE AIM OF THE INSTITUTION

Rabbinic literature constantly distinguishes the "companion" from *'am ha'ares*,[118] the man who is ignorant of the Law. The former is filled with an ideal of fidelity down to the minutest detail, and strives courageously to conform to all the rules of ceremonial cleanliness. Pious men who sought to resist an atmosphere of indifference bound themselves together into associations (*ḥabhûrôth*) that were nuclei of fervent piety.

The companion pledged himself, among other things, to observe scrupulously the law of tithes, and take care not to be contaminated with any food that might have been polluted.

Here are the most important rules laid down by the *Mishna*: "He that undertakes to be trustworthy (*ne'eman*) must give tithe from what he eats, from what he sells and from what he buys and he may not be the guest of a *'am ha'ares* . . ."[119]

"He that undertakes to be a companion (*ḥabher*) may not sell to a *'am ha'ares* foodstuff that is wet or dry, or buy from him foodstuff that is wet, and he may not be the guest of a *'am ha'ares*, nor may he receive him as a guest because of his raiment (which is a conveyor of uncleanness)."[120]

The *Tosephta* of the same treaty specifies that a companion was not allowed to pay his tithe to a priest held to be ignorant; that he might not touch meals prepared by a *'am ha'ares*, even if the prescribed offerings had been taken from them; and he must be in a state of legal cleanness even in partaking of his ordinary food (*ḥullîn*).[121]

CONDITIONS OF ADMITTANCE

The admittance into the *ḥabhûrah* had to be witnessed by three companions at least.[122] The *Tosephta* states simply: "before the company";[123] and the Jerusalem *Talmud*: "in public" (*barabbîm*).[124] An examination followed. If it was demonstrated that the candidate,

---

[118] Literally: "people of the land."   [119] *Dammai*, II, 2.
[120] *Ibid.*, II, 3.   [121] *Tos. Dam.*, II, 2.
[122] *Talmud bab.-Bekhoroth*, 30b.   [123] *Tos. Dam.*, II, 14.
[124] *Ibid.*, II, 22d. — Respecting this passage, S. Lieberman observes: "*Rabbim* is here synonymous with *Haberim*" (*Art. cit.*, p. 200). — The expression *barabbîm*, however, may mean simply "in public," "publicly."

even before he sought admittance into the *ḥabhûrah,* already conformed to the duties concerning tithes and purity, he was immediately proclaimed a companion; otherwise he was subject to a thirty days' probation. Shammai's more rigoristic school requested a whole year's probation before attaining the superior degrees of purity.[125]

There were, in fact, numerous classes in the company. One could accede at once to the higher degrees, provided the pledge to observe all the obligations of the inferior degrees was taken. It should be noted here, as a matter of special interest for us, that the most elevated degrees could be attained only by priests and Levites, since only they were allowed to touch the pure and holy offerings of sacrifices, later consuming the parts which were theirs by right.

THE LIFE OF THE COMPANIONS

Contrary to what has been observed of the Damascus and Qumrân Sect, the *ḥabhûrôth* did not live a communal life, properly speaking, under the guidance of established superiors. Neither was there any common ownership of property, other than that of pious men whose attitude was: "Mine is thine and thine is likewise thine!" [126]

Their main pursuit lay in safeguarding purity.

Hence the necessity of keeping aloof from the *'am haʾareṣ,* the same attitude we met in the case of the brethren of Damascus and Qumrân, since the contact of ignorant men offered a perpetual threat of contamination.

Among the countless prohibitions, many of which are no doubt of a later period,[127] it is enough to mention one also found in the *Damascus Document,* viz. to sell, at any price, the products of granary or wine press to the pagans.[128] It was due no doubt to the fear of the companions that their flour and wine be made unclean. In fact, this is what we find in the Jerusalem *Talmud:* "All agree that a whole stack of wheat, or a complete vintage of grapes or a complete harvest of olives, cannot be sold except to a learned companion." [129]

While keeping aloof from the common people, the companions, it seems, exercised proselytism among the pagans, as the Damascus brethren did, for we find a maxim, said to have been uttered by Rabbi Meir, to the effect that a pagan who abjured idolatry in the presence of three companions, should enjoy the status of a foreigner living within the Israelite Community.[130]

Again as in Damascus, the vow of a father bound the rest of the family, and his wife and children were supposed to observe the rules. The force of habit was generally trusted: a companion was allowed

---

[125] *Tos. Dam.,* II, 10. — *Talm. bab.-Bekhoroth,* 30b.
[126] *Mishna-Abhoth,* V, 10.
[127] This legislation originates to a large extent in the Rabbinical school of Usha (R. Meir), in the middle of the Second century A.D. — Cf. J. Bonsirven, *Le Judaïsme palestinien au temps de Jésus-Christ,* vol. I, Paris, 1935, p. 60.
[128] *D.D.,* VI, 6.   [129] *Dam.,* VI, 25c.
[130] *Talm. bab.* — *'Abhoda Zara,* 64b.

to eat at the table of a '*am ha'ares* who had married the daughter or the widow of a companion, though commercial transactions with the husband remained forbidden; and likewise, he could buy anything from a companion married to the daughter or the widow of a '*am ha'ares*, but not sit down at his table.[131]

A companion remained a member of the association as long as there was no doubt concerning his fidelitiy to the pledge he had taken. But if it was found that he failed to fulfill his obligations, he was excluded from the association, and his reinstatement depended on the subsequent improvement of his conduct. Rabbi Meir was the only one to advocate definitive exclusion, as he did not admit that a companion who had accepted the position of tax collector, could ever be received back.[132]

Thus the *habhûrôth* had points in common with the Damascus and Qumrân communities; for instance, purity was particularly insisted upon, giving thereby rise to segregation. Yet, it is obvious, beyond any shadow of doubt, that the two movements were very different. In Damascus and Qumrân we meet with an eschatological movement, while the companies were nothing of the sort. They may have had more points in common with the Damascus Sect than with that of the Qumrân,[133] but the divergencies were such that no confusion is possible.

It would be more interesting to find out whether, at their origin, they had not sprung from the same urge and been moved by the same influence.

The origin of the companies remains so far obscure, and is much disputed. For Schürer, the companions were tantamount to Pharisees.[134] A. Büchler, on the contrary, as well as Father Bonsirven, holds that the ordinances observed by a *habher*, "were not meant for all the Jews indiscriminately, but for the members of the priestly families only, who were obliged to observe stricter purity when partaking of the sacred food; and those rules of purity were later extended to the rest of the Jews." [135] J. Derenbourg has adopted an intermediate position: communal practices were of sacerdotal origin, and were later adopted by the lay Pharisees. "The priests," he writes, "who came each in turn to perform the Temple service in

---

[131] *Tos. Dam.*, II, 14–18.   [132] *Talm. bab. — Bekhoroth*, 31a.

[133] Professor Lieberman remarks nevertheless that *mašqeh harabbîm* — which I translate "banquet of the Great Ones" (*M.D.*, VI, 20) — might designate the liquid nourishment called *mašqîn* (cf. *Mishna-Makhshirin*, VI, 4), which the "companion" must not touch during the first period of his initiation. — Cf. *art. cit.*, p. 203. But this, in my opinion, does not hold good against the fact that the Community "banquet" was of a cultural character while touching the *mašqîn* was merely a matter of ceremonial purity. — Cf. *Tos. Dam.*, II, 12 and *Talm. bab.-Bekhor.*, 30b.

[134] *Geschichte des jüdischen Volkes im Zeitalter Jesu Christi*, 3rd edition, Leipzig, 1898, vol. II, p. 397.

[135] Cf. A. BÜCHLER, *Der galiläische 'Am-ha'ares des zweiten Jahrhunderts*, Wien, 1906, p. 3 and *passim;* J. BONSIRVEN, *op. cit.*, vol. I, p. 60.

Jerusalem, living away from their families, partook of their meals together; their high rank, the particular kind of food which was served to them, as coming from the offerings, tithe and sacrifices, lent to those repasts the character of a religious rite, and required, from both men and things, scrupulous care regarding purity. They washed before sitting down at the table, they blessed the bread and wine, since bread and flour were part of every sacrifice, they pronounced a benediction again after the repast was over, so that the table came to be considered a kind of altar. The Sabbaths and feast days were particularly suitable for these *syssities*, i.e., repasts taken in common, and their holiness made the religious character of those gatherings even more striking." [136] As for the meals of *ḥabhûrôth*, they are thought to have been instituted on the pattern of the Passover banquet, to which people gathered in groups of ten,[137] and in imitation of the priests' communal meals.[138]

No doubt Derenbourg's hypothesis concerning the origin of the companies oversimplifies matters. But his view of a priestly confraternity is not at variance with what we know of the laws of Damascus and Qumrân.

Regarding the origin of *ḥabhûrôth*, I feel inclined to agree with an opinion quoted by S. Mendelsohn, who believes that they were formed at the time of the Maccabean wars, among people particularly attached to piety and purity. The organization of the *ḥabhûrôth* would then have taken place in the last decades of the Second century B.C.[139]

To sum up: Jewish society, at a period not too distant from the beginnings of Christianity, was torn by separatist tendencies. Some of these groups contrived to maintain themselves within the Jewish community, for instance the Pharisees and the *ḥabherîm*, if indeed a distinction can be drawn between them. Others went to the length of breaking off completely with official Judaism. Obviously, the *"Sectarians"* were among the latter. And so were the Essenes, that group about which so little has been known, but which now, thanks above all to the Qumrân *Manual*, merges in quite a new light. How close the connection was between the brethren of Damascus, those of Qumrân, and the "monks" who dwelt on the shores of the Dead Sea, is the main riddle which we shall try to solve.

4. The Community of Essenes

Although many Jewish, pagan and Christian writers have dealt with Essenism at length, the sect has always remained a baffling and elusive mystery. The New Testament mentions it nowhere; Rabbinical literature is imprecise and vague; its origin, its decline, and even the

---

136 *Essai sur l'histoire et la géographie de la Palestine, d'après les Thalmuds et les autres sources rabbiniques*, vol. I, Paris, 1867, pp. 141–142.
137 JOSEPHUS, *B.J.*, VI, IX, 3.   138 J. DERENBOURG, *op. cit.*, p. 142.
139 Cf. the art. *Haber*, in the *Jew. Encycl.*, vol. VI, pp. 122–124.

etymology of its name remained obscure.[140] Both Philo and Josephus described the life of the Essenes, but one hesitated to accept their statements as it was not easy to draw a line between historical truth and idealization. The recent discoveries again raised the Essene problem; the Qumrân *Manual* shows, beyond any possible doubt, that we are dealing, if not with the same society, at least with identical surroundings. Even should it prove impossible to identify the Qumrân Sect with any historically known group, its close connection with the Essenes cannot, for all that, be gainsaid.[141] Professor Dupont-Sommer, in fact, does not hesitate to identify the Qumrân Sect with the Essenes of the ancient writers.[142] Father de Vaux, while adopting that view, holds however that it needs some tempering.[143]

ESSENISM AND ITS INSTITUTIONS

All classical Jewish and Christian writers are one in their admiration and praise of the Essenes, of their saintliness, communal discipline and chastity.

Philo, through a mistaken etymology, thought "Essenes" ('Εσσαῖοι) came from ὅσιοι, i.e., "holy ones." [144] They certainly had the reputation of excelling in piety as well as in all other virtues. Perhaps they did call themselves "Holy," as the Qumrân and Damascus brethren, who were considered "holy men," [145] even as "men of perfect holiness." [146]

The communal life led by the Sect was baffling to the men of antiquity. In whichever town or village of Syro-Palestine [147] its members settled, they lived the same peaceful existence under the guidance of overseers, and in total communion of spirit and prop-

---

[140] We find 'Εσσηνοί or 'Εσσαῖοι in Greek and *Esseni* in Latin. Most contemporary writers think that these forms derived from *hase'* (plural *hasên* or *hasaya'*) i.e., "pious." See discussion in the *Suppl. au Dict. de la Bible,* t. II, col. 1109–1110. It might be not unreasonable to suppose that some religious groups mentioned in the Rabbinical works, such as *senu'im* (the chaste ones), the *hassa'im* (the silent ones, those who keep the secrets), the *watiqim* (the steadfast ones), the *banna'im* (the builders) should be identified with the Essenes. Cf. art. *Essenes* in *The Jew. Encycl.,* vol. V, p. 226.

I. M. Grintz endeavors to identify the Beothusians of Rabbinical literature with the Essenes. The various Greek transcriptions ('Εσσαῖοι, 'Οσσαοιί 'Ιεσσαῖοι) would suggest, he thinks, that the name of an individual could be found at their origin (perhaps *'Issî*). Cf. *'Ansê "hayyahad"* — *'Issiyîm-Bêth ('() Sin, Sinai,* XVI, 1952, pp. 37–42.

[141] Cf. S. LIEBERMAN, *art. cit.* p. 206.

[142] *Aperçus préliminaires* . . . , pp. 105–117. *Nouveaux aperçus.* . . . *passim,* particularly p. 194: ". . . if Essenism properly said is the name of the Jewish Sect described by Philo and Josephus, i.e. the Jewish Sect of the Covenant, that of the documents of Qumrân. . . ."

[143] *R.B.,* January, 1953, p. 105.

[144] PHILO, *Quod omnis probus liber sit,* Ed. L. COHN and S. REITER, vol. VI, § 75.   [145] Cf. *M.D.,* V, 13; VIII, 17, etc.

[146] Cf. *D.D.,* XX, 2, 5, etc. — *M.D.,* VIII, 20.

[147] PHILO, *Quod omnis probus* . . . , § 75. — JOSEPHUS, *B.J.,* II, VIII, 4.

erty. The smallest assembly counted, as in Damascus and Qumrân, ten members at least; [148] the law of precedence likewise held good there.

For the Essenes also, communal life meant first of all prayers communally said. They began their days with addressing to God the first of their prayers as soon as the sun appeared on the horizon.[149] The Law of Moses was the object of the deepest reverence and was studied more particularly on the Sabbath, which they observed more strictly than the rest of the Jews.[150]

Their relations with the Temple of Jerusalem are not very clear. According to Philo, they rejected animal sacrifices,[151] while striving to preserve their minds in a state of priestly saintliness. It is the same negative attitude as is found in the Qumrân Manual. According to Josephus, the Essenes, "while sending offerings to the Temple, did not offer sacrifices therein . . . and offered them among themselves." [152] And, in fact, it would seem that their communal repast, the same as the one described in the Qumrân Manual, bore the stamp of a sacrificial banquet.

Before sitting down to the communal table, the brethren had to cleanse themselves and put on the white garment which was reserved for the ceremony.[153] "After that purification, they gather in a special hall into which no outsider is permitted to enter; neither would they themselves enter the refectory unless cleansed, as if it were some sacred precinct. They take their seats without any uproar, then the baker serves to each commensal his bread, the cook puts before him a dish with but one foodstuff therein. The priest recites a prayer before the repast, and no one may touch it before the prayer is said. After the repast, he prays anew; all, both at the beginning and at the end, return thanks to God, the bestower of the food which gives life." [154]

Nor was the blessing of food the only task incumbent upon the priests; they were the administrators of the Community's revenues, and also responsible for the bread and other food being prepared according to the strictest requisites of purity.[155] The corresponding passage in the Qumrân Manual apparently precludes the hypothe-

---

[148] B.J., II, VIII, 9.

[149] Ibid., II, VIII, 5. — It is no longer necessary to refute the fantastic interpretation according to which the Essenes worshipped the sun. The passage alludes to the morning prayer said at sunrise. The Babylonian Talmud praises the watiqîm (cf. supra, n. 140) who managed to conclude the Shema' ("Hearken Israel") at the very moment when the first rays of the sun appeared in the sky. Cf. Berakhoth, 9b. One of the two most ancient prayers — the Mishna presupposes them to be traditional (Berakhoth, I, 4) — which precede the Shema' is precisely addressed to the Creator of light, whence its name, Yôṣer 'ôr.

[150] B.J., II, VIII, 9.   [151] Quod omnis probus . . . , § 75.

[152] A.J., XVIII, I, 6. This obscure passage is much discussed: cf. M. DELCOR, R.B., pp. 544–546.

[153] B.J., II, VIII, 5.   [154] Ibid.   [155] A.J., XVIII, I, 5.

sis that the Essenes elected their priests; priestly descent, on the contrary, was required for a brother to be appointed caterer, or a superintendent of the communal table.[156]

Josephus hints that guests not belonging to the confraternity could be admitted to the evening meal and that they were greatly impressed by the calm and order that reigned in the house, also by the sobriety of those who partook of the meal, for they never ate or drank to excess.[157] This custom of admitting guests to the communal table is not mentioned in the *Damascus Document* or the Qumrân *Manual*.

Regarding Essene abstemiousness, the present state of Josephus' text does not at all convey the meaning of perpetual abstemiousness from meat and wine. The Essenes' remarkable sobriety in the use of wine suggests on the contrary that they did not condemn the use of it unconditionally. St. Jerome, however, quoting that same passage, expresses his admiration for those men who perpetually abstained from meat and wine, and had acquired the habit of everyday fasting.[158] That habit, it is true, is attested by the Therapeutes, whose connection with the Essenes cannot be doubted.[159] Nor must it be forgotten that the virtue Philo praises most in the Essenes is their frugality.[160] All this information, however, is far from conclusive.

The Qumrân *Manual* does not specify anything on this matter. The absence of such words as "wine" and "meat" cannot of course be accepted as evidence, but the use, by the author, of the word "must" (*tîrôš*) might not be without significance.[161] For it must be borne in mind that while *tîrôš* stands for "wine" in Biblical Hebrew, later Hebrew rather emphasizes the distinction between *tîrôš* and "wine." *Tîrôš* meant sweet unfermented liquors; "sweetness" was particularly characteristic, so that it came finally to designate even dry figs. "The Bible gives to the juice of the grape the name of must, and men give that name even to dry figs . . ."[162] "To him that

---

[156] Cf. *M.D.*, IX, 7–8. — Schürer's interpretation was right (*op. cit.*, II, p. 571, n. 63).   [157] *B.J.*, II, VIII, 5.   [158] *Adv. Jovinianum*, II, 14.

[159] Philo, *De vita contemplativa, passim*, and Eusebius, *Ecclesiastical History*, II, XVII. — These ascetics, each dwelling in his own small house, in the vicinity of Alexandria, led a life of perfect renunciation. They gave up all their property in order to dedicate themselves exclusively to prayer and study of the Law. They used to meet only on the Sabbath day. In the evening they partook of their only meal, a most frugal one, drinking nothing but water. Some would fast from one Sabbath to the other. All were unmarried, but with the men, there were also women, who remained virgins all their lives.

The picture outlined by Philo is of course somewhat idealized, but the skepticism professed by some modern writers (Lucius, Schürer, Lagrange) concerning the existence of Therapeutes, does not seem to me to be justified, even so. It is interesting to notice that Eusebius felt certain that these ascetics were Christian monks.

[160] *Quod omnis probus* . . . , § 84; Eusebius, *Praeparatio evangelica*, VIII, XI.
[161] I. M. Grintz, *Sinai*, XVI, 1952, p. 15.   [162] *Talm. jer.-Nazir*, II, 51d.

has vowed not to touch *tîrôš*, any kind of sweetmeat is forbidden, but he is free to drink wine." [163]

These remarks, however interesting, are inconclusive regarding the problem of the Essenes' abstemiousness; moreover, *tîrôš*, in the sense of "new wine," is mentioned among the products of the soil on which tithe should be given: "Thou shalt surely tithe all the increase of thy seed, that which cometh forth from the field year by year. And thou shalt eat before Yahweh thy God, in the place which He shall choose to cause His Name to dwell, the tithe of thy corn, thy new wine . . ." [164]

If all this is taken into account, a satisfactory explanation of Josephus' difficult passage, which has been quoted above, may be arrived at: "While sending offerings to the Temple, they did not themselves offer sacrifices therein, because of their greater purity, as they deemed, and for that same reason kept apart from the common (profane) precincts of the Temple; they offered sacrifices in their own abodes." [165] Once we understand that "sacrifice" implies "sacrificial repast," the whole passage becomes clear: as strict observers of the Law, the Essenes did send the prescribed gifts, but the sacrificial banquet was held in the Community refectory, for Jerusalem and the Sanctuary were considered insufficiently pure for so solemn an act. It is likely that they came to endow with that sacred character all their communal meals,[166] the more so as the meals were prepared by priests, as we have already seen.

Regarding judiciary customs, the Essenes possessed a Community tribunal which was composed of a hundred men at least.[167] They were not, as in Damascus, specially appointed; justice was exercised by the assembly of the Community, as was the Qumrân custom.

The deliberations were ruled by the law of precedence and a majority of the votes. As in Qumrân, the order of the day had to be previously approved, and attention was paid to proper behavior.[168]

Common ownership seems to have been substantially the same as in Qumrân. Most of our information is, as usual, supplied in the main by Josephus, but our other sources do not contradict him in any way. Members abandoned all their property to the Community, and its management was in the hands of a priest treasurer; any commercial activity among brethren was strictly prohibited; everything, in short, conforms to the Qumrân *Manual*.[169]

According to Josephus, almsgiving was encouraged: "They do nothing without the guidance of their superiors; but there are two virtues whose practice depends on themselves alone: the assistance of others, and mercy; for they are permitted of their own accord to

---

163 *Ibid.-Nedarîm*, VII, 40b. Both passages are quoted by Grintz.
164 *Deut.*, XIV, 22–23.   165 *A.J.*, XVIII, I, 5.
166 Thus Josephus emphasizes the fact that the Essenes used to enter the common refectory as into a sanctuary (*B.J.*, II, VIII, 5).
167 *B.J.*, II, VIII, 9.   168 *Ibid.*
169 *B.J.*, II, VIII, 3, 4, 6; *A.J.*, XVIII, I, 5.

afford succour to such as deserve it, when they stand in need of it, and to bestow food on those who are in distress; but they cannot give anything to their kindred without the permission of their superiors." [170] It has already been seen that charity was practiced in Damascus; [171] as for the Qumrân *Manual*, while not specifying any rules it certainly does not suggest anything that would exclude it.

That the Essenes practiced celibacy cannot be doubted: "*Sine ulla femina, omni venere abdicata . . . gens aeterna est in qua nemo nascitur . . .*" as Pliny put it.[172] Josephus takes care to observe that the Essenes "do not absolutely deny the fitness of marriage, and the succession of mankind thereby continued; but they guard against the lascivious behavior of women, and are persuaded that none of them preserve their fidelity to one man." [173] The same discourteous explanation is given by Philo, whose misogyny is notorious: women are selfish, jealous, hypocritical, false, beguiling, and if they have children, proud. "All of which," he remarks, "is harmful to communal life. He who is arrested by a woman's guiles takes care of himself, not of his fellows, and, little by little, from a free man he grows into being a slave." [174] But, as a matter of fact, we need not accept those ugly accusations in order to understand the celibacy which was the rule of the Essenes. Let us but realize that communal ways are hardly consonant with family life; and also that the pursuit of legal purity carried to its extreme leads inevitably to the renouncement of marriage.[175] Josephus, however, points to the existence of a class (τάγμα) of Essenes who did marry: "However, there is another order of Essenes, who agree with the rest as to their way of living, and customs and laws, but differ from them on the point of marriage, thinking that by not marrying they cut off the principal part of life, which is the propagation of the species; nay rather, that if all men should be of the same opinion, the whole race of mankind would fail. They try their spouses for three years; and after they have shown by three purifications (after menstruation) that they are likely to be fruitful, then they actually marry them." [176] It is stated, moreover, that conjugal intercourse remained forbidden throughout pregnancy,

---

[170] *Ibid.*, II, VIII, 6.   [171] *D.D.*, XIV, 14–16.   [172] *Hist. nat.*, V, 17.
[173] *B.J.*, II, VIII, 2.   [174] *Praep. ev.*, VIII, XI, 14–17.
[175] We must bear in mind that ritual uncleanness could be contracted involuntarily.
[176] *B.J.*, VIII, 13. — τριετίᾳ ("for three years") proves embarrassing to translators, as it appears to contradict what follows. But perhaps this passage might be understood differently. The Essenes for three years put their brides to proof (δοκιμάζοντες), i.e., submitted them just as the male candidates (δοκιμάζεται: II, VIII, 7) to a postulate (one year) and to a novitiate (two years), since women were also to know and to share Essene life. If moreover, the bride gave proof that she was able to bear children, marriage could take place.

A girl was considered in Talmudic Law to have attained the age of puberty when she was twelve years and one day old. Cf. S. Krauss, *Talmudische Archäologie*, t. II, Leipzig, p. 23. See also pp. 28–29.

since procreation was the only reason for marrying; and that women also were obliged to take ritual baths, clad in linen.

It has been seen that at the present stage we cannot know for certain whether the Qumrân brethren were married or not.[177] But we do know that, in either case, they could be regarded as Essenes.

Another characteristic feature was, according to Philo and Josephus, the Essenes' unconditional ban on slavery.[178] The Qumrân *Manual* does not mention the matter at all; the *Damascus Document*, on the other hand, does not object to slavery.[179]

CONDITIONS OF ADMITTANCE INTO THE ESSENE COMMUNITY

If Philo's and Josephus' testimony be accepted, candidates to Essenism were exclusively men of ripe age, anxious for a refuge where they might atone for their former life. "*Gens aeterna est in qua nemo nascitur, tam fecunda illis aliorum vitae poenitentia est.*" [180] According to Philo they were men nearing old age, freed from the passions of youth, and thus enabled to enjoy true freedom; [181] the Sectarians of Damascus and Qumrân, it may be remembered, were also styled "penitents." [182] Josephus, however, asserts that children were admitted, "while they are pliable and fit for learning." [183] With the married Essenes, just as in Damascus, children born within the Community were counted with candidates from the outside.[184]

Young and old, the newcomers had to submit to the prescribed probation. The "postulate," the duration of which is not specified in the Qumrân *Manual*, lasted for one year with the Essenes; the postulants, arrayed in a white garment and a belt and provided with a small hatchet,[185] were trained in the various practices of communal life. Then came a two years' "novitiate," during which contact between candidates and brethren grew much closer, through common participation in the ritual bathing before the meals; but candidates were not yet admitted to the banquet hall. To attain that supreme

---

177 Professor Brownlee supports the hypothesis that the Qumrân sectarians were married Essenes. Cf. *The Dead Sea Manual of Discipline, B.A.S.O.R., Suppl. Studies* 10–12, 1951, p. 4.

178 *Quod omnis probus* . . . , § 79. – A.J., XVIII, I, 5.

179 Cf. *D.D.*, XI, 12; XII, 10. It will be remembered that the *Damascus Document* authorizes in some cases the taking of oaths (IX, 8–16; XVI, 6–12). This is in formal contradiction of what both Philo (*op. cit.*, § 84) and Josephus (*B.J.*, II, VIII, 6) say of the Essenes.

180 *Hist. nat.*, V, 17: "This is an eternal nation wherein no one is born, so fecund for them proves the repentance that the others have of their own past."

181 *Praep. ev.*, VIII, XI, 3.   182 *D.D.*, IV, 2; XX, 17. – *M.D.*, X, 20.

183 *B.J.*, II, VIII, 2.

184 In the fragments that were detached from the *Manual of Discipline* scroll but do not appear to belong to that document, we find described the stages of the education of a youth born within the group. Cf. D. BARTHELEMY, *R.B.*, 1952, p. 204.

185 *B.J.*, II, VIII, 7. – They employed this hatchet to bury their excrement. They had to wrap themselves in their cloaks so as not to be seen (*B.J.*, II, VIII, 9). Cf. *M.D.*, VII, 13–14.

5. — The large cistern of Qumrân seen from the North.
The foreland of the cliff comes to an end at Râs Feshkha.

privilege "he is obliged to take tremendous oaths; that, in the first place, he will exercise piety towards God; and then, that he will observe justice towards all men; . . . that he will ever show fidelity to all men, and especially to those in authority . . . ; that he will be perpetually a lover of truth, and reprove those that tell lies, that he will keep his hands clean from theft, and his soul from unlawful gains, and that he will neither conceal anything from those of his own sect, nor discover any of their doctrines to others. . . . Moreover he swears to communicate their doctrines to no one otherwise than he has received them himself; . . . and will equally preserve the books belonging to the sect and the names of the angels." [186]

In the Qumrân *Manual*, the oath was required of the candidate not when he was finally accepted, but when he was admitted as a postulant; Josephus does not mention any such oath at all.

Neither do we find any mention in the Jewish historian's work of the penalties incurred by sins considered as forgivable. He only speaks of definitive exclusion as punishment for graver sins: "He who is thus separated from them, does often die after a miserable manner; for as he is bound by the oath he has taken, and by the customs he has been engaged in, he is not at liberty to partake of that food that he meets with elsewhere, but is forced to eat grass, and to famish his body with hunger till he perish; for which reason they receive many of them again when they are at their last gasp, out of compassion to them, as thinking the miseries they have endured almost to the brink of death sufficient punishment for the sin." [187]

These many and striking similarities justify a question: were the Qumrân brethren Essenes?

The geographical situation of Qumrân favors, as we have seen, an affirmative answer.

But what about the divergencies, which seem to hinder a pure and simple identification?

As a matter of fact, these divergencies are, in most cases, only small discrepancies or omissions.[188] A good many could be explained by the fact that the Essenism described by Philo and Josephus was posterior to the communal life codified by the Qumrân *Manual*.

Thus, no mention is found in the *Manual* of the white garment in which an Essene must always be arrayed,[189] but we must not forget that it was the distinctive attire of Jewish priests.[190] Nor is there any mention of the small hatchet which they must always carry when going to secret places: in fact this rule was prescribed in *Deuteronomy*,[191] and it was therefore not necessary to mention it, since the

---

[186] *B.J.*, II, VIII, 7.   [187] *Ibid.*, II, VIII, 8.

[188] We must not forget that Josephus gives us but a summary, and that the *Manual* does not present us either with an exhaustive description of all the aspects of the communal life. Thus it does not mention the observance of the Sabbath.   [189] *B.J.*, II, VIII, 3, 7.

[190] *Ex.*, XXVIII, 39–42. — Th. Reinach had already offered that opinion. Cf. *Oeuvres complètes de Fl. Josèphe*, t. V, Paris, 1912, p. 160, n. 2.

[191] *Deut.*, XXIII, 13–14.

sons of Zadok were pledged to observe the Law of Moses down to the smallest detail.

Another and more serious objection has been raised by Professor Dhorme: "It will be noted . . . that in the *exposés* of the Essene doctrine no mention is ever made of a New Covenant . . . ,"[192] or, in fact, of any Covenant whatever. On the other hand, everything is based, in the Qumrân *Manual*, on the Covenant of the priests, sons of Zadok.[193]

But on closer investigation the discrepancy, it will be found, might be due mainly to the literary style particular to Philo and Josephus. Their writings were intended for pagans, and they were anxious to offer a picture of Judaism which might appeal to them. The mention of a divine Covenant, a notion utterly foreign to the Greek-Roman world, would not have achieved such a purpose at all. Josephus was so well aware of this, that he went out of his way to give these Palestinian movements a Hellenic aspect. Were we to believe him, Pharisees, Sadducees, Essenes, were but the followers of three "philosophical schools."[194] The Pharisees, he bravely asserted, closely resembled Stoics;[195] as for Essenes, their ways were very much like Pythagoras' Greek disciples.[196] The Essenes, presented as models of virtue, were surely more attractive to the Greeks than some severe Jewish group, which observed the ordinances of a Covenant whose interpretation they held to be the only authentic one.

There can be no doubt that Essenism and Neo-Pythagorism have many points in common: pursuit of purity, baths, white garment, rejection of marriage, oaths and animal sacrifices. Scholars have supported the hypothesis of a Pythagorean influence of Essenism (Zeller, Schürer, Isidore, Lévy). Lagrange, for his part, was not so sure (*Le Judaïsme avant J.C.*, Paris, 1931, pp. 325–328). We must neither ignore the remark of A. J. Festugière, who hints that "Josephus, a scholar, might have imagined this likeness himself, in order to give a clearer idea of the Essenes to the Greek public," (*L'idéal religieux des Grecs et l'Evangile*, Paris, 1932, p. 76). It is certain at all events that the picture presented by Josephus contains more Pythagorean features than the Qumrân *Manual*.

A. Dupont-Sommer has for his part adopted the theory of a Pythagorean influence on the Community (*Aperçus préliminaires* . . . , pp. 111, 113.—*Nouveaux aperçus* . . . , pp. 153–156).

Without adopting at the present stage any definitive position upon that point, I would not dismiss the hypothesis which would ascribe all the peculiarities of the Sect as purely Jewish, or particular to this Community. However, it is beyond doubt that communal life in

---

192 *Comptes rendus de l'Académie des Inscriptions et Belles-Lettres*, 1951, p. 193.   193 Cf. V, 8–9.   194 *B.J.*, II, VIII, 2.

195 *De vita sua*, 2: . . . τῇ Φαρισαίων αἱρέσει κατακολουθῶν ἢ παραπλήσιός ἐστι τῇ παρ' Ἕλλησι Στοϊκῇ λεγομένῃ.

196 *A.J.*, XV, X, 4: Γένος δὲ τοῦτ' ἐστὶ διαίτῃ χρώμενον τῇ παρ' Ἕλλησιν ὑπὸ Πυθαγόρου καταδειγμένῃ.

Damascus—which in my opinion is the first stage—was substantially different from Neo-Pythagorism since it admitted marriage, the taking of oaths and bloody sacrifices.

Since Josephus did not mention the Covenant, he could not but omit the oath of Covenant taken by the candidates upon the admittance ceremony. But the tenor of the "tremendous oaths" taken by the Essenes upon their definitive admittance has many points in common with the "oath of the Covenant" mentioned by the Qumrân *Manual*.[197]

The *Manual* can thus be regarded as the code of a certain category of Essenes. It cannot, at the present stage, be decided whether they practiced total chastity or were married, though I feel personally inclined to the first opinion.

As for the Damascus Sect, many signs point to their having had a common origin with the Essenes. If this is correct, the *Damascus Document*, the Qumrân *Manual* and our information concerning the Essenes demonstrate three evolutionary phases:

a) *the Damascus stage*, resulting from a rupture within the ranks of the Jewish priesthood; striving after the strictest ceremonial purity, but so far entailing neither common ownership of property, nor celibacy;

b) *the Qumrân stage*, where a separation from the bulk of Judaism is much more marked, as well as a fully developed communal organization and an actual renunciation of private property and, probably, also of marriage;

c) the last stage of the Community's evolution brings us to the middle of the First century A.D. Little change is found since the Qumrân period; this is *Essenism* described by Philo, Josephus, Pliny and Hippolytus.

Such an evolution points to a relatively lengthy duration of the Essene movement. Of that past we know nothing so far. In the following pages we shall try to discover whether it is possible to gain some knowledge of this and of the historical facts which led to the birth of Essenism, properly speaking.

---

[197] Professor Dupont-Sommer has excellently proved it. Cf. *Observations sur le Manuel de Discipline découvert près de la Mer Morte*, Paris, 1951; pp. 19–22.

chapter four

THE HISTORICAL BACKGROUND

OF THE QUMRÂN MANUSCRIPTS

The identity of the Qumrân sect having thus been established with sufficient probability, let us now try to trace its history and to replace it within the framework of the history of Israel. The number and variety of hypotheses show this to be no easy task; which is but natural, considering that none of the documents in our possession are of a really historical type. Their style throughout is apocalyptic, and the events are supposed to happen in the ultimate period of history, "at the end of days" or at "the time of wrath." The meaning is conveyed through hints, good care is taken to avoid any proper names, and with the exception of the *Damascus Document,* no chronology is given.

Scholars are doing their best to shed some light upon the intentional obscurity fostered by the writers of the Community, and they have provided us with a good many theories. These are, of course, of unequal value, but even those which can be no longer defended have been useful in stressing some important feature in the complex history of the sect.

A rapid survey of these theories will not be superfluous, before we start to examine the documents. They can be divided into five groups, and appear in the following chronological order.

I. THE STRUGGLE AGAINST HELLENISM UNDER ANTIOCHUS EPIPHANES

The first theory [1] assigns the events to the reign of Antiochus IV, between 175 and 164 B.C. The *Kittim*, the conquerors of the *Habakkuk Commentary*, are identified with the armies of the Seleucid monarch, the "wicked Priests" with the Hellenized pontiffs Jason, Menelaus, or Alcimus. The "Teacher of Righteousness", according to a good many authors, is the High Priest Onias III, who was removed from office through the intrigues of Jason, and later assassinated at Menelaus' instigation; [2] and the community none other than the "Assembly of the Hassideans," the ancestors of the Essenes.

II. THE REIGN OF ALEXANDER JANNEUS

A good many authors [3] prefer the period of Alexander Janneus (103–76 B.C.), and identify the "wicked Priest" with that warlike pontiff from Jerusalem. Opinions differ concerning the *"Kittim"*: some think again they are the Seleucids with whom Janneus often had difficulties; [4] others hold that the enemies alluded to in the *Habakkuk Commentary* are the Romans. [5] The persecuted sect might designate either the Pharisees [6] or the Essenes. [7]

[1] B. REICKE, *Die Ta'âmire-Schriften und die Damaskus-Fragmente*, Studia Theologica, vol. II, fasc. I, Lund, 1949, pp. 45–70. — J. TRINQUET, *Les liens "sadocites" de l'Ecrit de Damas, des manuscrits de la Mer Morte et de l'Ecclésiastique*, V.T., 1951, pp. 287–292. — E. DHORME, *Comptes-rendus de l'Académie des Inscriptions et Belles-Lettres*, 1951, pp. 192–200. — G. LAMBERT, *Le Maître de Justice et la Communauté de l'Alliance*, N.R.Th., 1952, pp. 259–283. — I. RABINOWITZ, *The de Vaux Fragment of an unknown Work*, J.B.L., 1952, pp. 19–32; *Sequence and Dates of the extra-Biblical Dead Sea Scroll Texts and "Damascus" Fragments*, V.T., 1953, pp. 175–185. — H. H. ROWLEY, *The internal Dating of the Dead Sea Scrolls*, E.Th.L., 1952, pp. 257–276; *The historical Background of the Dead Sea Scrolls*, The Expository Times, September, 1952, pp. 378–384; *The Zadokite Fragments and the Dead Sea Scrolls*, Oxford, 1952, pp. 62–88. — H. BARDTKE, *Die Handschriftenfunde am Totem Meer*, Berlin, 1952, pp. 143–150. — A. MICHEL, *Le Maître de Justice*, Avignon, 1954, pp. 232–258.   [2] Reicke, Trinquet, Rowley, Michel.

[3] R. DE VAUX, *A propos des manuscrits de la Mer Morte*, R.B., 1950, pp. 428–429; ibid., 1951, pp. 442–443. — J. VAN DER PLOEG, *Les rouleaux de la Mer Morte*, Bi. Or., 1951, p. 10. — M. H. SEGAL, *The Habakkuk "Commentary" and the Damascus Fragments*, J.B.L., 1952, pp. 131–147. — M. DELCOR, *Essai sur le Midrash d'Habacuc*, Paris, 1951, pp. 56–61; *Le Midrash d'Habacuc*, R.B., 1951, pp. 521–549; *Où en est le problème du Midrash d'Habacuc?* R.H.R., t. 142, 1952, pp. 129–146. — W. H. BROWNLEE, *Biblical Interpretation among the Sectaries of the Dead Sea Scrolls*, B.A., 1951, p. 63. — D. BARTHELEMY, *Notes en marge de publications récentes sur les manuscrits de Qumrân*, R.B., 1952, pp. 207–218. — I. L. SEELIGMANN, Kirjath Sepher, vol. XXX, October 1954, p. 44.   [4] De Vaux, Delcor.

[5] Van der Ploeg, Segal, Brownlee, Barthélemy, etc.

[6] De Vaux, Delcor. — Fr. de Vaux has since then withdrawn the Pharisean label which he had at first bestowed upon the Sect (R.B., 1953, p. 105).

[7] Brownlee, Barthélemy.

III. THE CONQUEST OF POMPEY

A third hypothesis [8] favors the beginning of the Roman period in Palestine (63 B.C.), with Aristobulus II and Hyrcanus II as the "wicked Priests" who persecuted the Essenes. The "Teacher of Righteousness" has been tentatively identified with Onias the Thaumaturge, who was stoned by the mob in 65 B.C.[9] The *Kittim* are of course Pompey's legionaries.

A somewhat more complicated interpretation [10] would have it that the *Habakkuk Commentary* alludes to the various high priests from John Hyrcanus (134–104 B.C.) to Hyrcanus II (63–40 B.C.), and to Eleazar, the contemporary of John Hyrcanus, as the "Teacher of Righteousness." Otherwise, this hypothesis is in complete accord with that quoted above.

IV. FIRST CENTURY A.D.

Some have thought that the "Teacher of Righteousness" may stand for John the Baptist.[11] According to J. L. Teicher, the Community is that of the Ebionites, a Judeo-Christian sect which was in conflict with Pauline Christianity.[12] Jesus is the "Teacher of Righteousness" while St. Paul, the Apostle of the Gentiles, is labeled as "the Man of deception"; the *Kittim*, i.e., the Romans forming a background to the picture.

Some others have located the events at the time of the first Jewish war, from 66 to 70 A.D.: [13] we would then be dealing with the Zealots,

---

[8] A. DUPONT-SOMMER, *Observations sur le "Commentaire d'Habacuc" découvert près de la Mer Morte*, Paris, 1950; *Le "Commentaire d'Habacuc" découvert près de la Mer Morte*, R.H.R., t. 137, 1950, pp. 129–171; *Aperçus préliminaires sur les manuscrits de la Mer Morte*, Paris, 1950; *Nouveaux aperçus sur les manuscrits de la Mer Morte*, Paris, 1953. – R. GOOSSENS, *Onias le Juste, Messie de la Nouvelle Alliance . . .*, La Nouvelle Clio, 1950, pp. 336–353; *L'état actuel de la recherche sur les manuscrits de la Mer Morte . . .*, ibid., 1950, pp. 635–671; *Les Kittim du Commentaire d'Habacuc, ibid.*, 1952, pp. 137–170. – K. ELLIGER, *Studien zum Habakuk–Kommentar vom Toten Meer*, Tübingen, 1953, pp. 270–274 (the "wicked Priest": Hyrcan II).

[9] R. GOOSSENS, *Les éléments messianiques de la tradition sur Onias le Juste chez Josèphe et dans le Talmud*, Bulletin de l'Académie Royale de Belgique – Classe de Lettres – 1950, pp. 440–469.

[10] W. H. BROWNLEE, *The Historical Allusions of the Dead Sea Habakkuk Midrash*, B.A.S.O.R., 126, 1952, pp. 10–20.

[11] R. EISLER, *Letter to the Times*, 9.8.1949.

[12] J. L. TEICHER, *The Dead Sea Scrolls . . .*, J.J.S., 1951, p. 67–99; *The Damascus Fragments and the Origin of the Jewish-Christian Sect, ibid.*, 1951, p. 115–143; *Jesus in the Habakkuk Scroll, ibid.*, 1952, p. 53–55.

[13] R. TOURNAY, *Les anciens manuscrits hébreux récemment découverts*, R.B., 1949, pp. 232–233. – G. VERMÈS, *La Communauté de la Nouvelle Alliance . . .*, E.Th.L., 1951, pp. 70–82. – H. E. DEL MEDICO, *Deux manuscrits hébreux de la Mer Morte*, Paris, 1951.

who opposed the high priests of the epoch as well as the Romans of Vespasianus and Titus.

V. THE MIDDLE AGES

Finally, the Middle Ages [14] have been suggested as the historical setting of our documents. Thus, the *Kittim* would be the Crusaders, and the "wicked Priest" the Seljuk governor of Jerusalem.[15] The Community appears as some schismatic circle of medieval Judaism, the Karaites or the disciples of Abu Isa.

I do not intend to submit all these theories to a systematic examination, since it would be too technical, and inevitably boring. Let the readers rather take part in a sort of exploration, from which the eventful history of the sect will emerge sometimes clearly and sometimes dimly.

Let us, first, attempt to give a brief outline of a historical itinerary which extended through many centuries, and indicate its various stages. Then, from the allusions contained in our sources, we shall try to select those which might serve as a *terminus a quo* and a *terminus ad quem;* in other words, build up the frame within which the events mentioned in the manuscripts of Qumrân took place.

I. TERMINUS A QUO [16]

1. The Birth of the Community

The history of the world, so the author of the *Damascus Document* teaches us, is a succession of periods in which the fidelity of a small remnant alternates with the infidelity of the many. Each period is brought to an end by the punishment and ruin of the wicked, while the elect, those whom God "called by name," [17] escape annihilation and find their salvation.

The "celestial watchers," i.e. the Angels who had taken wives unto themselves, perished with their descendants, the "giants," in the days of the Flood. The sons of Noah came also to a sad end, for having transgressed the commandments of God. Abraham, Isaac and Jacob, on the contrary, the Patriarchs who observed the commandments and transmitted them to their sons, were named the friends of God. Again, the sons of Israel refused to obey the precepts, and perished in the desert. Neither would the survivors listen to Moses, bringing upon themselves thereby the wrath of God. Their sons continued their evil ways "and they perished and their kings were an-

---

[14] P. R. WEIS, *The Date of the Habakkuk Scroll, J.Q.R.*, t. 41, 1950, pp. 125–154. — S. ZEITLIN, *The Hebrew Scrolls: a Challenge to Scholarship, ibid.*, pp. 264–265.   [15] That of Weiss.
[16] Cf. my article: *Le cadre historique des manuscrits de la Mer Morte, R.Sc.R.*, 1953, pp. 14–29.   [17] *D.D.*, II, 11.

nihilated." [18] The very Law was forgotten until the advent of the High Priest Zadok, the "Anointed," who made it known anew among men. Some did follow him, but all the others remained stubborn.[19]

God's patience was finally exhausted, and His wrath devoured Israel, its land and its sanctuary. Only a small number were saved, through the sheer grace of God and because God "remembered the Covenant He had concluded with the Forefathers." [20] Wickedness was soon let loose again, finally culminating in the period in which we are particularly interested, because it is that of the birth of our sect. The men of iniquity "chose insolence, justified the wicked, and condemned the just, and all those who walked uprightly they held in abomination; they persecuted them with the sword and delighted in quarrelling with the people." [21] They also went astray in the observance of the "holy Sabbaths" and the "glorious feasts," and pronounced abominations against the precepts of the Covenant.[22] Thus, all through his exhortation, the author of the *Damascus Document* never tires of repeating his grievances.

There can be no doubt that we have to deal with a doctrinal crisis of an exceptional gravity, in which the existence of the Forefathers' Covenant is at stake.

Many a passage of the Qumrân scrolls gives the same warning. The traitors to the Covenant attempt to betray divine Law for the sake of "vanities" and pernicious innovations, by propagating "lies," "deception" and "folly." [23] Traditional doctrine is the object of their mockery; "They said of the vision of knowledge: This is not true! and of the way according to Thy heart: It is not that one!" [24]

The stress laid on the strictest observance of "their times" and "their feasts" [25] proves that the liturgical calendar was also much discussed.

These heretics, furthermore, not satisfied with freeing themselves from the legal observances, dared attack the very fundamentals of religion through displaying idolatrous propaganda in a foreign tongue:

"They walk with a stubborn heart, and seek Thee among idols. . . . They went to seek Thee through the mouth of prophets of deception . . . With barbarian lips and in a foreign tongue do they speak to Thy people so that through treachery they cause all their deeds to be but folly." [26]

The *Manual* also mentions a "purity of heart that loathes all impure idols." [27] We find further: "The fruit of holiness shall be upon my tongue and *abominations* shall not be found in it." [28]

To those who would not be seduced by beguiling words, the apostles of this new religion opposed violence and terror. That it

[18] *Ibid.*, II, 14–III,12.   [19] *Ibid.*, V, 4–5; II, 12–13.   [20] *Ibid.*, I, 3–5.
[21] *Ibid.*, I, 19–21.   [22] *Ibid.*, V, 12–13.
[23] Cf. *Hymn*, II, 12–13, 17; IV, 2–4, 6–7, etc.   [24] *Ibid.*, IV, 14.
[25] *M.D.*, I, 14–15.   [26] *Hymn*, IV, 11–13.   [27] *MD.*, IV, 5.
[28] *M.D.*, X, 22–23. — "Abominations" (*šiqqûṣîm*) is equivalent to "idols." Cf. "*abomination* that maketh desolate" in *Dan.*, XI, 31.

was a religious persecution in the true sense of the word is clearly indicated in the *Damascus Document,* while the newly found scrolls give a broad hint in the same direction. Here is one example out of many: "Thou hast saved the life of the poor man whom they intended to slay so that he would shed his blood for Thy service." [29]

The testimony of the *Damascus Document* is thus in full agreement with that of the Qumrân scrolls. We are confronted in both with the same doctrinal crisis and the same religious strife.

Those even slightly acquainted with the Jewish literature of the last two centuries B.C. will find at once that the picture drawn in the Damascus and Qumrân documents has many parallels in the writings of that period.

The last period of world history is to begin, according to the *Book of Enoch,* with the formation of a party of faithful Jews ("lambs born of white sheep") who cry in vain to their fellow countrymen (the "sheep"). "The sheep bleated not toward them and hearkened not to their word, but were entirely deaf, and their eyes grew blind to the extreme." [30]

If we are to believe the *Book of Jubilees,* the age of final salvation was to come after a particularly perverse generation, the deeds of which would be "impurity and fornication, defiling and abomination." The Covenant was to fall into oblivion. "They will fight against each other, the young man against the old . . . the poor man against the rich . . . the beggar against the prince, on the matter of the Law and of the Covenant, for they will have forgotten the commandment, the Covenant, the feasts, the months, the Sabbaths, the Jubilees and all the decrees." [31]

The *Testament of Levi* lets us have a glimpse at the gradual corruption of the priesthood, whose last representatives were to be "idolaters, adulterers, lovers of money, arrogant, miscreant, sensual." [32] This would be the seventh and last week of the priesthood before the advent of a new priest. It may be observed, to help us locate this last period within the frame of history, that the return from exile to the desolated land and the restoration of the sanctuary took place in the fifth week. [33]

Particular attention must be paid, among all these documents, to the *Assumption of Moses.* This work, too, mentions the same crisis at the end of the captivity, [34] at which time the Jews were divided concerning religion (*ad veritatem*): "They abandoned righteousness, embraced iniquity, defiled the sanctuary, and whored after foreign gods. For they followed not the truth of God. Some men defiled the altar . . . with the gifts which they offered up to the Lord, they who were not priests, but slaves born of slaves." [35]

---

[29] *Hymn,* II, 13–14.
[30] *En.,* XC, 6–7. Compare with *D.D.,* VIII, 16–17; XIX, 29–30.
[31] *Jub.,* XXIII, 14–19.   [32] *Test. of Levi,* XVII, 11.
[33] *Ibid.,* XVII, 10. Cf. also *Test. of Juda,* XXI, 6–XXIII.
[34] *Ass. of Moses,* IV, 6–8.   [35] *Ibid.,* V, 14.

But whereas in other documents the period of corruption immediately precedes the end of the world, it is, in the *Assumption of Moses,* inserted in past history, and followed by an age of priest-kings, culminating in the reign of an "impudent king" who is not of sacerdotal descent.[36]

Here no doubt could be entertained any longer. The "impudent king" (*rex petulans*) is most certainly Herod the Great; the priest-kings whom he deprived of office to reign in their stead are of course the Hasmoneans. Therefore the preceding religious strife which had left so deep an impression on contemporary literature can be nothing other than the Hellenistic crisis of the beginning of the Second century B.C.

The evidence is confirmed by the *Book of Daniel.* The struggle between the Persian, Greek, Lagid and Seleucid Empires involved at the same time a religious one within Israel, between those who betrayed the Covenant and were won over through deception to idolatry, and the "Wise men of the people." [37]

Indeed, no period of Israel's history would fit better into the situation as described in the *Damascus Document* and some Qumrân scrolls, than that which witnessed the strife between traditional religion and Hellenism.

Greek ideas and customs had spread with astounding swiftness throughout the East since the conquests of Alexander the Great. Jewish Palestine, ever distrustful of anything which came from the outside, did resist for some time. But in the beginning of the Second century B.C., the infiltration of Hellenism could no longer be resisted. This movement claimed to stand for progress and enlightenment, and gain considerable popularity.[38] Jesus ben Sirach, who wrote in about 180 B.C., was lavish in his curses upon the wicked who forsook the Law of the Most High.[39]

A few years later, in 175 B.C., Antiochus IV Epiphanes became the chief of the Seleucid Empire, to which Judea had belonged since the battle of Panaion in 198 B.C.[40] The advent of that accomplished Hellenist opened up very hopeful vistas for innovators within Israel.

"In those days," relates the *First Book of the Maccabees,* "there came forth prevaricators out of Israel, who seduced many, saying: 'Let us go and make a covenant with the nations that are round about us, for since we separated ourselves from them many many woes and evils have come upon us!' And these words appeared good in their eyes. Some of them hastened to go to the king who granted them the authorization to practice the customs of nations. They built a gymnasium in Jerusalem according to the manner of the nations;

---

36 *Ibid.,* VI, 1–4.   37 *Dan.,* X–XI.

38 Cf. E. Schürer, *Geschichte des jüdischen Volkes im Zeitalter Jesu Christi,* 3rd and 4th ed., t. I, Leipzig, 1901, pp. 189–190. – F. M. Abel, *Histoire de la Palestine depuis la conquête d'Alexandre jusqu'à l'invasion arabe,* t. I, Paris, 1952, pp. 109–111.

39 *Sir.,* XLI, 5–9.   40 Cf. F. M. Abel, *op. cit.,* I, p. 86.

they submitted themselves to uncircumcision, deviated from the
holy covenant, put themselves under the yoke of the nations, and
sold themselves to do evil." [41]

The chief of the Hellenistic party was no less a personage than
the high priest; the usurper Jason. He had bought for money the
supreme pontificate which his pious brother Onias had held until
174 B.C.[42] A good many priests neglected the Temple service, preferring to attend athletes' exhibitions in the gymnasiums.

Here then, are the "interpreters of falsehood," the seducers of the
people, those who wished to abandon the Mosaic Law for the fal-
lacious joys of the Greek way of life. We are now able to perceive
what was meant by "barbarous and uncircumcised lips" and the
"foreign tongue," which were so deeply abhorrent to those who remained faithful to the Covenant.[43]

Specialists in Israel's history, however, have come to the conclusion that the Hellenization inaugurated by Jason, spectacular though
it might appear, did not strike very deep. Innovations, it would seem,
were not imposed by force or universally. There is no sign testifying to an idolatrous cult in the Jerusalem Temple. The amateurish
trend of Jason's reform is well illustrated by the attitude of the
legates, whom he sent to Tyre with 300 silver drachmas to offer sacrifices in honor of Heracles. When they arrived, the emissaries were
so horrified by the sacrilegious task entrusted to them, that they
besought the Tyrians to make use of the sum for non-religious
ends.[44]

Jason fell into displeasure with the king through his lack of energy, and also because Menelaus offered a larger bribe. The new
high priest was not of Zadokite,[45] perhaps not even of priestly descent; [46] he was eager to prove his loyalty to the sovereign by inaugurating an era of enforced Hellenization.[47] The former high priest
Onias was among the first victims.[48]

Jason, thus dismissed, tried to create agitation in the country;
Antiochus, who had just conquered Egypt, marched on Jerusalem
and plundered the Temple, with Menelaus acting as his guide.

In the spring of 168 B.C., that monarch set out on a new campaign

---

[41] *I Macc.*, I, 11–15.   [42] Cf. *Dan.*, XI, 22. — *II Macc.*, IV, 7.
[43] Cf. J. T. Milik, *Verbum Domini*, 1950, p. 336, n. 1. — G. Lambert, *N.R.Th.*,
1952, pp. 277–278.   [44] Cf. *I Macc.*, IV, 18–19.
[45] Josephus certainly commits a mistake when he writes that Onias, said to be
a brother of Jason, was the successor of the latter. Cf. *Ant. Jud.*, XII, V, 1;
XII, IX, 7.
[46] According to the Greek text of *II Macc.*, III, 4, Menelaus' father Simon, the
provost of the Temple, sprang from the tribe of Benjamin. On the other hand,
the old Latin versions have *de tribu Balgea* or *de Balgei cognatione*, i.e. of
the sacerdotal class of Bilga. It is the reading adopted by F. M. Abel, *Les
livres des Maccabées*, Paris, 1949, p. 316.
[47] Cf. *II Macc.*, IV, 23 sq. — *I Macc.*, I, 52–53 unequivocally affirms that the
Hellenizing Jews themselves participated in idolatrous propaganda.
[48] Cf. *Dan.*, IX, 26 and *II Macc.*, IV, 34.

against Egypt, which was to end in failure because of the "Kittite ships." [49] In plain language, this is what happened. The king was stopped in Eleusis, an Alexandrian suburb, by Popilius Laenas, the Roman Senate's ambassador, who ordered him to leave Egyptian soil at once. The scene is well known; when asked for time to decide, the Roman, tracing with his stick a circle around the Seleucid, haughtily replied: "Then decide inside this!" Acquiescence was the only course: "I shall do what the Senate wishes." [50]

Antiochus avenged himself upon the Jews. Apollonius, his general, stormed Jerusalem in the spring of 167 B.C., and carried out a great slaughter. In the same year a royal ordinance was issued, declaring the Law of Moses to be null and void. On December 8th the "abomination of desolation," a statue of Olympian Zeus, was erected upon the altar of holocausts.[51] The Israelite cult was forbidden; idols were erected everywhere, even in the countryside, and the death penalty was in store for all those who still dared to practice their ancestors' religion or refused to carry out pagan rites.[52]

Such are the circumstances which appear best to explain the various facts hinted at by our documents. As has been said, a good many commentators have already come to the same conclusions.[53] The extra evidence found in these pages will, I hope, serve as an excuse for this somewhat lengthy account.

The fact that many passages in our documents reflect the situation at the time of Antiochus Epiphanes' persecution, does not, however, provide us with any information about the date on which the Community was formed, or the personality of the first members who flocked around a chief.

To shed light on this, let us now turn to the *Damascus Document*.

All the Qumrân scrolls, even when describing the remotest past, show us a society already strongly organized. Thus we find: "Thou hast not covered with shame the face of all my disciples that flock into Thy Covenant. Those who walked in the way according to Thy heart have hearkened to me and enrolled for Thy sake in the council of the saints." [54] Assuming that the poem, in which we hear the voice of the Leader, refers to facts which happened after 167 B.C., it would follow that the Community, which at the time was obviously quite young, was established sometime between 200 and 170 B.C.

Let us now listen to what the author of the *Damascus Document*

---

[49] *Dan.*, XI, 30.
[50] Cf. E. Schürer, *op. cit.*, I, p. 197. — F. M. Abel, *Histoire de la Palestine*, I, p. 121.   [51] *Dan.*, XI, 30. — *I Macc.*, I, 57.
[52] Cf. F. M. Abel, *op. cit.*, I, pp. 130–132. — E. Bikerman has excellently stated the Seleucid point of view: "What the government . . . reproached the Jews with at the time of the persecution was not so much the Law of Moses as such, as the fidelity to that Law after the Royal edict of December 167 had annulled it." Cf. *Un document relatif à la persécution d'Antiochus IV Epiphane, R.H.R.*, 1937, p. 222.
[53] Cf. *supra*, p. 64, n. 1.   [54] *Hymn*, IV, 19–21.

says about the matter, since he is the only one to have mentioned it explicitly.

"In the epoch of wrath, three hundred and ninety years after He had given them into the hands of Nebuchadnezzar, King of Babylon, He visited them and caused to grow forth from Israel and Aaron a root of cultivation to possess His land and wax fat in the goodness of His soil. They considered their trespass and knew that they were guilty and that they were as blind men and as those that had groped their way for twenty years. God considered their works, and that with all their heart they did seek Him, and He raised for them a Teacher of Righteousness to lead them in the way of His heart." [55]

If one could trust so precise a chronology, there would be no problem. The 390 years elapsed from 586 B.C., point to 196 B.C. as being the date when a nucleus of penitents was already in existence; then, twenty years later, on the vigil of Antiochus Epiphanes' accession to the throne, came the Teacher of Righteousness, the Community's master and organizer. It must be admitted, in the light of what has been seen above, that such a reconstitution of facts is anything but unlikely.

Nevertheless, when confronted with these figures, scholars profess some skepticism. This mistrust is best illustrated by E. Meyer, who rejects the chronology of the document as being an additional accretion, only to propose a chronology of his own which scarcely differs from it.[56]

The *Damascus Document* data are considered as problematic for two reasons:

a) Old Jewish historians lacked accurate knowledge concerning the length of the Persian epoch. Demetrius, a Jewish Hellenist of the end of the Third Century B.C., miscalculated its duration by seventy years; the *Book of Daniel* offers the same data and has its own system of computation; Josephus again miscalculates to the amount of fifty years; Rabbi Yose, in the *Seder 'Olam Rabba*, reckons three hundred and twenty-seven years from the beginning of the Babylonian exile (586 B.C.) to Herod's accession to power (37 B.C.).[57]

b) The 390 years of the *Damascus Document*, it would seem, were textually borrowed from *Ezek.*, IV, 5, where that figure stands as a symbol for the number of years of Israel's iniquity.[58]

On the other hand, it might be argued that members and relatives of the pontifical family would possess precise genealogical lists, which would permit a very accurate reckoning.

Discussions could thus be carried on endlessly, but it seems hardly worth it. Whether purposely or not, the Damascus chronology points

---

[55] *D.D.*, I, 5–11.   [56] *Die Gemeinde des Neuen Bundes*, Berlin, 1919, p. 14.
[57] Cf. A. BERTHOLET, *Zur Datierung der Damaskus-Schrift, Beihefte zur Z.A.W.*, 33, 1920, pp. 36–37.
[58] This was Fr. Lagrange's opinion: *R.B.*, 1912, p. 215, n. 4. S. Schechter on the contrary, preferred to read 490 years = 70 weeks of years, as *En.*, CIII, 9.

to a date which appears fairly certain, i.e. the beginning of the Second century B.C.

It was at that time that the splitting of Judaism into two antagonistic factions began to take shape. The *Book of Enoch*, the *Assumption of Moses* and the *Book of Daniel* convey as much.[59] The formation of the Hassidean group was surely an accomplished fact before the reign of Antiochus Epiphanes, and probably went back to the beginning of the century,[60] since they formed a Community at the time when they joined the Maccabees.[61]

2. The Hassidean Movement

Many scholars have linked, one way or another, the Damascus and Qumrân Community with the Hassideans.[62] Let us first of all make clear what we know about them.

The *Books of the Maccabees* provide us with very meager information, which is therefore all the more valuable.

Mattathias the Priest had scarcely raised the flag of revolt than the assembly of "Pious men" flocked to his side to help him.[63] "Then there were gathered unto them the community of Hassideans, mighty men in Israel who were wholly devoted to the Law." [64] They appear to have abandoned the towns to live in the desert like those "seeking righteousness and justice" mentioned in the *First Book of Maccabees*.[65] But however mighty, they were warriors only intermittently; here, as in many other respects, they appear as the forerunners of the military monastic orders in the Middle Ages.[66]

And in fact, as soon as the insurrection had ceased to be the holy war for freedom of worship, the Hassideans ceased to follow the Maccabeans, gathering instead around the High Priest Alcimus, Menelaus' successor, who pledged on oath to grant them peace. They paid a heavy price for the trust put into the last Hellenizing pontiff; sixty of them were killed [67] and Alcimus, in spite of his Aaronian descent, proved no better than his predecessor. It is not known whether the Hassideans, after this sad incident, went back to the Maccabean camp, for we find them no longer mentioned anywhere. Historians, however, think that they survived, and emerged later under the name of Pharisees.

It is hardly necessary to note that at the time of the Maccabean revolt, the Hassidean community had none of the characteristics which would denote a sect; they were, on the contrary, orthodoxy's staunchest defenders. Their intervention with Alcimus shows that

---

[59] Cf. *supra*, pp. 68–69.   [60] Cf. E. Schürer, *op. cit.*, I, p. 190.
[61] *I Macc.*, II, 42.
[62] Among others; Meyer, Bertholet, Dupont-Sommer, Dhorme, Lambert, Barthélemy, de Vaux, etc.
[63] *Hasîdîm.* — The name "Essenes" probably signifies "pious." Cf. supra, p. 58, n. 140.   [64] *I Macc.*, II, 42.   [65] *Ibid.*, II, 29 sq.
[66] Cf. F. M. Abel, *Le livre des Maccabées*, p. 44.
[67] Cf. *I Macc.*, VII, 13–17.

they had no intention of binding themselves unconditionally to the Maccabean cause, and that they did not attach any particular importance to a change in priestly *régime*, readily acknowledging a high priest who was not of Zadokite descent.

This portrait of the Hassideans offers many a point of undoubted likeness to the Community of our documents.

The members of the "Community council" were "volunteers" (*mithnaddebhîm*), just as Hassideans were ἐκουσιαζόμενο : [68] in both cases, men pursuing the same end—unswerving fidelity to the Law of Moses.

The Qumrân *Manual*, it is true, shows us peaceful men living in a monastic order; but this document, as has been pointed out, belongs to a more mature stage of the movement.[69]

To sum up: there can be no doubt that the Community was closely connected with the Hassidean movement, but their identification pure and simple would not, in my opinion, be justified by the facts.[70] If it were proved that the Hassideans were the ancestors of the Pharisees, it would not be unreasonable to suppose that their party, from the beginning, was mainly composed of laymen.

The Community's primitive nucleus, on the contrary, consisted of a sacerdotal *élite*, "the sons of Zadok, the priests."

3. *The Sons of Zadok*

Many authors have already remarked on the Zadokite stamp of the Community as being an all-important element.[71] My conviction concerning the point is very strong, viz., that we are dealing with a dissident clerical group. If we consider the importance of the problems connected with the cult and the celebration of the holy days "in their appointed times," the privileges enjoyed by priests in every field, the fierce opposition to the "wicked priesthood," the evidence compels us to admit that the sentence which recurs so often, not without pomposity: "the sons of Zadok, the priests, the keepers of the Covenant," [72] has to be taken literally.

The sons of Zadok are not unknown figures in history. This name was applied to the priestly families descending from the High Priest Zadok, a contemporary of David and Solomon.[73] The *Damascus Document*, it will be remembered, gives an eminent place to that eponymous ancestor of the Community.[74] Ever since, down to Onias III, and even to hellenizing Jason, the pontifical dignity has remained

---

68 The Septuagint rightly translates the different forms of *ndb* by ἐκουσιάζομαι and its derivatives.   69 Cf. *supra*, p. 61.
70 The recognition of Alcimus assumes, from that standpoint a particular importance.
71 Thus H. CAVAIGNAC, *R.H.R.*, t. 138, 1950, p. 152. — J. TRINQUET, *V.T.*, 1951, p. 289–291. — H. H. ROWLEY, *The Zadokite Fragments and the Dead Sea Scrolls*, p. 68, 76. — A. DUPONT-SOMMER, *Nouveaux aperçus* . . . , p. 98–103.
72 *M.D.*, V, 2, 9.   73 *II Sam.*, VIII, 17; XV, *passim*.   74 *D.D.*, V, 4–5.

their unquestioned privilege.[75] Ezekiel predicted that they would be the ministers of the new sanctuary in the last days, to the exclusion of all others.[76] Neither did the Community members fail to apply that gratifying prophecy to themselves.[77]

M. J. Trinquet has relevantly called attention to the praises paid by Ben-Sirach to the High Priest Simon III.[78] The Hebrew *Ecclesiasticus* wishes for him and his descendants a pontificate of eternal duration: "May the mercy (of God) be established with Simon, and keep for him the covenant of Pinhas: may it not be cut off from him or from his seed, as long as the skies shall last!" [79] In a thanksgiving Psalm, which is inserted after v. 12 in chapter LI of the Hebrew text, but does not figure in ancient translations, we read again: "Give praise to Him that chooses the sons of Zadok to be priests; His mercy is eternal!" [80]

It then appears highly probable that the Teacher of Righteousness and his first followers were intimately connected with the ancient pontifical family. This theory was very convincingly expounded by Israel Levi *à propos* of the *Damascus Document;* [81] in my opinion, it sheds light on a good many points of the Qumrân writings, which would otherwise remain obscure. For if the Community were connected with the Zadokite movement, we should have no difficulty in understanding how a group so strongly bound to Judaism and hitherto urged by a pure national feeling, should change suddenly into a sect, when we should expect it, once the riots and war were over, to regain its hereditary position within Israelite society.

But this coveted position had been usurped in the meanwhile by the Maccabees, and a return to the former *status quo* was no longer possible. The descendants of Simon and Onias, together with their very few partisans, were in no position to challenge the heroes of national resistance. They had inevitably to leave the scene and found a separatist conventicle, where they were free to maintain their hegemony and await the ultimate triumph of their cause.

The search of the *terminus a quo* of the historical facts alluded to in the documents enables us to stress some points with reasonable certainty.

1. There are many signs that the Community of the Covenant was formed at the period of anti-Hellenistic struggle, approximately, that is, between 200 and 170 B.C.

2. The Teacher of Righteousness, likewise, began to exercise his ministry at the time of Antiochus Epiphanes. According to the *Da-*

---

[75] The list of postexilian high priests is found in *Neh.*, XII, 10–11 (from Jesus to Iaddus, who was a contemporary of Alexander the Great). It can be completed with the help of *Jewish Antiquities* of Josephus.
[76] *Ezek.*, XLIV, 15–16.   [77] *D.D.*, III, 21–IV, 4.
[78] *Sir.*, L, 1–25. — Cf. *V.T.*, 1951, pp. 289–291.
[79] *Ibid.*, L, 24.   [80] *Ibid.*, LI, 12, IX.
[81] *Un écrit sadducéen antérieur à la destruction du Temple, R.E.J.*, 1912, pp. 3–4.

mascus Document, he appeared twenty years after the first nucleus was created, i.e., in the first years of the Sect. It is extremely likely, on the other hand, that the verses of *Hymn IV,* which allude constantly to the Hellenistic crisis, were meant by its author to have been spoken by the Teacher of Righteousness.

3. The Community and the Hassidean congregation stand for two movements that are perfectly parallel and resemble each other on every point save on their attitude toward Zadokite pontificate.

4. The Community, during its first period, could hardly be taken for a sect. Its ultimate dissidence has to be explained by other motives.

The historical setting of our documents opens therefore with the Hellenistic crisis. It now remains to be seen how it comes to an end.

Here again, a close investigation of the evidence at our disposal is required, before we make up our minds on the point.

II. TERMINUS AD QUEM

The *terminus ad quem* of facts alluded to depends in each case on the date at which each work was written. To gather evidence from the documents indiscriminately and at random would cause the most regrettable mistakes. I hope to be excused for recalling this self-evident truth.

I am not, at this stage, concerned with the Teacher of Righteousness or with the wicked Priest, but with the dating of the most recent events related in the documents. In order to do this, we shall try and discover the foreign nation to which the various documents allude, the fields of our investigation being again the *Damascus Document* and also the *Habakkuk Commentary.*

1. The Damascus Document

From the standpoint of external history the *Damascus Document* does not, it would seem, offer any particular problem. It opens, as has been seen, with the Hellenistic period, in the beginning of the Second century B.C. Israel's chiefs were led astray by novel and pernicious ideas, and were punished. It even informs us that a foreign prince was used as the agent of divine wrath.

"They have let themselves walk high-handedly in the ways of the wicked, of whom God hath said: *Their wine is the venom of dragons, the mortal poison of vipers.* The dragons are the kings of the nations; their wine is their ways; the poison of vipers is the chief of the kings of Yawan who has come to wreak vengeance upon them." [82]

Yawan being the Hebrew for Greece, the chief alluded to must be some Hellenistic prince or general. I am not trying to identify him here — I shall leave that for the following chapter — but only to situ-

[82] *D.D.,* VIII, 21–24.

ate him historically. As a working hypothesis, let us take the whole period during which the Seleucid threat hung over Judah, roughly from 175 to 140 B.C.

We find in the *Damascus Document* another somewhat vague indication when the author mentions the time elapsed between the death of the Teacher of Righteousness and the writing of his work: "From the day that the Teacher of the Community was gathered in until the destruction of all the men of war who have walked with the Man of Falsehood, it is about forty years." [83]

The *Damascus Document* does not apprise us of the precise moment at which the Teacher of Righteousness disappeared from the scene. I would venture the following tentative suggestion: supposing the Teacher of Righteousness began his public career sometime about 175 B.C. at the age of thirty-five, and that he died at the age of seventy, the *terminus ad quem* of the facts and of the date at which the *Damascus Document* was written, would be the last ten years of the Second century B.C. under the reign of John Hyrcanus. The margin of error could not be of any great importance, since the limiting points on either side could not extend beyond 130–80 B.C., that is, fifty years.

To sum up, all the events of which we find an echo in the *Damascus Document* took place during the Hellenistic period, with not so much as the shadow of a Roman on the horizon.

2. The Habakkuk Commentary

The *Habakkuk Commentary*, like the *Damascus Document*, relates facts from varying historical periods.[84]

That a long period elapsed between the earliest events recounted and the time at which the author wrote is obvious. He confesses that the "last days" continued well beyond the prophets' expectations.[85] Exhorting the Community, he calls out to its members not to be disheartened while awaiting the coming of the chosen time of God.[86] They must entertain no fear as to their salvation on the day of judgment, provided they persevere in their fidelity to the Teacher of Righteousness.[87]

This character, so often mentioned in the work, belongs to past and even remote history. As Fr. J. van der Ploeg very relevantly points out,[88] the verbs describing the Teacher's or his opponents' activities, are always in the past. Some chastisements, on the contrary, the nature of which is more or less eschatological,[89] the campaigns of the "last priests of Jerusalem," and the appearing upon the

---

83 *Ibid.*, XX, 13–15. — This period of forty years may be merely symbolical, recalling the forty years spent by the Hebrews in the desert.
84 Cf. my article in *R.Sc.R.*, 1953, pp. 203–230.
85 *H.C.*, VII, 8–9.   86 *Ibid.*, VII, 10–14.   87 *Ibid.*, VIII, 1–3.
88 *Les rouleaux de la Mer Morte, Bi. Or.*, 1951, p. 10.
89 For instance *H.C.*, X, 3–5; XI, 14–15 and XII, 5.

scene of the mysterious *Kittim* pertain to the future. Moreover, the interpretations proposed by the author being ascribed to the Teacher of Righteousness, it is quite possible that the passage from past to future marks the date of his death.

The passages concerning the long duration of the last days convey that the readers for whom the *Commentary* was written grew tired of waiting in vain. The author, as that of the *Damascus Document* before him, aimed at comforting those whose courage was faltering by reviving the hatred they nursed against their enemies.

a) THE "LAST PRIESTS OF JERUSALEM"

The Commentator does not blame the "last priests of Jerusalem," those adversaries of the Sect in the period following the death of the Teacher of Righteousness, for any particular crime against the Community. He just declares contemptuously that whatever riches and dishonest gains the priests have gathered through plundering the nations, will be, at the end of time, delivered over to the *Kittim*, that remnant of the peoples." [90]

According to him, the last representatives of a sacerdotal lineage were not only to enjoy prosperity, but would even be able to cause disturbance to their neighbors, and have them at their mercy: "they will plunder the nations."

Let us here proceed through elimination.

Hellenistic pontiffs seem to me out of the question. For one thing, they were the contemporaries of the Teacher of Righteousness. And they would have been ill-advised indeed, if they had attacked the foreign nations who were their allies.

Neither could the passage apply to the priestly chiefs at the time of the great Revolt against Rome (67–70 A.D.). Both archaeology and literary criteria exclude such an interpretation.

The Procurators' epoch, or the reign of Herod, would not suit the documents any better. At that time Jewish priests could not have become war chiefs. We are thus left with the Hasmonean period, from 152 to 37 B.C.

It is hardly likely, however, that the reproaches addressed to the "last priests" were intended for Antigonus or Hyrcan II, since any aggressive action by the high priests must have come to an end with the appearance in Palestine of Pompey's Roman legions in 63 B.C.

Were there, then, any other Hasmonean monarchs who could be considered as plunderers by the *Habakkuk* Commentator?

Such an accusation might have been addressed to the Maccabees Jonathan and Simon, if it were established that the Community felt hostile towards them. But these grievances would be particularly well founded during the period between the death of Simon (134 B.C.) and the first storming of Jerusalem by the Romans.

As a matter of fact, the situation changed altogether when John

---

[90] Cf. *H.C.*, IX, 2–7. — Perhaps the mutilated pericope of VI, 1–2 is also related to the "last priests."

Hyrcanus mounted the throne. "The Hasmoneans are also Macca-bees," as G. Ricciotti has pointed out, "but no longer the vagrant and heroic Maccabees of the desert; they were also to wage war, but those were dynastic rather than Yahwistic wars." [91]

Among Simon's descendants, many pursued a policy of territorial expansion, which brought them wealth by impoverishing the neigh-boring nations.

Here is a brief sketch of the Hasmonean conquests, according to Flavius Josephus' *Jewish Antiquities:*

John Hyrcanus (134–104 B.C.) stormed Madaba in Transjordan, conquered Samaria, destroying the Mount Garizim Temple, and waged war in Idumea.[92] Josephus remarks that at the end of his reign, John possessed incalculable wealth.[93]

Aristobulus exercised power for only one year (104–103 B.C.), in the course of which he succeeded in conquering the Itureans.[94]

The bellicose temper of Alexander Janneus (103–76 B.C.) was no-torious. He conquered Gadara, Amathont, Raphia, Anthedon and Gaza,[95] besieged Ptolemais [96] and waged war in Moab and Gilead,[97] where victory failed that priest-king.

Aristobulus II (67–63 B.C.) was accused before Pompey of making incursions into neighboring lands and of committing piracy on the seas.[98]

Very likely, then, the "last priests of Jerusalem" who plundered the riches of their neighbors were the successors of Simon the Maccabee. War chiefs rather than high-priests, they had indeed amassed huge wealth at the expense of their neighbors.

The encouraging progress of our inquest does not, for all that, complete the evidence as to the *terminus ad quem,* for the Commen-tator may not have known of all the *dramatis personae* just men-tioned.

The conquering people called *Kittim* have also so far remained an enigma. Let us not forget that the East changed masters during the period with which we are dealing. Were, then, the *Kittim* who were to seize the wealth plundered by the "last priests of Jerusalem" the Seleucids or the Romans?

The final fixing of the *terminus ad quem* will depend upon our choice.

b) THE KITTIM

Habakkuk the Prophet had revealed to his contemporaries that God had entrusted to the Babylonians the mission of chastising the wicked among His people. The hour of expiation was at hand.

The Commentator applied to the *Kittim* the passage in which Habakkuk spoke of the Chaldeans; to the *Kittim* was assigned the task of being agents of divine wrath at the end of time.

[91] *Histoire d'Israël,* t. II, Paris, 1948, p. 362.   [92] *A.J.,* XIII, IX, 1.
[93] *Ibid.,* XIII, X, 1.   [94] *Ibid.,* XIII, XI, 3.   [95] *Ibid.,* XIII, XIII, 3.
[96] *Ibid.,* XIII, XII.   [97] *Ibid.,* XIII, XIII, 5.   [98] *Ibid.,* XIV, III, 2.

The might of that invincible army is described dithyrambically by the author: valiant and ready for battle, sly and violent, haughty and sneering, they are truly the terror of nations. Their chiefs, each succeeding the other, set out from far-off islands to the conquest of lands. Tax collectors are not slow to follow on their tracks, which are marked with blood and destruction. They ascribe their triumphs to their flags and to their weapons, holding them in veneration and offering up sacrifices to them. Such is the nation that was to bring the exactions of the "last priests of Jerusalem" to an end.

Of these characteristics, some might suit any warlike and victorious people. Other indications, however, are more specific, such as those relating to their coming from remote and maritime lands; the succession of their chiefs (*môšelîm*) obeying the "House of Guilt"; above all, their worship of military insignia.

The *War* scroll also mentions the *Kittim* of Ashur and the "King of the North" as does the *Book of Daniel*.[99]

THE NAME

The genealogical table in *Genesis* mentions, among the descendants of Japheth, the four sons of Yawan: Elisha, Tarshish, *Kittim* and Dodanim.[100] *Kitti* (plural *kittim*, *kittiyim*, or *kitti'im*) in its strict sense designated the inhabitants of Kittion, an ancient Phoenician colony in Cyprus. This identification has been proved by many an ancient Phoenician inscription found on the spot.[101]

In Biblical Hebrew also, *Kittim* stands for Cyprus,[102] with the exception of the following two passages.

Numbers, XXIV, 25: "Ships shall come from the coast of *Kittim*, and they shall afflict Ashur, and shall afflict Egypt." This may, of course, only mean that the ships would come from the west, from the direction of Cyprus.[103] The verse, however, is somewhat mysterious and was used later: Jewish authors were to apply the name of *Kittim* to any conquering people of any epoch.

The author of *Daniel*, among others, had this passage in mind when he wrote: "Ships of *Kittim* shall come against him."[104] Some Biblical scholars have thought that this alluded to the well-known Eleusis scene, where Popilius Laenas forced Antiochus Epiphanes to evacuate Egypt.[105] Thus the "ships of *Kittim*," i.e. the Roman navy, did afflict Ashur, i.e. the Syrian king.

It would however be premature to consider the *Kittim* as synonymous with the Romans, for it must not be forgotten that Daniel used cryptic language and did not mention any proper names. The old Septuagint version, it is true, translates *Dan.*, XI, 30 by καὶ ἥξουσι 'Ρωμαῖοι giving thereby an interpretation, which is, in fact, historically

---

[99] Cf. *M.G.*, I, p. 18, and *Dan.*, XI.   [100] *Gen.*, X, 4.
[101] Cf. my article in *R.Sc.R.*, 1953, pp. 210–211.
[102] Cf. *Is.*, XXIII, 1, 12. — *Jer.*, II, 10. *Ezek.*, XXVII, 6.
[103] Cf. E. POWER, *Supplément au Dictionnaire de la Bible*, t. II, col. 21.
[104] *Dan.*, XI, 30.   [105] For instance Schürer, Montgomery, Dhorme, Abel.

accurate.[106] But I have proved, I think, in a recent article,[107] that *Kittim* became a synonym for Romans only after the sack of Jerusalem by the Romans in A.D. 70, this being a result of a semantic evolutionary process which had been going on for centuries.

What meaning, then, did pre-Christian writers ascribe to this name?

Many scholars, stressing the *First Book of the Maccabees* [108] and the *Book of Jubilees*,[109] hold that *Kittim* meant Greeks in the Second century and in the beginning of the First century B.C.[110]

It is, then, highly probable that *Kittim*, in about 100 B.C. signified Greeks, being in fact used as a proper name, for the author of the *First Book of the Maccabees* would have hardly sought to disguise Alexander the Great's nationality by calling him "the king of *Kittim*." [111]

With the *Habakkuk Commentary*, the situation is altogether different. Being a cryptographic work, any precise or clear indications are avoided with the greatest care. Besides, its literary connections with the *Book of Daniel* cannot be doubted,[112] and it is therefore not unreasonable to suppose that both used *Kittim* as a cryptogram for the Romans.

CHARACTERISTICS OF THE KITTIM

It is every day more generally admitted that the characteristics of the *Kittim* suit the Romans much better than the Seleucids of whatever period.

Kittim cannot stand for the armies of Antiochus Epiphanes. For one thing, they are never seen to cross the path of the Teacher of Righteousness or his adversaries. It is in fact remarkable that, when speaking of the captivity of the wicked Priests, the Commentator takes care not to mention the *Kittim*, only saying that he was delivered into the hands of his enemies.[113] And besides, how then could the fact be explained that the author did not accuse them of any crime committed against Israel? He only spoke of the cruelty they exerted towards the *nations*. Such an attitude, on the part of hyperorthodox Jews toward Antiochus Epiphanes would indeed be incomprehensible. Both *Daniel* and the *First Book of the Maccabees* use a very different language.[114]

Neither could the *Kittim* be the last Seleucids, i.e. the contempo-

---

[106] St. Jerome translates: *"et venient super eum trieres et Romani."*
[107] *R.Sc.R.*, 1953, pp. 212–214.   [108] *I Macc.*, I, 1; VIII, 5.
[109] *Jub.*, XXIV, 28–29; XXXVII, 10.
[110] Cf. R. DE VAUX, *R.B.*, 1951, p. 442. — M. DELCOR, *Essai sur le Midrash d'Habacuc*, Paris, 1951, pp. 41–42; *Le Midrash d'Habacuc, R.B.*, 1951, pp. 525–526.   [111] Cf. *I Macc.*, I, 1.
[112] Cf. H. H. ROWLEY, *The Zadokite Fragments* . . . , pp. 70–71, 85–86.
[113] *H.C.*, IX, 10.
[114] Cf. *Dan.*, XI, 28–31. — *I Macc.*, I, 11, 21–25, etc. — *II Macc.*, V, 1–20, etc.

raries of Alexander Janneus.[115] Antiochus Epiphanes could still be considered, though not without some exaggeration, as the chief of an invincible army; [116] "while round about 100 B.C., Seleucid history is merely a monotonous repetition of vicissitudes . . . The dynasty is agonizing in a fray of passions and hereditary feuds, among which the historian is at a loss to know where to attach his sympathies." [117] An empire verging on the tomb, kings that are defeated more often than victorious . . . how could they possibly be the *Kittim* of the *Commentary*, the unconquerable warriors who sowed panic everywhere on their path, mocking at kings and their strongholds, proudly humiliating great and small? This is indeed unlikely.

The *Kittim* come from lands that are maritime and remote; [118] this again implicitly recalls the "ships of *Kittim*." To exclude a possible illusion to the Phoenician coast might be unwise, but if we take it to stand for Italy, the sentence appears in quite a new light.

The *Kittim* obey rules (*môšelîm*) who are sent and recalled by the "House of Guilt" (*bêth'asmah*); surely this can be better applied to the Roman proconsuls and to the Senate,[119] than to the Seleucids and to the intrigues of their councils.[120]

And, lastly, it is stated that the *Kittim* offer up sacrifices to their military insignia.

That such a cult existed in Greece has not so far been proved; all endeavors in that direction have been inconclusive.[121]

With the Romans, on the contrary, such a cult is well attested: both epigraphic and literary documents testify that the *signa* were deified, and that cult was offered to them.

Roman eagles were *dii*[122] and *numina*,[123] the *insignia* were sacred,[124] and adored by the soldiers who took oaths on them.[125]

---

115 Cf. M. Delcor, *op. cit.*, pp. 56–61.
116 After the victory won by Lucius Cornelius Scipio over Antiochus the Great at Magnesia in 190 B.C., the Seleucid Empire was forced to acknowledge the supremacy of Rome. See the clauses of the treaty of Sardes in F. M. Abel, *Histoire de la Palestine*, I, pp. 103–104. Let us remember that Antiochus Epiphanes does not try to oppose the order which is dictated to him by the envoy of the Senate. Cf. *supra*, p. 74.
117 A. Bouché-Leclercq, *Histoire des Séleucides*, Paris, 1913, p. 418.
118 *H.C.*, III, 10–11.
119 This interpretation was proposed at first by J. van der Ploeg, *Bi. Or.*, 1951, p. 10 and by M. H. Segal, *J.B.L.*, 1951, p. 134.
120 Cf. M. Delcor, *op. cit.*, pp. 56–58.
121 E. Stauffer, *Zur Frühdatierung des Habakukmidrash, Th.L.Z.*, 1951, cols. 667–674 and H. H. Rowley, *The Zadokite Fragments . . .*, pp. 73–74 refer to *Ps.*, LXXIV, 4, where mention is made of enemy emblems set up in the middle of the "assembly." Even if that very doubtful interpretation were accepted, no hint can be found of any sacrifices offered to the *signa*. Cf. my article in *R.Sc.R.*, 1953, p. 219.
122 *Corpus Inscriptionum Latinarum*, III, n. 6224 and 7591.
123 Tacitus, *Annales*, II, 17.   124 Josephus, *B.J.*, III, VI, 2.
125 Tertullianus, *Apol.*, XVI, 8.

There is moreover a passage in Josephus which requires no comment:

". . . the Romans brought their insignia to the holy precincts (of the Jerusalem Temple) and set them up close against the eastern gate; there they offered sacrifices in their honor and amidst prodigious acclamations hailed Titus with the name of *Imperator*."[126]

And let no one object that the quoted passage dates from the Christian era;[127] Professor R. Goossens[128] has shown that the cult of *signa* is attested at the epoch when Triumvir Crassus was fighting the Parthans (53 B.C.),[129] and that Cicero ascribed it to Catilina in the following terms:

"I know that you have also sent forward that silver eagle which, I trust, will be a cause of ruin and a curse for all your band. . . . For this eagle a shrine of iniquities has been set up in your own home. Is it possible that you could longer be separated from this to which you were wont to pay homage as you set forth to murder, from whose altars you often have lifted that impious right hand of yours for the slaughter of the citizens?"[130]

This passage does not in the least mean that the cult of the eagle was a private devotion of Catilina's, as Professor H. H. Rowley would lead us to believe.[131] Cicero does not at all reproach his adversary with the extravagance of offering sacrifices to the emblem of the Roman people, but he accuses him of daring to slaughter his fellow citizens under the cover of that powerful emblem.

The Roman cult of the military insignia is therefore sufficiently proved, not only during the Christian era, but much earlier, back to the time of the Republic in the first half of the First century B.C.

Professor A. Dupont-Sommer has the merit of having been the first to call attention to so important a feature in helping to identify the *Kittim*.[132] This theory has ever since been gaining ground, and is, in my opinion, at least, the only possible one.[133]

The *Kittim* of the *Habakkuk Commentary* are therefore the Romans, at the period of their expansion throughout the East; they do

---

[126] *B.J.*, VI, VI, 1.
[127] Cf. H. H. ROWLEY, *The Zadokite Fragments* . . . , p. 73, where he supposes that the cult of the *signa* was closely related to that of the Caesars.
[128] *Les Kittim du Commentaire d'Habacuc, La Nouvelle Clio*, 1952, pp. 137–170.   [129] *Ibid.*, p. 149.
[130] *Ibid.*, p. 152. The passage is quoted from *Catilin.*, I, IX, 24; see also *Catilin*, II, VI, 13.   [131] *Op. cit.*, p. 73, n. 1.
[132] Cf. *Le "Commentaire d'Habacuc" découvert près de la Mer Morte, R.H.R.*, t. 137, 1950, p. 159.
[133] Other objections have been made against identifying the *Kittim* with the Romans, such as an allusion in the *H.C.* to the war elephants of the Seleucids: it does not seem necessary to resume the argument here. The reader may refer to *R.Sc.R.*, 1953, pp. 223–227 and to A. Dupont-Sommer in *Nouveaux aperçus* . . . , pp. 48–50.

not seem, however, to have actually conquered Judea yet; they are *ante portas.*

Their spectacular march through the land, the submission of peoples and kings, a reputation for invincibility; this description suits perfectly the sentiments of an Oriental at the sight of Licinius Lucullus' and Pompey's victories, which reduced the powerful Armenian Kingdom of Tigranes and the Seleucid Empire to the condition of a Roman province (69–65 B.C.).[134]

In 65 B.C., Scaurus, one of Pompey's generals, intervened in the conflict between Aristobulus II and Hyrcanus II, and in exchange for a substantial sum, pronounced for the former.[135] Henceforth, gifts flowed in a steady stream from Jerusalem to the envoys of Rome: 300 silver talents for General Gabinius; [136] 500 golden talents for buying the good will of Pompey.[137] And this was but a beginning.

When the author of the *Habakkuk Commentary* predicted that the riches of the "last priests of Jerusalem" would pass into the hands of the *Kittim,* he made a shrewd guess: the money with which the Hasmonean bribed the Roman generals excited the insatiable greed of the new masters of the world. It did not take a prophet to foresee and foretell the sequence of events. In 63 B.C., Pompey made his entry into Jerusalem.

Since the Romans whom the *Commentary* had in view were Pompey's legionaires, the sequence of the "last priests" must extend down to Aristobulus II.

Concerning the date at which the *Commentary* was written, I estimate it to be shortly before Jerusalem fell to the Romans, preferably between 65 and 63 B.C.[138] It might possibly have been written sometime later,[139] but in any case not after 37 B.C., at which time the Hasmonean dynasty came to an end.

The fight against Hellenism under Antiochus Epiphanes and Pompey's advance toward the frontiers of Judea, these are the two limits of the historical perspective which we believe we have discovered in the writings of the Covenant Community.

As well as the historical setting, we have been able to establish the date of the composition of the two most precious documents—the *Damascus Document* and the *Habakkuk Commentary*—at respectively between 110 and 100 B.C. and between 65 and 63 B.C.

The century of Jewish history which saw the birth of this literature

---

134 R. Goossens has come to very much the same conclusions. The passages from Latin writers (Cicero, Sallust) which he has collected have enabled him to make some interesting comparisons.

135 Cf. *A.J.*, XIV, II, 3.   136 *Ibid.*, XIV, III, 2.   137 *Ibid.*, XIV, III, 1.

138 A very similar solution has been offered by J. VAN DER PLOEG, *Bi. Or.*, 1951, p. 10; H. M. SEGAL, *J.B.L.*, 1951, pp. 134–135 and W. H. BROWNLEE, *B.A.S.O.R.*, 126, 1952, pp. 15–16.

139 Perhaps the commentator abstained from announcing the total ruin of the "last priests," because Pompey merely replaced Aristobulus II by Hyrcanus II.

was in many respects a decisive one for the evolution of doctrines and the change in the structure of Judaism.

We know now the beginning of the story and its end, the Hellenistic crisis and the decline of the "last priests of Jerusalem." But what happened in the meantime, while the Teacher of Righteousness presided over the destiny of the Community? Can the manuscripts of the Sect throw any light on this problem?

chapter five

THE TEACHER

OF RIGHTEOUSNESS

We felt fairly secure in the last chapter, following, as it were, the well-beaten track of general history. The Hellenistic crisis and the Roman conquest of the Near East, which seem to mark the two limits of the historical perspective, are both events about which we are well informed.

The internal history of the Community is, on the contrary, a *terra incognita*, which must be explored. The movement created by the Teacher of Righteousness came into contact, no doubt, with the historical personalities whose existence is revealed in the *Book of Maccabees* and by Josephus, but the writers of the Sect took, we feel, good care to conceal their identity.

I must, therefore, emphasize once more that the historical reconstruction which I am going to propose can be but a tentative one. At the same time, I hope to prove that these hypotheses are extremely likely, supported as they are by the clear evidence of the texts.

Granted that the Teacher of Righteousness began his public activities about 170 B.C. as has been suggested, and that the period of the "last Priests of Jerusalem" opened with the death of Simon the Maccabee (134 B.C.), the inference is that the conflict between the Teacher of Righteousness and his opponents occurred in the intermediate period.

The *Habakkuk Commentary* will be our main source and its data will be compared with those figuring in the *Damascus Document* and the *Hymns*.

We shall, with the help of these documents, first endeavor to identify the opponents of the Teacher of Righteousness, then to trace, as closely as possible, the path followed by the Sect until A.D. 70 when communal life in Qumrân was brought to an end; or even, if possible, down to the Middle Ages, when Zadokite leanings unexpectedly reappeared again, culminating in the Karaite schism.

1. The Opponents of the Teacher of Righteousness

It is, *a priori*, impossible to tell whether the Teacher quarreled with one or more of Judah's leading men. "The best exegesis," it has been said, "will of course try to refer to one person only, in order to account for the character of the High Priest (the "wicked Priest")." [1] Such a conclusion may be reached at the end of an investigation; but to consider it as axiomatic from the start, would not be wise.

The enemies of the Community have many pseudonyms: "the Man (or Men) of Mockery" and the "Man of Deception" in the *Damascus Document;* [2] the "Man of Deception," the "Liemonger," and most frequent of all, the "Wicked Priest" in the *Habakkuk Commentary*.[3] Such cryptic language was often used in apocalyptic *milieux*, as for instance the "King of the North" and the "King of the South" in the *Book of Daniel*.[4]

From what has been said in the last chapter, it follows that the allusions, in some cases at least, must refer to the Hellenistic high priests. The "Man of Mockery" for instance, who at the time when the Teacher of Righteousness appeared on the scene, "poured out upon Israel waters of falsehood and led them astray into chaos without way, swerving from the pathways of righteousness and removing the landmarks which their forefathers had set up in their inheritance"; [5] and the "Man of Deception," surrounded by bellicose "traitors," who did not hearken to the Teacher's admonitions,[6] might well be one or the other of the Hellenizing priests, Menelaus or Alcimus. And it was natural that the Community writers should deny him the title of priest.

The wicked priest's character and career are described more precisely. At first irreproachable, he did wrong when he took into his hands the government of Israel. As a chastisement for his misdeeds, God gave him over to his enemies, who inflicted upon him a dreadful death.[7]

To whom among the priests are these facts applicable?

---

[1] Cf. M. M. DELCOR, *Essai sur le Midrash d'Habacuc*, p. 44.
[2] *D.D.*, I, 14; XX, 11, 15.
[3] *H.C.*, II, 1–2; V, 9–12; X, 9–13; VIII, 8–13; VIII, 16–IX, 2; IX, 9–12; XI, 4–8; XI, 12–15; XII, 2–6; XII, 8–10.
[4] W. H. BROWNLEE, *B.A.S.O.R.*, 126, 1952, p. 11.
[5] *D.D.*, I, 14–16.   [6] *H.C.*, II, 1–2; V, 9–12.
[7] *Ibid.*, VIII, 8–13; VIII, 16–IX, 2; IX, 9–12.

THE HELLENIZING PONTIFFS

Inevitably, our thoughts turn first to the age of Antiochus Epiphanes. Were not Jason, Menelaus and Alcimus all traitors, who had betrayed the Law, and mocked and persecuted those who clung to the faith of the Fathers?

The man, whom the portrait of the "wicked Priest" resembles most, is undoubtedly Menelaus. A faithful satellite of Antiochus, he plotted the assassination of Onias III and criminally guided that king when he plundered and profaned the Temple; he was well qualified for the title of "wicked." His end also resembles that of the "wicked Priest" from the *Commentary*, in that he was finally tormented and put to death by his Syrian masters in 162 B.C.[8]

I do not, however, consider that identification as acceptable. For one thing, how could Menelaus be accused of having plundered the riches of *peoples*, whereas he was in the pay of the pagans and the friend of Gentiles? Neither are we clear about the "men of violence that revolted against God" and whom Menelaus would have plundered. And lastly, the "wicked Priest" is supposed to have been "irreproachable" at the beginning of his career, which would not fit Menelaus at all.

To attempt to identify the priest with Jason or Alcimus would only increase the problem, since neither of them was delivered into the hands of his enemies, or put to death. Jason, who was dismissed, died in exile,[9] and Alcimus was in office when he died of a stroke.[10]

Hence a search for the "wicked Priest" among the Hellenizing pontiffs brings us to a standstill. Whether one examines them individually, or all three together, the enquiry leads us nowhere. I do not doubt that some passages may allude to them, but it seems that they are not the only persons to be considered.

THE MACCABEES

The identification of the "last priests of Jerusalem" with the Hasmoneans, from John Hyrcanus down to Aristobulus II, which was proposed above, may have a bearing on the present problem.

It is a remarkable fact that the wickedness which is laid at their door is of the same kind exactly as that which caused the "wicked Priest" to abandon God by betraying His commandments. Does the author not hint that the last representatives of an abhorred sacerdotal race did but follow the example set them by their elders? In other words, the "wicked Priest" who was "called by the name of Truth at the beginning of his activities," should be sought among the founders of the Hasmonean dynasty.

This bold solution, proposed by Israel Lévi for the *Damascus Docu-*

---

[8] Cf. *II Macc.*, V, 13; XIII, 3–8.
[9] Cf. *II Macc.*, V, 9–10.   [10] Cf. *I Macc.*, IX, 54–56.

ment some time ago,[11] was adopted on the publication of the first texts of Qumrân by I. L. Seeligmann.

"In my opinion," he wrote in January 1949, "some characteristics . . . of the wicked Priest would not fit any pre-Maccabean high priest; more particularly (*H.C.*), 8, 9–13 . . . rather reminds one of some representative of the Maccabean dynasty or of one of the posterior Maccabean princes, whose unduly secularized, worldly and violent policy of conquest, aroused, on the part of his religious subjects, a fierce resistance." [12]

Professor H. Bardtke has, more recently, echoed the same opinion: "Are we to assume that the 'wicked Priest' played a part in the Maccabean wars and amassed his wealth thereby; or that the description points to some Hasmonean king who assumed the pontifical office, as was indeed the case with Jonathan in 153 B.C.?" [13] For my part, I have ventured to reply in the affirmative.[14] I say "venture," for the hypothesis calls for an inevitable objection: how could the heroes of a holy war come to be called "wicked"?

Yet, the glory which surrounds the Maccabees must not cause us to forget that they lived in one of the most troubled periods of Jewish history, a period full of hatred and hereditary feuds.

It should not be forgotten that the Hassideans had already parted company with the Maccabees during Alcimus' pontificate; that their successors, the Pharisees, called upon John Hyrcanus, the son of Simon the Maccabee, to give up the pontificate, his accession being illegal; [15] and that some apocrypha, the *Psalms of Solomon* and above all the *Assumption of Moses*, of which more will be said later, judged with great severity the dynasty founded by the Maccabees.[16]

Nevertheless, the accusations voiced by the Pharisees were not so grave as those uttered by the members of the Community, who claimed to speak in the name of the ancient pontifical family whom the Maccabees had supplanted. The "sons of Zadok" could not accept lightheartedly the loss of their secular rights. It amounted, in their eyes, to the rejection by the usurper of the divine oracle delivered by Ezekiel, making light of the Covenant that God made with Pinhas and of which the descendants of Zadok were the sole heirs.[17]

---

11 *Un écrit sadducéen antérieur à la destruction du Temple*, R.E.J., 1912, pp. 2–4.

12 *The Epoch-making Discovery of Hebrew Scrolls in the Judean Desert*, Bi.Or., 1949, p. 6.

13 *Die Handschriftenfunde am Toten Meer*, Berlin, 1952, p. 142.

14 *Où en est la question des manuscrits de la Mer Morte?* C.S., 1953, pp. 71–74.

15 Josephus, *A.J.*, XIII, X, 5.   16 *Ass. of Moses*, VI, 1.

17 In order to understand the claims of Ezekiel and of the Community, it is necessary to remember that the Aaronids descended from their ancestor through either Eleazar or Ithamar, the sons of Aaron. Cf. *Num.*, III, 2–4. Pinhas the son of Eleazar received, however, as a reward for his zeal, the promise of an eternal priesthood for himself and his posterity. (*Num.*, XXV, 6–13; *Ps.*, CVI, 30–31; *Sir.*, L, 24 Hebrew). Lastly, in the Pinhas lineage, the descendants of Zadok claimed the exclusive right to perpetual priesthood (*Ezek.*, XLIV, 15–16).

Father Lagrange wrote more than twenty years ago: "One would be inclined to think that a covert opposition continued among the families who were despoiled of pontifical power. But their complicity with Antiochus Epiphanes, their continued intrigues, had been exposed and made them powerless." [18]

How much more bitter must have been the feelings of the true "sons of Zadok," who so far from seeking a compromise with Hellenism had, during the darkest hours, been the most faithful defenders of the Law, vowing to atone for the crimes perpetrated by their brethren. Nothing would be more natural than that these Zadokites should "covert opposition" against the Maccabean intruders, expressing it, as is often the case, in cryptic writings such as the *Habakkuk Commentary*.

The Maccabean hypothesis cannot, thus, be *a priori* put aside. It remains to be seen whether it explains, better than the other theories, all the data of the documents. For my part, I think it does, and I hope to be able to prove it.

This is how the Commentator interprets *Hab.*, II, 5:

"Its meaning concerns the wicked Priest who claimed the name of Truth unto himself at the beginning of his assumption of office. But when he ruled in Israel, his heart became proud, he abandoned God and betrayed the commandments for the sake of wealth. He robbed and amassed the wealth of the men of violence who had rebelled against God, and he took the wealth of the peoples, heaping upon himself the burden of transgression. He showed a detestable activity in the ways of abominations, carrying out every impurity of defilement." [19]

Thus the good Priest, who at the beginning of his career was attached to true religion, became wicked on assuming the rule over Israel, and usurping the office of the high priest. His love of profit caused his downfall, he plundered the "violent men that revolted against God" and the "peoples," i.e., the foreigners. Through this criminal behavior, he became guilty of all manner of defilements and impurities.[20]

The most likely model for this description is, in my opinion, Jonathan the Maccabee, judged, of course, by "Zadokite" standards.

His public life had the most auspicious beginnings, since he carried on the struggle against the Syrians after his brother Judah's glorious death. He refused staunchly to recognize Alcimus as High Priest, which in Zadokite eyes was the highest virtue. He succeeded in defeating the formidable Bacchides at Bethbassi.[21]

The Syrian general lost heart, and concluded peace with the Mac-

[18] *Le judaïsme avant Jésus-Christ*, Paris, 1931, p. 105.   [19] *H.C.*, VIII, 8–13.
[20] These "defilements" and "impurities" do not necessarily imply dissolute morals. All the works of the man who does not keep all the laws of the Community will be "defilement" (*niddah*) before God, and his property will be reckoned as "impurity" (*tame'*). Cf. *M.D.*, V, 18–20; see also *D.D.*, IV, 20–21; V, 6–11.   [21] Cf. *I Macc.*, IX, 43–69.

cabee; the latter was to settle at Michmas, from whence he was to
"judge" (govern) Israel and harass the renegade Jews.[22]

Having thus achieved religious freedom, Jonathan's mission was
at an end; he had nothing left except to reinstate the legitimate pontiff. But the Maccabee showed no sign that he intended to do so,
and when Alexander Balas, the usurper of the Seleucid throne,
offered him the pontifical office, he accepted it at once and unhesi-
tatingly.[23] "The dubious character of his patron," in Fr. Abel's words,
"does not lend glamour to his (Jonathan's) promotion." [24] Despoiling pontiffs who thought themselves elect for all eternity was tantamount, for the members of the Community, to forsaking God and
betraying His decrees.

"During the feast of the Tabernacles in 152 B.C.," wrote E. Bicker-
mann, the author of the standard works on the Seleucid era,[25] "Jonathan . . . put on the sacred ornament of the High Priest. Judah had
fiercely fought Alcimus . . . because the latter was unclean. Eight
years later, Jonathan set himself up as a pontiff, though not belonging
to the Zadokite family to whom the office belonged by right. That
priests should be invested by civil power was a Greek rather than a
Jewish custom. Once more, those who had fought for the Torah
adapted it finally to pagan ways." [26]

Such was Jonathan's sin, a most grievous one; to accept the pontifical stole and purple from the hands of Alexander Balas was truly
to "abandon God and forsake His decrees."

The other crime mentioned by the Commentator, that of having
robbed the wealth of the "men of violence that revolted against God,"
might also be ascribed to Jonathan.

These men of violence could not, of course, be robbers, but rather
apostate Jews allied to the Syrian generals, and fiercely hated by
Jonathan.[27] The wealth of these traitors, the Community members
probably considered as the "soiled goods of iniquity" which must be
destroyed, according to the ancient *herem* law. The Maccabee,
when he kept the booty for his own use, incurred the reproach of
being a grasping man who fought only to increase his own wealth.

Concerning the riches "taken from the peoples," this might mean
on the one hand the plunder which Jonathan won through his numerous victories; [28] on the other hand, it might refer to the gifts with

[22] *Ibid.*, IX, 73.   [23] *Ibid.*, X, 15–21.   [24] *Histoire de la Palestine*, I, p. 173.
[25] Cf. *Institutions séleucides*, Paris, 1938, and *Der Gott des Makkabäer*, Berlin,
    1937. The author's name is spelt BIKERMAN or BICKERMANN according to
    whether it is written in French or German.
[26] *Die Makkabäer*, Berlin, 1935, p. 42.
[27] Cf. *I Macc.*, IX, 61, 73. — A. Dupont-Sommer has thought of bandits, yet
    confesses that the allusion is lacking in precision. Cf. *R.H.R.*, 1950, t. 137,
    p. 163.
[28] *I Macc.*, X, 74: After his victory over Apollonius, Jonathan and his followers
    returned loaded with booty; *I Macc.*, XI, 51: so did the levy sent by Jona-
    than to Antiochia; *I Macc.*, XII, 31–32 shows Jonathan plundering the
    Zabadeans, etc.

which the Seleucid kings bribed him in order to have him on their side.[29] This was another and no less serious crime: the usurper had sold himself to the enemies of his nation in order to secure political and religious power.

The end of the passage, however, seems at first sight disconcerting: does not the author ascribe to the wicked Priest detestable deeds and all manner of defilements and impurities?

But let us not forget that Zadokite language differs totally from our own way of speaking; that to them the action of anyone not belonging to their group was defiled with impurity; [30] that any property not belonging to the Community could not be entirely pure. If we are to see those accusations in their true proportion, it should be remembered that the *Damascus Document* holds polygamy to be lustful, although polygamy was allowed by the Law,[31] and that it taxes as "defilement of the sanctuary," the unobservance of certain prescriptions concerning conjugal intercourse or prohibited marriages.[32]

It would not, therefore, have been surprising that Jonathan should be accused of being unclean, since many characteristics of some of the dynasty's later representatives might have been ascribed to him.[33]

The "wicked Priest's" sad end is described in two passages of the *Habakkuk Commentary.*

The first shows him delivered over by God into the hands of his enemies, who scorned him and tormented him to death; thus the wicked man who behaved impiously with the Teacher of Righteousness and his disciples met an ignominious and well-deserved fate.[34]

This, again, fits Jonathan admirably, and him only, among the first Hasmoneans.

General Tryphon, that treacherous pretender to the Seleucid throne, foreseeing that Jonathan would stand in his way, tried to get rid of him. Jonathan mistrusted the Syrian and went to meet him at the head of an army of 40,000 men. He found at Bethsan a Tryphon, who was all smiles. The general offered him the town of Ptolemais and "other strongholds," but, since they were friends, requested the dismissal of his soldiery.

Jonathan fell into the trap. He made his entry into Ptolemais escorted by only a few soldiers; they were massacred on the spot, and he himself was taken prisoner.[35] He certainly experienced "bitterness of soul" and "grief unto death" while meditating on his misfortunes.

His brother Simon did everything in his power to save him, accepting Tryphon's every demand: Jonathan's two sons were sent as hostages, and a ransom paid amounting to a hundred silver talents,

---

[29] Thus Alexander Balas, the young Antiochus and Tryphon. Cf. *I Macc.*, X, 88–89; XI, 58; XII, 43.   [30] Cf. *M.D.*, V, 18–20.   [31] *D.D.*, IV, 20–21.
[32] *Ibid.*, V, 6–11. These rules are stricter than those of the Pentateuch.
[33] For instance Alexander Janneus and the *Ps. of Solomon*, VIII, 13.
[34] *H.C.*, IX, 8–12.   [35] *I Macc.*, XII, 46–68.

all to no avail. Simon then decided to fight; but before fleeing, the Syrian general caused his prisoner to be executed.[36]

The Commentator no doubt had that gruesome scene in mind when he alluded in another passage to the punishment inflicted on the wicked Priest. The general sense is clear, even though the text is mutilated, for the missing passage does not even amount to a whole line.[37]

It alludes to a Priest who revolted against the commandments of God, and was, it seems, delivered into the hands of his enemies. They chastised him in a wicked manner, "atrocities and horrible woes they executed upon him and vengeance upon his body and flesh." [38]

This would imply that Jonathan was tortured before being put to death. Historically, this is not only likely but even probable. That the *First Book of the Maccabees* mentions nothing of the sort is not surprising; one does not like to lessen the glory of a venerated figure.

This, then, is my tentative interpretation of the three passages, which seem to give us the key to the *Habakkuk Commentary;* they apply to Jonathan better than to any other historical character.

But what about the other passages concerning the wicked Priest?

There would be no major difficulty in maintaining that they refer to the same person, and it would not raise any new problem. The indications are, however, that they refer more probably to Simon, the last survivor of the Maccabee brothers.

As A. Dupont-Sommer has already observed, the punishment of the wicked Priest appears in a number of passages to be in the future.[39] The punishment, it is true, is of an eschatological nature, viz.: sulphurous fire, the cup of God's wrath. . . .[40] One feels, for all that, that even after Jonathan's death, somebody had yet to be punished.

Such a feeling is confirmed by several passages; we find, among others, an eschatological picture which looks like an extraordinarily accurate story of Simon's murder.

There is, lastly, a reason which is suggested by the interpretation as a whole.

---

[36] *Ibid.,* XIII, 17–24.

[37] *H.C.,* VIII, 16–IX, 2. — Cf. my article in *C.S.,* 1951, p. 66. I propose a purely conjectural reconstitution of the second part of the mutilated line: ". . . the commandments [of God and he has delivered him into the hands of his enemies and they have attack]ed him to [accomplish]." In Hebrew: . . . *hûqqê* ['*el wayyittenehû beyadh 'ôyebhaw wayyithgô*]*llelû bhô la* ['*aśôth*].

[38] This could not possibly allude to any sufferings of the Teacher of Righteousness. The idea of revenge is always associated in the documents with the punishment of sinners who are to be annihilated by the "revengers of revenge," through the medium of Belial. Thus it was the "chief of the kings of Yawan" (Hellenistic kings) who came to execute vengeance on the traitors to the Covenant (*D.D.,* VIII, 11–12).

[39] *Aperçus préliminaires* . . . , p. 52.   [40] *H.C.,* X, 5, 13; XI, 14.

(Photo Starcky)

6. — A hall in the main building.

The history of the Community, as it is suggested in the *Commentary*, opens with the Hellenistic crisis.[41] Some allusions referring to Jonathan have been identified, and the Hasmoneans, from John Hyrcanus to Aristobulus II, recognized as the "last priests of Jerusalem." All the enemies of the Zadokites, in short, have been mentioned in the documents: it would be surprising indeed, if Simon proved the sole exception, since the Sectarians must have considered him their bitterest foe, as he was responsible for their final eviction.

In my opinion, these arguments amply justify the conclusions at which I have finally arrived.

The character designated sometimes as the "Liemonger," sometimes as the "wicked Priest," is accused of having misled a multitude of men "into building through bloodshed a city of vanity, and into raising up a congregation through deceit," and of having made use of them all, with an eye to his own glory. His followers, intoxicated with the "deeds of deceit," dedicated themselves to a "work of vanity," for their sin of deriding the "elect of God" would certainly be punished.[42] The persecution carried out against the Teacher of Righteousness and his disciples was also to be laid at his door: "He robbed the property of the poor" and intended to ruin their Community.[43]

He committed "abominations," just like his predecessor, and "defiled the sanctuary of God." [44]

The "city of vanity," built in blood, corresponds to the "assembly" raised through deceit, as M. Delcor has aptly remarked.[45] It cannot be doubted that the "builders of walls," whom the *Damascus Document* taxes with lust, defilement of the sanctuary and the profanation of the holy spirit within them, are not merely the masons or their employers.[46] It seems much more likely that this "assembly" signifies the new priestly society of which Simon, invested with the hereditary title of High Priest, became the head when he consented "to become pontiff, and captain and the governor of the Jews and of the priests, and to be at the head of all." [47]

What was meant by "abominations" and "defiling of the sanctuary" has already been seen.[48] In the case of Simon, we seem to possess an historical proof of these complaints. Josephus relates that under John Hyrcanus a rumor had spread that the high priest's mother, i.e., Simon's wife, had been led into captivity during the reign of Anti-

---

41 Cf. *supra*, p. 89.   42 *H.C.*, X, 9–13.   43 *Ibid.*, XII, 2–10.
44 *Ibid.*, XII, 7–9.   45 *Essai sur le Midrash d'Habacuc*, p. 35.
46 Cf. *D.D.*, IV, 19; VIII, 12. – According to A. Dupont-Sommer (*Aperçus préliminaires* . . . , p. 50) and to H. H. Rowley (*The Zadokite Fragments* . . . , pp. 66–67) however, the author had in view repairs carried out in Jerusalem. Neither must we forget that Rabbinic writings do mention a group of pietists called the "builders" (*banna'im*), whom historians tentatively identified with the Essenes (cf. *supra*, p. 58, n. 140). Those whom the *Damascus Document* envisages, were not merely "builders," but also covered the "walls" with plaster, as if to conceal their lack of solidity.
47 Cf. *I Macc.*, XIV, 25–48.   48 Cf. *supra*, p. 93.

ochus Epiphanes.[49] Now, a high priest may not marry such a woman, according at least to the interpretation of the doctors of the Law.[50]

This story, true or false, was taken seriously, and brought about the rupture between John Hyrcanus and the Pharisees: they considered that Simon had contracted a prohibited marriage. People held their tongues because they feared the father's authority, but let them loose when his son succeeded him.

Such a rumor, of course, would not have fallen upon deaf ears amongst the members of the Community.

What must have exasperated them most was Simon's popularity and the glory that surrounded him. He must truly have deceived the masses and intoxicated them, that they should readily undergo so many useless efforts for the sake of his "glory." His reign was described in Messianic terms: "His glorious name was proclaimed to the end of the earth." [51] So much the worse for his blinded people, the Commentator thought, who extol the renown of this Priest; his ignominy shall be even greater. His heart is uncircumcised, his soul intoxicated with distorted doctrine, and he thirsts for truth no longer; he must be punished. His chastisement shall be such as his iniquities merit. He, who had "intoxicated" multitudes, should drain the "cup of God's wrath which will make him totter." [52]

While admitting that the chastisement is presented eschatologically, one cannot fail to notice that this punishment through drunkenness bears a curious likeness to the historical event, which the *First Book of the Maccabees* relates in the following words:

Simon "went down to Jericho, he himself and his sons . . . in the one hundred and seventy-seventh year, in the eleventh month (at the beginning of 134 B.C.). The son of Abubos (Ptolemy, Simon's son-in-law) received them deceitfully into the little stronghold that is called Dôk. . . . He made them a great banquet and he hid men there. And when Simon and his sons were drunk, Ptolemy and his men rose up and took their arms, and coming upon Simon in the banqueting hall, they slew him together with his two sons and some of his servants." [53]

Jonathan's cupidity had brought him to ruin through his coveting Ptolemais and other strongholds; drunkenness proved as fatal to Simon, and his death was unworthy of a high priest. It would not be at all surprising that so fierce an adversary of the Maccabean cause, as was the Commentator, should see in that disgraceful end the finger of God.

In a small hill-fortress, a few miles from Jericho, the Community's arch-enemy paid with his life for the wrong he had committed toward

---

49 A.J., XII, X, 5. See also *Talmud bab.-Qiddushin,* 66a.
50 Women taken into captivity were presumed to have been violated, unless witnesses could testify to the contrary. Cf. *Mishna-Kethubhoth,* I, 4; II, 5–6, 9.   51 *I Macc.,* XIV, 10. See the whole pericopa from 4 to 15.
52 *H.C.,* XI, 12–15.   53 *I Macc.,* XVI, 14–16.

"God's elect." But his race was not entirely extinguished through Ptolemy's treachery. His son John, surnamed Hyrcanus, frustrated the plot of those who were after his life, and succeeded his father in his office at the altar.[54]

And so the pontificate, instead of returning to the "sons of Zadok," passed into the hands of the "last priests of Jerusalem."

It would seem that at that critical stage the Teacher of Righteousness was no longer alive, his death having probably preceded that of Simon.[55]

The identity of his adversaries thus tentatively established, the time has come for an attempted reconstruction of the Teacher's career.

2. The Teacher of Righteousness

This great priest [56] appeared at a most tragic stage of Israelite sacerdotal history. The ruling class was contaminated by Hellenism: the legitimate pontiff had been set aside, his usurping brother driven away in his turn, and upstarts were officiating at the altar. Religion itself was gravely injured and its very existence threatened.

The Teacher of Righteousness was also a member, if my previous conclusions be accepted,[57] of that illustrious family which had produced reformers and men of genius such as Zadok, most probably Ezekiel, and Ezra who was at once a priest, a scribe, and a doctor of the Law of Moses.

He was ill-treated and mocked by his fellow citizens, who were imbued with novel ideas. He was made to leave his own people, seeking refuge with those who, like himself, refused to submit. But soon, devoted disciples flocked around him and listened religiously to every word he uttered.[58]

His teaching consisted mainly of the interpretation of the word of God, and, most of all, of the writings of the Prophets. The understanding of mysteries was, according to the *Habakkuk Commentary*, revealed to him not by an angel, as was the case with Daniel,[59] but directly by God.[60] He had a better knowledge than even the Prophets of the events concerning the end of time, or so at least his followers firmly believed.

His teaching, apparently, was also devoted to the explanation of the commandments of Moses and he must have played his part in the transmission of the "revelations" pertaining to the Law, of which the "sons of Zadok" were so proud.[61] His initial influence is probably

---

54 *Ibid.*, XVI, 18–24.   55 Cf. *supra*, p. 77.   56 Cf. *H.C.*, II, 8.
57 Cf. *supra*, pp. 74–75.
58 See *Hymn*, IV, the words of which are, in all likelihood, attributed to the Teacher of Righteousness.
59 *Dan.*, IX, 20 sq.   60 *H.C.*, II, 2–3; VII, 4–5.
61 Cf. *M.D.*, I, 9; V, 9, 12; VIII, 1, 15; IX, 13, 19.

reflected in some passages of the *Damascus Document* and of the *Manual*. The reforms he had in mind bear, on many points, a strong likeness to those promulgated by Ezra: a ban on prohibited marriages, a rigorous discrimination between things pure and impure, and segregation from the unfaithful.[62]

His influence must have been so profound that the Community members felt secure about their salvation, provided they kept their loyalty and faith to the Teacher of Righteousness.[63]

The congregation which he organized also vowed to atone for the misdeeds committed by the wicked in Israel, by the Hellenists particularly, and to do penance.[64]

Thus supported by a group of fervent disciples, and feeling sure of God's favor through what he took for unmistakable signs, the Teacher of Righteousness rose against his scoffers crying: "My hand will be upon those that despise me." [65]

Such an attitude is fully consistent with that of the Hassideans, the Maccabees, and all those who clung to the Covenant of the Forefathers.

How did they react to the national insurrection? The scroll of the *War of the Sons of Light against the Sons of Darkness* leads one to believe that the group joined the revolt under the leadership of the Maccabees. Did such a collaboration excite a certain amount of rivalry? We are inclined to think so. Whereas in the *Books of the Maccabees* the direction of military action is ascribed to Judah (who exhorts the fighters, prays to God for victory, and curses the enemy), in the *War* scroll that privilege is ascribed solely to the High Priest, with the priests his brethren, and the inspectors of the camps.[66] It is to be noted that the Pontiff is called the "High Priest" (*kôhen harô's*), while the Hasmoneans used the title "Great Priest" (*kôhen gadôl*).[67]

How long did the Zadokites and the Maccabees remain together? We may conjecture that they probably parted company as soon as Bacchides left for good. The peace he signed with Jonathan spelt the end of the Syrian danger. While the Zadokites confidently expected to resume their functions, Jonathan took an unequivocal step, by assuming the pontifical office himself. Henceforward, from 152 B.C., the rupture was an accomplished fact.

Thus, in all probability, the Community of the Teacher of Righteousness was transformed into a sect of convinced dissidents, which

---

62 Cf. *Ezr.*, IX–X. – *D.D.*, VI, 14–VII, 6.   63 *H.C.*, VIII, 1–3. Cf. *infra*, p.
64 Cf. *M.D.*, VIII, 4–7.   65 *Hymn*, IV, 18.
66 Compare *I Macc.*, III, 18 sq.; IV, 30 sq. – *II Macc.*, VIII, 18 sq.; XII, 37, etc. with *M.G.*, I, p. 20.
67 Cf. *I Macc.*, XIV, 27: ἀρχιερεὺς μέγας. "If . . . μέγας signifies *gadol*, . . . the epithet *great* would then aim at raising even higher the dignity of Simon over all the other high priests of the East, or above the other high priests of his own lineage and all his predecessors." (F. M. ABEL, *Les livres des Maccabées*, pp. 256–257). The same title is found on John Hyrcanus' coins.

remained in opposition, although the Hellenistic threat hovered over Judaism no longer. Their hostility toward those in power placed them, however, in an unenviable plight.

The supporters of Jonathan and of Simon ridiculed in every way those who claimed the privilege of being, to the exclusion of all others, "God's elect," and made them an object of continual vexation and affront. Then, little by little, the matter became serious. The Teacher of Righteousness had, some time since, retired into exile and was living, together with his disciples, in some peaceful corner of Judea.

In this "abode of exile," he was visited by the "wicked Priest," that is, Simon the Maccabee. Exasperated by the passive resistance which the Community offered him, he arrived on the day on which the sectarians were celebrating the feast of the great Atonement, a day of fasting, expiation and penitence, and presented them with an ultimatum: let them listen to reason, or else be prepared to be annihilated. "And upon the resting day of Yôm Kippurim, he appeared to them for the purpose of leading them astray, that they might stumble on that fast day, the Sabbath of their resting." [68]

The feast of Kippur was thus turned from a day of penitence into a day of mourning for the followers of the Teacher of Righteousness. As for the latter, a good many authors think the incident cost him his life.[69] This is of course possible, but no proof is given. His death,

---

[68] The expression "their Sabbath" and the fact that the high priest was able to journey on so holy a feast will be more easily understood if, together with S. Talmon (*Yom Hakkipurim in the Habakkuk Scroll, Bibl.*, 1951, pp. 549–563), one presumes the existence of two different calendars, the one adopted by the Community, and the other by official Judaism. This is corroborated by *M.D.*, I, 14–15, and even more by *D.D.*, VI, 18–19; XVI, 3–4. The latter passage quotes the *Book of Jubilees*, extolling the solar year: twelve months of thirty days each, plus four intercalary days at the beginning of each season; whilst orthodox Jewry followed a lunar-solar calendar: a year of 354 days and a supplementary month every three years. The Community calendar has been studied by A. Dupont-Sommer, *Nouveaux aperçus . . .*, pp. 140–156, and A. Jaubert, *Le calendrier des Jubiles et de la secte de Qumrân. Ses origines bibliques*, V.T., 1953, pp. 250–264. For the calendar of the Karaites, see *infra*, p. 107. In order to understand the importance of this controversy, it is necessary to remember the dispute in the second century A.D. between the Church of Asia and the Church of the West, concerning the correct date of the Feast of Easter.

[69] Dupont-Sommer, Goossens, del Medico. — Professor Dupont-Sommer has found in the *Testament of Levi* a new argument to corroborate his hypothesis that the Teacher of Righteousness was put to death in the reign of Aristobulus II (*Nouveaux aperçus*, pp. 63–84); I should like here to make some remarks on this subject.

The seven priesthoods of chapter XVII in the *Test. of Levi*, are interpreted as seven successive pontificates, from Judah the Maccabee to Aristobulus II. The particularly serious crime committed under Aristobulus would be the murder of the Teacher of Righteousness.

Such an interpretation appears to me vulnerable on two points. 1) The seven priesthoods, which correspond to seven jubilees, would seem to apply to periods rather than to individuals. 2) Prof. Dupont-Sommer very properly

either a violent or a natural one, occurred probably under the pontificate of Simon, between 142 and 134 B.C.

It was, in all probability, at the same period that the exodus of a Zadokite group to the Damascene land took place. This province was part of the Seleucid Empire, which being hostile to the Hasmoneans would have provided a secure place of refuge for the enemies of the *régime*. In that country they were to adopt the name of the "Community of the New Covenant in the land of Damascus." [70] All those who were later to join them took their oath on that renewed Covenant, according to the authentic interpretation of the Law and the Prophets given by the "sons of Zadok."

The first literary works of the Sect appeared at the time of the Damascus exile: the *Hymns*, the *Damascus Document*, and also most probably, the *Habakkuk Commentary*. It is not irrelevant to remark here that when Pompey was about to settle the conflict between Hyrcanus and Aristobulus, a group of Jews appealed to him to abolish the kingship and return the power into the hands of the priests.[71] It could mean but one thing, a change of *régime* within the hierarchy, since the Hasmoneans were themselves priests. The scene moreover occurred, according to Josephus, in Damascus.

The return of the exiles to their homeland was to follow shortly. But they found that Judaism had undergone tremendous changes in the meantime: the new Doctors of the Law were now lay Pharisees.

When they returned to Judea, the Zadokites found other disciples of the Teacher of Righteousness, who had perhaps never left the country. Together they formed a Community living outside Jewish society, and were henceforward known as the "Essenes." The Qumrân "monastery" was founded, it must not be forgotten, not later than the end of the Second century B.C.[72] This was, it seems, the center of the Sect, and the meeting place for other communities disseminated

---

separates the last two verses from the preceding ones, considering them to be remains of an apocalypse of weeks which is now lost. But I think he is wrong in not recognizing that they are two parallel texts which explain each other. The series of seven jubilees and that of the seven weeks both end with a generation of criminal priests, which ought probably to be applied to the era of Hellenizing pontiffs, since the return from the Babylonian exile is situated in the fifth week.

As for the title "Savior of the world" which Prof. Dupont-Sommer applies to the Teacher of Righteousness, I am not certain that it is not, as R. H. Charles thought, of Christian origin. The expression "Savior of the Gentiles," which is found in the *Testament of Dan* (VI, 9), would confirm this assumption. The *Testaments* contain many other manifestly Christian interpolations, such as "God took on a body" (*Test. of Simeon*, VI, 7); "Until the Most-High shall visit the earth, coming in person — as a man, eating and drinking with men" — (*Test. of Asher*, VII, 3).

[70] Cf. *D.D.*, VI, 5; XX, 12. — D. Flusser, in a very evocative article, shows that the author of the *Ascension of Isaiah* also testifies to an exodus of a persecuted Jewish group which took refuge in the North. Cf. *Yedi'oth hahebhrah lahaqirath 'Eres Yiśra'el*, 1952, pp. 26–46.

[71] JOSEPHUS, *A.J.*, XIV, III, 2.   [72] Cf. *supra*, p. 16.

throughout Palestinian towns and villages. Communal life was maintained there until the Roman war, i.e., between A.D. 66 and 70.

Did they take part in the Revolt? One would be tempted to doubt this, but, on the other hand, Josephus mentions an Essene called John, who became governor of the Thamna toparchy and was eventually killed in action at Askalon.[73] There is, however, no question of their general participation in this Revolt.

But at the same time, Josephus also speaks of the atrocious tortures to which the Essenes were subjected by the Roman soldiers, and says they chose death rather than curse the Lawgiver (Moses) or taste prohibited food.[74] One may conclude that in May, A.D. 68, Vespasian's legions, which were stationed in Jericho,[75] descended to Qumrân, a distance of only eight miles, and maltreated the Essenes they caught, while the others took to flight. It is reasonable to suppose that the valuable manuscripts of the Qumrân library were concealed in the neighboring caves as soon as the Roman incursions came dangerously near.

A hecatomb of Essenes . . . a mere hypothesis of course, but it would account for the sudden and mysterious disappearance of that sect. The mother-community once annihilated, the others disintegrated in their turn.

In this history of the Community from the reign of Antiochus Epiphanes to the time of the first Revolt, some events are clearly traced, while others remain obscure and uncertain. Details are nearly always lacking, or at best too vague to be of any use. To fill the gaps, it is often necessary to make conjectures, and problematic comparisons. However, my purpose will be attained if this sketchy portrait affords some likeness to historical reality.

The quest has been an exceptionally difficult one, owing first to the sibylline language of the documents, and above all to what may be called the confusion of perspectives. The *Damascus Document* and the Qumrân writings both profess the same abhorrence toward enemies so bitterly opposed to each other as the Hellenists and the Maccabees.

These two parties, so utterly alien to each other, have one important point in common: their opposition to the Zadokite priesthood. Therefore, in the eyes of the Teacher of Righteousness and his disciples, they were both to be placed in the same category: both were usurpers of the pontifical power.[76]

---

[73] Cf. JOSEPHUS, *B.J.*, II, XX, 4; III, II, 1.
[74] *Ibid.*, II, VIII, 10.   [75] *Ibid.*, IV, VIII, 1; IX, 1.
[76] An attitude of mind which is strangely similar is found in the *Assumption of Moses*. The author, having first deplored the misdeeds of the Hellenists, goes on in his barbaric Latin: *"Tunc exurgent illis reges imperantes et in sacerdotes summi dei vocabuntur, facient facientes impietatem ab sancto sanctitatis"* (VI, 1: Then kings will arise that will call themselves priests of the Most-High God, but they will commit wickedness in the Holy of Holies). These *reges imperantes* are the Maccabees and the Hasmoneans, all of whom

It is now also apparent why the Maccabees were even more bitterly objected to than the Hellenists; the tragic story of Jason and Menelaus was already a thing of the past at the time the documents were written, whereas the Hasmonean pontificate remained a disturbing reality.

3. *The Community of the "Sons of Zadok" and the Karaites*

The year A.D. 70 marked the decline of Essenism. Although I have put forward the opinion that the main Community was brutally and thoroughly annihilated, the possibility of a much slower agony is not to be excluded. But whatever the cause, and in spite of the sporadic survival of a group here and there, their extinction long before the Middle Ages is a certainty. The Sadducees, their hostile brethren, who while claiming Zadokite descent had accepted the various sacerdotal régimes, had ceased to exist as an organized party shortly after the destruction of the Temple.[77] Only the Pharisees survived the crisis, and became the uncontested masters of Judaism's destinies.

Yet, during the Eighth, Ninth, and Tenth centuries A.D., sacerdotal traditions were brought back to life. In his controversy with the Pharisees' successors, the Rabbanites, Anan, the founder of the Karaite sect, claimed to be the heir to Zadokite doctrine, and maintained that his teaching was founded on a tradition more ancient than that of his adversaries. Like the Sadducees he held the Bible to be the sole source of the faith, and the only guide to the religious life.

Anan died about A.D. 800, but his disciples carried on the struggle. It was at about this same time that the Hebrew manuscripts were discovered in a cave near Jericho, a fact mentioned in a letter by the Metropolitan Timotheus.[78]

It is a remarkable fact that the Karaite writers of the Tenth century A.D. speak of one or more writings of Zadok, a disciple of Antigonos of Sokho (Third century B.C.), who was considered to be the founder of the Sadducees.[79] Mention is also made, at the same epoch, of a sect called the "men of the cave" (*al-Maghariya*), because their

---

the author deems guilty, considering them the successors of the Hellenists. The word "king" offers no difficulty, as it is used in this work in the broader sense of "chief." The "mighty king of the West," mentioned later (VI, 8), is none other than Varus, the governor of Syria.

[77] The "House of Absalom" of *H.C.*, V, 9, applies, I think, to the priestly families that did not support the Teacher of Righteousness.

[78] Cf. *supra*, p. 12.

[79] Cf. JACOB AL-QIRQISÂNÎ, *Kitâb al-anwâr wal-marâqib* (Book of the Lights and the Watchtowers), which I quote from L. NEMOY's *Karaite Anthology*, New Haven, 1952, p. 50. — Most of the texts of which I shall make use have been collected by Fr. Lagrange (*R.B.*, 1912, pp. 332–335), Fr. de Vaux (*R.B.*, 1950, pp. 420–426) and Professor P. Kahle (*V.T.*, 1951, pp. 44–46). I have also used S. Poznanski's article, *Anan et ses écrits, R.E.J.*, XLIV, 1902, pp. 160–187; XLV, 1902, pp. 50–69; pp. 176–203.

books, which included those of the "Alexandrine" (Philo), were
found in a cave.[80] Qirqisânî ascribes the origin of this sect to the
same period as that of the Sadducees, i.e., around 200 B.C.[81]

These ancient writings, which caused such a stir, probably originated from some of the hiding places of Qumrân; they were
Zadokite, not Sadducean.

Anan's immediate successor, Benjamin al-Nahâwendî (Ninth century A.D.), appears to have been the first Karaite writer to have known
of them. He modified many points of his master's teaching, and may
well therefore be considered as the second founder of Karaism.[82]
Some passages of his work bear a Philonian stamp, and it was seen
that the writings of the "Alexandrine" were treasured by the
Maghariya.

A hundred years later, in A.D. 937, Jacob-al-Qirqisânî sums up the
contents of the *Book of Zadok* as follows:

"Zadok was the first to expose the errors of the Rabbanites. He
openly disagreed with them and he discovered part of the truth; he
also composed a book in which he strongly reproved and attacked
them. However, he produced no proof for anything that he claimed,
but merely set it forth in the manner of an assertion, except for one
thing, namely, the prohibition of marrying one's niece, which he de-
duced from her being analogous to the paternal or maternal aunts." [83]

This passage, in S. Schechter's opinion, alludes to the *Damascus
Document*, which likewise prohibited a marriage between uncle and
niece.[84]

Another Tenth-century Karaite, Abû al-Surrî Sahl ben Maṣliaḥ,
contested the statement of Sa'adia, when that famous Rabbanite ascribed to Zadok and Boethus the difficulties in fixing the date of the
new moon: "But the works of the Sadducees are known to all," Sahl
pleaded, "and contain nothing of what that man affirms." [85] Zadok's
books were then popular and widely known among the Karaites, and
Sa'adia himself entertained no doubt as to their existence.[86]

Karaite and Moslem writers state that the Sadducees and the
Maghariya differed from the Rabbanites in the matter of reckoning
the months and determining the new moon. Their manner of reckoning is found in the *Damascus Document* and the Qumrân *Manual*,
which are both dependent on the *Book of Jubilees*.[87]

The Sadducees, according to Qirqisânî, banned divorce; the same
ban is found in the law of Damascus.[88]

[80] QIRQISÂNÎ, *loc. cit.*
[81] *Ibid.* — Al-Shahrastânî, the Arab historiographer, asserts that the sect was
    already flourishing four hundred years before Arius (who died in A.D. 336).
    Cf. P. KAHLE, *art. cit.*, p. 45.
[82] Cf. NEMOY, *op. cit.*, p. 21. — P. KAHLE, *art. cit.*, p. 45.
[83] L. NEMOY, *op. cit.*, p. 50.
[84] *Fragments of a Zadokite Work*, p. XVIII. Cf. *D.D.*, V, 8–11.
[85] Cf. S. POZNANSKI, *art. cit.*, *R.E.J.*, XLIV, 1902, pp. 176–177.
[86] *Ibid.*   [87] Cf. P. KAHLE, *art. cit.*, p. 45.
[88] L. NEMOY, *op. cit.*, p. 333. — *D.D.*, IV, 20–21.

Again, Daniel al-Qûmisî (Ninth-Tenth centuries A.D.) forbids eating the blood of a fish, which was also forbidden by the Damascus code.[89]

Some Karaites went further, and prohibited the sacrifice of the Paschal lamb when Nisan 14th occurred on a Friday.[90] Correspondingly, we find in the *Damascus Document:* "Let no man offer on the altar on the Sabbath; except the burnt offering of the Sabbath." [91]

Lastly let it be observed that the title, "Teacher of Righteousness," was equally used by the Karaites, who applied it to the Prophet Elijah, the Messiah's precursor. Daniel al-Qûmisî was the first to use it in his commentary of *Joel*, II, 23: "In my opinion, it is the Teacher of Righteousness, Elijah, that will be sent into Israel to teach him the ordinances." [92]

It can hardly, therefore, be contested that the first two centuries of the Karaite schism were deeply influenced by the Zadokite-Essene literature. The influence could be only literary, since Qirqisânî states explicitly that neither Maghariya nor Sadducees any longer existed in his day.[93] It was due rather to the discovery of manuscripts which, many centuries earlier, the Essenes had hidden in Qumrân. This explanation is supported by the discovery, in the Cairo Geniza, at the end of the Nineteenth century, of two fragmentary copies of the *Damascus Document*, one from the Tenth, the other from the Twelfth centuries, together with a good many Karaite texts.[94]

Thus, quite by chance, the heritage of the Community of the "Sons of Zadok" came into the hands of new masters, more than seven hundred years after the Qumrân "monastery" was destroyed. Communal life, of course, was not resumed, but many customs peculiar to the Sect were resurrected. Borrowings from the *Damascus Document* appear to have been particularly important.

The Teacher of Righteousness was, long ago, attacked by the troops of the wicked Priest while he was celebrating the day of Kippur in accordance with a calendar different from that of official Judaism. In our own day, "Karaite and Rabbanite holidays, including the most sacred day in the Jewish year, the Day of Atonement, do not always coincide." [95]

The Karaites likewise refuse to celebrate the Feast of Hanukkah, which recalls the deliverance of Jerusalem by the Maccabees. Professor Nemoy offers the explanation that this is due to the feast being post-Biblical in origin,[96] but this may not be the only reason.

Karaite communities still exist. Some tens of thousands used to

---

[89] Cf. L. NEMOY, *op. cit.*, p. 31. — *D.D.*, XII, 13–14.
[90] Cf. S. POZNANSKI, *art. cit.*, *R.E.J.*, XLV, 1902, pp. 178–181.
[91] *D.D.*, XI, 17–18.
[92] This passage is quoted by P. R. WEIS, *J.Q.R.*, XLI, 1950, p. 135. — Cf. also S. SZYSZMAN, *V.T.*, 1952, pp. 343–348.
[93] Cf. L. NEMOY, *op. cit.*, p. 336.
[94] Cf. J. MANN, *Texts and Studies in Jewish Historical Literature*, vol. II, *Karaitica*, Philadelphia, 1935.
[95] L. NEMOY, *op. cit.*, p. XXIV.   [96] *Ibid.*

live in Russia. Their great Synagogue in the Old City of Jerusalem has been destroyed and abandoned. The Cairo Community treasures among its possessions the oldest complete manuscript of the Prophets, written in A.D. 895 by Moshe ben Asher, the most celebrated of the Masoretes.

The flame which was kindled by the Teacher of Righteousness more than two thousand years ago, has not yet been extinguished.

chapter six

THE SEARCH FOR GOD

This study would be incomplete if it did not contain a sketch, at least, of the religious beliefs of the Sect. It would be premature at the present stage to attempt an exhaustive analysis of the Community's theological doctrine. In order to deal with so complex and involved a problem, we must wait for the whole literature of the Sect to be published.

In the following pages I shall confine myself to the examination of the documents already at our disposal in order to distinguish the principal characteristics of the spiritual life of the Sect.

I shall therefore endeavor to underline the great theological truths which directed the "search for God." To this end, I shall discuss the attitude of the Sect towards the Law of Moses, its doctrine of election and grace, the part played by the mediators, and lastly its eschatology and teaching concerning union with God.

Let it be made clear once more that this is but a tentative sketch. Our conclusions are bound to be conjectural and temporary. The discovery of new documents may complete or modify them.

I hope, nevertheless, to offer a not inaccurate description of the religious life of the Teacher of Righteousness and his disciples.

1. The Sect's Attitude toward the Law

The spiritual life of the brethren established in Qumrân and Damascus was inserted into an historical context of "legal piety." In post-exilic Judaism, the first place in the scale of religious values is given incontestably to the Law.

The supreme ideal was to study the Torah and to possess it in all its detail, in order to make of it a standard of life. To the *knowledge* of the scholar or the theologian, Israel prefers the perfect conduct of the wise man who conforms his actions to the will of God.

It is perfectly natural that we find the same conception in the writings of the Community; it would indeed be surprising if we did not.

Total obedience to the Law is the most characteristic feature of the brethren's religious attitude. From the beginning, their love for the Torah caused them to break away from the rest of the people, and the whole life of the Sect was dedicated to the scrutiny of God's commandments and to putting them into practice.

The *Damascus Document* makes it quite clear that obedience to the commandments was the keystone of the whole spiritual structure of the Community.[1] The history of the world, to its author, is but an alternation of fidelity and infidelity on the part of creatures toward the celestial decrees:

"And now, children, hearken unto me, and I shall uncover your eyes to see and consider the works of God; to choose that in which He delights and to reject that which He hates; *to walk uprightly in all His ways* and not to wander conforming to the designs of guilty inclination and the allurement of lustfulness. For many went astray through these, and mighty heroes stumbled through them from old times until now."[2]

The "celestial watchers," the giants, the sons of Noah had all transgressed the commandments, thus incurring the wrath of God. On the other hand,

"Abraham did not walk thus and was raised to the rank of a friend through keeping the commandments of God and not choosing the desire of his own spirit. He handed them down to Isaac and to Jacob who kept them and were written down as friends of God and His Covenant for eternity."[3]

From the time of the Patriarchs down to the foundation of the Sect, Israel's whole history was nothing but rebellion and disobedience. The teachers of the people, Moses and Zadok, were not listened to. The Law given on Mount Sinai was quickly forgotten; David, for instance, had no knowledge of it since he practiced polygamy, and down to the advent of the Teacher of Righteousness, crimes were succeeded by chastisements, and infidelity to the Covenant by the devastation of the land and the annihilation of its inhabitants.

A return to the Law of Moses was the first objective of the reform program adopted. The members of the Community endeavored to submit anew to the commandments of God, to be reckoned with the upright, to be sanctified and justified,[4] and to scrutinize the Torah in order to "level a highway for the Lord,"[5] persevering in the integral observance of the rules prescribed, until the advent of the Messianic era.[6]

---

[1] Cf. *D.D.*, II, 2–IV, 12.   [2] *Ibid.*, II, 14–17.   [3] *Ibid.*, III, 2–4.
[4] Cf. *M.D.*, III, 1–4.   [5] Cf. *Ibid.*, VIII, 15.   [6] *Ibid.*, IX, 9.

All those who became, either in Damascus or Qumrân, members of the Community, were pledged by oath to be converted to the Law of Moses.[7] To enter the Sect without a firm decision to conform to all the commandments, was both folly and a sacrilegious crime.[8]

How earnest the Community was in its intention of making the Torah respected might be inferred from the penalties that awaited transgressors:

"Any one of them who transgresses a word of the Law of Moses, insolently or with guile, shall be banished from the Council of the Community never to return. Nor shall any of the holy men be in touch with him . . . — If he has transgressed through inadvertence, he shall be excluded from the purification . . . !"[9]

"Legal piety" culminated in the scrupulous pursuit of ritual purity. It accounts, in my opinion, for the brethren's segregation from men of the outside world, for their breaking away from the Temple, and for their probable renouncement of marriage.[10]

If the Sect's spirituality bore a legal character, it was not, for all that, confined to a merely external observance; the Community demanded much more than a mechanical fulfillment of the precepts of the Law. To submit to the various ablution rites "in the pools and the rivers," for instance, was not enough, "for they will not be cleansed unless they have turned from their wickedness."[11] The spirit was not less important than the letter of the Law.

Does it mean that a spirituality of this nature was merely a religion of deeds, an *orthopraxy*? The problem is serious not in regard to the Qumrân Sect only; it concerns Judaism itself and its whole religious attitude.

On this subject, we can do no better than repeat the conclusions at which Father P. Démann arrived in his article: *Foi juive et foi chrétienne:*

"The faith of Israel," we read, "has a very definite and particular stamp, which corresponds exactly to the revelation given to Israel, a Revelation that is essentially a Law and a Promise. When I say "Law," I do not in the least intend to reduce the *Torah* to a mere legislation, to a juridical reality, to the Greek *nomos*. The *Torah*, the Law, is a revelation, a revelation of the will of God, and therefore, the revelation of God, continuing and diversifying God's first and decisive Word to Abraham: 'Get thee out of thy country . . . unto the land that I will show thee'; not a truth to be believed in, but a thing to be *done*. To respond to this Word, however, is faith, and all

---

[7] *Ibid.*, V, 7 sq.   [8] *Ibid.*, II, 17.   [9] *Ibid.*, VIII, 21 sq.

[10] The fear of contamination through contact with impure men explains the segregated life led by the brethren. The Essenes' refusal to offer sacrifices in the Temple receives the same interpretation from Josephus. Perhaps they also disagreed with the conduct of the priests of Jerusalem. With respect to celibacy, let us recall that according to the Law, conjugal intercourse resulted in ritual impurity which, however slight, did not permit acts of worship. Cf. *Ex.*, XIX, 15; *Lev.*, XV, 18; *I Sam.*, XXI, 4. An uninterrupted cult required a total and perpetual continence.   [11] *Ibid.*, V, 13.

the more so because the manifestation of God's will cannot be separated from His Promise: man obeys Him by putting his trust in
His Word and in His Promise. The fulfillment of the will of God,
obedience to His Law, is an act of trust in His Promise, in His tran-
scendent fidelity, might and goodness: this is faith." [12]

The "legal" piety of the Qumrân brethren implied then, not only
faith through obedience, but also the total surrender of the self and
a striving toward union with God.

But does this mean that the spirituality of the Sect was merely
that of the official Judaism of the time?

By no means. On close investigation, and compared to official
Judaism, it is essentially the spirituality of a *sect*. Union with God
could only be achieved through the exact observance of the Law of
Moses: but, and this is the main point, man could not observe the
Torah or obey the will of God except within the Community. The
members of the Community were the only ones predestined to be
saved.

2.   The Doctrine of Election

The theology of history set out in the *Damascus Document* divides
the "ages of the world" into five periods: the first ended with the
Flood; the second, with the Exodus from Egypt; the third with the destruction of the Temple by Nebuchadnezzar; the fourth, with the
crisis which led to the birth of the Community; while the last opened
with the advent of the Teacher of Righteousness, and was to see the
appearing of the Messiahs of Aaron and Israel.

At each period, God again and again set apart a nucleus of the
elect, a "remnant," "in order to leave (a group of) survivors for the
land and fill the face of the universe with their seed." [13]

These elect were Noah, Abraham, Isaac, Jacob, Moses, Zadok, the
"first penitents" who founded the Community, and lastly the Teacher
of Righteousness and his disciples.

Ever since the coming of the Teacher of Righteousness, sent by
God to the faithful in order to teach them the true way, and unveil
truths hitherto hidden from Israel, it was no longer possible to observe
the Law fittingly outside the Community. Only there, were known
the "mysteries" of the Law and of the Prophets, the genuine calendar,
and the true rules of purity and justice. When new members undertook to observe the Law, they promised to act "according to all that
is revealed to the sons of Zadok, the priests who keep the Covenant,
and to the great assembly of the men of their Covenant, who communally dedicate themselves to His truth." [14]

Adherence to the Community therefore meant election, predestination, and the token of salvation.

"To those whom God has chosen, He has given (wisdom, justice,

---

[12] *C.S.*, 1952, p. 98.   [13] *D.D.*, II, 11–12.   [14] *M.D.*, V, 9–10.

glory) as an eternal inheritance, and has given them to share the destiny of the saints. He has associated their assembly with the sons of Heaven, to establish the Council of the Community, the foundation of a sanctuary, an eternal planting for all the time to come." [15]

The "sons of Zadok" believed they possessed proofs of their election. One, for example, they found in Ezekiel:

"The priests, the Levites, the sons of Zadok, that kept the charge of my sanctuary when the children of Israel went astray from me . . . shall offer unto me the fat and the blood." [16]

Referring to this passage, the *Damascus Document* adds that the "sons of Zadok" are Israel's elect who shall be again in office at the end of time.[17]

Another evidence of their election they found in their historical experience. While the traitors to the Law were delivered over to the sword of vengeance, the penitents had escaped annihilation, and God had saved them.

Henceforth, Israel's inheritance, they declared, was exclusively theirs. The Old Covenant had, through Israel's fall, become obsolete. The Sect was founded on the basis of a *New Covenant*.

The repercussions of such a conviction on the brethren's theology, and therefore on their spiritual life, may well be imagined.

Israel's election was that of a nation. The promise God made to Abraham concerned both him and his posterity, i.e., all the sons of Israel. All men belonging by birth to the people of God were elect by right. They had of course to obey God and observe His Law, but the privilege of being the children of God, submitted to the Law, was their birthright.

In Qumrân, on the contrary, the brethren were "dedicated men" who adhered to the Community through an act of free will, and a total surrender of their own selves. All the brethren were Jews, but all the Jews were not brethren. And if it were proved that the members of the Sect lived in the state of celibacy, the fact of their being elect had even less to do with carnal descent. The Community of the elect was thus made up of individuals who were directly chosen by God.

Such a conception reminds one of the *Epistle to the Romans:*

"For they are not all Israel, which are of Israel, neither because they are Abraham's seed, are they all children. That is, it is not the children of the flesh that are children of God, but the children of the promise are reckoned for a seed." [18]

The privilege of the brethren was not due to a fleshly sonship, but to God's direct benevolence toward every one of them. In other words, every vocation was held to be God's gracious gift; it follows that the spirituality of the Sect was deeply impregnated with the idea of grace.

---

[15] *Ibid.*, XI, 7–9.   [16] *Ezek.*, XLIV, 15.   [17] *D.D.*, IV, 3–4.
[18] *Rom.*, IX, 7–9.

3. Grace

The spiritual life of the Community was wholly based on personal vocation; each member had been called and set aside by God. They were, every one of them, the "children of grace."

However eminent the part they assigned to the study and the practice of the Law, they were nonetheless convinced that wisdom, justice and sanctity were the fruits of grace.

This is best illustrated by the following passages from their Psalms; these prayers are of great spiritual importance, as they reflect better than any other literary work, the religious attitude of the brethren.

"As for me, I know that justice is not of man,
  nor of the son of man the perfection of way:
  'Tis to God Most High that pertains every righteous deed,
  whilst the way of man is not strengthened,
  unless through the spirit that God created for him.
  to make perfect the way of the children of man,
  so that all His creatures may know
  the strength of His might and the greatness of His bounty
  towards all the children of His grace." [19]

And again:

"For I say: My justification belongs to God,
  the perfection of my way and the uprightness of my heart are in
      His hand;
  through His favor shall my sins be blotted out.
  For from the fountain of His knowledge my light has sprung forth;
  my eyes have beheld His wonders;
  my heart has been illumined by the mysteries that are to come,
  and He who exists unto eternity is the support of my right hand.
  Upon the rock of strength is the way of my steps,
  and they shall not be shaken by aught.
  For the truth of God is the rock I tread,
  and His might is the support of my right hand.
  From the fountain of His justice flow my heart's judgments of light;
  From His wondrous mysteries my eyes have beheld Him who exists
      unto eternity,
  a wisdom which is hidden from men, a knowledge and a purpose
      illuminated,
  (hidden from) the sons of man.
  A fountain of righteousness, a store of strength,
  an abode of glory (hidden) from the assembly of flesh." [20]

Through considering God's mercies towards them, the brethren were brought to the knowledge of their own nothingness, and abased

---

[19] *Hymn*, IV, 26–29.   [20] *M.D.*, XI, 2–7.

themselves before the infinite greatness of God. Such an attitude is diametrically opposed to what is (inaccurately) described as "Pharisaic" piety. Yet, the sectarians were stricter than even the Doctors of the Law; Essenism, in fact, has even been considered as hyper-Pharisaic.

A brother, so far from boasting of his scrupulous observance of the Law, was ever tormented by the recollection of his past faults, and felt unworthy of the mercy shown to him by God. He was well aware of his weakness and evil inclinations, and was urged thereby to surrender his whole self to God completely. In his relations with God, humility and trust were his most outstanding characteristics.

But let the members of the Community again speak for themselves:

"Trembling and fright have seized me and all my bones are broken; my heart is melting wax near the fire;
my knees slip as water going down a slope,
for I have remembered my faults and the infidelity of my fathers.
But remembering the strength of Thy hand and the multitude of Thy mercies,
I rose and stood erect again and my spirit persevered at its place before the trial.
For I have relied upon Thy grace and the multitude of Thy mercies,
For thou wilt forgive iniquity and purify man from his guilt by Thy justice." [21]

Again, from the final blessing in the *Manual*:

"Blessed art Thou, O my God, who openest unto knowledge the heart of Thy servant.
Strengthen all his deeds in righteousness,
and grant to the son of Thy handmaid . . . to stand before Thee for ever.
For without Thee the way is not perfect
and apart from Thy good pleasure can nothing be accomplished.
Thou hast taught all knowledge;
all that exists, exists by Thy good pleasure.
Without Thee there is no one who can decide anything contrary to Thy council,
understand all Thy holy purposes, behold the depths of Thy mysteries,
Comprehend all Thy marvels and the strength of Thy might.
Who could bear Thy glory?
What indeed is the son of man amidst Thy wondrous works,
and how can he who is born of a woman stay before Thee?
For his clay is but dust and his body the nourishment of worms.
He is not made of rock; he is but fashioned clay and his longing is for the dust.

[21] *Hymn,* IV, 29–33.

What will clay which is shaped by the hand reply?
What counsel could it understand?" [22]

Those prayers reflect the Sect's deepest aspirations which would
only be fulfilled when the brethren would stand before God, together with the other "elect of mankind." [23]

Knowledge and *understanding*, the divine gifts which lead men to
union with God, are often mentioned. It has been inferred, somewhat
overhastily, that the doctrine professed in Qumrân is of a gnostical
character, and very different from the Rabbinic-Pharisaic teaching.[24]

Here, perhaps there is danger of accepting too hastily the *Mishna*
and the *Talmuds* as the only mirror of Palestinian Judaism; it is important to remember the liturgical tradition of the Synagogue.

I mention in this connection the special prayer for "knowledge"
or "gnosis" in the *Shemoneh 'esreh* or *Tephillah*, that has been recited
daily ever since pre-Christian times and quote the fourth of the eight-
een blessings from the old Palestinian version, found in the Cario
Geniza:

"Deign to grant us, our Father, a *knowledge* that cometh from Thee,
and *understanding* and *wisdom* from Thy Torah,
Blessed be Thou, O Lord, who givest us *knowledge!*" [25]

This blessing may be compared to a passage from the *Manual:*

"May (God) bless thee with all good things, keep thee from every
evil, illumine thy heart with life-giving wisdom and deign to grant
thee the knowledge of eternity!" [26]

The science and justice which the Community Psalms implore are
the tokens of union with God.

However, before we speak of their eschatological hopes, it is
necessary to say a few words about the spiritual guides who were
to show the brethren their way.

4. The Rôle of the Mediators

Of these guides the first was Moses, the Law-giver, who faithfully
transmitted God's will regarding all things. So holy was his Law that
the *Damascus Document* forbade it to be used, together with the
names of God, in the taking of oaths.[27] It may be noted here that the
law of the Essenes condemned to death those who cursed the Law-
giver.[28]

The second guide was the High Priest Zadok, that eponymous ancestor of the Community. It was he who, since the death of Eleazar
and Joshua, re-opened the Law which had been sealed.[29] He was, as

---

[22] *M.D.*, XI, 15–22.   [23] *Ibid.*, XI, 16.
[24] Cf. K. G. KUHN, *Die in Palästina gefundenen hebräischen Texte und das
Neue Testament, Zeitschrift für Theol. und Kirche,* 1952, p. 209.
[25] Cf. W. STAERK, *Altjüdische liturgische Gebete,* 2nd edition, Berlin, 1930,
p. 12.   [26] *M.D.*, II, 2–5.   [27] *D.D.*, XV, 1–3.
[28] JOSEPHUS, *B.J.*, II, VIII, 9.   [29] *D.D.*, V, 4–5.

Father Lagrange rightly observed, the true "Anointed One" of the *Damascus Document*, through whom God manifested the holy spirit which was to remain with the faithful.[30] The *Document* says, for instance, that the Sects' enemies, called the "builders of walls," soiled the holy spirit that was in them by rebelling against the precepts of the Covenant.[31] The elect were to be called by the name of this Anointed One, a transparent allusion to the "Community of the Sons of Zadock."

The Teacher of Righteousness' mission as a mediator is of particular interest to us. The various documents show that his disciples ascribed to him revelations, especially regarding the mysterious words of the Prophets. As a revealer of the way of the heart of God, the Teacher of Righteousness was held the supreme guide.

But what was his rôle regarding salvation? This is stated clearly enough in two passages, the first from the *Damascus Document*:

"All they that hold fast to these rules, inasmuch as they go out and go in according to the Law, *who shall have listened to the voice of the Teacher of Righteousness,* and confessed before God (saying): "We have sinned, we have been wicked . . . ; who will not act high-handedly against the holy precepts . . . , who will *give ear to the voice of the Teacher of Righteousness,* and will not have spoken against the righteous precepts when they shall have heard them, they shall rejoice . . . they shall overcome all the inhabitants of the universe. God shall forgive them and they shall witness His salvation for they shall have taken refuge in His holy name." [32]

The *Habakkuk Commentary* likewise reproves the Man of deception and his accomplices because they did not believe in the words which the Teacher of Righteousness heard from the mouth of God.[33]

It follows from these passages that faith in the mission of the Teacher of Righteousness and fidelity to his doctrine were considered indispensable to salvation.

The idea is plainly formulated in the *Habakkuk Commentary* with respect to the famous verse, "The just shall live by his faith." The Commentator then goes on:

"Its meaning concerns all those who practice the Law in the house of Judah, whom God shall save from the house of condemnation, for the sake of their sufferings, and *their faith in the Teacher of Righteousness.*" [34]

It is clear, therefore, that the Community demanded from its members faith in the Teacher of Righteousness, the recognition of his mission as legislator and interpreter, as well as a total fidelity to his message. His redemptive rôle was that of a master who taught righteousness.

But was he considered as the Messiah? In a broad sense, yes. Zadok had been so considered before him, and also Moses; and the

---

[30] *Ibid.*, II, 12–13. — Cf. M. J. LAGRANGE, *La secte juive de la Nouvelle Alliance au pays de Damas*, R.B., 1912, p. 322.   [31] *Ibid.*, V, 11–12.
[32] *Ibid.*, XX, 27–34.   [33] *H.C.*, II, 1–2.   [34] *Ibid.*, VIII, 1–3.

Teacher of Righteousness was a new Moses. He must not, for all that, be confused with the Messiah, or rather the Messiahs, who were expected at the end of time.[35]

For it must be borne in mind that the Community believed in the advent of two Messiahs, one of them descending from Aaron, the other from Israel. J. T. MILIK correctly offers *"usque ad adventum . . . (duorum) Unctorum: (ex) Aaron et Israel"* as the translation of *'ad bo' . . . mešîḥê 'Aharôn w-Iśra' el.*[36] The title of "Messiah of Aaron and Israel" in the singular, which we find in the *Damascus Document*,[37] is due, no doubt, to the medieval scribe who held a more orthodox view about the matter.[38] On the other hand, it is unequivocally specified in the *Testament of the Twelve Patriarchs* that beside the Davidic Messiah, and superior to him, a Levitic Messiah was also expected.[39]

The Messiah of Israel is mentioned in a document called the *Two Columns:* [40] he takes part in the banquet of the Community, but is inferior to a Priest whom J. T. MILIK wishes to identify with the Messiah of Aaron.[41] Regarding the Messianic banquet, it is found in the New Testament as well as in Rabbinic literature.[42]

As long as the Sect's other texts remain unpublished, there is no possibility of forming a precise idea of the Messianic doctrine.[43]

However, even now it is clear that the part played by the mediators was exclusively confined to teaching. Intimate union between the faithful and God is achieved through no human channel, not even through the Messiahs, but through the agency of the spirits of light and truth.

5. Union with God

According to the doctrine of the Community, salvation is governed by an absolute predestination, *ante praevisa merita.*

"From the God of knowledge comes all that is and all that is to be

---

[35] Cf. J. VAN DER PLOEG, *Bi. Or.*, 1951, p. 13. — An opposite opinion has been advanced by A. DUPONT-SOMMER, *Aperçus préliminaires . . .* , pp. 78–80; *Nouveaux aperçus . . .* , pp. 81–83. — For the doctrine concerning the New Moses, see my article, *La figure de Moïse au tournant des deux Testaments* in *Moïse, l'homme de l'Alliance*, C.S., N° 2–3–4, 1954, pp. 80–84.

[36] *Verb. Dom.*, 1951, p. 152. The passage is quoted from *M.D.*, IX, 11. Cf. also M. BURROWS, *The Messiahs of Aaron and Israel*, Anglican Theol. Review, 1952, pp. 203–206.

[37] *D.D.*, XIX, 10–11; XX, 1; XII, 23–XIII, 1; XIV, 19.

[38] Cf. J. T. MILIK, *R.B.*, 1953, p. 291.

[39] Cf. *Test. of Ruben*, VI, 7–12. — *Test. of Levi*, VIII, 14; XVIII. — *Test. of Judah*, XXIV, 1–3. — *Test. of Dan.*, V, 10–11. — *Test. of Joseph*, XIX, 5–91. See R. H. CHARLES, *The Apocrypha and Pseudepigrapha of the Old Testament*, vol. II, Oxford, 1913, p. 294.

[40] Cf. D. BARTHÉLEMY, *R.B.*, 1952, p. 203–205.   [41] *R.B.*, 1953, p. 291.

[42] Cf. *Luc.*, XXII, 30. — For Rabbinical texts see J. BLOCH, *On the Apocalyptic in Judaism*, J.Q.R., Monograph Series, n. II, Philadelphia, 1952, p. 96–100.

[43] For further detailed and complementary information, cf. *infra*, p. 222.

and even before they existed God had established their whole lot. They exist according to their (respective) rules, conforming to His glorious purpose, in which they change nothing, and will thus fulfill their actions. In the hands of God are the laws of all beings and He will sustain them in all their pursuits. He created man for the domination of the world and assigned him two spirits by which to walk until the season of His visitation: they are the spirits of truth and iniquity." [44]

The "sons of justice" or the "sons of light" are governed by the spirit of truth, also called "Prince of light" or the "Angel of truth"; while the "sons of iniquity" or the "sons of darkness" obey Belial who is the "Angel of darkness." Man acts righteously or wrongly according to whether he is of one spirit or the other. The *duae viae*, what the *Manual* calls "the respective ways of the two spirits in the world," [45] are illustrated at length, in the same passage, by two lists of virtues and vices; those "*duae viae*" are found, as Father Audet has conclusively shown, in the *Didachè* and in the *Epistle of Barnabas*.[46]

An implacable enmity separates the two classes of humanity, belonging respectively to the two spirits. Those in the camp of light and truth have to submit to trials, temptations, and attacks by Belial and his terrestrial auxiliaries, the "sons of darkness." In this way is explained the fact that the just, i.e., the Community members, were unceasingly tempted, insulted and persecuted. They must not murmur, for God Himself ordered the course of human history this way by assigning the two spirits in equal proportion. They need not, nevertheless, be frightened or disheartened: God had set a limit to the reign of iniquity, and at the end of time, it would vanish for ever.

"Until then the spirits of truth and iniquity will contend for the heart of man. He will walk in wisdom or in folly: if a man's inheritance is truth and righteousness, he will hate iniquity; but if his heritage is the portion of iniquity, then he will be wicked and will abominate truth. For God has set the two spirits in equal parts until the decreed end and the renewal of all things. He does know the merit of their deeds for all eternity and He has given them to mankind for their inheritance so that they may know good and evil, that He may allot the destiny of all the living according to the spirit within them at the season of visitation." [47]

Kuhn,[48] Grossouw,[49] and Brownlee [50] have all, in recent publications, stressed points common to the doctrine of the two spirits in the *Manual* and to the theology of St. Paul and St. John. They think

---

[44] M.D., III, 15–19.   [45] Ibid., IV, 2.   [46] R.B., 1952, pp. 219–238.
[47] M.D., IV, 23–26.   [48] Art. cit., p. 192–211.
[49] The Dead Sea Scrolls and the New Testament, Studia Catholica, 1951, pp. 289–299; 1952, pp. 1–8.
[50] See the several references to parallel passages in his translation of the Manual: The Dead Sea Manual of Discipline, B.A.S.O.R., Supplementary Studies Nos. 10–12, New Haven, 1951.

that the origin of this doctrine might be found in Persia.[51] As found in the *Manual*, however, it is wholly Jewish, since the two spirits were both created by the God of Israel. But this theology might have originated with those exiles who had been in prolonged touch with Persian civilization before coming back to Palestine under the guidance of Ezra.

The whole theology of the Sect is based on the belief in the influence of these two spirits. To participate in the destiny of light, man had to be chosen; and to enjoy the inspirations of the spirit of truth implied the experience, within a man's self, of the grace of God. The spirit abiding in the faithful man was an intimate link between himself and God. The same spirit of light was the foundation of all good works:

"One (spirit) God has loved throughout all eternity, and He shall delight in all his deeds for ever." [52]

How moving is the thanksgiving song of the "sons of light," praising God, who had separated them from the wicked and abhorred "sons of darkness." The reprobates are destined for a dreadful end, indeed:

"The visitation of all those who shall walk by the spirit of iniquity shall consist in a multitude of plagues inflicted by the angels of destruction, eternal damnation through the burning anger of God's vengeance, everlasting torture and perpetual disgrace together with the shame of destruction in the fire of dark regions. All the years of their life shall be of grievous mourning and bitter misfortune, in an existence of darkness until their destruction without remnant or survivor." [53]

The lot of the "sons of darkness" was, therefore, total annihilation, in the obscurity of everlasting fire.

What was the ultimate end of the "sons of light," and what was the eternal reward in store for those who obeyed the spirit of truth?

Such expressions as "wisdom of life," "knowledge of eternity," "eternal life," "eternal bliss," "eternal destiny," are used in the documents again and again, and as Father van der Ploeg has shown, testify to a faith in immortality.

"In a visible fashion, the community is here, in this world; but it continues beyond this world. The idea that the Community, or the Sect, is "eternal" is closely connected with the belief that the individual souls of its members are immortal." [54]

It was the brethren's hope to stand before God on an "eternal height," [55] together with the "sons of heaven," [56] singing with them the praises of God during all eternity.[57]

[51] K. G. KUHN, *art. cit.*, p. 211; *Die Sektenschrift und die iranische Religion*, ibid., 1952, pp. 296–316. — A. DUPONT-SOMMER, *L'instruction sur les deux Esprits dans le Manuel de Discipline*, R.H.R., t. 142, 1952, pp. 5–35; *Nouveaux aperçus* . . . , pp. 156–172.

[52] *M.D.*, III, 26–IV, 1.   [53] *Ibid.*, IV, 11–14.   [54] *V.T.*, 1952, p. 173.
[55] Cf. *Hymn*, III, 3.   [56] *Ibid.*, III, 5.   [57] *Ibid.*, III, 6.

It might perhaps be said that such a hope presupposed a faith in the immortality of the soul, but not of the whole man. Such a doctrine is foreign to Judaism, but Josephus explicitly ascribed it to the Essenes.

"It is a belief that is firmly established among them that the body is corruptible, and that the matter of which it is composed is inconsistent, but that the soul is immortal and cannot be destroyed, that it dwelt in the most subtile ether, and that drawn into the body as into a prison, it becomes united to it through a sort of natural attraction; that this soul, once detached from the bonds of flesh, freed, so to speak, from this lengthy slavery, takes its joyful flight toward the heavens." [58]

Such a Platonic conception, strange as it may appear, cannot, *a priori*, be waived aside. We know that the doctrine of the pre-existence of souls is found in some ancient Jewish writings, in, for instance, the *Second Book of Enoch*, the *Apocalypse of Baruch*, and in some passages of Rabbinic literature.[59]

But faith in the resurrection of the flesh is not, for all that, suppressed.

We might be tempted, however, as I have pointed out, to understand the eschatological doctrine of the Community in a purely spiritual sense. But that such a conclusion is unavoidable I, for one, am inclined to doubt.

This apparent contradiction might perhaps be explained in the following way:

The author of the *Manual* and the Community Psalmist did not deal with the resurrection of bodies, not because they did not believe in it, but because they expected universal Judgment to occur before their own generation had passed away. And so, entering into eternity was an *assumption* of the purified and sanctified body, rather than a *resurrection*.

This is, of course, but a conjecture, but not, I think, an unlikely one. It presumes an eschatological expectation within the Community analogous to that which is expressed in the first *Epistle to the Corinthians*. The mystery Saint Paul announced was that "we shall not all die, but we shall all be changed." [60]

Such are the most characteristic features of the beliefs and piety of the brethren of the Covenant.

They sought God through the practice of the Law, being enabled to do so by God's gratuitous election; an election proving that everything was due to grace.

---

[58] *B.J.*, II, VIII, 11. — See also lines 12–15 of the inscription n. 1510 from *Corpus Inscriptionum Iudaicarum* (vol. II) by J. B. FREY: "This tomb conceals within it my body which was reared in purity; but the soul has departed to the saints." The funerary inscription, dating probably from 5 B.C. comes from the Jewish necropolis at Tell el-Yehoudieh, the ancient Leontopolis.
[59] Cf. J. BLOCH, *op. cit.*, pp. 103–104.   [60] *I Cor.*, XV, 51.

At the end of the journey, which they travelled under the leadership of Guides chosen by God, light and joy and eternal life awaited them. This was an authentic religious attitude, a breathing of the Spirit which prepares in the desert the way of the Lord.

And we know that their expectation of the imminent coming of the Lord was, whether they knew it or not, soon to be truly fulfilled.

THE TEXTS

THE "HABAKKUK COMMENTARY"

Translator's Note

For the translation of the Qumrân documents, I have had before me both the original Hebrew, and also Father Vermès' French translations.

I have, in addition, frequently consulted some of the available English translations, principally Mr. C. Rabin's *The Zadokite Documents* (Oxford, 1954), and I wish to express my gratitude to him, and to the Clarendon Press, Oxford, for allowing me to borrow from this excellent work.

Roman numerals in the Notes indicate the column number in the manuscript, and Arabic numerals, the line.

COLUMN I   ¹ [*The oracle of Habakkuk. How long O Lord shall I c*]*ry and thou wilt not* ² *hear* (*Hab.*, I, 1–2 a)

Its meaning concerns . . . . at the beginning of the generation ³ [the last . . . .] upon them.

⁴ [*Cry out unto thee because of the violence and thou wilt not save* (*Hab.*, I, 2b)

Its meaning concerns those who cr]ied because of the ⁵ [violence.

Why dost thou show me iniquity and lo]*o*[*k upon pa*]*in?* (*Hab.* I, 3a)

⁶ [Its meaning concerns those who . . . .] God in oppression and infidelity ⁷ [. . . . .]

⁸ *Spoiling and violence are before me, and there is strife and contention* (*Hab.*, I, 3b)

Its meaning concerns those who have] . . . . violence and strife ⁹ [. . . . .] him ¹⁰ [. . . . .].

Therefore the Law is slacked ¹¹ *and righteousness does never go forth* (*Hab.*, I, 4a)

Its meaning, concerns those who have despised the Law of God.

¹² [. . . . . *For the wicked man circumve*]*nts the righteous one* (*Hab.*, I, 4b)

¹³ Its meaning is that the wicked is the wicked Priest and the righteous is the teacher of righteousness. . . . .

¹⁴ [*The*]*refore judgment goes forth* ¹⁵ [*perverted* (*Hab.*, I, 4b) Its meaning . . . .] and not [. . . . .

¹⁶⁻¹⁷ *Behold them ye among the nations and regard them and wonder marvellously for I work a work in your days. ye will not believe when*]

COLUMN II   ¹ *it will be told unto you* (*Hab.*, I, 5)

[Its meaning concerns] the traitors with the Man ² of deceit, for they did not [believe] in all that the Teacher of righteousness [had heard] from the mouth ³ of God; and those traitors to the new [Covenant,] for they have not ⁴ believed in the Covenant of God [and have profaned] His [h]oly [Na]me. ⁵ Likewise, the meaning of this word [concerns those trai]tors at the end ⁶ of time: there will be violen[t . . . .] who will not believe ⁷ when they hear all that [will come to pass in] the last generation from the mouth ⁸ of the priest whom God has given to [. . . . .] to give the meaning of all ⁹ the words of His servants the prophets, for it is through them that God has related all ¹⁰ that is to come upon His people and upon their [His land.]

[*F*]*or lo I raise up the* ¹¹ *Chaldeans, that bit*[*ter and impl*]*acable nation* (*Hab.*, I, 6b)

¹² Its meaning concerns the Kittim [who are] swift and valiant

---

II, 1–10   The interpretation, rather damaged again, refers to the last part of the commented Biblical verse.

The unbelievers are: 1) the followers of the Man of deceit (cf. *H.C.*, V, 11; X, 9 — *D.D.*, XIX, 25–26; XX, 14–15) who opposed the Teacher of Righteousness, the charismatic interpreter of God's word; 2) the traitors to the "New Covenant" (i.e., the Community; cf. *D.D.*, VI, 19; VIII, 21; XX, 12); 3) the traitors of the last days (the Commentator's contemporaries) who rejected the explanations of the Prophets, which the priest-interpreter, God's disciple, propounded. *H.C.*, VII, 4–5 hints that the Teacher of Righteousness is alluded to.

II, 12–14   The *Kittim* are the enemy of the last days, typified by the Babylonians. Cf. *supra*, p. 84, sq. They were to be swift, valiant and invincible.

II, 12   *Its meaning* (*pišrô*) is the introductory formula which begins the interpretation of each pericopa. Cf. also *D.D.*, IV, 14. The primitive sense of *pešer* is found in Arabic where it signifies to find out that which is hidden, to interpret plainly (the Koran). In the Bible, as also in Akkadian and

[13] in war to destroy many men [. . . . .] under the domination [14] of the Kittim and . . . . and they will not believe [15-17] in the ordinances [of God . . . .

Which march through the breadth of the earth, to possess dwelling places that are not theirs. (Hab., I, 7)

Its meaning concerns the Kittim who . . . .]
COLUMN III   [1] will advance through the plain, smiting and despoiling the cities of the earth. [2] For that is what he has said: "to possess what is not theirs."

They are terrible [3] and dreadful: their might and their magnificence proceed from themselves (Hab., I, 7)

[4] Its meaning concerns, the Kittim, whose fear and terror (will be heavy) upon all [5] nations. All their purposes to do evil are deliberate. With cunning and violence [6] will they walk toward all peoples.

Their horses also are swifter than leopards and nimbler than [7] the evening wolves. Their horsemen spread themselves and come from far; [8] they fly as an eagle that hasteth to devour. They come, all of them, for violence: [9] the countenance of their face is like the east wind. (Hab., I, 8–9a)

[Its meaning] concerns the Kittim who [10] trampled the earth with the feet of [their] horses and their beasts. From afar [11] they will come — from the isles of the sea — to devo[ur al]l the peoples as an eagle. [12] And still unsatisfied, with wrath and an[ger, with fu]ry and rage, [13] they will handle all [nations. Fo]r this is what he [14] has said: "The co[untenance of their face is as the east wind."

They will gather] captives as the sand (Hab., I, 9b)

[15-17] [Its meaning concerns the Kittim who . . . .
. . . .
. . . .
. . . .
And he at kings]

Syriac, this term refers to the interpretation of dreams. In *Eccl.*, VIII, 1, however, it means to "solve enigmas," and in *Dan.*, V (Balthazar's banquet) to "explain a cryptic text." Cf. also *Matth.*, XIII, 36. The exact meaning of this introductory formula seems to be the following: to convey to the ordinary reader the exact signification received by revelation (cf. VII, 3–5), of the "mystery" of a prophecy. Cf. *C.S.*, 1951, pp. 340–341.

III, 4–6   The spectacular march of the *Kittim* through the plain, leaving behind them destroyed and plundered cities.
    Here and in line 10, *ha ares* ought probably be rendered by "earth," not by "the land" (i.e., Palestine).

III, 4–6   The *Kittim*, both crafty and violent, were to spread round them dismay among the nations. It should be noted that the passage refers to the "peoples" and "nations," not to the Israelites.

III, 9–14   The *Kittim*, from "the islands of the sea," an important detail not found in the Biblical verse, were to spread terror among the nations as well as exploit them.
    The end of *Hab.*, I, 9 is different in the M.T., but is confirmed by Symmachus, Theodotion, the Vulgate and the Targum.

COLUMN IV   ¹ *will scoff and princes will be derision unto him* (*Hab.*, I, 10 b)

Its meaning concerns those who ² deride a multitude of men and will be scornful of the dignitaries. Kings ³ and princes they will despise and they will scoff at a mighty people.

And he ⁴ *will deride every stronghold, he will heap up dust and take them* (*Hab.*, I, 10a)

⁵ Its meaning concerns the rulers of the Kittim who will scorn ⁶ the strongholds of the peoples and proudly laugh at them. ⁷ With a mighty army they will surround them to take them. And because of the terror and the fear, ⁸ they will give themselves up into their hands and they will destroy them in consideration of the wickedness of their ⁹ inhabitants.

Then the wind changed and was removed and he made his strength ¹⁰ *his god* (*Hab.*, I, 11)

Its meaning [con]cerns the rulers of the Kittim ¹¹ who, through the decree of the "House of gui[lt]" will withdraw a man ¹² from before his fellow. Their rul[ers, this one after that] one, will come ¹³ to lay waste the ea[rth.]

[*And he*] *made his strength his god.*

¹⁴ Its meaning [concerns . . . .] upon the peoples ¹⁵⁻¹⁷ [. . . . .

. . . .

Art thou not from the beginning, O Yahweh, my God, my Holy One? We shall not die! Yahweh,]

COLUMN V   ¹ *thou hast ordained him for judgment; O Rock,*

IV, 1–13   The *Kittim* will treat kings haughtily, and seize strongholds with a disconcerting facility.

The chiefs (or rulers) of the *Kittim* would change, one retiring before the other, according to the decisions of the "house of guilt" (perhaps a tribunal that pronounces on their guilt). But when one is recalled, his place is filled by another who will carry on his conquest of the world.

The passage of *Hab.*, I, 11 offers, when compared to the Massoretic recension a curiously variant reading ("The wind changed and passed over, and he whose might was his god became guilty"). Instead of *we'ašam* (he became guilty) the manuscript has *wayyasem* (he put). The explanation, on the other hand, reads again *beth 'ašmah* (house of *guilt*).

V, 1–8   An eschatological view of the end of history: the Community members who remain attached, in spite of their ordeals, to the laws, shall condemn both the nations and Israel's apostates (cf. *M.D.*, VIII, 6–7; X, 19 – *D.D.*, II, 15–18). They manifested their fidelity by refusing the attractions of impurity. "Lust" must be interpreted, although perhaps not exclusively, in a doctrinal sense. Cf. *M.D.*, I, 6; IV, 10. – *D.D.*, III, 3, etc.

V, 1   The word *lemôkhihô* may be, as YALON believes, an Aramaising infinitive.

V, 4   *Bhyrw* may be read *behirô* (his elect, sing.) or *behirâw* (his elects, plur., *scriptio defectiva*). *H.C.*, X, 13 and *M.D.*, VIII, 6; IX, 14 suggest the plural.

V, 8–12   The "house of Absalom" (cf. *supra*, p. 105. n. 77) refused to intervene in the quarrel between the Teacher of Righteousness and the Man of deceit (cf. II, 1).

thou hast established him for correction, with eyes too pure [2] to behold evil; thou canst not look on pain. (Hab., I, 12–13a)

[3] The meaning of this word is that God will not destroy His people by the hand of the nations [4] but by the hands of His elected one(s) God will give judgment upon all the nations. And through their reproach [5] those who will have kept His commandments [6] in their distress will pronounce guilty all the wicked of His people.

And what he has said: *with eyes too pure to behold* [7] *evil.*

Its meaning is that they did not follow the lust of their eyes in the time [8] of wickedness.

Wherefore look ye, ye traitors, and holdest thy peace when the wicked man [9] *leads astray one more righteous than he? (Hab., I, 13b)*

Its meaning concerns the "House of Absalom" [10] and the men of their counsel who were silent at the reproof of the Teacher of righteousness, [11] and did not help him against the Man of deceit who had scorned [12] the Law amidst all their con[grega]tion.

Thou hast handled man as the fishes of the sea, [13] *as the creeping things, to rule over him. He shall take up [all of them with the ang]le, and will drag them [with his net* [14] *and will gather them into his drag. Therefore he shall sacrifice] unto his net. Therefore he will rejoice* [15] *[and burn incense unto his drag; because of them] his portion [is fat* [16–17] *and his meat plenteous. (Hab., I, 14–16)*

Its meaning concerns . . . .
. . . .]

COLUMN VI   [1] of the Kittim; and they will gather their wealth and their booty [2] as the fish of the sea.

What he has said: *Therefore he will sacrifice to his net* [3] *and burn incense unto his drag.*

Its meaning is that they [4] do offer sacrifice to their standards and that their instruments of war are the object [5] of their worship.

Because of them his portion is fat and his meat plenteous.

[6] Its meaning is that they will distribute their yoke and [7] their tax-burden — their nourishment — upon all the peoples, year by year, [8] to bring ruin on many lands.

V, 13–14   Two important variants in the Biblical text: *limšol bô* (to dominate over him, cf. *Gen.*, I, 28) instead of *lo' mošel bô* ("that have no master" — M.T.); *Hab.*, I, 15–16, as given in the manuscript, differs in order from the M.T., but is confirmed by the Lucian version of the Septuagint (VAN DER PLOEG).

VI, 3–8   Here the Commentator substitutes the insignia and the weapons of the *Kittim* for the net and drag to which the fisherman offered sacrifices. Cf. the Targum on *Hab.*, I, 16: "this is why he sacrificeth into his weapons and burneth incense to his insignia." Cf. N. WIEDER, *J.J.S.*, 1953, pp. 14–18. — By nourishment is meant the annual repartition of taxes.

VI, 8–12   The victims of the *Kittim*. Once again, no allusion is made to the inhabitants of Judah.

VI, 8   For *Hab.*, I, 17 the manuscript gives *yariq harbô* (he shall draw his sword) instead of *yariq hermô* (he shall draw his net, M.T.).

He shall therefore draw his sword continually ⁹*to slay nations and he shall show them no mercy* (*Hab.*, I, 17)

¹⁰ Its meaning concerns the Kittim who will destroy a multitude of men with the sword: ¹¹ youths, adults and old men, women and little children; toward the fruit ¹² of the womb they shall not show mercy.

I will stand upon my watch ¹³ *and set me upon my tower. I will look forth to see what he will speak with me* ¹⁴ [*and what he shall answer*] *to my complaint. And Yahweh answered me* ¹⁵ [*and said: Write the vision and make it plain*] *upon tables that he may run that* ¹⁶⁻¹⁷ [*readeth it.* (*Hab.*, I, 1–2)

Its meaning concerns . . . .
. . . .]

COLUMN VII   ¹ And God commanded Habakkuk to write the things that would come upon ² the last generation, but He did not make known to him the end of time.

³ And what he has said: *That he may run that readeth it.*

⁴ Its meaning concerns the Teacher of righteousness to whom God made known ⁵ all the mysteries of the words of His servants, the prophets.

For there is vision yet ⁶ *for an appointed time; it hasteth toward the end and shall not lie* (*Hab.*, II, 3a)

⁷ Its meaning is that the last days shall be longer than all that ⁸ the prophets have predicted, for wondrous are the mysteries of God.

⁹ *Though it tarry, wait for it, because it will surely come and will not* ¹⁰ *delay.* (*Hab.*, II, 3b)

Its meaning concerns the men of the Truth, ¹¹ those who practice the Law, whose hands have not slackened in the service ¹² the Truth even though the last days shall delay for them, for ¹³ all the appointed times of God shall duly come, as He has established ¹⁴ for them in the mystery of His wisdom.

Behold it is puffed up, it is not upright, ¹⁵ [*his soul within him.*] (*Hab.*, II, 4b)

Its meaning is that they will double upon themselves ¹⁶ [. . . . . .
. . . . wi]ll be destroyed at the time of their judgment [. . . . .
¹⁷ . . . .

But the just man shall live by his faith. (*Hab.*, II, 4b)

COLUMN VIII   ¹ Its meaning concerns all those who practice

VII, 15   What God did not reveal to Habakkuk He revealed to the Teacher of righteousness, to whom nothing of the prophetic "mysteries" was hidden.

VII, 7–8   God's plan is ever disconcerting. Thus the last days stretched out beyond the time that was previously foreseen. For *wondrous mysteries* cf. *M.D.*, IX, 18; XI, 5. – *D.D.*, III, 18. – *Hymn*, IV, 23–24.

VII, 10–14   The only practical conclusion to be drawn here is that they should wait patiently for God's hour and faithfully observe His Commandments.

VIII, 1–3   Members of the Community shall secure salvation through their sufferings and their fidelity to the doctrine of the Teacher of righteousness. Cf. *D.D.*, XX, 27–34 and *supra*, pp. 115–116.

the Law in the house of Judah, whom [2] God shall deliver from the house of condemnation for the sake of their sufferings and their faith [3] in the Teacher of righteousness.

Moreover, wealth shall lead the arrogant man to treachery. He will not [4] live, who has enlarged his mouth as the Sheol, who is as death, and cannot be satisfied. [5] All the nations shall be gathered toward him and all the peoples will assemble close to him. [6] Shall not all these take up a parable against him? He will have expounders of visions [7] who will say: "Woe to him that increaseth that which is not his! How long shall he load himself [8] with a pledge?" (*Hab.*, 2, 5–6)

Its meaning concerns the wicked Priest who [9] claimed the name of Truth unto himself in the beginning of his assumption of office. But when he ruled [10] in Israel his heart became proud, he abandoned God and betrayed the commandment for the sake of [11] wealth. He robbed and amassed the wealth of the men of violence who had rebelled against God, [12] and he took the wealth of the peoples, loading upon himself the burden of transgressions. His actions were detestable in the ways of [13] abominations, in every impurity and defilement.

Suddenly shall not those that [oppress] thee [14] rise up; they that torment thee, shall they not awake, and shalt thou not become their prey? [15] Because thou hast spoiled many nations, all the remnant of the people shall spoil thee. (*Hab.*, II, 7–8a)

[16] [Its meaning con]cerns the Priest who has rebelled [17] [against . . . . the commandments of God . . . .]

COLUMN IX   have attacked him to [fulfill] [1] his chastisement in a wicked way. Atrocities of terrible [2] diseases they have executed upon him and vengeance upon his body of flesh.

And what [3] he has said: *Because thou hast spoiled many nations, all [4] the remnant of the people shall spoil thee.*

Its meaning concerns the last priests of Jerusalem [5] who will gather wealth and dishonest riches by plundering the peoples. [6] But in the last days their wealth and their spoil shall be delivered to [7] the army of the Kittim. For they are the "remnant of the peoples."

[8] *Because of men's blood, and because of the violence done to the land, to the city and to all that dwell therein.* (*Hab.*, II, 8b)

VIII, 8–13   The "wicked Priest," blameless at the beginning of his career, went astray when he became Israel's chief. He was, according to the Commentator, moved to this "treason" by his greed for money. The unworthy priest plundered the "men of violence that had rebelled against God" and the peoples, and because of this, all his conduct was judged impure and defiled.

VIII, 16; IX, 2   The wicked Priest who had rebelled against God's ordinances did not escape the punishment he deserved. He fell into the hands of his enemies (cf. IX, 10) who submitted him to abominable tortures.

VIII, 17; IX, 2   Cf. *supra*, p. 94, n. 37. Compare *mahalîm* (diseases) with *mahaliyîm* (diseases caused by wounds) of *II Chron.*, XXIV, 24–25. — The root *nqm* is found frequently in *M.D.* to signify the vengeance in store for the wicked. — For *body of flesh* (*gewiath baśar*): cf. *Sir.* (Greek), XXIII, 16 and *Coloss.*, II, 11: ὥμα σ (τῆς) σαρκός.

⁹ Its meaning concerns the wicked Priest whom, because of the iniquity committed against the Teacher ¹⁰ of righteousness and the members of his Community, God delivered into the hands of his enemies to torment him ¹¹ with a mortal blow — his soul being full of bitterness — because he had done evil ¹² against His chosen ones.

Woe to him that getteth an evil gain [for] his [hou]se, that he may set ¹³ his nest on high that he may be delivered from the fingers of evil. Thou hast conceived a shameful purpose ¹⁴ for thy house. By cutting off many peoples thou hast sinned against thy soul. For ¹⁵ the st[one] cries out [of] the wall [and] the beam out of the timber [answers] it (*Hab.,* II, 9–11)

¹⁶⁻¹⁷ [Its meaning] concerns the [Priest] who [. . . . .
. . . .]

COLUMN X   ¹ that its stone should be laid in oppression and the wood of its timber in robbery.

And what ² he has said: *By cutting off many peoples, thy soul hath sinned.*

³ Its meaning concerns the house of judgment, where God will give ⁴ His judgment among many peoples. Then shall He bring him to judgment ⁵ and in their midst shall He pronounce him guilty and condemn him to the fire of brimstone.

Woe ⁶ to him that buildeth a town in blood and establisheth a city in iniquity. Is it not ⁷ of the Lord of hosts: the peoples labor for the fire ⁸ and the nations weary themselves for vanity. (*Hab.,* II, 12–13)

⁹ Its meaning concerns the Liemonger who led astray many men ¹⁰ into building in blood a city of vanity, and into raising up an assembly through deceit, ¹¹ causing many men to labor for the sake of his glory in a labor of vanity and making them drunk ¹² with works of falsehood, so that their labor should be for nothing, and that they should enter ¹³ the judgment of fire, those who had derided and insulted the elect of God.

IX, 9–12   The wicked Priest, because he behaved wickedly toward the Teacher of righteousness is delivered over to his enemies and put to death (cf. VIII, 16–IX, 2).

IX, 11   *Mortal blow:* literally "a blow of destruction." The expression *bitterness of soul* (*merôrê* or *merîrî nepheš*) may perhaps also mean death (cf. *Targum of Is.,* XXXVIII, 15: (God) "hath saved my soul from bitterness" (*wĕšezêbh mimmerîr naphši.* — "His elect": *beḥîrâw* (the Teacher of Righteousness and his Community); cf. V, 4 note.

IX, 16–X, 1   This concerns, it would seem, a "builder" priest; cf. X, 9–13.

X, 3–5   The eschatological condemnation of the wicked Priest (STERN, DELCOR). Note that the verbs are in the future.

X, 9–13   The Liemonger (cf. *D.D.,* XIX, 25–26) builds a city in blood and founds an assembly through deceit. The efforts of his deceived followers shall be of no avail, and the insults they have heaped on the Community shall not remain unpunished.

X, 11   *Saturating them (harôtham)* comes from *rwh* (saturate with drink, intoxicate). Cf. XI, 14 (*rewiyah* = drunkenness).

X, 15–XI, 2   The final victory of the "knowledge" of God over falsehood. Cf. *M.D.,* IV, 19. — *Fragm. from the Victory of Justice,* 6.

7. — The *Commentary* of *Habakkuk* Scroll, column XI.

[14] *For the earth shall be filled with the knowledge of the glory of Yahweh as the waters* [15] *cover the* [sea.] (*Hab.*, II, 14)
The meaning of these words is that [16] when they shall be converted

. . . .
. . . .

COLUMN XI   [1] the lie. And afterwards the knowledge shall be revealed to them as abundantly as the waters [2] of the sea.

Woe unto him that causeth his neighbors to drink of the mixture [3] *of his fury unto drunkenness that he may look on their feasts (stumbling)* (*Hab.*, II, 15)

[4] Its meaning concerns the wicked Priest who [5] persecuted the Teacher of Righteousness in order to confuse him in the passion [6] of his fury, in the house of his exile. And upon the solemn holy day [7] of *Yom Kippurim*, he appeared before them to confuse them [8] that they might stumble on that fast day, the sabbath of their resting.

Thou art sated [9] *with shame instead of glory. Drink thou too, and reel!* [10] *The cup of the Lord's right hand shall be turned against thee and shame* [11] *against thy glory* (*Hab.*, II, 16)

[12] Its meaning concerns the priest whose shame exceeded his glory.
[13] For he did not circumcise the uncircumcision of his heart and

---

XI, 2–8   An implacable enemy, the wicked Priest hunted the Teacher of Righteousness even to his exile. He chose the feast of the Community Atonement Day (cf. *D.D.*, VI, 18), because he wished to force them to profane their feast. Cf. *Hymn*, IV, 8.

XI, 2–3   There are three interesting variants for *Hab.*, II, 15: 1) *his neighbors* instead of "his neighbor" (M.T.); 2) *his fury* (cf. Symmachus and the Vulgate) for "thy fury" (M.T.); 3) *to look at their feasts* instead of "to look at their nakedness" (M.T.). The latter correction may be ascribed to two reasons: a) the word rendered by "nakedness" must have been thought offensive (the euphemistic bent well attested in the Greek versions and in the Targums); b) a doctrinal motive, attributing to Habakkuk a prediction of the *Yom Kippur*. The Commentator was perhaps playing on the double meaning of *mô'adêhem*, "their feast" (Atonement Day) and "their totterings" (from *ma'ad* "to totter," "to stumble," a clever euphemism).

XI, 5   I propose to translate the *piel* of *bl'* by "to confuse." While not claiming that there were two different roots, one meaning "to swallow up," and the other "to disturb," a semantic evolution in the direction of the latter term can be traced already in the Bible. The parallelism of *bl'* (to confuse) with *kšl* (to stumble) substantiates that hypothesis.

XI, 6   *In the house of his exile* (*abbêth gelûthô*) is proposed by YALON and HABERMANN: *'abbêth = 'al bêth*. Change of *'ayin* into *'aleph* is often found in Punic and Aramaic; for Mishnaic Hebrew cf. M. H. SEGAL, *A Grammar of Mishnaic Hebrew*, Oxford, 1927, p. 27–28. A Murabba'at papyrus has since confirmed the interpretation of YALON and HABERMANN. Cf. *infra*, Appendix.

XI, 8–15   In his quest for vain glory, (cf. X, 11) the Priest quenched his thirst for truth with the intoxicating drink of wickedness (cf. *Hymn*, IV, 7–8 and *M.D.*, II, 13–14. The cup of God's wrath shall cause him to totter.

XI, 9   A euphemism similar to *Hab.*, II, 15 is found in the Biblical verse: *hera'el* (stumble thou!" — cf. the Septuagint, Aquila, Peshitta) instead of *he'arel* ("show thy uncircumcision" — M.T.) The Commentator has both meanings: a) "ways of drunkenness"; b) "uncircumcision of the heart."

XI, 14   For "drunkenness" (*rewiyah*) cf. X, 11.

walked in the ways [14] of drunkenness to quench (his) thirst. But the cup of the wrath [15] of God will make him totter through cha[stising him . . . .] and a plague [16-17] [deadly . . . .

COLUMN XII   *For the violence done to Lebanon shall cover thee and the destruction of the beasts]* [1] *shall make thee afraid. Because of men's blood, and for the violence done to the land, to the city, and to all that dwell therein.* (*Hab.*, II, 17)

[2] The meaning of this word concerns the wicked Priest, to make him repay [3] the ill-treatment which he inflicted upon the poor; for Lebanon [4] is the Council of the Community, and the beasts are the simple ones of Judah, those who practice the Law. [5] And God shall condemn him to destruction [6] inasmuch as he had plotted to destroy the poor.

And what he has said: *Because of the bloodshed* [7] *in the city and the violence done to the land.*

Its meaning: the city is Jerusalem [8] wherein the wicked Priest wrought works of abomination and defiled [9] the sanctuary of God. And the violence done to the land, they are the cities of Judah where [10] he robbed the property of the poor.

What profiteth the graven image that the maker thereof hath graven it, [11] *the molten image, rebellion of lie, that the heart of the maker thereof trusteth therein,* [12] *to make dumb idols?* (*Hab.*, II, 18)

The meaning of this word concerns all [13] the images of the nations which they have fashioned so that they may worship them and bow down [14] to them. But they shall not save them on the day of judgment.

Woe unto him [15-17] *[that saith to the wood:] awake! [To the] dumb [stone: Arise! Behold it is laid over with gold and silver, and there is no breath at all in the midst of it. But Yahweh is in his holy temple:]*

COLUMN XIII   [1] *hush! all the earth before him.* (*Hab.*, II, 19–20)

Its meaning concerns all the nations [2] who worship stone and wood. But on the day [3] of judgment God will destroy all the servants of the idols [4] and the wicked upon the earth.

XII, 1–10   The wicked Priest, guilty of having persecuted the Community of the "Poor," (cf. *M.D.*, VI, 19–22, IX, 22. — *Hymn*, II, 15; III, 8), of having seized their property, and of having defiled the Holy City, shall be condemned by God to the eternal destruction that is the lot of the wicked.

XII, 3–4   The identification of the Lebanon with the Council of the Community results from a Jewish exegetical tradition according to which the Lebanon is a symbolical name for the Temple of Jerusalem. See my forthcoming article, "*Car le Liban, c'est le Conseil de la Communauté*" in the *Mémorial Robert.*

XII, 12–XIII, 4   The uselessness of idolatry. Cf. *I Hen.*, XCIX, 7.

THE MANUAL OF DISCIPLINE

COLUMN I   ¹. to live according to the rule of the Community; to seek ² God . . . . ;
to do what is good and right before Him, as ³ He commanded
through Moses and all His servants the prophets; and to love everything ⁴ that He has chosen, and to hate everything that He has rejected, to keep far from every evil, ⁵ and to be attached to every good
deed; to practice truth, righteousness and justice ⁶ in the land; to
walk no more in the stubbornness of a guilty heart and lustful eyes
⁷ so as to do any evil; to bring those who volunteer to do God's ordinances ⁸ into the Covenant of grace in harmony with the counsel of
God, to walk before Him perfectly in all that ⁹ has been revealed to
their "solemn assemblies"; to love all the sons of light, each ¹⁰ accord-

---

I, 1–2   BROWNLEE proposes to fill the gaps as follows: [These are the
ordinances] ¹ for [the whole assembly, including children and wom]en. . . . . . .
² [in His ordinances, dedicating themselves in Community] . . ." This is
very conjectural, since the fragments which BROWNLEE employs for his reconstitution probably do not belong to the Manual. Cf. D. BARTHELEMY, R.B.,
1952, p. 203.
I, 1   Rule (serekh), cf. I, 16; II, 20–21; V, 1, 23; VI, 8, 22 — D.D., XII, 19.
I, 3–6   Cf. V, 4–5. — D.D., II, 15–16.
I, 6   Cf. D.D., II, 16; III, 5–11; XIX, 20. — H.C., V, 7. See also Test. of
Benjamin, VIII, 2.
I, 7   Volunteer: joining the Community was a spontaneous act, a surrender of
one's self to God. The Hassideans were also volunteers: cf. I Macc. II, 42.
I, 8   Cf. D.D., XII, 2.
I, 9   Solemn assemblies: literally, "assemblies of testimony."
I, 9–10   The lot of every man is pre-established: cf. III, 15–16.
      Sons of light: cf. Luke, XVI, 8. — John, XII, 36. — I Thess., V, 5. — Eph.,
V, 8. — The lot: cf. II, 2, 5, 17, 23; IV, 24, 26; V, 3; VI, 16, 18, 22; IX, 7.
— D.D., XX, 4.

ing to his lot in God's counsel, and to hate all the sons of darkness, each according to his guilt [11] in God's vengeance.

All who volunteer for the sake of His truth shall bring all their knowledge, all their mind, [12] and all their property into the community of God to clarify their knowledge by the truth of God's ordinances, to regulate (the use of) their mind [13] according to the perfection of His ways, and (that of) their property according to His righteous counsel. Let them not transgress a single [14] one word of God concerning their periods: let them not advance their times, nor lag behind [15] any of their feasts. Let them not swerve from His true ordinances to go either right or left.

[16] All those who enter the order of the Community shall enter the Covenant in God's presence to act [17] according to all that He commanded and not to turn aside from Him out of any terror or fright or ordeal [18] roused by the dominion of Belial.

As they are entering into the Covenant, the priests [19] and the Levites shall bless the God of deliverances and all His deeds of truth. All those [20] who enter into the Covenant shall say after them: Amen; amen!

The Ritual of Entry into the Covenant

[21] The priests shall recount God's benevolences through His deeds of might [22] and shall announce His merciful graces unto Israel. The Levites shall recount [23] the iniquities of the children of Israel, all their guilty revolts and their sin [24] under the dominion of Belial. All those who enter the Covenant shall confess after them saying: "We have been corrupt, [25] we have rebelled, we have sinned, we have been wicked, we and our fathers before us, in walking [26] [contrary to the ordinances] of truth. [God is] righteous; [He has executed] His justice upon us and our fathers,

---

I, 14–15   The Community used a liturgical calendar which differed from that of official Judaism; cf. *H.C.*, XI, 8. — *D.D.*, VI, 18–19. — *Jub.*, VI, 23–38. — *I Enoch*, LXXII; LXXX, 2–6.

I, 16   Not the *Covenant* God concluded with the people on Mount Sinai, but a new covenant within the Community.

I, 18   *Belial*, i.e., Satan, a name often found in the Apocrypha (*D.D.*, *Jub.*, *Test. of the Twelve Patriarchs*, etc.); it is also found in *N.T.* (*II Cor.*, VI, 15).

I, 20   A sign in the margin of the manuscript marks the end of the section, the last two sentences being used as a transition.

I, 20–II, 18   After the priests and Levites had recalled God's mercies and Israel's infidelities, the candidates had to make a public confession. Then followed a series of blessings (upon the members of God's party) and curses (upon the party of Belial). A special curse was aimed at those who pretended to be converted. Blessings and curses ended with the liturgical response of a double *amen*. The passage is an imitation of *Deut.*, XXVII–XXX.

I, 21   Cf. *D.D.*, XIII, 8.

I, 24–26   Cf. *D.D.*, XX, 28–30.

COLUMN II   ¹ but He has rewarded us with the mercies of His grace for ever and ever.

The priests bless ² all the men of God, who walk perfectly in all His ways and they say: "May He bless thee with every ³ good, keep thee from every evil, illumine thy heart with life-giving wisdom and deign to grant thee the knowledge of eternity ⁴ and lift up His face of mercy toward thee for eternal bliss!"

The Levites curse all the men ⁵ of Belial and shall respond and say: "Cursed be thou for all thy guilty wicked deeds! May God make thee ⁶ an object of shuddering through all exactors of vengeance! May He cause thee to be visited, for thy destruction, by all who render ⁷ retribution! Cursed be thou for ever: thy deeds are like darkness! Be thou chastised ⁸ in the gloom of eternal fire! May God deign not to pay heed when thou callest Him, nor to pardon thee by forgiving thy iniquities! ⁹ May He show a face of anger for vengeance on thee and may no one who clings to the Fathers wish thee peace!" ¹⁰ All those who enter into the Covenant shall say after the blessings and the curses: Amen, amen!

¹¹ The priests and the Levites shall resume and say: "Cursed by he who, (retaining) the idols of his heart (which cause him) to transgress, ¹² enters into this Covenant and (thus) puts the stumbling-block of his guilt before him, causing (him) to swerve (from the Covenant). *And it will come to pass* ¹³ *that when he hears the words of the Covenant, he will congratulate himself in his heart, saying:* "*May I possess peace* ¹⁴ *even when I walk in the stubbornness of my heart!*" — May his spirit, which is possessed with thirst together with intoxication, perish ¹⁵ forever! May the wrath of God and His

---

II, 1   *For ever and ever* (*min 'ôlam we'ad 'ôlam*): cf. *Mishna-Berakhôth,* IX, 5: "At the end of every blessing in the Temple, they said: 'For ever' (*'ad 'ôlam*); but since the heretics had taught corruptly and said that there is but one world (the one here below), it was ordained that they should say: 'For ever and ever' (*min 'ôlam we'ad 'ôlam*)."

II, 2–3   Cf. the fourth blessing of the Jewish prayer *Shemoneh 'eśreh,* the blessing upon wisdom, in its Palestinian version. Cf. *supra,* p. 114.

II, 6   Cf. *D.D.,* VIII, 2.

II, 8   In the kingdom of darkness even the fire is dark.

II, 11–12   Cf. *Deut.,* XXVII, 14–15. — *Ezech.,* XIV, 3. — *D.D.,* XX, 8–10.

II, 13–14   *Deut.,* XXIX, 18–19. Cf. *H.C.,* XI, 14–15.

II, 16   Cf. *D.D.,* XX, 26.

II, 18   A sign indicating the end of the section.

II, 19–22   The Community was divided into three categories: priests, Levites and the people. Cf. *D.D.,* XIV, 3–6 (with the proselytes forming a fourth class). The priests ranked according to the perfection of their spirit; Israel's traditional divisions were used for the people: thousands, hundreds, fifties, tens (cf. *Ex.,* XVIII, 21–25. — *D.D.,* XIII, 1–2; XIV, 3–6). The same classification was used for the world of Angels: *I Enoch,* LXIX, 3. Every member occupied, within his own group, the place pre-established for him. That hierarchy was apparently unchangeable; nevertheless, see V, 24.

II, 21–22   Cf. *D.D.,* XII, 23–XIII, 1.

II, 25–III, 4   One had to submit sincerely to the Law of the Covenant in order to be counted with the righteous.

zeal for His judgments be kindled against him for (his) eternal destruction! May the curses of the Covenant [16] cling to him! May God set him apart for disaster! May he be cut off from the midst of the sons of light because he swerved from following [17] God because of his idols and because of that which casts him into iniquity. May He place his lot in the midst of the eternally cursed!" [18] All those entering the Covenant shall respond and say after the: Amen, amen!

The Laws of Precedence

[19] Thus shall they do year by year all the days of the dominion of Belial:

The priests shall walk [20] first in the order according to the (perfection of) their spirit, one after another. After them shall walk the Levites [21] and thirdly all the people shall walk, one after another, by thousands, and hundreds, [22] and fifties, and tens. — Let every man of Israel know the status of his office in God's Community [23] according to the eternal counsel. Let no one step down from the status of his office nor rise from his allotted place. [24] For everything shall be in common: truth, humble goodness, benevolent charity, and righteous purpose [25] of each toward his fellow according to the holy counsel and (as) members of the eternal assembly.

Conditions of Admittance and Purification

COLUMN III   Whoever shall disdain to enter [26] [into the Covenant of Go]d that he may walk in the stubbornness of his heart, [let him not enter] into the Community of His Truth, for his soul [1] has rejected the intelligent instructions of righteous laws; he has not held fast to the Restorer of his life; may he not be reckoned with the upright.[2] Let him not bring his knowledge, his mind, and his property into the Council of the Community, for all his doings are wicked strife, and defilement [3] his quietness. Let him not be justified because of the plotting of his stubborn heart. Let him look upon darkness as though upon the ways of light; to the fount of perfection [4] let him not approach.

Let him not be purified by atonement, nor washed by the waters of purification; may he not be sanctified in pools [5] and rivers; may he not be cleansed with any water for washing. Let him remain impure, impure for as long as he rejects the decrees [6] of God and does not correct his ways in the Community of His Counsel.

For it is through the spirit of God's true counsel concerning the ways of man that all his iniquities will be atoned [7] so that he may

---

III, 1   Cf. *D.D.*, XIX, 35.
III, 2–3   The passage is obscure; nothing will profit the obstinate man.
III, 4–6   No rite of purification will cleanse his impurity.
III, 5   Cf. *D.D.*, II, 2.
III, 6–12   A man cannot be made clean by purifying water alone, but must also observe the laws of the Covenant. Cf. V, 13–14.

look upon the life-giving light; united through the holy spirit to His truth, man shall be cleansed of all [8] his iniquities; because of an upright and humble spirit his sin shall be atoned; through the submission of his soul to all God's ordinances his flesh shall be cleansed [9] when he shall be sprinkled with water for impurity and be sanctified by waters of purification. He shall direct his steps so as to walk perfectly [10] in all God's ways, as He has commanded to their solemn assemblies. Let him not swerve either to the right or to the left, nor [11] transgress a single one of God's words. Then shall he find grace before God because of the agreeable atonements and this will become for him a Covenant of [12] eternal Community.

Mankind and the Two Spirits

[13] To the teacher. Let him instruct and teach all the sons of light concerning the orders of men [14] with regard to all varieties of their spirits, their distinctive marks with regard to their deeds in their lifetime, also their punishment or [15] bliss to come.

From the God of knowledge comes all that is and all that is to be and even before they existed He had established their whole lot. [16] They exist according to their (respective) rules, conforming to His glorious purpose, in which they change nothing, and they shall thus fulfill their actions. In His hands are [17] the laws of all beings and He will sustain them in all their pursuits. — He created man for the domination [18] of the world and assigned him two spirits by which to walk until the season of His visitation: they are the spirits [19] of truth and iniquity.

From the fountain of truth (issue) the generations of truth and

---

III, 12   A sign indicating the end of the section.

III, 13–15   The spirit of truth and the spirit of iniquity divide men into two hostile clans. The spirit to which a man adheres, is shown, in his lifetime, by his good or evil deeds, and at his judgment, by his eternal reward or damnation.

III, 15–17   God is the Creator of all things, and the predestination He pronounces absolute. Cf. *D.D.*, III, 7.

III, 17–19   Man, created master of the universe, is governed by one spirit or the other. Cf. *Test. of Judah*, XX, 1–5. — *I John*, IV, 6.

III, 19   A sign indicating the end of the section.

III, 19–21   The world, made by the One and Only God, is dualistic: fountain of truth, spring of darkness; the Prince of light (cf. *D.D.*, V, 18. — *I Enoch*, LXI, 12), the Angel of darkness (cf. *Test. of Simeon*, II, 7. — *Test. of Judah*, XIX, 4); ways of light (cf. *II Enoch*, XXX, 15. — *Eph.*, V, 8. — *I John*, I, 7), ways of darkness (cf. *Rom.*, XIII, 13. — *John*, VIII, 12. — *I John*, I, 6, etc.). For *Two ways*, cf. *I Enoch*, XCI, 18 sq.; *Test. of Asher*, I, 3–9. *Epistle of Barnabas*, XVIII–XX. — *Didache*, I–V (in Greek and above all, in Latin). "Truth-light" and "error-darkness" are synonymous and interchangeable conceptions.

III, 21–IV, 1   The spirits of darkness persecute the sons of light, beguile and lead them astray. But God and His Angel (Michael?) come to the help of the sons of light. This is a monotheistic dualism, since both spirits were created by the God of Israel.

III, 21–23   Cf. *D.D.*, XVI, 5.

from the fountain of darkness (issue) the generations of iniquity. [20] Within the hands of the prince of light is the rule over all the sons of righteousness: they shall walk in the ways of light. Within the hands of the Angel [21] of darkness is all the rule over the sons of iniquity: they shall walk in the ways of darkness. It is the Angel of darkness that causes [22] all the sons of righteousness to go astray; all their sins and their iniquities, and their guilt and their wicked deeds are under his dominion [23] according to God's mysteries until the end of time; all trials and their seasons of distress are under the dominion of his hostility. [24] All the spirits allotted him (exist to) cause the downfall of the sons of light. But the God of Israel and His Angel of truth come to the help of all [25] the sons of light. He created the spirits of light and darkness. Upon them He founded every work [26] and upon their ways every deed (. . .) One (spirit) God has loved throughout all

COLUMN IV   [1] eternity, and He shall delight in all his deeds forever; He has loathed the counsel of the other and all His ways He has hated forever.

COLUMN IV   [1] the duration of ages and in all his activities He delights forever; He has loathed the counsel of the other and all His ways He has hated forever.

[2] These are (respectively) their ways in the world:

To enlighten the heart of man, to make straight before him all the ways of true righteousness, to make his heart tremble with the judgments [3] of God, a spirit of humility and slowness to anger, great mercy, eternal goodness, knowledge, intelligence, a mighty wisdom which trusts nothing [4] but God's works and leans upon His abundant mercy, an enlightened spirit in every purposeful work, zeal for righteous laws, holy [5] purposes with steadfast intent, abundant graces toward all the children of truth, resplendent purity that loathes all impure idols, wise [6] modesty, unfailing discretion concerning all the mysteries of knowledge. These are the counsels of the spirit for the sons of truth in the world. — The visitation of all those who walk by this spirit shall be healing, [7] abundant and enduring bliss, fruitfulness with all everlasting blessings, eternal joy in the life without end, a crown of glory [8] and raiment of majesty in eternal light.

IV, 2–15   The works of both spirits (virtues – sins) are universally valid, as well as their respective retribution, and concern the whole of mankind. Concerning rewards, the prospect of eternal life (cf. *D.D.*, III, 20) is added to the customary benedictions of the O.T. (well-being, a long life, a numerous posterity). The resurrection of the wicked is not mentioned; they appear to be destined to annihilation.

IV, 5   Sons of truth: cf. *Test. of Judah*, XXIV, 3.

IV, 7   *Crown of glory*: cf. *Test. of Benjamin*, IV, 1. *Ascens. of Is.*, IX, 9–10.

IV, 7–8   Cf. *D.D.*, XIII, 12.

IV, 8   *Raiment of majesty*: cf. *I Enoch*, LXII, 15–16. — *II Enoch*, XXII, 8. A sign indicating the end of the section.

⁹ To the spirit of iniquity (belong) greediness, slackening in the service of righteousness, wickedness and falsehood, pride and haughtiness of heart, lying and deceit, cruelty ¹⁰ and great perversity, anger and abundant folly, arrogant jealousy, loathsome works (that are perpetrated) in a spirit of lust, ways of pollution in the service of uncleanness, ¹¹ a mocking tongue, blindness of eyes and dullness of ears, stiffness of neck and hardening of the heart to walk but in the ways of darkness and in the prudence of evil. — The visitation ¹² of all those who walk by it (this spirit) shall consist in a multitude of plagues inflicted by the angels of destruction, eternal damnation through the burning anger of the God of vengeance, everlasting torture and perpetual ¹³ disgrace together with the shame of destruction in the fire of dark regions. All the years of their life shall be of grievous mourning and bitter misfortune, in an existence of darkness, until their ¹⁴ destruction without remnant or survivor.

¹⁵ These are the (two spirits) that preside over the history of all mankind; and with one or the other shall, during their lifetime, all their hosts be divided, and in the ways of one or the other shall they walk. All the merit ¹⁶ of their deeds shall be according to their divisions, according to the inheritance of each, whether much or small, for all the periods of eternity. For God has set them (the two spirits) in equal parts until the end ¹⁷ of time, and He has set eternal enmity between their divisions: abomination of truth is the work of iniquity; abomination of iniquity is the way of truth. Jealous strife ¹⁸ sets them in mutual opposition concerning their (respective) laws, for they (can) not walk together.

But God, through the mysteries of His intelligence and His glorious wisdom has appointed an end for the existence of iniquity and at the season ¹⁹ of visitation He will destroy it forever. Then shall truth in triumph gain the world, for (until then) it was drawn into the ways of wickedness under the influence of iniquity until ²⁰ the season or the ordained judgment.

Then shall God purify in His truth all the works of *the Man*, and shall render pure unto Himself the body of the Man, rooting out all

---

IV, 12   *Angels of destruction:* cf. *D.D.*, II, 6. — *Talmud bab.-Sanhedrin,* 106b: "Three angels of destruction appeared before Doeg: one caused him to forget his learning; the second burnt his soul; and the third scattered his ashes."

IV, 14   Cf. *D.D.*, II, 6–7. — A sign indicating the end of the section.

IV, 15–18   The two spirits having been created in equal numbers, the history of humanity must be a ceaseless strife between good and evil, and its issue cannot be foreseen where individual souls are concerned.

IV, 18–23   At the end of time, justice and the commandments of God will be taught to the elect by the *Man* (*gebher*) whom God will have justified and sanctified. This *Man* is probably the *Teacher of Righteousness:* cf. *Comm. of Ps.* XXXVII, fragm. 2, 11, 14–16, and also *Hymn*, VI, 8–9.

The elect were to enjoy the glory of the innocent, unfallen Adam (cf. *D.D.*, III, 20. — *Gen Rabba*, XI, 2; XII, 6; XVII, 4, etc.) in an eternal Covenant (cf. *D.D.*, II, 7).

spirit of iniquity from ²¹ his flesh and purifying it of all impurity by the holy spirit. As the waters of purification shall He pour over him the spirit of truth. He shall clothe himself ²² in the spirit of purification, in order to teach the knowledge of the Most High unto the just and to teach unto the perfect the wisdom of the sons of heaven. For God has chosen them for an eternal Covenant, ²³ and all the glory of Adam is theirs. There will be iniquity no more, and all the works of deceit shall become shameful.

Until then the spirits of truth and iniquity will contend for the heart of man. ²⁴ He will walk in wisdom or in folly; if a man's inheritance is truth and righteousness, he will hate iniquity; but if his heritage is the portion of iniquity, then he will be wicked ²⁵ and will abominate truth. For God has set them (the two spirits) in equal parts until the decreed end and the renewal of all things. He does know the merit of their deeds for all ²⁶ [eternity], and He has given them to mankind for their inheritance so that they may know [good and evil, that He may all]ot the destiny of all the living according to the spirit within them at the season of visitation.

The Program of the Community

COLUMN V   ¹ This is the rule for all the men of the Community who dedicate themselves to turn from evil and to hold firmly to all that He has commanded according to His good pleasure:

Let them separate themselves from the congregation ² of perverse men and be united in matters of doctrine and property; conforming in their decisions to the sons of Zadok, the priests who keep the Covenant and with the great (assembly) of men ³ of the Community who hold firmly to the Covenant. According to their advice shall be established the lot of every thing, doctrine, property and laws. Let them practice common truth and humility, ⁴ righteousness and justice, benevolent charity and modesty in all their ways. Let none walk in the stubbornness of his heart to go astray after his own heart, ⁵ his own eyes and the scheming of his evil inclination, but let them circumcise together the uncircumcision of an evil inclina-

---

IV, 23–26   The struggle shall continue until its established end and until the renewal of all things, and each man's eternal lot shall be established according to the spirit which he obeyed.

V, 1–7   The members of the Sect, leading a communal life and professing a common doctrine, undertake to amend all their ways so as to atone for all their brethren.

V, 1   A special mark is here found in the margin to indicate the beginning of a new chapter. — *Community: yaḥad.* Cf. *D.D.,* XX, 1, 14, 32.

V, 2   *Conforming in their decisions to . . .* — literally, answer after the manner of one. Cf. V, 15–16.

V, 3   *The great (assembly),* in Hebrew *robh.* Since members of the assembly were called the "Great ones," *robh* may be considered as the assembly's name.

V, 4–5   Cf. *DD.,* II, 15–16.

V, 6   The Community consisted of the sons of Aaron (priests and Levites) and the sons of Israel (laymen). — Cf. *D.D.,* III, 19.

tion and a stiff neck, so as to lay a foundation of truth for Israel for a Community of eternal [6] Covenant and so as to be granted forgiveness for all those who dedicate themselves to the sanctuary among Aaron and in the house of truth in Israel and for those who join them, in a common life, common lawsuits and judgments, [7] so as to condemn all transgressors of the rule.

The Oath of Admission

This is the rule of their conduct concerning all these ordinances:
    When they are admitted into the Community: whoever enters into the Council of the Community, [8] shall enter into the Covenant of God in the presence of all the dedicated ones and shall take a binding oath to return to the Law of Moses — according to all that which He has commanded — with [9] wholeness of heart and wholeness of soul — according to all that is revealed of it to the sons of Zadok, the priests who keep the Covenant and who seek His good pleasure, and to the great (assembly) of the men of their Covenant, [10] who communally dedicate themselves to His truth — and to walk according to His good pleasure. Let him bind himself by the Covenant to separate himself from all perverse men who walk [11] in the ways of wickedness, for these are not reckoned in His Covenant; for they have not sought or scrutinized His ordinances to know the secrets on account of which they have gone astray. [12] They have treated with insolence that which has been revealed so as to excite the wrath of judgment, and that vengeance might be executed by all the curses of the Covenant, bringing upon them great [13] chastisement unto an eternal destruction without remnant.

Separation from the Wicked

Let him not come to the waters to share in the purification of the holy men — for they will not be cleansed [14] unless they have turned from their wickedness! — for he is impure among all those who transgress His word. Likewise let no one have to do with him in matters of labor and property, lest he cause him to carry [15] a burden of

V, 7–13   The oath of admittance required a conversion to the Law of Moses as completed by the "revelations" made by God to the Zadokite priests, and a total breaking off from all "men of iniquity," Jews or Pagans.
V, 8   Cf. *D.D.*, XV, 2–3.
V, 11   *The secrets:* cf. *D.D.*, III, 14.
V, 12   *The curses of the Covenant:* Cf. *D.D.*, I, 17; XV, 2–3.
    Insolently: cf. *DD.*, XX, 30.
V, 13   A sign indicating the end of the section.
V, 13–20   Every man entering the Covenant must stop any intercourse with the wicked in matters of purification, work, property and doctrine. He must accept nothing from them, any relationship being considered as sin and impurity.
V, 13   Purification required an inner conversion of man: cf. III, 4–6.
V, 15   *A burden of transgression:* cf. VII, 24–25; VIII, 23.
    Thou shalt keep far . . . : Ex., XXIII, 7.

transgression, for one must keep far from him in every matter, for this is what is written: *Thou shalt keep far from every false matter!* Likewise, no man of the men of the Community may take a decision [16] according to their opinion in regard to any teaching or judgment. Likewise, may he not eat anything of theirs, nor drink, nor take from their hand anything whatsoever [17] except for a price, for it is written: *Cease ye from man whose breath is in his nostrils, for of what value is he to be reckoned?* For [18] all those who are not reckoned in His Covenant, are to be separated, both they and all they have. Likewise, may the holy man not rely upon any deed of [19] vanity, for all they are vanity who have not recognized His Covenant and He shall destroy from the world all those who despise His word. All their deeds become uncleanness [20] before Him and uncleanness all their property.

Behavior Towards Those Entering the Community

But if anyone enters into the Covenant to walk according to all these ordinances, to be united to the holy congregation, let them examine [21] his spirit, in common, among themselves, regarding his instruction and his works in the Law, in accordance with the sons of Zadok who have dedicated themselves to establish [22] His Covenant and to keep the ordinances which He has commanded, and in accordance with the great (assembly) of Israel, together with those who have dedicated themselves to return jointly to His Covenant. [23] Let them enroll them in order, each after the other, according to their instruction and their deeds. Let every man obey the other, the inferior his superior. They shall [24] examine their spirit and their deeds year by year to promote each according to his understanding and the perfection of his ways or to retard him according to his swerving. Let them reprove [25] each other in truth, with humility and a benevolent charity toward everyone.

Let him not speak to the other in anger or in wrath, [26] or with pride [hardness of heart and] a wicked spirit. He shall not hate him

---

V, 16–17   Cf. *D.D.*, XIII, 14–15.

V, 17   *Cease ye from man . . .* : *Is.*, II, 22.

V, 20–25   The attitude of members towards those who wish to join the Community must be the following: after an investigation, they are assigned to their places, and have to obey their elders. At the end of a year, they are promoted or degraded according to their behavior. This would seem to be contradictory to II, 22–23, where everyone's post is supposed to be predestined, and therefore unchangeable. We are here perhaps dealing with two different sources which testify to two diverging practices. Or perhaps, and I think it more probable, V, 20 sq. are concerned with the candidate's promotion through the various stages of his initiation: the "postulate," and the first and second year of the "novitiate." Cf. VI, 13–23. Reproofs and rebukes should truly be brotherly.

V, 24   Cf. *D.D.*, VII, 2; XX, 4.

V, 25   A sign indicating the end of the section.

[for the uncircumcision] of his heart, for on the day when he shall have reproved him, he shall not

COLUMN VI   ¹be guilty any longer. Likewise, no man shall bring accusation against his fellow in the presence of the Great Ones without having reproved him before (two?) witnesses.

The Common Life

This is how they shall ²walk in all their dwellings of exile, all those who are there, each with his fellow:

The lesser shall obey the greater with regard to labor and wealth. Let them eat communally, ³bless communally, and take counsel communally. In every place where there are ten men of the Council of the Community, let there be among them a man ⁴who is a priest and let each according to his rank sit before him: this is how they shall take counsel with regard to every matter. — When the table is laid for the meal or ⁵for the must to drink, the priest shall be the first to stretch out his hand to invoke a blessing upon the first of the bread and the must. ⁶(. . . . .). And in whatever place the ten are found, let there be a man who studies the Law day and night, ⁷continually, for the improvement of all. — Let the Great Ones keep awake in common during a third of every night of the year to read the Book, study the Law ⁸and recite the blessings in common.

The Meetings

This is the procedure for the gathering of the Great Ones, each in his assigned position:

V, 25–VI, 1   All manifestations of bad temper are strictly banned. Hatred or denunciation of an unfaithful brother is not permitted, unless efforts have been made charitably to rebuke him. Cf. *D.D.*, IX, 28.

VI, 1   The *Great Ones* (*rabbîm*), who enjoyed full rights, were entitled to seats in the great assembly (*rôbh*): cf. *D.D.*, XIII, 7. — We may read either ʿ*edayîm* (two witnesses) or ʿ*edîm* (witnesses). Cf. *D.D.*, IX, 3.

VI, 1–8   Communal life concerned work and property, deliberations, meals and prayer. The smallest community must consist of at least ten men (a "ten"), with a priest at its head to preside over the councils. Cf. *D.D.*, XIII, 1–2.

Bread and *tirôš* were blessed by a priest before being served at the communal meal: that the meal was of a somewhat sacred nature cannot be doubted, since the *Great Ones* alone could be present. Concerning *tirôš*, cf. *supra*, pp. 55–56.

One member out of ten has to be wholly dedicated to the study of the Law. The office is mentioned in *D.D.*, VI, 7; VII, 18.

A third of a night was dedicated to studying Holy Scriptures and communal prayer. According to the *Testament of the Twelve Patriarchs*, Levi charged his sons with the uninterrupted study of the Law. Cf. *Test. of Levi*, XIII, 2.

VI, 6   The full stops indicate a repetition.

VI, 7   The *Book* is most probably the Bible.

VI, 8   A sign indicating the end of the section.

The priests shall sit first, the elders second, and the rest of all [9] the people shall sit each according to his position. Thus they shall deliberate with regard to judgment, counsel or any matter brought before the Great Ones: each shall express his opinion [10] before the Council of the Community. No man shall interrupt the speech of another before his brother finishes speaking. Neither shall he speak before his fellow whose position is inscribed [11] above him; may he who is questioned speak in his turn. In the gathering of the Great Ones no one shall speak any word without the assent of the Great Ones, with the exception (?) [12] of the Overseer of the Great Ones. Whoever has a word to speak to the Great Ones — if he is not in the office of a man who (may) take advice with the Council [13] of the Community, — let him stand upon his feet and say: "I have a word to speak to the Great ones." If they grant it to him, he shall speak.

The Stages of Admittance into the Community

[14] Let the Supervisor at the head of the Great Ones examine every man of Israel who is to be admitted into the Community as to his understanding and his works, and if he is equal to discipline they

---

VI, 8–13   Every Great One was entitled to speak according to his order of precedence. It was forbidden to interrupt a speech (cf. VII, 9). The matter to be discussed had to be first approved of by the assembly, unless it was proposed by the Overseer (*mebhaqqer*: cf. VI, 19–20. — D.D., IX, 18; XIII, 6–13; XIV, 8; XV, 8, 14), an uncertain, but fairly probable, translation. Brethren who had sinned against the Law inadvertently, and perhaps the novices, were admitted to the meetings but were not allowed to speak, unless by special authorization.

VI, 11–12   Cf. *D.D.*, XIV, 11–12.

VI, 13–23   There were four stages before acceptance as a full member: 1) the candidate was examined as to his aptitude, accepted in the Covenant (cf. I, 16–II, 18) and received instruction; 2) he was examined again and underwent his first year of "novitiate" (the novice remained impure and was owner of his property); 3) a second year of novitiate followed upon a new examination (the novice's property was handed over to the treasurer, but he still remained its owner; he was not yet admitted to the "banquet": cf. VI, 4–5); 4) the novice was finally admitted after a last examination (he renounced his right to private property, and was admitted to an active participation in the deliberations and judgments). — Regarding the age of judges, see *D.D.*, X, 4–10.

VI, 13–14   Cf. *D.D.*, XIII, 11.

VI, 20   Cf. *D.D.*, IX, 18.

VI, 22   Cf. *D.D.*, XIII, 12.

VI, 23   A sign indicating the end of the section.

VI, 24–VII, 26   Temporary penalties consisted in depriving the culprit of a fourth part of his food ration and excluding him from purification. Graver faults might involve expulsion. In certain cases the culprit might be readmitted after two years' probation; in others, expulsion was final. A part of the code will be found again in VIII, 16–IX, 2.

VI, 24–25   Cf. *D.D.*, XX, 6; XIV, 20; IX, 21.

VI, 27–VII, 1   It was absolutely forbidden to pronounce the ineffable Name (YHWH). The brethren even refrained from writing it: cf. VIII, 14. See also *D.D.*, XV, 1.

shall bring him [15] into the Covenant to turn to the truth and to turn away from all iniquity. Let him expound to him all the laws of the Community. When he has been admitted, let him stand before the Great Ones, and let them inquire about [16] him. According to the lot established in the Council of the Community, let him be either admitted or dismissed. If he is admitted into the Council of the Community, let him not partake of the purification [17] of the Great Ones before they have examined him as to his spirit and his deeds, and before he has accomplished a full year. Neither shall he share in the property of the Great Ones. [18] Upon the completion of a year in the midst of the Community, let the Great Ones inquire concerning his affairs as to his understanding and his deeds regarding the Law, and if it is decided [19] that he shall be admitted into the congregation of the Community, according to the judgment of the priests and the great (assembly) of the men of their Covenant, let his wealth and his wages be conveyed into the hands [20] of the treasurer of the Great Ones who shall enter them to his credit in the account book, but shall not spend them for the Great Ones. Let him not partake of the banquet of the Great Ones until [21] the completion of his second year among the men of the Community. Upon the completion of his second year, they shall examine him according to the judgment of the Great Ones. If it is decided [22] that he shall be admitted into the Community, they shall enroll him in the order of his assigned position among his brethren, for the law, doctrine and purity; let his wealth be poured (into that of the Community) and his counsel [23] and judgment be valid in the Council.

The Penal Code

[24] These are the laws by which they shall judge in common scrutiny according to the cases:

If there be found among them a man who shall have lied [25] in the matter of wealth — and this knowingly — they shall exclude him from the purification of the Great Ones for one year and he shall be deprived of one-fourth of his food allowance. Whoever shall answer [26] his neighbor with arrogance or speak to him with anger belittling the dignity of his brother by disobeying his brother who is enrolled before him [27] [or will take the law into his own han]ds, he shall be punished for a year and set [apart. He who] swears by the Name of the Honored One that is above all honored ones;

COLUMN VII   [1] if he curses either because he is terrified of persecution or because of any other reason which he may have, he who reads the Book or pronounces the blessings, he shall be put aside [2] and he shall return no more to the Council of the Community. If anyone has spoken in wrath against one of the priests enrolled in the book, he shall be punished for one year [3] and excluded from the purification of the Great Ones. If he has spoken through inadvertence, he shall be punished for six months. He who lies knowingly, [4] let him be punished for six months. He who unjustly calumniates his fellow, knowingly, shall be punished for one year [5] and be set apart. He who speaks bitterly to his fellow or deceives him knowingly, shall be punished for six months. If [6] he is guilty of neglect toward his fellow, he shall be punished for three months. If he is guilty of neglect concerning the property of the Community so as to destroy it, he shall repay it [7] in full; [8] if he is unable to repay it, he shall be punished for sixty days. Whoever bears a grudge against his fellow unjustly, shall be punished for six months (one year). [9] Likewise, he who takes vengeance for himself in any way. Whoever utters a vain word, shall be punished for three months. Whoever interrupts his fellow, [10] for ten days. Whoever lies down and sleeps during a gathering of the Great Ones, for thirty days. As for him who departs from the gathering of the Great Ones [11] without permission and without good reason for as many as three times at a single gathering, he shall be punished for ten days. If they make him stand [12] and he departs, he shall be punished for thirty days. Whoever walks naked before his fellow without being sick, shall be punished for six months. [13] Whoever spits in the midst of a gathering of the Great Ones, shall be punished for thirty days. Whoever brings out his "hand" from under his garment [14] and stirs so that his nakedness becomes apparent, shall be punished for thirty days. Whoever laughs foolishly with a loud voice, shall be punished for thirty [15] days. Whoever brings forth his left hand to make gestures with it, shall be punished for ten days. Whoever slanders his fellow, [16] shall be excluded for one year from the purification of the Great Ones, and shall be punished. Whoever slanders the Great Ones shall be banished [17] and return no more. Whoever murmurs against the authority of the Community, shall be banished and shall return no more. If he murmurs against his fellow [18] unjustly, he shall be punished for six months. The man whose spirit is so frightened by the authority of the Community that he becomes traitor to the truth [19] to walk in the stubbornness of his own heart, if he returns he shall be punished for two years: in the first he shall not participate in the purification of the Great Ones; [20] in the second he shall not participate in the banquet of the Great Ones and he shall sit after all the

---

VII, 8   A correction is found above the line, showing that the penalty was increased from six months to a year.

VII, 8–9   *Grudge* and *vengeance:* cf. *DD.*, IX, 4.

VII, 9   *He who utters a vain word* . . . : cf. *D.D.*, X, 17–18. — *He who interrupts his fellow:* cf. VI, 10.

VII, 10   *He who departs* . . . *(ha'iš hanniphṭar).* MILIK, VAN DER PLOEG and LAMBERT, think this hints at some improper behavior.

VII, 11   *If they make him stand:* to watch him. LAMBERT: "if they remark to him." HABERMANN: "if they appoint him as a guardian" (after *Mishna-Soṭah*, VIII, 6).

VII, 12   *Without being sick:* cf. *Sir.* XXXI, 21. We might translate also thus: "unless this be due to an accident." Cf. *Talmud bab.—Nedarîm*, 27b.

VII, 13–14   Sticking to proper behavior when satisfying a natural necessity.

men of the Community. Upon [21] the completion of the two years, the Great Ones shall inquire into his case. If they admit him, he shall be enrolled in his assigned order, and after that he shall inquire concerning the law. [22] Whosoever, after having been in the Council of the Community for the space of ten years [23] turns away and becomes traitor to the Community, shall be brought before [24] the Great Ones to walk in the stubbornness of his own heart. He shall never return to the Council of the Community. Whosoever among the men of the Commu[nity who is in] touch [25] with him concerning purification or property which is not in the hands of the Council of the Great Ones, his judgment shall be the same: he shall be ba[nished].

The Supreme Council

COLUMN VIII   [There shall be] [1] in the Council of the Community twelve men and three priests perfectly conversant with all that is revealed of the whole [2] Law, who practice truth, righteousness and justice, benevolent charity and modesty among the brethren, [3] who maintain faithfulness upon the earth with an unshaken purpose and with a contrite spirit, who expiate guilt by practising justice [4] and by the anguish of ordeal, and who behave towards all men according to the measure of truth and to the rule of the time.

The Community during the Eschatological Period

When all these things shall come to pass in Israel, [5] the Council of the Community shall be established in truth as an eternal planting, a sanctuary for Israel and a foundation of the holy [6] of holies for Aaron, witnesses of truth in view of the judgment, the elect chosen by grace to atone for the earth and to render [7] retribution to the wicked. This is the proven wall, the precious corner-stone, [8] whose foundations shall not be shaken nor dislodged from their place. This is the place of the holy of holies [9] for Aaron: they know, all, the Covenant of justice and the offering of fragrant odor. It is a house of perfection and truth in Israel [10] for the sealing of a Covenant

---

VII, 15   *His fellow:* one not belonging to the Great ones. Cf. the sequel.
VII, 18–21   Discouragement due to the harsh discipline is forgivable; accordingly, the brother who repented of it could be admitted back.
VII, 22–25   A betrayal, following upon ten years of communal life, admitted of no extenuating circumstances.
VII, 25–VIII, 4   There were three priests, and twelve laymen, standing, no doubt, for the twelve tribes of Israel. The Community pursued the maintenance of good doctrine and atonement. Cf. *Jub.*, VI, 2.
VIII, 1   All that is revealed. Cf. V, 9. — *D.D.*, XV, 13.
VIII, 4–10   An *eternal planting* and *the cornerstone* of the true sanctuary, the Community was called to atone for the wickedness of the world, to accuse sinners before the tribunal of God, and to judge them on the day of the annihilation of iniquity. Cf. *H.C.*, V, 3–6.

according to the eternal decrees. They shall agree to atone for the earth and to pronounce judgment on the wicked so that there may be wrongdoing no more.

The Separate Life and Flight into the Desert

When the (members) shall be established in the institution of the Community for two years, in perfect conduct, [11] they shall be separated (as) holy ones within the Council of the men of the Community. As for every matter hidden from Israel but uncovered by the man who [12] seeks, let him not hide it from them out of fear of the spirit of rebellion.

When these things shall come to pass in the Community in Israel, [13] according to these rules, they shall withdraw from the city of the men of iniquity to go into the wilderness to clear the way of HE [14] as it is written: *In the wilderness clear the way of . . . . , level in the desert a highway for our God.* [15] This is the study of the Law which He has commanded through Moses, so that all may be done according to all that which is revealed in each age [16] and according to that which the prophets have revealed through His holy spirit.

Temporary Exclusion

Whosoever among the men of the Community — of the Covenant [17] of the Community — turns away insolently from any commandment, he shall not participate in the purification of the holy men [18] nor shall he have any knowledge of any of their deliberations until his deeds are purified from all iniquity and until he walks in perfection of way. He shall (then) be admitted to the Council [19] accord-

---

VIII, 5   The *plant* (cf. XI, 8) was the symbol of the assembly of the elect; it is also found in D.D., I, 7 and I Enoch, X, 6; LXXXIV, 6; XCIII, 2–10. In a Christian passage of the Ascens. of Is. the plant represents the Church (IV, 3).

VIII, 7   The *wall.* . . . Cf. Is., XXVIII, 16.

VIII, 10–12   A separate life was necessary (cf. D.D., XIV, 10–12). Within the Community, however, it was the teacher's duty to impart to his brethren any mystery revealed to him.

VIII, 12   A sign indicating the end of the section.

VIII, 12–16   In establishing itself in the solitude of the desert (of Judah), the Community effectively cut itself off from the men of iniquity. The way of God was prepared in the desert through the study and the correct practice of the Law.

VIII, 13   HE (*hû'ha'*), i.e., God.

VIII, 14   In the desert . . . : Is., XL, 3. Four full stops replace the Tetragram, as also in the great Isaiah scroll of Qumrân (XL, 7 and XLII, 6). The verse was applied in the N.T. to John the Baptist (Mark, I, 3. — Matth., III, 3. — Luke, III, 4–6. — John, I, 23). The theme of the flight into the desert is found in the Ascens. of Is., II, 7–11; IV, 1–3.

VIII, 15   The *study* (*midraš*) of the Law: cf. D.D., XX, 6.

VIII, 16–19   The neglect of a single rule sufficed to expel the culprit from the Community until he sincerely amended his ways. Cf. D.D., X, 3.

ing to the judgment of the Great Ones, and afterwards he shall be enrolled in his assigned position. This same rule shall be enforced on all those who join the Community.

Excommunication and Penalty for Faults Committed through Inadvertence

[20] Now these are the laws by which the men of perfect holiness shall walk each with his fellow, [21] all those who have entered into the holy Council, who walk in perfection of way as He has commanded:

Any one of them [22] who transgresses a word of the Law of Moses, insolently or with guile, shall be banished from the Council of the Community [23] never to return. Nor shall any of the holy men come in touch with him in matter of wealth or counsel or any (other) [24] matter. If he has transgressed through inadvertence, he shall be excluded from the purification and from the Council and they shall inquire into his case: [25] he shall not judge nor take any active part in the Council for the space of two years. If his way becomes perfect again, [26] he shall return to the gathering, to the study and to the council, according to the judgment of the Great Ones, provided he has not inadvertently sinned for the space of two years;

COLUMN IX   [1] because for every sin of inadvertence he shall be punished for two years, whereas whosoever acts insolently shall return no more. But whoever sins inadvertently, [2] shall be on trial for two years concerning the perfection of his way and of his counsel, according to the judgment of the Great Ones, and afterwards he shall be enrolled in his assigned position within the holy Community.

Atonement

[3] When these things shall come to pass in Israel, according to these rules, the holy spirit shall be a foundation for eternal [4] truth in order to make atonement for guilty rebellion and sinful infidelity and in order to obtain mercy on earth without the flesh of whole burnt offerings and the fats of sacrifice. The offering [5] of the lips accord-

VIII, 19   A sign indicating the end of the section.
VIII, 20–IX, 2   Whoever purposely violated the Law was expelled for ever; all contact with him was strictly forbidden. Whoever sinned through inadvertence was excluded from purification and council meetings, and was subject to two years' probation.
VIII, 20   *Men of perfect holiness:* cf. *D.D.*, XX, 2, 5, 7.
VIII, 21–23   Cf. *D.D.*, XX, 3.
VIII, 24–IX, 2   Cf. *D.D.*, XII, 3–6.
IX, 3–5   The work of atonement must be founded on the holy spirit, not on bloody sacrifice, and prayer shall provisionally take the place of offerings. Cf. *D.D.*, VI, 11–14.
IX, 3   A special mark indicating the beginning of a new chapter.
IX, 5   A sign indicating the end of the section.
IX, 5–11   Separate life under the leadership of priests shall last until the

ing to the law shall be as a fragrance of righteousness and perfection of way as the gift of an agreeable offering.

A Separated Life under the Guidance of Priests until the Messianic Age

At that time the men of the Community shall be set apart [6] as a sanctuary for Aaron, being united to the holy of holies, and those who walk in perfection [7] as a house of community for Israel. Only the sons of Aaron shall have authority in matters of law and property and according to their judgment the lot shall be established for every group of the men of the Community [8] and for the property of the holy men who walk in perfection. Let their property not be mixed with the property of the men of deceit [9] who have not purified their way by separating themselves from iniquity and by walking in perfection of way. Let them not depart from any counsel of the Law to walk [10] in a stubbornness of heart, but let them conform to the ancient decrees by which the men of the Community have begun to perfect themselves [11] until the coming of a Prophet and of the Anointed Ones from Aaron and Israel.

Rules for the Instructor

[12] These are the rules concerning the instructor, according to which he is to walk with every living being, according to the law of every age and to the worth of every man.
    [13] Let him do God's will according to what is revealed at every epoch; let him teach all the knowledge manifested at every age and [14] the rule of the age. Let him discern and weigh the sons of Zadok according to their spirit so that they may persevere among those chosen ones of the age according to [15] His will as He has commanded. Let him judge each man according to his spirit; let him bring him in according to the cleanness of his hands, according to his understanding [16] let him approach him, and let him thus regulate his love and his hatred. Let him not admonish the men of perdi-

---

advent of the prophet who was to be the forerunner (cf. *Deut.*, XVIII, 15. — *I Macc.*, IV, 46. — *John*, I, 21; VII, 40) and of the two Messiahs, that of Aaron (or Levi) and that of Israel (or Judah). Cf. *supra*, p. 115.

IX, 10–11   Cf. *D.D.*, XX, 31–32; IV, 8.

IX, 11   A sign indicating the end of the section.

IX, 12–19   The instructor must conform to the rules revealed for each period. He must choose new members with discernment. He must avoid all argument with people outside the Community, and in no case reveal to them the true doctrine, but he must instruct the breathren in all the mysteries of God.

IX, 12   Cf. *DD.*, XII, 21.

IX, 13   *Every age*: cf. *D.D.*, X, 5.

IX, 14   *Sons of Zadok* (*benê haṣṣadôq*), reading *benê sadôq*. But "Sons of justice" (*benê haṣṣedeq*) is equally possible: cf. III, 20, 22, also "the sons of the just" (*benê haṣṣadîq*).

IX, 16   *Men of perdition*: cf. *D.D.*, VI, 15.

tion nor dispute with them, [17] but let him conceal the counsel of the Law from the men of iniquity. Let him teach true knowledge and righteous law to those who choose [18] the way, each according to his spirit, according to the rule of the time, to lead them unto wisdom. Let him instruct them in the true and wondrous mysteries in the midst [19] of the men of the Community so that they may walk perfectly each with his fellow in all that has been revealed to them.

Concerning the Last Days

This is the time for the clearing of the way [20] in the wilderness; let him instruct them concerning that which is to be done at that time: to be separated from whomsoever has not turned away [21] from every iniquity.

These are the rules of conduct for the instructor in those times for the regulating of his love and his hatred:

Let him bear an eternal hatred [22] toward the men of perdition, hiding the secret, abandoning to them property, and wages as a slave (does) to his master and as the oppressed [23] to his lord. Let every man be filled with zeal for the rule, and let his time become the day of judgment. Let him fulfill the will (of God) in every gesture of his hands [24] and in all his activities, as He has commanded. Let him rejoice in everything that comes to pass unto him as though it were a gift, and apart from the will of God let him have no pleasure. [25] Let him delight in every word that proceeds from his mouth and desire nothing but that which He has commanded. Let him give constant attention to God's decrees. [26] [At every moment of the future] let him bless his Maker and, wherever he is, let him speak of [God] and bless him [with the offering] of the lips

COLUMN X   [1] during the times which He has ordained.

The Sacred Times of Prayer

At the beginning of the dominion of light; in its middle; and when it withdraws toward the place which is assigned to it; at the begin-

IX, 18   *Wondrous mysteries:* cf. *H.C.,* VII, 8. — *Hymn,* IV, 23–24; V, 4. — *D.D.,* III, 18.

IX, 19   A sign indicating the end of the section.

IX, 19–X, 1   One must hate the wicked, keep the doctrine secret from them, leaving wealth to them; observe the ordinances so as to hasten the day of judgment; trust entirely in God, and bless Him at the times which He has Himself ordained. This is the introduction to the passage concerning the calendar.

IX, 20   Cf. *D.D.,* XV, 10.

X, 1   *During the times which He has ordained* ('*im qissim 'ašer haqqaqo'*). The *aleph* added to the verb is thought by MILIK and BROWNLEE to designate God ('*El* or '*Elohîm*); but it may be merely the suffix pronoun of the third person masc. sing. *Waw* and *Aleph* are often confused in the scrolls.

X, 1–8   The beginning, the middle, and the end of each period (i.e., of the day, the night, the month, etc.) were the established times of prayer. These

ning [2] of the night watches, — for (God) opens the storehouse (of darkness) and sets it up upon it (the light); — in their middle; and when darkness withdraws before the light. When the heavenly lights issue [3] forth from the abode of holiness; and when they withdraw toward the habitation of glory.

At the beginning of the months; in their middle; and at the time of their passing [4] from one to the other. At the time of the new moon, a great day for the Holy of Holies and a sign for the unlocking of His mercies (. . . . .), for the beginning [5] of all periods for ever.

At the beginning of the months and for their duration; on the holy days appointed unto remembrance: at these seasons [6] I bless (God) with the offering of the lips, according to the ordinance engraved for ever.

At the beginning of the years; in their middle, and when they fulfill the law that has been [7] established for them, on the established day (of their passing) from one to the other: from the season of

---

periods were indicated by signs (cf. *Gen.*, I, 14): the sun represents the day, the stars the night, and the moon the months. Concerning the seasons of the year or the year itself, as well as the weeks of years, the rules, although less detailed, seem to be laid down according to the same principles: the beginning, the middle and the transition. The Jubilee, it appears, occurred at the beginning of a week of years, i.e., the 50th year.

X, 1   *The place which is assigned to it,* i.e., to the sun: cf. *I Enoch*, XLI, 4–5; LXXI, 4.

X, 2   *The storehouse* of darkness: this storehouse is not mentioned in *I Enoch*, although storehouses of the sun, the moon, the winds and clouds, etc., are referred to.

Sets them up upon it: a very difficult passage. I agree with HABERMANN reading *'alâw* (upon it) instead of *'lt*.

X, 3   The heavenly lights *issue forth,* i.e., through the gates of the firmament. Cf. *D.D.*, X, 16. — *I Enoch*, XXXIII–XXXVI, LXXII, 3.

X, 4   *The great day:* reading *yôm gadhol* together with MILIK, VAN DER PLOEG, and LAMBERT.

A sign n: *ôth* (sign) is followed by a *nun,* separated from the following word by a short interval. BROWNLEE holds that *nun* to be the third character of an acrostic: *Amen.* BARTHELEMY is of the same opinion and remarks that the numerical value of the Hebrew characters gives 91 (*aleph* = 1 + *mem* = 40 + *nun* = 50). Others think that the *n* is the first character of a word, an abbreviation (MILIK, VAN DER PLOEG, LAMBERT, HABERMANN). According to DUPONT-SOMMER the *sign n* means 50, a number held sacred by the Pythagoreans. — But the *n* might also be due merely to the fact that the copyist associated in his memory some word beginning with an *n* (*ne'eman* for instance) with *'ôth.* The whole passage, moreover, appears to be faulty. *Hasdâw 'ôlam* is grammatically impossible. We must read either *hasdê 'ôlam* (eternal mercies) or, perhaps more probably, *we'ôth ôlam lemip̄taḥ ḥasdâw* (and an eternal sign for the unlocking of His mercies). See in Ben Sira the whole passage concerning the moon (XLIII, 6–8).

X, 5   *Holy days,* the feasts, or perhaps the Sabbaths (DUPONT-SOMMER). A sign indicating the end of the section.

X, 6   *The ordinance engraved for ever:* the true calendar, engraved on the heavenly tablets, according to *Jub.*, VI, 30, 35.

X, 7   The Sabbatical year: cf. *Lev.*, XXV, 8–55.

reaping to the season of summer, from the season of sowing to the season of green herbage; from the periods of years to the Sabbatical year, [8] and at the beginning of the weeks (of years) at the Jubilee.

For as long as I live, the engraved ordinance is upon my tongue (bearing) the fruit of praise and the offering of my lips.

Final Canticle

[9] I sing with skill; all the music of my harp glorifies God, and my cithern His holy decree, and I praise the rule of His justice with the flute of my lips. [10] At the beginning of the day and of the night, I enter into the Covenant of God; when the morning ceases and the night ends, I retell His Commandments, and for as long as they shall exist shall I make of them [11] my boundary and shall not go out from it. I declare His judgment concerning my swervings, and my faults are before me, according to the engraved law.

I say to God: "My Righteousness!" and [12] to the Most High: "Author of my well-being, source of knowledge, fount of holiness, height of glory, all-mightiness of eternal splendor!" I shall choose that which [13] He shall have taught me and I shall rejoice in that which He shall have appointed unto me. When I put forth my hands and my feet, I shall bless His Name; when I go out or when I go in, [14] when I sit down or when I rise up, and upon my bed shall I sing unto Him. I shall bless Him with the offering which comes forth from my lips for the sake of all which He has established unto men, [15] and before I lift up my hands to partake of the delicious fruits of the earth.

At the beginning of terror or fear and in the place of anguish and desolation [16] shall I bless Him; I shall render thanks unto Him for His marvellous works, and I shall praise Him for His power's sake. Every day shall I lean upon His mercies and I shall know that within His Hand lies the justification [17] of all the living, and that all His works are truth. At the beginning of anguish shall I praise Him, and I shall sing to Him also for my deliverance sake.

Behavior Toward the Wicked and Those Who Repent

I shall repay no man with [18] evil; I shall pursue man with good, for with God is the judgment of all the living, and He shall give unto every man his due. I shall not envy because of a spirit [19] of wicked-

---

X, 8   *The Jubilee:* cf. *Lev.,* XXV, 8–55.
X, 9–XI, 22   This poem is closely related to the *Thanksgiving Hymns.*
X, 9–17   God must be blessed at all times and in every circumstance.
X, 11   *My boundary:* cf. X, 25. — *D.D.,* XX, 25.
X, 12   *Fount of knowledge:* cf. *M.G.,* I, pl. XII, line 1. — *I En.,* XLVIII, 1.
X, 16–17   Justification is the work of God. Cf. *Hymn,* IV, 27.
X, 19   One must not quarrel with the wicked. Cf. IX, 16.

ness and my soul shall not covet wealth (acquired) by violence. I desire not the upper hand in a quarrel with men of perdition until the day of vengeance; nevertheless [20] I shall turn back from the men of iniquity and shall not rejoice until their judgment is established. I shall not bear any grudge against those who have repented of their sin, but I shall have no compassion [21] on whomsoever turns aside from the way. I shall not console them that are stricken until they make their way perfect. I shall not keep Belial in my heart; no man shall hear, coming forth from my mouth [22] futile words, and guilty deceits, falsehoods and lies shall not be found upon my lips. The fruit of holiness shall be upon my tongue and abominations [23] shall not be found thereon. I shall open my mouth with thankful praise, my tongue shall tell forever the mercies of God and the treachery of men until they turn back [24] from their sins. I shall shut out vain things from my lips, impurities and falsehoods from the knowledge of my heart. According to the counsel of wisdom I shall conceal (tell) knowledge [25] and I shall hedge [wisdom] with a steadfast boundary to maintain faithfulness and protection of laws. According to the righteousness of God I spre[ad ab]road [26] the precept with the help of the measuring-cord of the time, [practising truth and righteous judgment,] benevolent charity toward the humble and strengthening the hands of the timid [of heart in order to teach] COLUMN XI   [1] wisdom to those whose spirits are gone astray and to bring understanding of the instruction unto those who murmur; to respond humbly to the proud and with a contrite spirit to [2] those who hold the staff of authority, to those who threaten, speak insults, and acquire property.

Leaning on God

For I (say): "My justification belongs to God; the perfection of my way and the uprightness of my heart are in His hand; [3] through His favor shall my sins be blotted out. For from the fountain of His knowledge my light has sprung forth; my eyes have beheld His wonders; my heart has been illumined by the mysteries [4] that are to come and He Who exists unto eternity is the support of my right hand. Upon the rock of strength is the way of my steps and they shall

---

X, 20   The necessity of breaking with the wicked was one of the Community's main dogmas, which its teachers never tired of repeating. — *Those who have repented of their sin:* cf. D.D., II, 6; IV, 2; XX, 17.

X, 21   *Turns aside from the way:* cf. D.D., II, 6; VIII, 16; XIX, 29.
        Them that are stricken: the wicked were chastised already in their lifetime. Cf. IV, 12.

X, 22   *Abominations (šiqqûṣim):* a word meaning idols. Cf. "the abomination of desolation" in *Dan.*, IX, 27; XI, 31; XII, 11.

X, 24   *I shall conceal:* a correction above the line says "I shall recount."

X, 26–XI, 1   Cf. *Is.*, XXXV, 4 and XXIX, 24.

XI, 2–15   Religious thought reaches here its culmination.

XI, 2–5   For *justification:* cf. X, 16–17 and *Hymn*, IV, 27.

not be shaken by aught. For the truth of God is [5] the rock I tread and His might is the support of my right hand. From the fountain of His justice (flow) my heart's judgments of light; from His wondrous mysteries, Him Who exists unto eternity my eyes [6] have beheld: a wisdom which is hidden from men, a knowledge and a purpose illuminated, (hidden from) the son of men, a fountain of righteousness, a store [7] of strength, an abode of glory, (hidden) from the assembly of flesh. To those whom God has chosen, He has given (all) that as an eternal inheritance, and has given them to share the destiny [8] of the saints and He has associated their assembly with the sons of Heaven to establish the Council of the Community, the foundation of a sanctuary, an eternal planting for all [9] the time to come.

The Unworthiness of Man and Divine Love

I (say): "Wickedness pertains to man, and iniquity to the assembly of man. Because of my sins, my rebellions, my transgressions and the iniquity of my heart am I part of the assembly (delivered over) [10] to worms, and associated with those who walk in darkness. For does man have his own path, he does not strengthen his own steps: for to God belongs justice and from His hand [11] comes perfection of way. By His knowledge do all things exist, by this purpose He establishes every being, and apart from Him shall nothing be done.

As for me, if [12] I stumble, the mercies of God shall come to my help forever; if I fall because of the sin of the flesh, my justification shall be established through the righteousness of God forever. [13] If anguish invade me, He shall deliver my soul out of the pit, and He shall establish my steps upon the way. With His mercies shall He reach me, and according to His compassion [14] He shall judge me. With true justice shall He judge me and in His great goodness He shall pardon me all my iniquities. In His righteousness He shall cleanse me from the impurity [15] of man so that I may praise God for His righteousness sake, and the Most High for His majesty.

Final Blessing

Blessed art Thou, O My God, who openest unto knowledge [16] the heart of Thy servant. Strengthen all his deeds in righteousness and

---

XI, 4   *Support* of the righteous: cf. *I Enoch,* XLVIII, 4 (the Son of Man).
    Shaken: reading *yizda'za'.*
XI, 5   *Fountain of justice:* cf. *I Enoch,* XLVIII, 1.
XI, 7–8   The privilege of pertaining to the Community was due to God's supreme mercy.
    The foundation of a sanctuary: yesôd mabhnîth qôdeš.
XI, 9–15   The same theme is found in *Hymn,* IV, 25–34; V.
XI, 11   Cf. *Hymn,* V, 1–2.
XI, 15   A sign indicating the end of the section.
XI, 16   Cf. *I Enoch,* LXII, 8.
XI, 17–22   Cf. *Hymn,* V.

grant to the son of Thy handmaid — as Thou hast been pleased to do to the elect of mankind — to stand [17] before Thee for ever. For without Thee the way is not perfect and apart from Thy good pleasure can nothing be accomplished. Thou hast taught [18] all knowledge; all that exists, exists by Thy good pleasure and without Thee there is no one who can decide anything contrary to Thy counsel, or understand [19] all Thy holy purposes or behold the depth of Thy mysteries, or comprehend all Thy marvels [20] and the strength of Thy might. Who could bear Thy glory? What indeed is the son of man among Thy wondrous works [21] and how can he who is born of woman stay before Thee? For his clay is but dust and his body the nourishment of worms. He is not made of rock; he is but [22] fashioned clay and his longing is for the dust. What shall clay which is shaped by hand reply? What counsel could it understand?

XI, 21   *He is not made of rock (wehû'a miṣṣûr):* accepting HABERMANN's interpretation (ṣûr = rock, with min as the depriving particle).
XI, 22   A sign to indicate the end.

THE DAMASCUS DOCUMENT

I THE ADMONITION

COLUMN I   [1] And now hearken all ye that know righteousness and consider the works [2] of God. For He has entered into dispute with all flesh and He will execute judgment upon all those that despise Him.

[3] For because they sinned in forsaking Him, He hid His face from Israel and from His sanctuary [4] and gave them to the sword. But remembering the Covenant He had concluded with the forefathers, He preserved a remnant [5] of Israel and gave them not up to destruction.

The Birth of the Community

In the age of wrath, three hundred [6] and ninety years after He had given them into the hands of Nebuchadnezzar, king of Babylon, [7] He visited them and caused to grow forth from Israel and Aaron the root of a plant to possess [8] His land and wax fat in the goodness of His soil. They considered their trespass and knew that they were [9] guilty and that they were like the blind and those that grope their way [10] for twenty years. God considered their works, and that

I, 1–2   Hearken: The Document opens with an admonition as the judgment was thought to be at hand.
        Ye that know justice: Is., LI, 7.
I, 3–4   This alludes to the destruction of Jerusalem and the Temple by Nebuchadnezzar in 587 B.C.
I, 4–5   The small remnant to be saved: the faithful Jews, particularly the priests, who returned from exile.
I, 5–6   390 years: cf. Ezek., IV, 5.
I, 7   The root of a plant: cf. M.D., VIII, 5.
I, 8–10   Intermediary period between the birth of the Community and the coming of the Teacher of Righteousness.

with all their heart did they seek Him, [11] and He raised for them a
Teacher of Righteousness to lead them in the way of His heart. He
made known [12] unto the later generations that which He had accomplished concerning the last generation, the congregation of traitors,
[13] those who had backslided from the way. This is the time about
which it was written: *Like a backsliding heifer,* [14] *thus did Israel
slide back.* Then arose the Man of mockery who poured out upon
Israel [15] the waters of falsehood and led them astray into a chaos
without way, swerving [16] from the pathways of righteousness and
removing the landmarks which the forefathers had set up in their
inheritance: in order [17] to cause the curses of His Covenant to
cleave to them and deliver them to the avenging sword that exe-
cutes the vengeance [18] of the Covenant. Because they had sought
deceptions, chosen impostures and recovered the breaches. [19] They
chose insolence, justified the wicked and condemned the just,
[20] broke the Covenant, transgressed against the law, threatened the
life of the just, and all those who walked [21] uprightly they held in
abomination; they persecuted them with the sword and delighted
in quarreling with the people. But the wrath of God was kindled.

COLUMN II   [1] against their congregation, so as to annihilate

all their multitude, and their works were an impurity before His
eyes.

Repentance and Infidelity — The Elect

[2] And now hearken unto me, all ye that are of the Covenant, and I
shall uncover your ears concerning the ways [3] of the wicked. God
has loved knowledge; wisdom and counsel He has set up before
Him; [4] understanding and knowledge minister unto Him; longsuf-
fering is with Him and much mercy [5] to pardon those that repent
them of their sin. But power and might and great wrath with flames
of fire [6] are in Him — all the angels of destruction — against them

---

I, 11   The Teacher laid down the doctrinal foundations of the group.
I, 12–II, 1   An epoch of doctrinal innovation, of violence and strife. *The
Man of mockery* was the chief of the rebels. Their revolt was drowned in
blood.
I, 13–14   *Like a backsliding heifer* . . . : *Hos.,* IV, 16.
I, 17   *The curses of His Covenant:* cf. XV, 2–3. — *Deut.,* XXIX, 20. — *M.D.,*
V, 12.
       The avenging sword: Lev., XXVI, 25.
I, 20   *Threatened the life of the just: Ps.,* XCIV, 21.
II, 2   God loves the repentant sinner, but He abhors the wicked, whose
deeds have been known from the beginning (cf. *M.D.,* III, 15). He has
raised, at every period, a nucleus of righteous men among sinners, and con-
veyed to them His teaching through His Anointed One (the high-priest
Zadok, who will be mentioned in V, 6).
II, 5   *Those that repent:* cf. IV, 12; XX, 17. — *M.D.,* X, 20.
II, 6–7   Cf. *M.D.,* IV, 12–14, 22; X, 21.

that backslide from the way and hold the law in abomination: there shall be no remnant [7] or survivor of them. For God chose them not from the beginning of the world and before they were created He already knew [8] their works. He held in abomination the generations of their congregation and hid His face from the land [9] (at) the time of their destruction. He knew the years of (their) office, the number and exact epochs of their appointed times from all [10] eternity and for ever more, that which shall befall at the appointed times of all the years of the world. [11] And in each of them He raised up for Himself (men) called by name in order to leave (a group of) survivors for the land and people [12] the face of the universe with their seed. He made known His holy spirit unto them through His Anointed One. He is [13] truth and by his name their names are determined. But those whom He has hated, has He led astray.

A Theology of History

[14] And now, children, hearken unto me, and I shall uncover your eyes to see and consider the works of [15] God; to choose that in which He delights and to rejects that which He hates, to walk uprightly [16] in all His ways and not to wander according to the designs of a guilty inclination and the allurement of lust. For many [17] went astray through these, and mighty heroes stumbled because of them from old times even until now.

The Watchers and the Giants

Walking in the stubbornness [18] of their hearts, the Heavenly Watchers fell and were entangled, while they did not keep the commandments of God. [19] Their sons, tall as a cedar and great as a mountain, fell. [20] All flesh that was on dry land perished. They became as though they had not been, because they had followed [21] their own

---

II, 8   *The generations of their (assembly): dôrôth mdm*, rectified as *sodam*. Other writers change *mdm* into *miqqedem* (from the origin): SCHECHTER, CHARLES, HABERMANN, etc., or *dôrôtham:* LEVI; *'omdam* (when they arose): RABIN. LAGRANGE translates: "sanguinary generations" (*dôrôth middam?*).

II, 9   (*At*) *the time of their annihilation:* if we read (*be)mo'ed.* The manuscript gives *my* (or *mw*) *'d.* The sense is clear, in spite of this uncertainty.

II, 9–10   God knows all that is to come. — The passage refers to the elect.

II, 13   *By his name* (Zadok's) *their names* (the sons of Zadok) *are determined.*

II, 14   The author begins his historical commentary, starting with the episode of the "Watchers" and continuing down to his own time.

II, 15–16   Cf. *M.D.,* I, 3–6; V, 4–5. — *H.C.,* V, 7.

II, 18   *The Heavenly Watchers:* cf. *Enoch,* VI–X. — *Test. of Ruben,* V, 6–7. — *Test. of Nephtali,* III, 5.

II, 19   The flood was due to the wickedness of the giants, the offspring of Watchers and the daughters of man: cf. *Gen.,* VI, 4–7.

II, 20–21   The flood, a punishment of wickedness.

will and had not kept the commandments of their Maker until His
anger was kindled against them.

The Sons of Noah

COLUMN III   [1] Thus did the sons of Noah go astray and their
families also; because of this were they destroyed.

The Patriarchs

[2] Abraham did not walk thus and was raised to the dignity of a
friend because he had kept the commandments of God and had not
chosen [3] the desire of his own spirit. He handed them down to
Isaac and to Jacob who kept them and were written down as friends
[4] of God and His covenanters for eternity.

The Sons of Israel

The sons of Jacob went astray and were punished for [5] their errors.
Their sons in Egypt walked in the stubbornness of their hearts
scheming against [6] the commandments of God, and doing each that
which was right in his own eyes, and they ate blood. He destroyed
[7] their males in the desert, (when He spoke) unto them in Kadesh:
Go ye up and take possession . . . of their spirit. But they obeyed
not [8] the voice of their Maker, nor the commandments of their
teachers, and they murmured in their tents. And the anger of God
was kindled [9] against their congregation.

And their sons perished through it and their kings were annihilated. Through it their heroes [10] perished and their land became
desolate. Through it the first members of the Covenant became
culpable and were given over [11] to the sword: because they had for-

---

III, 1   The author, not mentioning Noah, the first of the elect, passes on
immediately to the latter's unfaithful offspring.

III, 2–4   Noah's election is not mentioned, so that Abraham should appear
as the first of the elect. Abraham, Isaac and Jacob were the first righteous
men, shining characters in the dark and interminable ranks of the wicked.

III, 4–9   The sins and punishments of Jacob's sons and of the Hebrews in
Egypt and in the desert.

III, 6   *Ate blood:* cf. *I Enoch*, VII, 5.

III, 7   *in the desert (when he) (spoke) unto them: bammidbar (bedabberô)
lahem:* the word in parenthesis may have been dropped through haplography.
Go up and possess . . . . their spirits: cf. *Deut.*, IX, 23 (Go up and possess
their land). An abbreviated quotation.

III, 8   *And they murmured in their tents:* Ps., CVI, 25.

III, 9–12   A brief review of Israel's history from the conquest of Canaan
to the storm of Jerusalem by Nebuchadnezzar, presenting it as a sequence
of infidelities and punishments. David and Zadok are to be mentioned later.

III, 12–IV, 12   The creation of the Community by the faithful priests of
Zadokite lineage, to whom was revealed a cult and a way of life agreeable
to God. Those who persevered at their side, even after their secession and
their rupture with the house of Judah, could feel secure of their salvation.

saken the Covenant of God, chosen their own desire and gone astray in the stubbornness [12] of their hearts, each doing what it pleased him to do.

The Community of the Sons of Zadok

But among them that held fast to the commandments of God — [13] those that remained — God established His Covenant with Israel even until eternity, revealing unto them [14] the hidden things concerning which all Israel had gone astray: His holy Sabbaths and His glorious feasts, [15] His righteous testimonies and His true ways. The desires of His will, which if any man accomplish them [16] he shall live, showed He unto them. They digged a well of plentiful waters: [17] and he who despises them shall not live. But they let themselves be carried away by the sin of man whose ways are impure, [18] and they said: "This is ours." But God in His wonderful mysteries forgave them their trespass and pardoned their sin. [19] He built them a sure house in Israel, the like of which has not stood from ancient times and even until [20] now. They who hold fast to it shall possess eternal life and all the glory of Adam, as [21] God has established for them through Ezekiel the Prophet, saying: *"The priests, the Levites, the sons*
COLUMN IV   [1] *of Zadok who kept the charge of My sanctuary when the children of Israel strayed* [2] *in their infidelity, will offer Me fat and blood."*
The priests are the penitents of Israel, [3] who went out from the land of Judah and those that went with them. The sons of Zadok are the elect [4] of Israel, those that have been called by their name, who shall be in office at the end of time. Behold the exact statement [5] of their names according to their generations, the epoch of their office, the number of their tribulations, the years [6] of their exile and

III, 14   *Hidden things:* cf. M.D., V, 11.
III, 14–15   *His sabbaths,* etc.: cf. *Jub.,* I, 14; II, 29–30; VI, 33–34; XXIII, 19.
III, 16   The *well of plentiful waters* signifies the Law. Cf. VI, 3–5; XIX, 34.
III, 17–18   Cf. I, 8–10.
    Wondrous mysteries: cf. H.C., VIII, 8. — M.D., IX, 11; XI, 5. — Hymn, IV, 23–24; V, 4, etc.
III, 19   *A firm house:* the Community. Cf. XX, 10–13. — M.D., V, 6; VIII, 4–5; IX, 6.
III, 20   Cf. M.D., IV, 7, 23.
III, 21–IV, 2   *The priests . . . :* Ezek., XLIV, 15.
IV, 2   *The penitents:* cf. II, 5.
IV, 3   *Those that went with them (nilwîm):* a pun on *lewiyyîm* (*Levites*).
IV, 4   *Called by their name:* cf. II, 11.
    The sons of Zadok, after a temporary exile, were to resume their office in the sanctuary before the judgment.
IV, 4–6   Cf. II, 9.
IV, 6   *(They are the first) holy (men):* accepting Habermann's interpretation of an otherwise unintelligible passage: *(hem 'anšê) haqqôdeš (hari')šônîm* instead of *hqwdš šwnym.*

the exact statement of their works. [They are the first holy men] whom God has forgiven. [7] They have justified the righteous and condemned the wicked. Let all those who follow them [8] act according to the prescription of the Law as it was taught unto the forefathers until the period of these years shall be accomplished. [9] According to the Covenant which God established with the forefathers to pardon them [10] their iniquities, thus shall He forgive them. When this epoch is completed according to the number of these years, [11] there shall be no more uniting with the house of Judah, but each man must stand within [12] his own stronghold: the wall is built, the law is removed.

The Wickedness of Israel at the Time
of the Formation of the Community

And during all these years [13] shall Belial be let loose upon Israel, as God has spoken by the hand of the prophet Isaiah son [14] of Amoz saying: *"Fear, and the pit, and the snare are upon thee, O inhabitant of the land."* Its explanation: [15] the three nets of Belial, — of which Levi, son of Jacob, has spoken, — [16] with which he ensnared the Israelites. He made them appear unto them as three kinds [17] of righteousness. The first is lust; the second is profit; the third is [18] the profanation of the sanctuary. Whoever escapes from the one is caught in the second, and whoever is delivered from the second is caught [19] in the third. The "builders of walls," they who "followed the *saw*" — the *saw* is the preacher [20] of whom it was said: *they will do nothing but preach* — are caught in two (of these snares): in the

---

IV, 7–8   The contrary of I, 15–21.
IV, 8   Cf. VII, 4–5; XX, 31–32. — *M.D.*, IX, 10–11.
IV, 10–12   A separated life: cf. *M.D.*, VIII, 10–13; IX, 20–21, etc.
IV, 12   *The wall is built* . . . : cf. *Mic.*, VII, 11.
IV, 12–VI, 2   The period of tribulation preceding the end of the world was to be characterized by three capital sins, which the wicked would try to pass as virtues: lust (polygamy), love of gain, and the profanation of the Temple (by entering it while impure). A fourth sin is here added by the author, viz. the profanation of the holy spirit that is in man through rebellion against the commandments of God.
IV, 14   *Fear, pit* . . . : cf. *Is.*, XXIV, 17.
      Its interpretation (pišrô): cf. *H.C.*, passim.
IV, 15   *Levi, son of Jacob:* alludes to the *Test. of Levi.* The verse quoted here is not found in the text in its present condition, but similar remarks are found in IX, 9; XIV, 5–8; XV, 1; XVI.
IV, 18–19   *Whoever escapes* . . . : cf. XXIV, 17.
IV, 19   *"Builders of walls":* cf. VIII, 12, 16. — *Ezek.*, XIII, 10. These are the Jews whom a teacher of lies led astray by a false commandment (*șaw*). This passage concerning the *șaw* is inspired by *Hos.*, V, 11 and must be understood in the light of the ancient Versions, where we find *saw* translated as "vanity" (LXX, Pesh.), "riches of falsehood" (Targ.), "dirt" (Vulg.). Cf. *Is.*, XXVIII, 10, 13.
IV, 20   *They will do nothing but preach:* *Mic.*, II, 6.

snare of lust — by marrying [21] two women each of them being alive
— whereas the principle of creation is: *Male and female created He
them.*

COLUMN V   [1] Those that entered into the ark went therein two
by two. Concerning the prince it is written: [2] *Let him not multiply
wives unto himself.* David read not the sealed book of the Law
which [3] was inside the ark because it had not been opened for Israel
since the death of Eleazar [4] and Joshua — the ancients having served
Ashtoreth — and revelation [5] had been concealed until the coming
of Zadok. The works of David profited unto him except for the
blood of Uriah, [6] for God did not upbraid him for them.

They also profane the sanctuary inasmuch as they do not [7] discern
according to the Law, but lie with her that has an issue of blood;
they marry [8] the daughters of their brothers or the daughters of
their sisters. Now Moses has said: [9] *Thou shalt not approach unto
thy mother's sister! She is thy mother's kin.* The "law of nakedness"
written for men [10] applies equally to women, and if the brother's
daughter uncover the nakedness of her father's brother, [11] that is
also prohibited.

They have also rendered unclean the holy spirit within them and
with a scoffing tongue [12] they have spoken against the precepts of
the Covenant of God saying: "They are not true!" and [13] they have
proffered abominations against them. They are all kindlers of fire
and setters alight of darts; spider [14] webs are their webs and vipers'
eggs their eggs. He that approaches unto them [15] shall not go un-

---

IV, 21   According to the author's exegesis, polygamy arises from lust. He
perhaps disapproved even of divorce followed by a second marriage, if the
first wife was still alive.

Each of them being alive (*behayyêhem*): for a masculine suffix referring
to a feminine subject, cf. P. JOÜON, *Grammaire de l'hébreu biblique,* § 149b.
M. H. SEGAL, *Gramm. of Mishnaic Hebr.,* § 71.

Male and female . . . : Gen., I, 27. Cf. *Jub.,* III, 7. — Matth., XIX, 3–7;
Mark, X, 2–12.

V, 1   Cf. *Gen.,* VII, 9.

V, 2   *Deut.,* XVII, 17.

V, 4   The *ancients:* from Joshua to David and Zadok.

V, 4–5   Note the vital part ascribed to the eponymous ancestor of the "sons
of Zadok."

V, 5   *Profited unto him (wayya'alû):* as in *Sir.,* XXX, 25 (quoted by HABER-
MANN). Since the Law was sealed, David could not be aware of its prescriptions; His transgressions therefore, with the exception of Uriah's assassination,
were not conscious and deliberate sins (polygamy, for instance). The sons of
Zadok had little respect for the monarchy.

V, 7   Cf. *Lev.,* XV, 19. — *Ps. of Solomon,* VIII, 12 (13).

V, 9   Cf. *Lev.,* XVIII, 13.

V, 9–10   The "*law of nakedness*": i.e., the law regarding prohibited marriages. *Lev.* prohibited the marriage of a man with his aunt; the author infers
that the marriage of a man with his niece is equally banned. This view was
accepted by the Sadducean priests, and later, by the Karaites. Cf. *supra,* p. 103.

V, 12   Cf. *Hymn,* IV, 14. *Test. of Levi,* XIV, 4.

V, 13–14   *They are all kindlers . . .* : cf. *Is.,* L, 11 and LIX, 5.

V, 15   *As his posterity (ketharbithô):* HABERMANN's correction for *khr bytw.*

punished, as (also) his posterity, he shall be exterminated, verily
he shall be crushed. For (. . . .) since ancient times God has examined [16] their deeds and His wrath has been kindled against their
practices, *for it is a people of no understanding,* [17] *it is a nation
void of counsel,* inasmuch as there is no understanding in them. For
even before [18] Moses and Aaron had been raised by the hand of the
Prince of Lights, Belial raised Jannes and [19] his brother by his evil
device, when Israel was delivered for the first time. [20] Whereas at
the time of the destruction of the land there arose the removers of
the boundary and they led Israel astray. [21] The land became desolate, for they preached revolt against the commandments of God
given by the hand of Moses and also
COLUMN VI   [1] by the hand of His holy Anointed One. They
prophesied falsehood in order to cause Israel to turn away from
[2] God.

The Exiles of Damascus and their Study of the Law

But God remembered the Covenant (He had made) with the forefathers and He raised up from Aaron men of understanding and
from Israel [3] men of wisdom and He called upon them to dig the
well: *the well which princes digged,* [4] *which the nobles of the
people delved with the Master.*
    The well is the Law; those that digged it are [5] the penitents of
Israel, who went out from the land of Judah and exiled themselves
to the land of Damascus; [6] God named them princes because they
did seek Him, but [7] their fame has been told by the mouth of no
man. The Master is the Interpreter of the Law, of whom [8] Isaiah
has said: *He has made manifest the tool for his work.* The nobles
of the people are [9] they that have come to dig the well according

---

V, 16, 17   *A people of understanding: Is.,* XXVII, 11 and *Deut.,* XXXII, 25.
V, 18   *The Prince of lights:* cf. *M.D.,* III, 20.
V, 18–19   *Jannes and his brother:* two magicians from Egypt. Cf. II, *Tim.,*
    III, 8. – Cf. R. Bloch, *Quelques aspects de la figure de Moïse dans la lit-
    térature rabbinique,* in *Moïse, l'Homme de l'Alliance,* Special Number of
    C.S., 1954, pp. 105–106, n. 21.
V, 20–21   Cf. I, 14–17; V, 12.
VI, 1   *The Anointed One:* Zadok, cf. II, 12.
VI, 2–11   Recalls how the Community was founded. Cf. I, 7 sq.; III, 12 sq.
VI, 3   *The well:* cf. III, 16.
VI, 3–4   *The well which the Princes . . . :* Numbers, XXI, 18. – Cf. my
    study *La figure de Moïse au tournant des deux Testaments* in *Moïse,
    l'Homme de l'Alliance,* pp. 81–82.
VI, 5   *The penitents of Israel:* cf. II, 5.
VI, 7   *Their fame:* the passage is unintelligible. Rabin: "and their fame
    was not rejected by the mouth of anyone."
    The Interpreter of Law: cf. VII, 18. – *M.D.,* VI, 6.
VI, 8   *He has made: Is.,* LIV, 16.

to the orders which the Master has given, [10] and in which they must
walk during all the time of iniquity, without this they shall not live
until the coming [11] of him who shall teach righteousness at the end
of time.

Rules to be Observed

All they that have entered into the Covenant [12] (vowing) to come
not into the sanctuary in order to kindle fire on its altar needlessly,
and have shut [13] the door about whom God has said: *Who amongst
you will shut the door?* and *You shall not kindle fire on My altar
[14] needlessly* — let them take care to act according to the exact interpretation of the Law which is fit during the time of wickedness,
to keep apart [15] from the children of perdition, to refrain by a vow,
an interdict, [16] or *qorban* from the impure riches of unrighteousness
not to rob the poor of His people, making of widows their spoil
[17] and murdering orphans; to distinguish between the pure and the
impure, and to teach the difference between [18] that which is holy
and that which is profane; to keep the Sabbath day according to its
exact interpretation, the feasts [19] and the fast day according to the
computation of the members of the new Covenant in the land of
Damascus; [20] to set aside the holy things as it is fit; to love each man

VI, 10–11   *Who shall teach righteousness (yôreh haṣṣedeq):* perhaps the
Messiah of Aaron.
VI, 11–VII, 6   The priests who left the Temple were to observe the ordi-
nances of the Covenant scrupulously if they wanted to share the Messianic
bliss.
VI, 11–14   Cf. *M.D.,* IX, 3–5.
VI, 13–14   *Mal.,* I, 10.
    Let them take care ('im lo' yišmerû): a form of pledge (cf. Joüon, § 165b),
as recognized by Lagrange.
VI, 15–16   *Children of perdition:* cf. XIII, 14. — *M.D.,* IX, 16–22; X, 19.
— *Jub.,* X, 3; XV, 26.
    Riches of unrighteousness: cf. VIII, 5; XIX, 17. — *Luke,* XVI, 9. — *Targum
of Is.,* V, 23.
    *By a vow, an interdict, or by the wealth of the sanctuary (banneder
ûbhaḥerem ûbhehôn hammiqdaš):* three forms of pledge. For an oath taken
on the "wealth of the sanctuary" cf. *Matth.,* XXIII, 16: "Whosoever shall
swear by the Temple, it is nothing; but whosoever shall swear by the gold of
the Temple, he is a debtor." Cf. S. Lieberman, *Greek in Jewish Palestine,*
New York, 1942, pp. 134–135.
VI, 18   Cf. *H.C.,* XI, 8. — *M.D.,* I, 14–15.
VI, 19   *The fast day (yôm hatta'anîth),* i.e., the day of Atonement. According to the computation (kemîna'): Other transcriptions give *bmš'.* The root
mnh (*mn'*) signifies "to count," "to calculate." A parallel may be found in
the adverbial locution *kemîn* (likewise, in the same way as). Rabin reads
kmṣt which means in Mishnaic Hebrew: "to arrive at a conclusion," "to hold
a legal opinion," and translates here: "according to the finding."
    The New Covenant: cf. XIX, 33–34; XX, 12. — *H.C.,* II, 3.
VI, 20   *To set aside the holy things:* Lev., XXII, 15.
    To love each man his brother: Lev., XIX, 18.

his brother ²¹ like himself; to support the poor, the needy and the stranger; to seek each man the well-being of
COLUMN VII   ¹ his brethren; not to sin through forbidden intercourse (with women); to refrain from lewdness ² as it is fit; *to reprove each man his brother* according to the commandment and to bear no rancor ³ from one day to the next; to keep away from all forms of impurity according to the rule; not to defile ⁴ the holy spirit within them, since God has set them apart, all they that walk ⁵ thus in a holy perfection, according to all the teachings of the Covenant of God,

are assured ⁶ of life for a thousand generations.

COLUMN XIX   ¹ are assured of life for thousands of generations, as is written: *He keepeth the Covenant and mercy* ² *with them that love Him and keep His commandments to a thousand generations* (*Deut.*, VII, 9).

Familial Law

If they dwell in camps according to the custom of the land, if they marry ⁷ and beget children — let them walk according to the rule ⁸ of the instructions, according to the rule of the Law as He has said: *Between a man and his wife, between a father* ⁹ *and his son.*

If they dwell in camps according to the custom ³ of the land, as it was from ancient times, if they marry according to the rule of the Law and beget children, ⁴ let them walk according to the Law, according to the rule of the instructions, according to the custom of the Law, ⁵ as He has said: *Between a man and his wife, between a father and his son.*

VII, 2   *To reprove* . . . : *Lev.*, XIX, 17. – *M.D.*, V, 24–VI, 1.
  To bear no rancor: Lev., XIX, 18. – *M.D.*, VII, 8; X, 20.
VII, 4   *The holy spirit:* cf. V, 11.
VII, 5   *Are assured* . . . : we possess, from now on, two versions which we present in adjacent columns.
VII, 5–6   Cf. XIV, 2.
VII, 6–9   The exiles' family life must conform to the Law, as well as to their own particular rules.
VII, 6   *According to the custom of the land:* the "sons of Zadok," it seems, had left the towns even before their secession and had settled in camps.
VII, 6–7   The passage proves beyond dispute that the exiles were married and had children.
VII, 8   *Between a man* . . . : *Numb.*, XXX, 17.
VII, 9–VIII, 1   When Ephraim separated from Judah, the unfaithful were put to death, whereas those who remained faithful found salvation through fleeing to the north, towards Damascus.

Chastisement of the Wicked — Reward of the Faithful

To all those that despise (them) shall God render the retribution of the wicked when He shall visit the land, [10] when the word shall be accomplished which is written in the prophet Isaiah son of Amoz, [11] who said: *There will come upon thee and upon thy people and upon thy father's house days that have* [12] *(not) come from the day that Ephraim departed from Judah.* When the two houses of Israel were divided, [13] and Ephraim turned away from Judah, all the unfaithful were given over to the sword but they that remained faithful [14] escaped to the land of the north, as He has said: *I shall transfer the 'sikkûth' of your king* [15] *and the 'Kiyyûn' of your images (beyond) the tents of Damascus.* The books of the Law are the tent (*sûkkath*) [16] of the King — as He has said: *I will raise up the tabernacle of David that is fallen.* The king [17] is the assembly; the *Kiyyûn* of the images are the books of the prophets [18] whose words Israel did despise. The Star is the Interpreter of the Law, [19] who came to the land of Damascus — as it is written: *A Star came out of Jacob and a sceptre* [20] *has risen*

To all those that despise the commandments [6] and the precepts, shall God render the retribution of the wicked when He shall visit the land, [7] when the word written by the prophet Zachariah shall be accomplished: *Awake O sword, against* [8] *my shepherd and against the man that is my fellow — saith God. Smite the shepherd and the sheep shall be scattered,* [9] *but I will turn my hand upon the little ones* (*Zach.,* XII, 7). They that have remained faithful unto Him are the poor of the flock. [10] They shall escape in the time of the visitation, while the remnant shall be given over to the sword when shall come the Messiah [11] of Aaron and Israel, as it happened in the time of the first visitation of which He said [12] by the hand of Ezekiel *to set a mark upon the foreheads of such as sigh and groan* (*Ezek.,* IX, 4), [13] while the remnant was delivered to the avenging sword of the Covenant.

VII, 11–12   *There will come . . .* : Is., VII, 17.

VII, 14–15   *I shall transfer . . .* : Am., V, 26. — This difficult passage could be translated as: "Ye shall bear *Sikkûth*, your king, and *Yiyyûn*, your idol, the star of your gods which ye made unto yourselves, and I shall cause ye to go into exile beyond Damascus" . . . The author of *D.D.* quotes an altered text and interprets it allegorically. For Davidic Messianism he had very little regard.

VII, 16   *I will raise up . . .* : Am., IX, 11.

VII, 18   *The Star:* an historical character and expounder of the Law. Cf. VI, 7.

VII, 19   *A star came forth . . .* : Numb., XXIV, 17.

VII, 20, 21   *He shall smite . . .* : Numb., XXIV, 17.

out of Israel. The sceptre is the prince of all the congregation; when he shall come he shall smite in pieces ²¹ all the sons of devastation. — Those others escaped at the time of the first visitation,

COLUMN VIII   ¹ but the faithless were delivered to the sword.

This shall be the lot of all members of His Covenant, ² who shall not be steadfast in these precepts: they shall be visited by destruction at the hand of Belial. This is the day ³ when God shall make His visitation. — *It is upon the princes of Judah over whom the wrath shall be poured out.* ⁴ For they hoped for healing, but He has crushed all the rebels because they did not forsake the way ⁵ of the traitors and have let themselves be led away into the paths of lewdness, towards wicked wealth, towards taking vengeance and bearing rancor ⁶ each man against his brother, and towards hating each man his neighbor; they have contracted forbidden marriages ⁷ and have come together to do shameful things. They have boasted of wealth and gain and each man has done that which seemed good in his own eyes. ⁸ Every man has chosen the stubbornness of his own heart and has not withdrawn from the people. They have let themselves walk high-handedly ⁹ in the way of the wicked of

This shall also be the lot of all members of His ¹⁴ Covenant who shall not pay heed to the malediction (that pertains) to the precepts: they shall be visited by the hand of Belial. ¹⁵ This is the day when God shall make His visitation, as He hath said: *The princes of Judah were like them that remove* ¹⁶ *the bound; upon them I shall pour out My wrath.* For they have entered into the Covenant of repentance, ¹⁷ but they have not forsaken the way of the traitors and have let themselves be led away into the paths of lewdness, towards wicked wealth, ¹⁸ towards taking vengeance and bearing rancor each man against his brother, and towards hating each man his neighbor. ¹⁹ They have contracted forbidden marriages and have come together to do shameless things. They have boasted of wealth and gain and ²⁰ each man has done that which seemed good in his own eyes. Every man has chosen the stubbornness of his own heart and has not withdrawn from the people ²¹ and their sins. They

VIII, 1–13   Those who, instead of holding fast to the observance of the rules, were led astray, brought thereby God's wrath upon themselves. Divine vengeance was executed by the Chief of the Kings of Yawan (i.e., the Hellenistic world).

VIII, 2   Cf. *M.D.*, II, 6.

VIII, 3   *The princes of Judah.: Hos.*, V, 10. This passage is abridged.

VIII, 4–9   Cf., III, 8, sq., 17; VI, 15–VII, 3.

whom God hath said: *Their wine is the venom of a dragon,* [10] *the mortal poison of a viper.* The dragons are the kings of the nations; their wine is [11] their conduct. The poison of a viper is the "chief" of the kings of Yawan come to wreak [12] vengeance upon them.

All this, "the builders of walls and those who daub them with plaster" did not understand, for [13] he who weighs the wind and spreads falsehood, spread (it) upon them, so that the wrath of God was kindled against all his congregation.

[14] And even as Moses has said: *Not for thy righteousness nor for the uprightness of thy heart dost thou go to possess* [15] *these nations, but because He loved thy fathers and because He would keep His oath:* [16] such is also the case with those among Israel that have repented, and forsaken the way of the people. Because of the love which God had for [17] the forefathers, who had called (upon the people) to follow Him, He has loved also them that came after them, for theirs [18] is the Covenant of the fathers.

have let themselves walk high-handedly in the ways of the wicked, of whom [22] God hath said: *Their wine is the venom of a dragon, the mortal poison of a viper.* The dragons are [23] the kings of the nations; their wine is their conduct; the poison of a viper is the "chief" [24] of the kings of Yawan come to wreak vengeance upon them.

All this, "the builders [25] of the walls and those who daub them with plaster" did not understand (because of) him who runs after the wind, weighs the storm and spreads [26] falsehood upon men, so that the wrath of God was kindled against all his congregation.

Even as Moses has said [27] unto Israel: *Not for thy righteousness nor for the uprightness of thy heart dost thou go to possess these nations,* [28] *but because He loved thy fathers and because He would keep (His) oath:* such is also [29] the case with those among Israel that have repented and forsaken the way of the people because of the love which God had for the forefathers, [30] who had encouraged the people to follow God; He has loved them also that came after them for theirs is [31] the Covenant of the fathers.

VIII, 9–10   *Their wine . . .* : cf. *Deut.,* XXXII, 33.
VIII, 11   *The chief*: a pun on *rôš* (poison *or* chief).
VIII, 12   *The builders . . .* : cf. IV, 19. — *Ezek.,* XIII, 10.
VIII, 13   *He who weighs . . .* : cf. I, 14. — *Mic.,* II, 11. — *H.C.,* II, 1; V, 11.
VIII, 14–18   Because of His love for the just men of the past, God granted to the Community His Covenant and the grace of a true doctrine.
VIII, 14–15   *Not for thy righteousness . . .* : *Deut.,* IX, 5 and VII, 8.
VIII, 18   *The builders*: cf. IV, 19.
VIII, 18–21   The "builders of the walls" merited the divine wrath which is the consequence of all those who disobey the commandments. Document A ends at VIII, 21. Its continuation will be found in Document B, XIX, 34.

Because of His hatred for the "builders of walls," His wrath has been kindled. [19] This also is how He acts toward all those who have despised the commandments of God: He has forsaken them and they have gone after the stubbornness of their hearts. [20] This is the word which Jeremiah said unto Baruch, the son of Neriah, and Elisha [21] unto his servant Gehazi.

He hates and abhors the "builders of walls" and His wrath has been kindled against them and against all those [32] that walk after them. This is also how He acts toward all those who have despised the commandments of God: [33] He has forsaken them and they have gone after the stubbornness of their hearts.

The Lot of the Traitors to the New Covenant

All the men that have entered into the New Covenant in the land of Damascus . . .

It is thus also with all men that have entered into the New Covenant in the land of Damascus . . .

who have turned back and have acted faithlessly, and have withdrawn from the well of living water: [35] they shall not be reckoned within the gathering of the people and shall not be written down on their roll from the day of the disappearance of COLUMN XX   [1] the Teacher of the Community until a Messiah shall rise out of Aaron and from Israel.

XIX, 33–XX, 1   This passage is only preserved in Document B.
　　The death of the Teacher of Righteousness inaugurated the ultimate period of world history which was to last down to Messianic times. During that period, The *People,* the true Israel, was to be found in the Community alone. Those who left it would be punished as traitors.
XIX, 34   The *well:* cf. III, 16.
XIX, 35   Cf. *M.D.,* III, 1; V, 11, 18.
　　The *disappearance (heʾaseph):* a term implying death. Cf. XX, 14. — *Num.,* XX, 26. — *Sir.,* VIII, 7; XL, 28. — *Num. Rabba,* XIV, 4.
XX, 1   The *Teacher of the Community* (cf. X, 14, 32). I read *môreh hayyahad* instead of *hayyahîd* (the Unique Teacher) of the transcriptions. For *yahad* (community), cf. *M.D., passim.* This correction is unavoidable when *D.D.,* XX, 31–32 is compared with *M.D.,* IX, 10–11. The word which is unknown in medieval Hebrew, was not understood by the copyist, who wrote *yahîd,* or more probably, *yihûd,* as Milik has lately observed (*R.B.,* 1953, p. 283). *Yihûd,* in medieval Hebrew, signifies "unity," the unity of God (cf. the New Year prayer, *Abhînû Malkenû,* in W. Staerk, *Altjüd. liturg. Gebete,* p. 29, line 29), and through metonymy, the true religion (cf. *Targ. of the Lamentations,* III, 28).
　　The *Messiah.* . . . : cf. XIX, 10–11.
XX, 1–17   The traitors are the members of the Community who abandoned the observance of the rule and were excommunicated. This section has many points in common with the *M.D.*

Such also is the case ²of those who have entered the congregation of the men of perfect holiness and who were loath to carry out the precepts of the just: ³he is the man that is melted in the furnace. When his deeds become manifest, let him be sent away from the congregation, ⁴like one whose lot had not been established in the midst of the disciples of God. Men of knowledge shall reprove him according to his faithlessness ⁵until the day when he shall stand again in the conclave of the men of perfect holiness. ⁶When his deeds become manifest according to the interpretation of the Law, in which walk ⁷the men of perfect holiness, let no man come to an agreement with him concerning property or work, ⁸for all the holy men of the Most High have cursed him. And this applies also to all those who have despised the first men ⁹and the lost men, who have concerned themselves with idols and have walked in the stubbornness ¹⁰of their hearts. They have no share in the House of the Law: in the same manner as their fellows who have turned back ¹¹with the men of mockery, they shall be judged. For they have spoken falsely concerning the righteous precepts and have despised ¹²the sure Covenant which has been established in the land of Damascus, which is the New Covenant. ¹³They and their families shall have no share in the House of the Law. From the day ¹⁴of the disappearance of the Teacher of the Community until the destruction of all the men of war who walked ¹⁵with the Man of Falsehood, it is about forty years. At that time will be kindled ¹⁶the wrath of God against Israel, as He has said: *There is neither king nor ruler*, nor judge, nor ¹⁷anybody to reprove in righteousness.

But the men of Jacob that repented their iniquity have kept the

---

XX, 2   *The men of perfect holiness:* cf. VII, 5; XX, 5, 7. — M.D., VIII, 20.
XX, 3   Cf. XX, 6, 25. — M.D., VIII, 16–19, 21–23.
XX, 4   *The lot:* cf. M.D., I, 10; II, 2; IV, 26; VI, 16, 18, 21; IX, 7.
    Shall reprove him: instead of the *yzkyrwwhw* found in the transcriptions, I here follow HABERMANN and RABIN's reading *yôkhîhûhû*. Cf. M.D., V, 24, 26; VI, 24.
XX, 5   Cf. M.D., VIII, 16–19.
XX, 6   *Interpretation of the Law:* cf. M.D., VIII, 15, 26; VI, 24.
XX, 7   *Let no one come to an agreement with him (ʾal yeʾôth ʾiš ʿimmô):* the *niphal* of *ʾwt* signifies "to agree, be in accord, rejoice." M.D. has *ʾal yithʿarebh* instead (cf. VIII, 23; IX, 8).
XX, 8–9   *The first men and the last men:* the members of the Old Covenant and those of the New.
XX, 8–10   Cf. M.D., II, 11–12.
XX, 10   *The House of the Law*, i.e., the Community (cf. XX, 13).
XX, 11   *The men of mockery:* cf. I, 14. *For they have spoken falsely . . . :* Cf. *Hymn*, IV, 12–13.
XX, 12   *The sure Covenant:* cf. VI, 19.
XX, 13   Cf. XX, 10.
XX, 13–14   Cf. XIX, 35–XX, 1.
XX, 15   *The Man of Falsehood:* cf. VIII, 13.
XX, 16–17   *There is neither king . . . :* Hos., III, 4. — Cf. Is., XI, 4.

Covenant of God. *Then one man shall say* [18] *to his fellow: "Let each man strengthen his brother* and turn their feet toward the way of God."* [19] *God has hearkened to their words; He has heard (them) and a book of remembrance has been written before Him for those that fear God and have regard* [20] *for His Name,* until salvation and righteousness shall be revealed to them that fear God. *Ye shall again discern between the righteous* [21] *and the wicked, between him that serveth God and him that serveth Him not. He shall show mercy a thousand times to them that love Him* [22] *and to those who remain faithful unto Him for a thousand generations.*

Those who went out from the House of discord — that is the Holy City — [23] and put their trust in God at the time when Israel trespassed and defiled the sanctuary, but who have turned again [24] toward the way of the people with wicked words, shall be judged each man according to his spirit, in His holy [25] council. All those among the members of the Covenant who will have opened a breach in the boundary of the Law, when [26] the glory of God will appear unto Israel, they shall be cut off from the midst of the camp, and with them, those that caused wickedness [27] in Judah in the days of its ordeal.

Repentance and Salvation

But all they that hold fast to these rules, inasmuch as they go out [28] and go in according to the Law, who shall have listened to the voice of the Teacher and confessed before God (saying): "We have sinned, [29] we have been wicked, both we and our fathers, by walking contrariwise against the precepts of the Covenant. [The righteousness] [30] and the truth of Thy judgments have overtaken us"; who

---

XX, 17–27   Israel's penitents, i.e., the Community, had separated themselves from the people in order to remain faithful to the Covenant. Whoever opens a breach in the traditions which protect the Law, will be held as guilty as the seducers of Israel.

XX, 17   *That repented . . . :* cf. II, 5.

XX, 17–18   *Then one man shall say . . . :* cf. *Mal.,* III, 18.

XX, 19–20   *Mal.,* III, 18.

XX, 20–22   *Ye shall discern . . . :* cf. *Mal.,* III, 18. — *Ex.,* XX, 6 and *Deut.,* VII, 9.

XX, 22–25   A difficult passage. According to the proposed interpretation, it seems to refer to the traitors of the Community after the exodus to Damascus.

XX, 22   *The House of discord (bêth pelegh):* the Holy City of Jerusalem, divided into several antagonistic factions.

XX, 23   *Again:* I read here *'ôd* with a *waw* added above the line.

XX, 24   *Toward the way . . . all those:* reading *'el derekh ha'am bidebharîm ra'îm kullam.* Cf. VIII, 16; XIX, 29.

XX, 25   *The boundary of the Law:* cf. I, 16. — *M.D.,* X, 10–11, 25.

XX, 26   *They shall be cut off . . . :* cf. *M.D.,* II, 16.

XX, 27–34   The true and persevering penitents who obey the Community regulations and embrace the teaching of the Teacher of Righteousness, will be granted God's forgiveness and partake of His salvation.

will not act high-handedly against His holy precepts, His righteous [31] judgments and His true testimonies, who will learn from the ancient decrees [32] according to which the members of the Community had walked, who will give ear to the voice of the Teacher of Righteousness and will not have spoken [33] against the righteous precepts when they shall have heard them — they shall rejoice and be glad, their heart shall be strengthened and they shall overcome [34] all the inhabitants of the universe. God shall forgive them and they shall witness His salvation, for they shall have taken refuge in His holy Name.

II. Laws and Customs of the Community

Pagan Courts of Justice

COLUMN IX   [1] Whosoever shall cause another to be delivered up to the justice of the nations, shall be put to death.

Vengeance

[2] As to that which He has said: *Thou shalt not avenge nor bear any grudge against the children of thy people,* — whosoever among the members [3] of the Covenant who shall bring an accusation against his neighbor without having reproved him before (two) witnesses, [4] shall accuse him out of anger or denounce him to his elders to make him contemptible — he avenges himself and bears a grudge. [5] But it is written: *He taketh vengeance on his adversaries*

XX, 28   *The vioce of the Teacher (qôl môreh):* the word "Teacher" has no article. It is employed in this connection as a proper name. Cf. M. A. Segal, *Gramm. of Mishnaic Hebr.,* § 378, p. 184.

XX, 28–30   *"We have sinned . . .":* cf. *M.D.,* I, 24–26.

XX, 30   *High-handedly:* cf. *M.D.,* V, 12; VIII, 17, 22; IX, 1.

XX, 30–32   Cf. III, 15; IV, 8. — *M.D.,* IX, 10–11.

XX, 32   *The members of the Community:* cf. XX, 1.

XX, 34   End of Document B. From this point the text is resumed in Document A.

IX–XVI   A legal document begins abruptly on page IX. It is possible that the lost portion of Document A contained the transition from the exhortation to this collection of laws and customs. Points in common with the *M.D.* are many.

IX, 1   It was forbidden to bring anyone before a pagan tribunal. Rabin, as a result of a correction inspired by *Lev.,* XXVII, 29, has reached a very different conclusion concerning this most difficult passage; i.e., that every man who had been condemned to death was to be handed over to the Gentiles.

IX, 2   *Thou shalt not take vengeance . . . : Lev.,* XIX, 18.

IX, 3   Cf. VII, 2. — *M.D.,* VI, 1.

IX, 4   Cf. *M.D.,* VIII, 8–9.

IX, 5   He taketh vengeance . . . : *Nah.,* I, 2. This certainly refers to God: cf. *M.D.,* X, 17–19.

and he reserveth wrath to his enemies. [6] If he keeps silent concerning him from one day to another, but accuses him out of anger, [7] he will accuse himself of a capital crime, because he did not observe the commandment of God who said unto him: [8] *Thou shalt surely reprove thy neighbor and not bear sin because of him.*

Concerning the Oath:

As to that which [9] He has said: *Thy hand shall not save thee —* whosoever shall cause another to swear an oath in the open field, [10] and not before the judges or at their decree, his own hand shall have saved him. (Concerning) anything that is lost, [11] without it being known who stole it from the property of the camp in which it has been stolen, let its owner pronounce [12] an oath of cursing — and anyone who shall hear it, if he knows and does not tell, will be guilty. [13] Anything acquired in an unlawful manner that should be returned, if there be no owner, let the man who returns it confess to the priest, [14] who shall take it for himself, beside the ram of atonement. Likewise anything lost which has been found and has no [15] owner, shall go to the priests, for he who finds it knows not to whom it belongs by right; [16] if there be no owners, the priests shall keep it.

Witnesses

If a man commits an offence [17] against the Law, and his neighbor, being alone, sees it, if it is a capital crime he shall make it known [18] in the (culprit's) presence, as a rebuke, to the Overseer. The

---

IX, 6–8   To avoid any suspicion of personal revenge, the culprit must be rebuked immediately.

IX, 8   *Rebuke thy brother . . .* : *Lev.,* XIX, 17.

IX, 9   *Thy hand . . . I Sam.,* XXV, 26.

IX, 10   I.e., he will have taken the law into his own hands.

IX, 12   *An oath of cursing: Numb.,* V, 21. Cf. *Lev.,* V, 1.

IX, 13–14   If the owner is unknown, the thief must hand the stolen article over to the priest.

IX, 14   *Beside . . .* : cf. *Numb.,* V, 8.

IX, 14–16   Anything found must be handed over to a priest, who will become its owner unless the loser makes himself known. The right of ownership by discovery does not figure in this code. Cf. on the other hand *Mishna-Baba Meṣi̧a,* I, 3–5; II, 1.

IX, 16–X, 3   If a capital crime was committed against the Law, three successive witnesses, each testifying to a different case, sufficed for the culprit to be condemned to death. If there were but two trustworthy witnesses, the guilty man was pronounced impure. In the case of an offence concerning property, the testimony of two consecutive witnesses brought condemnation, and the testimony of one witness, exclusion from purification. The witness in a capital lawsuit had to be of age, i.e., have appeared before the surveyors, and pious. The testimony of a man undergoing punishment himself could not be accepted.

IX, 18   *As a rebuke:* cf. IX, 3. The Overseer (*mebhaqqer*): cf. XIII, 3, 13; XIV, 8; XV, 8, 14. — *M.D.,* VI, 12, 20.

To his account (beyadhô): cf. *M.D.,* VI, 20.

Overseer shall write it down against him. If he do it [19] again before
one person, the latter will again inform the Overseer. If he repeats
the offence and is apprehended by [20] one person, his judgment is
ruled. If they be two, but testify [21] each man about a different matter, let the man be set apart from the purification only, provided
they (the witnesses) are reliable [22] and have reported him to the
Overseer on the same day that they have seen him (the culprit).
Concerning property let them accept two [23] reliable witnesses – if
there be only one – let him (the culprit) be set apart from purification. Let no witness be accepted
COLUMN X   [1] by the judges, to condemn to death by his testimony, unless he has attained the age of passing [2] before the surveyors, (and is) a God-fearing man. Let no man be considered [3] a
reliable witness, if he has transgressed high-handedly any commandment before his purification (which shall allow him) to return.

The Judges

[4] This is the rule for the judges of the congregation: up to ten men
selected [5] from the congregation according to (the rule) of the
time; four from the tribe of Levi and Aaron and six from Israel,
[6] instructed in the book of HHGW and the principles of the Cove-

IX, 21   Cf. X, 23. – *M.D.*, VI, 25; VII, 3, 16; VIII, 24.
IX, 22   Cf. IX, 6.
X, 1–2   *The age of passing before the surveyors:* cf. XV, 6. The age must
be about twenty. At the age of twenty-five, one might be appointed a judge:
cf. X, 7.
X, 3   *Before his purification . . . :* I here rectify *'ad zekhôthô* for *'d zkw.*
Cf. *M.D.*, VIII, 17–18.
X, 4–10   The tribunal was composed of ten judges, four priests and Levites
and six laymen; they had to be learned and not more than sixty years old.
The Community, apparently, did not credit old people with strong intel-
lectual capacity. The *M.D.* mentions a council of fifteen members, but this
was not a tribunal: cf. VIII, 1–4.
X, 4–5   *Men selected ('anasîm berûrîm):* cf. *Targum Ps. Jonathan* on *Deut.*,
I, 23 (*gubherîn berîrîn*).
    According (to the rule) of the time (bephî ha'eth): cf. *M.D.*, IX, 13.
X, 6   *The book of HHGW:* cf. XIII, 2; XIV, 7–8. The same book is mentioned in an unpublished text: cf. R. De Vaux, *R.B.*, 1950, p. 427. HHGW
has not, so far, received a satisfactory explanation. Levi suggested that it
might be a document named after its *incipit: hegû* (meditate); the Jews
named the books of the Law in this manner: e.g., *bereshîth* (Genesis). But
if so, why the article *he?* I cannot, for the same reason, accept the interpretation of Charles, who saw in it the name of Prophet Haggai with a *heth.* I
feel certain that it is neither a verb nor a proper name, but a common name
with its article. If we read *HHGW,* it might be translated as *The Meditation*
(*sepher he-hegî*). The verb *hgh* or *hg'* is chiefly used to signify meditation,
the study of the Bible. Cf. *Jerus. Talmud.* – *Meghilla,* IV, 74d. Rabin has
reached the same conclusion. HHGW would then be a commentary on the
Law, perhaps also of the Prophets. – Dupont-Sommer's interpretation (cf.
Nouveaux aperçus . . . p. 88, n. 9): *hegu* = a transcription of the Greek
ἡγούμενος (spiritual Leader) is far-fetched.

nant, from twenty-five [7] years old to sixty years old. And let no man [8] remain in office after the age of sixty to judge the congregation. For because of the faithlessness of man [9] his days have been shortened and in His wrath against the inhabitants of the earth, God has decided to remove [10] their understanding even before they have completed their days.

Concerning the purification with water:

Let no [11] man bathe in water that is dirty or whose quantity is less than a mar'îl (for) each one. [12] Let no man purify himself with water from a vessel; with water from a hole in the rock of which there is not the quantity of a [13] mar'îl; (with water) touched by one who is impure: these waters are as unclean as the water from a vessel.

[14] Concerning the Sabbath to observe it as it is fit:

Let no man on the sixth day do [15] any work from the time when the orb of the sun [16] is distant from the gate by its own fullness, for this is what He has said: Keep [17] the Sabbath day to sanctify it. Let no man on the Sabbath day speak [18] vain and empty words. Let him not lend anything to his neighbor. Let him not deal in property and gain. [19] Let him not speak about labor or work to be done on the morrow. [20] Let no man walk about in the fields carrying out the work which he has in mind. [21] Let no man walk about outside his town above one thousand cubits on the Sabbath day. [22] Let no man eat on the Sabbath day except that which has been prepared previously or of that which would be lost [23] in the fields. Let him not eat and let him not drink unless it be in the camp.

X, 9–10   Cf. *Jub.*, XXIII, 11: "All the generations which shall arise from that time (the time of Abraham) until the day of the great judgment, shall grow old quickly, and their knowledge shall forsake them by reason of their old age."

X, 10–13   Both the quality and quantity of the water used for ablution rites were fixed.

X, 11   *Less than the quantity of a mar'îl:* the *mar'îl* or *marhîl* was a measure of capacity, according to S. LIEBERMANN, *Greek in Jewish Palestine,* p. 135, n. 151.

X, 14–XII, 1   The regulations figuring in this section have, for their greater part, a parallel in the Bible as well as in Rabbinic literature.

(For) each one: (le) 'îš. The *lamed* is dropped through haplography.

X, 14–16   The Sabbatical repose commences when the disk of the sun touches the horizon (LAGRANGE). For the *gate of the sun* cf. *M.D.*, X, 3.

X, 16–17   *Keep the Sabbath Day* . . . : *Deut.*, V, 12.

X, 17–18   *Vain and empty words:* cf. *M.D.*, VII, 9; X, 22, 24. — *Talmud bab.* — *Shabbath,* 150a.

X, 18   *Let him not lend anything:* cf. *Deut.*, XV, 2; XXIV, 10.

X, 19   *The morrow (lemaškêm):* cf. *Mishna-Bikkurîm,* III, 2. — S. LIEBERMANN, *loc. cit.*

X, 21   Cf. XI, 6 (concerning two thousands cubits). — *Mishna-'Erubhîn,* IV, 3; V, 7.

X, 22–23   Cf. *Mishna-Beṣa,* I, 2. — *Jub.,* II, 29–30; L, 9.

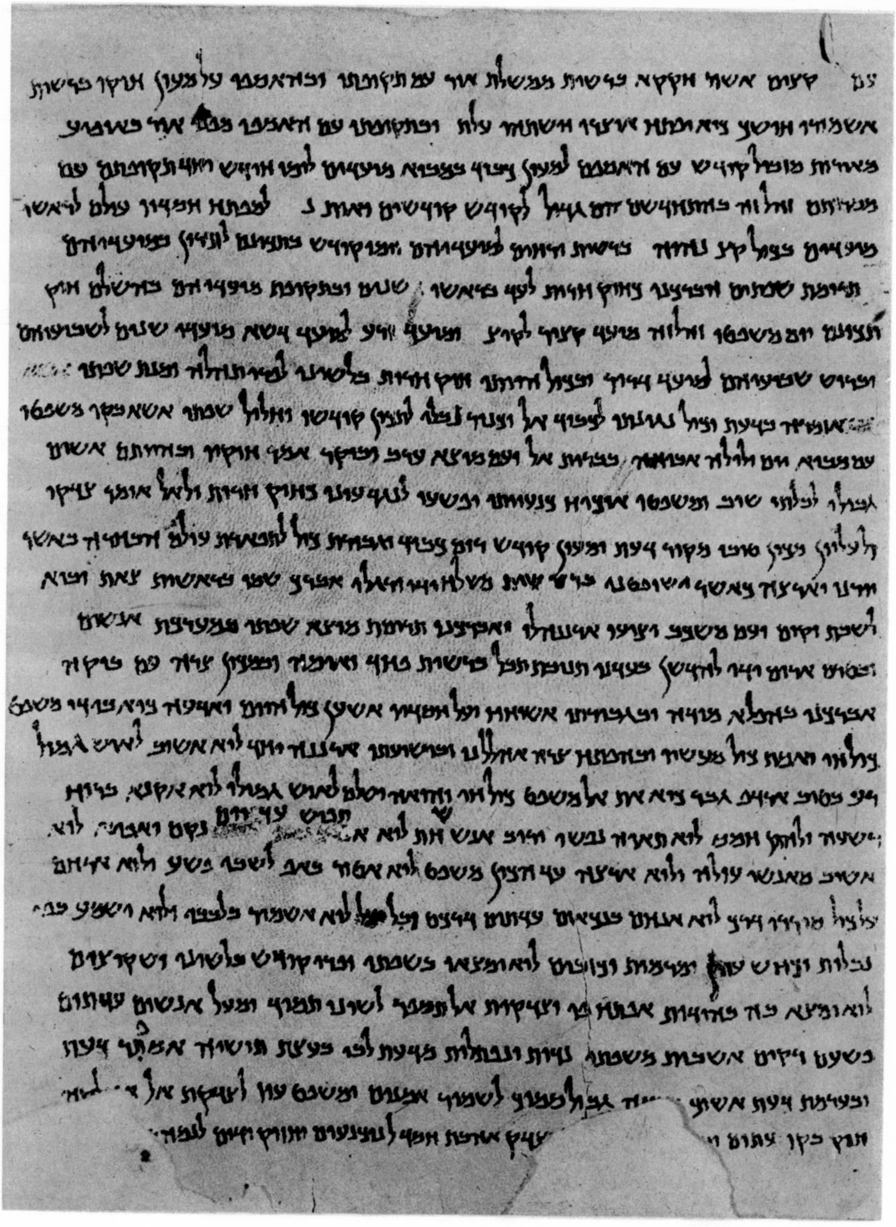

(Cliché American Schools of Oriental Research)

8. — The *Manual of Discipline* Scroll, column X.

COLUMN XI   [1] Whilst traveling, if he goes down to wash, let him drink as long as he stands there, but let him not draw water into [2] any vessel. Let him not send the son of a stranger to do that which he requires on the Sabbath day. [3] Let no man put upon himself dirty clothes or such as have been worn by another man, unless [4] they have been washed in water or rubbed with frankincense. Let no man mingle voluntarily (with strangers) [5] on the Sabbath. Let no man go after cattle to pasture them outside his town farther than [6] two thousand cubits. Let him not raise his hand to strike it with his fist. If (the beast) [7] is unruly, let him not take it out of his house. Let no man take anything out which is inside the house, [8] nor bring anything in which is outside. If he is in the tent, let him not take anything out of it [9] nor bring anything into it. Let him not open a pitch (sealed) vessel on the Sabbath. Let no man carry [10] upon himself perfumes when he walks about on the Sabbath. Let no man move, in a dwelling house, [11] either stone or dust. Let the father not carry his nursling to walk about on the Sabbath. [12] Let no man give orders to his servant or his maidservant or his hired laborer on the Sabbath. [13] Let no man assist a beast to drop its young on the Sabbath day. If it falls into a cistern [14] or into a well, let him not pull it out on the Sabbath. Let no man celebrate the Sabbath in the neighborhood [15] of gentiles. Let no man profane the Sabbath for the sake of property and gain. [16] If any human person falls into a place (full) of water or into a "cistern" on the Sabbath, [17] let no man pull him out with a ladder, or a rope, or any object. Let no man offer on the altar on the Sabbath [18] except the burnt offering of the Sabbath, for thus it is written: *apart from your Sabbath offerings.*

XI, 1–2   Cf. *Jub.*, L, 8.

XI, 3   *Worn by another man (baggew):* by the body (HABERMANN).

XI, 4   *Let no man mingle ('al yith'arebh 'iš):* in the *M.D.*, the *hithpaël* of *'rb* means "to mix, to be in contact with."

XI, 6   Cf. X, 21.

XI, 7   *Let no man take anything out:* cf. *Jub.*, II, 30. — *Mishna-Shabbath,* I, 1; VII, 2.

XI, 8   *If he is in the tent:* during the Feast of Tabernacles. Cf. *Mishna-Sukkah,* III, 12–15. It was permitted, however, to carry a *lulabh* (a palm branch).

XI, 10   *Perfumes:* cf. *Mishna-Shabbath,* XVIII, 3; XXI, 1.

XI, 11   Prohibiting the carrying of a *nursling:* cf. on the other hand, *Mishna-Shabbath,* XVIII, 3; XXII, 1.

XI, 13   Cf. *Mishna-Shabbath,* XVIII, 3.

XI, 13–14   Cf. *Talmud bab.* — *Shabbath,* 128b. — *Matth.,* XII, 11. — *Mishna-Besa,* III, 4.

XI, 14–15   The same prohibition is found among the Samaritans and the Karaites (SCHECHTER).

XI, 15   Cf. *Neh.,* XIII, 15–18.

XI, 16–17   Prohibiting the use of any instrument of rescue. The *Talmud bab.* — *Yoma,* 84b permits the use of a net or of a ladder for the rescue of a child fallen into the sea or into a pit.

XI, 18   *Apart from your Sabbath-offerings:* cf. *Lev.,* XXIII, 38. — The real meaning of the Biblical passage is quite different: on feast days, specific

Profanation of the Sanctuary

Let no man send [19] to the altar a burnt offering, or an offering, or frankincense or wood by the hand of a man impure with one [20] of the impurities, thus allowing him to defile the altar, for it is written: *The sacrifice* [21] *of the wicked is an abomination, but the prayer of the righteous is an offering of delight.* All those who enter [22] into the House of obeisance, let them not enter in a state of impurity, (even though) washed. When the trumpets of the assembly [23] shall sound, whether they be early or late, let them not interrupt the whole service: it is a holy service.

COLUMN XII   [1] Let no man lie with a woman in the city of the sanctuary in order not to defile [2] the city of the sanctuary by his impurity.

Persons Possessed

Whosoever shall be under the dominion of the spirits of Belial [3] and shall proffer words of rebellion, shall be judged according to the law relating to magicians and soothsayers.

The Sin of Inadvertence

[4] Every man who, through error, shall profane the Sabbaths or the feasts, shall not be put to death; nevertheless men shall be charged [5] to watch him. If he makes amends, let him be watched during seven years; [6] let him then (re)turn into the assembly.

Relations with the Gentiles

Let no man put forth his hand to shed the blood of a Gentile [7] for the sake of property and gain. Also let no man carry off anything of

---

sacrifices had to be offered, independently of the Sabbatical sacrifices, the gifts, vows, etc.

XI, 18–XII, 2   The sanctuary must not be defiled either by entering it in a state of impurity oneself, or by employing any other person in a state of impurity to make offering there. Marital intercourse was therefore forbidden in the Temple city, so that any such defilement was impossible.

XI, 20–21   *The sacrifice of the wicked . . . :* cf. *Prov.,* XV, 8.

XI, 22   *The House of obeisance,* i.e., the Temple. According to *Mishna-Sheqalîm,* VI, 1, 3, thirteen obeisances were made in the Temple: four towards the north, four towards the south, three towards the east, and two towards the west.

XI, 22–23   The exact meaning of this rule escapes me.

XII, 1   Cf. V, 6–7.

XII, 2   *Whosoever shall be under the dominion of the spirits of Belial:* cf. *M.D.,* 1, 18, 24; II, 19; X, 11.

XII, 3   Cf. *Lev.,* XX, 27. — *Deut.,* XVIII, 11: the death penalty.

XII, 3–6   Cf. *M.D.,* VIII, 24–IX, 2. The length of the period of probation is not the same in the two documents: seven years and two years respectively.

their property in order that they may not [8] blaspheme, unless it be decided upon by the congregation of Israel. Let no man sell pure beasts [9] or birds to the Gentiles, in order that they may not sacrifice them. Let no man sell to them anything from his granary [10] or from his wine press, at whatever price. Let no man sell to them his slave or his maidservant [11] who have entered with him into the Covenant of Abraham.

Purity

Let no man defile himself [12] by eating any wild beast or reptile from beehives to all living [13] beings that move in water. And let them not eat fish unless they have been split [14] while alive and their blood poured away. All the locusts in their various kinds shall be put into fire or water [15] while they are alive, for this is the manner of their creation.

All wood and stone [16] and dust contaminated by the impurity of a man, [17] shall contaminate him who shall touch them. Every nail or peg in the wall [18] of a house where lies a dead man shall contract the impurity of a manufactured object.

The Rules

[19] This is the constitutive rule for the cities of Israel concerning the statutes, so as to distinguish between [20] the pure and the impure, and to make known the (difference) between that which is holy and that which is profane.

These are the precepts [21] for the teacher in which he shall walk with every living being according to the rule proper to every age. According to this rule [22] shall all the posterity of Israel walk, and they shall not be cursed.

XII, 8–9   Cf. *Mishna-'Aboda Zara,* I, 5–6.

XII, 10–11   Cf. *Ex.,* XXI, 8.

XII, 11–13   *Reptile:* the author had in mind any small insects which might be swallowed through inadvertence with honey or liquids. Rabbi Judah (Second century) considered anyone who filtered wine and vinegar as a heretic. Cf. *Tosephta-Terumoth,* VII, 11 as S. LIEBERMAN has indicated in *Proceedings of the American Academy of Jewish Research,* vol. XX, 1951, pp. 396–398.

XII, 14   *Their blood poured away:* cf. *Pirqe R. Eliezer,* chap. IX.

XII, 14–15   Cf. *Talmud bab.-Ḥullin,* 27b.

XII, 15–18   Cf. *Mishna-Kelim,* VI, 1; XII, 5. Our document is stricter than the *Mishna.*

XII, 19–22   After the laws concerning the Sabbath and purity come the regulations governing communal life and the organization of the group.

XII, 19–20   This sentence is both the conclusion of the preceding section and the beginning of a new one, that of the rules (*serakhîm*): cf. XII, 22; XIII, 7; XIV, 3–12. — *M.D.,* I, 1; V, 1; VI, 8, etc.

XII, 20–21   Cf. *M.D.,* IX, 12.

The Organization of the Camps

This is the constitutive rule for [23] the camps, according to which they shall walk during the time of wickedness until there shall arise the Messiah of Aaron

COLUMN XIII   [1] and Israel, a rule that shall be applicable to ten men as the minimum, to the thousands and hundreds and fifties [2] and tens.

Wheresoever there be ten men, let there never be absent a priest instructed in the book of HHGW; [3] all shall be ruled by his word. If he is not expert in all these things and a man of the Levites is expert [4] in these things, the fate concerning the proceedings of the members of the camp shall be established according to his word. If [5] the law concerning leprosy must be applied to any man, then the priest shall come and shall stand in the camp; [6] the Overseer shall instruct him in the exact meaning of the Law. Even if he (the priest) is a fool, it is he who shall lock him up, for theirs is [7] the right.

The Task of the Overseer

This is the rule for the camp Overseer: he shall instruct the Great Ones in the works [8] of God and instruct them concerning the wonders of His might; he shall recount before them the events of former times in all their "detail." [9] He shall love them as a father loves his sons, and shall carry (the burden of) their anguish as does a shepherd for his flock. [10] He shall untie all the knots of their bonds so that there shall be none oppressed or broken in his congregation.

[11] Whosoever shall join his congregation, let him examine him concerning his deeds, his understanding, his ability, his strength,

---

XII, 23–XIII, 1   Cf. XIV, 19; XX, 10–11; XX, 1. — *M.D.*, IX, 11.

XIII, 2–7   Each group must normally be governed by a learned priest. If there was no such priest a Levite could take his place. The right to apply the law of leprosy, however, belonged to the priests alone.

XIII, 2   Cf. *M.D.*, VI, 3–4 — Rost's transcription is inaccurate; the word should be read as *wbmqwm*.

A *priest*: literally a "man priest," — "*Dominus sacerdos.*" Cf. *Mishna-Yoma*, I, 3–5.

The *book of HHGW*: cf. X, 6.

XIII, 4   The *fate* . . . : cf. XX, 4.

XIII, 6   Cf. *Mishna-Nega'im*, III, 1, — *Hos.*, V, 1.

XIII, 7–16   The Overseer was both the teacher and the shepherd. On him depended the admission of new members. His authorization was also required in financial transactions.

XIII, 7   The *Great Ones*: cf. *M.D.*, VI, 1.

XIII, 8   Cf. *M.D.*, I, 21.

XIII, 9   Cf. *Is.*, XL, 11.

XIII, 10   Cf. *Is.*, LVIII, 6.

XIII, 11   Cf. *M.D.*, VI, 13–14; I, 11–12; III, 2.

courage, and his property. [12] They shall write him down, according to his integrity, in his place in the destiny of light. Let no man claim the right [13] among the members of the camp, to bring any man into the congregation without the permission of the camp Overseer. [14] Let no man of the members of the Covenant of God take anything from a son of perdition, nor give anything unto him unless [15] from hand to hand. Let no man do any buying or selling without having told [16] the Overseer in the camp, let him (then) settle his agreement.

Let not . . . . God [17] . . . .
. . . . and thus to the plot of land he . . . .
[18] . . . . they have humiliated him. For the sake of sin let him not bear rancor unto them . . . .
[19] . . . . and he who is not tied
[20] This is the dwelling of the camp. All . . . .
[21] . . . . they shall not succeed in dwelling in the land . . . . [22] . . . .
to the teacher . . . . . [23] . . . .
COLUMN XIV   [1] *that have not come from the day that Ephraim departed from Judah.* To all those who walk thus [2] the Covenant of God stands fast with them so as to save them from all snares of the pit, for (their prayers) will be granted at once.

The Laws of Precedence

[3] The constitutive rule for all the camps. They shall all be numbered by name: the priests first, [4] the Levites second, the children of Israel third, the proselyte fourth. They shall be written down by name [5] each man after his brother: the priests first, the Levites second, the children of Israel [6] third, the proselyte fourth. In this order shall they sit and shall they question concerning every affair.

XIII, 12   Cf. *M.D.*, VI, 22; V, 23, etc.
     The destiny of light: I read *gôral ha'ôr.* Cf. *M.D.*, IV, 7–8. RABIN: "lot of truth" (*gôral ha'emeth*).
XIII, 13   *Without the permission:* reading *zûlath pî.*
XIII, 14–15   Prohibiting the exchange of gifts with one not belonging to the Community. Cf. *M.D.*, V, 16–17.
     Children of perdition: cf. VI, 15.
XIII, 15–16   The Overseer's leave was requested before conducting business of any kind. The passage has been reconstructed by HABERMANN.
XIII, 16–23   The passage is badly damaged; only fragments of the sentences can be deciphered. Line 23, which is completely missing, begins with a quotation from *Is.*, VII, 17: "The Lord shall bring upon thee, and upon thy people, and upon thy father's house, . . ." Cf. VII, 11. The end of the quotation is found on the following line. — RABIN puts forward a tentative reconstruction of lines 20–23.
XIV, 1–2   Cf. VII, 4–5.
     All snares of the pit: cf. *Hymn*, I, 2.
XIV, 3–6   Concerning the numbering of the members and the establishing of their rank.
XIV, 3–6   Cf. XII, 12. — *M.D.*, II, 19–22; VI, 8–10.

The Overseers

The priests that shall inspect [7] the Great Ones shall be from thirty to sixty years old, instructed in the book [8] of HHGW and in all the decrees of the Law to direct the congregation according to the decrees which concern it. The Overseer [9] in charge of all the camps shall be from thirty to fifty years old; he shall be master [10] of all the secrets of men and of all tongues according to their number. According to his word shall all the members of the congregation come [11] each man in his rank. If a man wish to speak of any matter, let him speak of it to the Overseer [12] with regard to all litigation or judgment.

The Common Purse

This is the rule for the Great Ones for the provision of all their needs: [13] they shall give the wages of two days in every month (according to the rule) to the Overseer and to the judges. [14] From it they shall take for their (lucrative) transactions and they shall support with it the poor and the needy; the old man who [15] . . . . ; the man who is stricken (with leprosy) and he that has been taken prisoner by a foreign people; the virgin [who [16] has no] redeemer and the [orphan] of whom no one takes care.

All the work of their hands and not . . . . . . [17] . . . .
. . . . This is the constitutive statement . . . .
. . . . [18] . . . . God. This is the interpretation of the decrees according to which [they shall walk during the age [19] of wickedness, until there shall arise the Mess]iah of Aaron and of Israel. He shall forgive their sin . . . .
[20] . . . . [whosoever shall de]ceive wittingly concerning money . . . .
[21] . . . . he shall be punished for six days. Whoever speaks . . . .
[22] . . . . unjustly . . . . [23] . . . .

XIV, 8   The book of *HHGW*: cf. X, 6.
XIV, 10   *According to their number*: reading *lemisperêha* with HABERMANN. RABIN: *lemišpehôtham* (according to their families).
XIV, 11   *Each man in his rank* (*'iš bethorô*): cf. *M.D.*, VI, 11.
XIV, 11–12   The matter to be discussed was to be previously approved: cf. *M.D.*, VI, 11–12.
XIV, 12–16   Common ownership of property was applied only in part. A part of the members' revenues was set aside to be handed over to the Overseer, the judges, and to the needy.
XIV, 14   *For their lucrative (transactions)*: reading *be'adhh[bish]'am.*
XIV, 17–20   The text is damaged. It is probably the end of the section.
XIV, 19   Cf. XIX, 10–11.
XIV, 20–23   A small penal code to be compared with *M.D.*, VI, 24–VII, 25.
XIV, 20   *Whosoever shall deceive* . . . : cf. *M.D.*, VI, 24–25.

The Oath of the Covenant

COLUMN XV   ¹ [He shall not swe]ar by *Aleph* and *Lamed,* or by *Aleph* and *Daleth,* but with the oath of the Covenant, ² by the curses of the Covenant. Let him not mention the Law of Moses, for in it . . . . ³ If he swears and then transgresses, he will profane the Name. If he does so by the curses of the Covenant, [he will be brought before] ⁴ the judges. If he has transgressed, he is guilty; but if he confesses and makes restitution, he will not bring upon himself the charge of ⁵ a capital [crime]. Whosoever enters into the Covenant of all Israel, according to the eternal precept, with his sons, when they attain ⁶ the age of presentation before the surveyors, he will cause them to take the oath of the Covenant. This is ⁷ the decree during the whole period of wickedness for all those who turn from their corrupt ways. On the day that he shall speak ⁸ to the Overseer of the Great Ones, the oath of the Covenant shall be imposed upon him, the Covenant which Moses ⁹ established with Israel, the Covenant to return to the Law of Moses with an whole heart and ¹⁰ an whole soul, to that which is found therein to be observed during the period [of wickedness]. Let no man make known to him ¹¹ the decrees before he has presented himself to the surveyor, lest he be led astray while learning them. ¹² But when he will have pledged himself to return to the Law of Moses with all his heart and all his soul, ¹³ if he betray it let (all) withdraw from him.

All that is revealed in the Law concerning litigations ¹⁴ [and the judgments] . . . . if he bears testimony against him, the Overseer . . . . him . . . . and will command him and . . . .

XV, 1–13   The manner of taking an oath was carefully regulated. It seems that the Community was opposed to swearing. The only oath they appreciated was the one by which members pledged themselves to be converted to the Law of Moses.

XV, 1   *Aleph and Lamed:* '*elohîm* (God). *Aleph and Daleth:* '*adônaî* (Lord). Cf. *Tosephta-Berakhôth,* VII, 6, quoted by S. LIEBERMANN, *art. cit.,* pp. 395–396, 400–401.

XV, 2–3   Cf. I, 17. — M.D., V, 8; II, 4–17.

The Law of Moses, for in it: HABERMANN completes it thus: "he explains the Name" (*Ex.,* III, 14).

XV, 3   *(He will be brought before):* wehûbha' 'el (HABERMANN).

XV, 5–6   This concerns a man whose children were under age at the time of his joining the Covenant. They were to take their oath on reaching the age of enlistment.

XV, 7–13   Cf. M.D., V, 7–13.

XV, 10   Cf. M.D., IX, 20.

XV, 10–11   Cf. M.D., IX, 17.

XV, 13   *If he betray it let (all) withdraw from him:* [reḥeq]îm [hem] mimmennû 'im y[im]'al.

All that is . . . : cf. M.D., VIII, 1–2.

15 . . . . according to his knowledge: "I have been a fool and a madman." Every simpleton . . . .
16 . . . . and faint-hearted . . . .
until . . . . 17-20 . . . .
COLUMN XVI   ¹ with you a Covenant and with all Israel. Therefore let every man pledge himself to return to ² the Law of Moses, for in it all things are most carefully ordered.

The Calendar

The determination of their times concerning the blindness ³ of Israel in this (domain), behold it is minutely ordered in the "Book of the Divisions of Times ⁴ according to their jubilees and weeks." On the day that any man shall pledge himself to return ⁵ to the Law of Moses, the Angel of Hostility will depart from him, for as long as he will keep his word. ⁶ For this reason Abraham circumcised himself on the same day that he knew it.

Keeping and Annulling an Oath

And as for what which He has said: *That which is come out of thy lips ⁷ thou shalt observe*, every binding oath with which a man will have pledged himself ⁸ to carry out a prescription of the Law, let him not redeem himself even at the price of death. Every (oath) by which ⁹ a man has pledged himself to depart from the Law, let him not carry it out even at the price of death.

¹⁰ Concerning the oath of a woman to whom her husband has commanded to annul her oath:

¹¹ Let no husband annul an oath which does not cause her to be wicked . . . . it is to be observed. If it has to be annulled —
¹² if it is such as to lead to transgression of the Covenant — let the husband annul it, it is not to be observed. Likewise is the right of the father (of the woman).

XV, 15   *I have been a fool:* I complete *hayyîthî 'awîl.*
XVI, 1–6   One must return to the Law of Moses and respect the times according to their authentic computation.
XVI, 3   *The "Book of the Divisions . . . ,"* i.e., the *Book of Jubilees.* In the Prologue of this book, it says: "This is the history of the division of the days . . . of the events of the years, of their weeks, of their Jubilees, throughout all the years of the world . . ."
XVI, 5   *The Angel of Hostility (mal'akh hammaśṭemah):* cf. *M.D.,* III, 21–23. — *War,* XII, 8.
XVI, 6   When he learnt that the sign of the Covenant would rescue him from every infernal power. Cf. *Jub.,* XV, 31–32.
XVI, 6–7   On the obligation of keeping oaths.
XVI, 6–7   *That which is come out . . . Deut.,* XXIII, 24.
XVI, 10–12   *Numb.,* XXX, 6–9, authorizes the husband or father of a woman to annul her vows. This right is restricted here only to oaths which might tend towards a transgression of the Covenant.

¹³ Concerning the rules relative to voluntary offerings:

Let no man offer on the altar anything which has been stolen nor ¹⁴ shall the priests accept it from Israel. Let no man vow the food ¹⁵ of his house to God, because of that is what He has said: *Man hunts his servant with an anathema.*

Let him not ¹⁶ vow it without . . . .
. . . . his property, ¹⁷ he shall sanctify . . . . shall be punished ¹⁸ whosoever offers . . . . ¹⁹ of the judge . . . .
20-23 . . . .

XVI, 13–15   Prohibiting the offering of stolen goods, or of food needed by the offerer's family.

XVI, 14–15   Cf. *Mark*, VII, 11 (*Qorban*).

XVI, 15   *Man hunts . . . :* cf. *Mic.*, VII, 2. Micah employs the word *ḥerem* as signifying "net," here it means "anathema."

XVI, 16–23   A damaged passage.

THANKSGIVING HYMNS

HYMN I

(*M.G.*, II, plate VII — *Oṣar M.G.*, plate 36, 20–30)

[1] I will extol Thee, O Lord, because Thou hast bound me in the
bundle of life

[2] and hast sheltered me (through Thy protection) from all the
snares of the pit.

Men of violence have threatened my life, whilst I relied upon
[3] Thy Covenant.

For they, a gang of deceit, a company of Belial, know not that my
rank comes from Thee,
[4] and that in Thy goodness, Thou wilt save me, since Thou Thyself
dost direct my steps.

They assail me with Thy leave [5] that Thou mayest manifest Thyself
in glory through the condemnation of the wicked
and show Thy might in my favor before the children [6] of men:
for my assurance (springs) from Thy mercy.

I, 1   The Hymns begin with the word: "I extol Thee, Lord" . . . (*'ôdekhah
'Adonaî*); thence they are called *Thanksgiving Hymns* (or *Psalms*): *Hôdayôth*
(SUKENIK).
The bundle of life: cf. I Sam., XXV, 29.
I, 2   It may also be translated: "among those who relied on Thy Covenant."
The snares of the pit: cf. D.D., XIV, 1–2.
I, 6   A description of a war which develops into an apocalyptical vision.
Surrounded: reading *sobhebhîm;* others read this word as *sabhabhûnî*
(they surrounded me).

I said: "Valiant men have set up their camp against me,
surrounded by all [7] their implements of war.
They have shot their arrows unceasingly;
the flame of their spears was as a fire that devours the trees;
[8] as the roar of many waters, the clamor of their cries;
a devastating storm to destroy a multitude of men.
[9] Naught and nothingness spring even to the stars, when their
waves rise up."
And I, even when my heart melted like water, have persevered in
Thy Covenant.
[10] They have laid for me a trap: may their feet be taken therein!
They have set a snare for me: and have fallen themselves therein!
My foot has stayed in the righteous path: [11] (in) the assembly
shall I bless Thy name.

Hymn II

(M.G., II, plate VII – Oṣar M.G., plate 36, 31–39)

[12] I extol Thee, O Lord, because [Thou hast set] Thine eye upon me,
Thou hast shielded me from the rage of the liemongers,
[13] and from the company of those who seek to lead me astray.
Thou hast saved the life of him who is poor when they sought to
put to death
[14] shedding his blood because of Thy service.
But they knew not that my steps (were directed) by Thee.

They have exposed me to shame [15] and derision by the mouth of
all those who were seeking deceit.
But Thou, my God, hast succoured him who is wretched and poor
[16] against one that is stronger than he.
Thou hast delivered me from the hands of the mighty,
and by their insults Thou hast not disheartened me

I, 9   A very difficult passage, and the translation is conjectural. For *maz-zûrôth* (stars), cf. *Job*, XXXVIII, 32, and *II Kings*, XXIII, 5. The vocalization is confirmed by Greek transcriptions (Septuagint and Theodotion): μαζουρωθ (M.T.: *mazzarôth*).

I, 10   Accepting Sukenik's slight correction. Otherwise the sentence would read "away from their assembly" (presumably the assembly of the wicked). Cf. *Ps.*, XXVI, 12.

II, 12   Hymns I and II are found in the same column in the manuscript. The numbering of lines, therefore, is continued.

The psalmist is persecuted because of his attachment to the Covenant of God. His was a doctrinal struggle against enemies who sought to impose "deceit," "seduction" and "folly." Cf. IV, 3–4, 6, 13. — *I Enoch*, XCIV, 5; XCIX, 2, 14; CIV, 10.

[*Thou hast set*] *Thine eye upon me: a[ṣithah]* 'ênekhah 'al naphši. Cf. the Septuagint, Aquila and Theodotion in *Prov.*, XVI, 30 (στηριζεῖν). See also the Versions for *Ps.*, XXXII, 8 (for instance Vulg.: *firmabo super te oculos meos*).

[17] so that I might abandon Thy service through fear of the malice
of wickedness;
and barter my steadfast heart for folly. . . .

Hymn III

(*M.G.*, II, plate VIII — *Oṣar M.G.*, plate 37, 19–36)

[1] . . . .
[2] I extol Thee, O Lord, because Thou hast saved me from the pit,
[3] and from the hell of Abaddon hast Thou raised me up unto the
eternal heights.

And I walk in the righteous and boundless path and I know
that there remains hope for him [4] whom Thou hast shaped from
clay, that he may join the eternal assembly.
Thou hast cleansed from the perverse spirit a multitude of sins
that it may keep watch with [5] the army of the saints,
and that it may come together with the assembly of the sons of
heaven.
Thou hast allotted to each man an eternal destiny with the spirits
[6] of knowledge
to praise Thy name with them in jubilation and to recount Thy
marvels regarding all Thy works.

[7] And I, a vessel of clay, what am I?
Kneaded in water, what is my value and my strength?

II, 18–20   The end of the Hymn is badly damaged; all we can read is:
" [18] . . . commandments and they have been written as a testimony in order
to make known [19] . . . to all his descendants [20] . . . . . in Thy disciples."
III, 1   The first line found on the present plate is the last line of Hymn VI.
Cf. *infra*, p. 196.
III, 3   *Abhaddón* (perdition), signifies — as does the "pit" — the lowest
part of the infernal regions: *Apoc.*, XX, 1–5. — *Ascens. of Is.*, X, 8. *The
eternal height*, i.e., heaven. The same word is found in the ancient Jewish
prayer *Yôṣer*: Cf. W. Staerk, *Altjüdische liturgische Gebete, Kleine Texte 58*
(published by H. Lietzmann), Berlin, 1930, p. 5, line 6.
III, 4–6   In addition to the promise of an *eternal destiny*, the member of
the Community was united to a *spirit of knowledge* or "spirit of truth," which
would lead him into the "ways of truth": cf. *M.D.*, 19–20; IV, 2–8, 24–25.
Cf. also *I Enoch*, XXXVII, 4.
    That he may join the eternal assembly, i.e., predestinated. For the purifica-
tion of the spirit, see *M.D.*, III, 6–9; IV, 20–23. *The army of the saints* and
the assembly of the sons of heaven, i.e., the heavenly spirits. Cf. *I Enoch*,
CI, 1.
III, 7   No man is worthy of salvation: before he was called by God, his destiny was bound with that of the wicked, and subject to a thousand trials. We
find here a magnificent description of the torments of the wicked, culminating in their destruction by fire.
    The realm of wickedness: probably the earthly kingdoms of the wicked,
where the psalmist lived before joining the Community.

For I stood in the realm of wickedness [8] and my lot was with the damned.

The soul of the poor one passed, like a stranger, amidst great tribulations

and miseries of torment (accompanied) my steps:

[9] When all the snares of the pit were opened, and the traps of wickedness were set up,

and the nets of the damned upon the waters;

[10] When all the arrows of the pit flew irrevocably,

and struck, leaving no hope.

When the cord fell down upon the "condemned,"

and the fate of wrath [11] upon the forsaken,

and the venting of fury upon the forlorn.

This was a time of wrath for all Belial: the bonds of death were tightened, leaving no escape.

[12] The torrents of Belial overflowed all the banks of the heights;

as a fire devouring all them that drew water, destroying every tree, green [13] or barren, on their shores;

It scourged with bright flames until there was no man left to drink.

(Fire) devours the foundations of clay [14] and the surface of the dry earth;

The floors of the mountains dissolve and the roots of rocks are become torrents of pitch.

But the fire runs on, devouring, even down to the great [15] Ocean, and the torrents of Belial shall rush forth even into Abaddon,

The "schemers" of the Ocean lament in the roar of waves of mud.

And the earth [16] cries out because of the disaster which is come upon the world:

all its "schemers" howl, all its inhabitants shriek [17] and stagger in the midst of the [great] disaster.

For God makes to resound His mighty voice, and His holy abode to speak the truth [18] of His glory.

The heavenly host gives voice also;

The foundations of the world stagger and reel.

The war [19] of the valiant of heaven scourges the world

and shall not cease before the decreed destruction shall be accomplished,

which shall be for evermore and nothing shall be like unto it.

III, 12–19   Fire devours the trees, the earth, and even the seas. Their guilty inhabitants are terrified, and expect their final annihilation.

The torrents of Belial, i.e., the fiery rivers of Sheol. Cf. *II Sam.,* XXII, 5; *I Enoch,* XVII, 5 and the *Apocalypse of Peter,* ch. V, in E. HENNECKE's *Neutestamentliche Apokryphen,* Tübingen, 1924, pp. 320 and 325.

HYMN IV

(*M.G.*, II, plate IX — *Oṣar M.G.*, plate 38, 5–40)

[1] I extol Thee, O Lord, because Thou hast gladdened me with Thy
Covenant . . .

[2] I seek Thee: and like the true dawn, (so) at the daybreak Thou
hast appeared unto me.

But they, Thy people, [3] [the liemongers] have beguiled them with
words,

Interpreters of falsehood have misled them and they have let themselves be caught with no understanding,

for . . . . [4] their works (are) folly.

For I was despised by them and they did not consider me, when
Thou didst manifest Thyself mighty within me.

They did send me out from my land [5] even as a bird from its nest.

All my friends and brethren did abandon me and held me for a
broken vessel.

Lie-mongers [6] and false seers have conceived against me a scheme
of Belial, that I should barter the Law which Thou hast engraved upon my heart

for the words of seduction which (they addressed to) [7] Thy people.

They have withheld the draught of knowledge from the thirsty

and with liquor that leads them astray have they assuaged their
thirst:

to contemplate [8] their drunkenness, that they should celebrate their
feasts in frenzy,

so that they be captured in their snares.

But Thou, O God, Thou laughest at the schemes [9] of Belial;

IV, 2   *At daybreak ('ortayîm):* we understand this term, together with
YALON and MILIK, to be an adverbial locution with the dual form of *'ôrah*
(light). The same grammatical form is found in *ṣohorayîm* (noon) and
'arbayîm (a fixed time of the evening, important to religious rites).

IV, 3   The same situation and the same reproaches are found in *Hymn*, II.

IV, 4   Those words are uttered by, or ascribed to, a leader, most probably
the Teacher of Righteousness. Cf. IV, 19–20.

IV, 4–5   The leader was forced into exile. For the exile of the Teacher of
Righteousness, cf. *H.C.*, XI, 5–6.

   A broken vessel: cf. *Ps.*, XXXI, 13.

IV, 6   Cf. *Hymn*, II, 12.

IV, 7–8   *The draught of knowledge,* i.e., the true doctrine (cf. "fount of
knowledge," *M.D.*, X, 12). The *thirsty* sought after truth, and were made
drunk with error. Cf. *M.D.*, II, 13–14. — *H.C.*, XI, 4–8, 13–16. — *I En.*,
XLVIII, 1.

IV, 9   The *design* of God is immutable; cf. *M.D.*, III, 15–16.

IV, 9–11   The Jews beguiled by the psalmist's enemies, also claimed to be
serving God. But theirs was a hypocritical and false religion, and the practices to which they clung caused them to be wicked. Cf. *M.D.*, II, 11–17. —
Test. of Asher, II, 2 sq.; IV.

IV, 9   *They conceive designs of Belial:* reading *zimmat Beliyyaʿal yaḥṣôbhû.*

Thy purpose shall be fulfilled and the plan of Thy heart is established for ever.

As for them, they are forsaken, they conceive designs of Belial,
     [10] and seek Thee with a double heart:
they are not established in Thy truth.
A root bearing poison and absinth is within their plotting;
     [11] they walk, with a stubborn heart, and seek Thee among idols;
and keep before them that which hurls them into iniquity.
They [12] have sought Thee in the word of prophets of falsehood who
     speak untruth.
With barbarian lips and a foreign tongue do they address Thy people
     [13] that by cunning they should cause all their deeds to be folly.
For they have not [hearkened to Thy voi]ce nor lent an ear to
     Thy word
since they said [14] of the vision of knowledge: "It is not true!"
and of the way according to Thy heart they said: "It is not the way!"

But Thou, O God, shalt answer them by chastising them [15] in Thy
     might,
[according] to their idols and to the multitude of their sins,
so that they may be caught in their own scheming, they that have
     turned away from Thy Covenant.
[16] Thou shalt destroy by [judgm]ent all the men of deceit
and there shall be found no more any false seer:
For in Thy works there is no folly, [17] nor craftiness in the thoughts
     of Thy heart.

But those whom Thou lovest will stand before Thee for evermore,
and those who walk in the way according to Thy heart [18] will be
     established forever.
[And I] — Thou supporting me — shall stand firm, and shall rise up
     against those who mock me
and my hand shall be upon those who despise me,
for [19] they have no regard for me until Thou showest Thyself mighty
     within me.

In Thy strength Thou didst appear to me at daybreak,
and Thou didst not cover with shame the face [20] of all my disci[ples],
who gathered together in Thy Covenant.

IV, 12   *The prophets of falsehood* addressed the Jews *with barbarian lips
and in a foreign tongue,* in order to lead them into error. We read in a fragment of a *Hymn* (cf. *M.G.*, I, pl. XII, 1–2) ". . . thou hast put [in] my
heart to open the fountain of knowledge to the understanding. But they have
given them in exchange, to the people without understanding, an *uncircumcised lip* and a *foreign tongue* . . ." Cf. also *D.D.*, XX, 11.
IV, 14   Cf. *D.D.*, V, 12. — *I Enoch,* XCVIII, 14.
IV, 20   *Adhering to Thee:* accepting LAMBERT's interpretation.

They who walked in the way which is after Thy heart hearkened
 unto me
adhering to Thee [21] in the counsel of the saints.
Thou shalt bring their cause and truth to triumph according to Thy
 justice.
Thou shalt not permit them to be led astray by the wicked, [22] when
 they plot against them.
Thou hast placed their fear upon Thy people and destruction upon
 all the peoples of the lands
to annihilate by judgment all [23] the transgressors of Thy word.
Through me hast Thou rejoiced a multitude; Thou hast manifested
 Thyself infinitely mighty
because Thou hast caused me to know Thy wondrous [24] mysteries
and in Thy wondrous secret Thou hast shown Thy might toward me.
Thou hast acted wondrously toward a multitude for the sake of
 Thy glory
to make known [25] Thy might to all the living.

What is flesh (that it should deserve) such a thing?
What is a vessel of clay that it should be favored with such marvels?
Man is in iniquity [26] from his birth and in guilty infidelity even to
 his old age.

As for me, I know that justice is not of man, nor of the son of man
 the perfection [27] of way.
To the Most High God pertains every righteous deed,
whereas the way of man is not established;
unless through the spirit that God created for him [28] to make perfect
 the way of the children of man,
so that all His creatures may know the strength of His might
and the greatness of His bounty toward all the children [29] of His
 grace.

IV, 22 *Thou hast placed* their *fear:* the suffix pronoun (*their*) remains
vague, and may apply either to the faithful of the Covenant whom the Jews,
in general, shunned (LAMBERT), or to the wicked who filled the "people of
God," i.e., the Community, with such fear that they cut themselves off from
Israel.

IV, 23-24 *The wondrous secrets* and *mysteries* of God, probably refer to
the plan of salvation to be fulfilled within the Community. Cf. *H.C.*, VII,
8. — *M.D.*, IX, 18; XI, 5. — *D.D.*, III, 18.

IV, 25-34 The Hymn concludes by praising the infinite mercy of God,
who does not withhold Himself from sinful man. Justice is not from man but
from God; it is a grace. Cf. *M.D.*, X, 16-17. Perseverance in goodness is the
work of the spirit which God created for man: cf. *M.D.*, IV, 23-26. Nothing
could be farther from the theory of justification by a mere fulfilment of the
prescriptions of the law. Election was considered as an act of God's benevolence, and the glory of God its sole and ultimate end. Cf. *Hymn*, V, 12, and
supra, pp. 112-113.

IV, 26 Cf. *Is.*, XLVI, 3-4.

IV, 29-30 Cf. *Mic.*, I, 4.

As for me, [trembling] and fear have seized upon me and all my
    bones are broken;
my heart melts as wax beside the fire,
my knees slip [30] as water down a slope;
for I have remembered my faults and the infidelity of my fathers.
When sinners rose up against Thy Covenant [31] and the wicked
    against Thy word;
I also told myself in my sin: "I am cut off from Thy Covenant."

But remembering the strength of Thy hand [32] and the multitude of
    Thy mercies,
I rose up and stood erect and my spirit persevered in its place in
    the midst of my anguish.
For I have relied [33] on Thy mercy and upon Thy great goodness.
For Thou shalt forgive iniquity [and purify m]an of his guilt
    through Thy justice.
[34] Not for the sake of man hast Thou done (so), [but for the sake
    of Thy glory], since Thou hast created both the just man and
    the sinner . . . .

Hymn V

(*M.G.*, II, plate X — *Oṣar M.G.*, plate 44, 1–12)

[1] [According to Thy purpose were all things made and according to
    the thought of Thy heart hast Thou established all things,
and without Thee [2] nothing was shaped] and without Thy will
    nothing does exist.
No man may understand [Thy deep secrets], [3] [and Thy mys]teries,
    (can) no man contemplate.

What then is man—he is of earth; of dust [4] he was shaped and he
    returns unto dust, —
that Thou shouldst instruct me concerning such marvels
and that the secret of . . . . [5] Thou shouldst cause me to know?

And I, clay and dust, what can I purpose if Thou shouldst not
    desire it,
what can I think [6] unless it pleases Thee?
How may I persevere if Thou strengthenest me not,

IV, 34–36   From the second half of line 34 the text is damaged. We can
    only decipher: [35] . . . . . I cling to Thy Covenant until . . . . . [36] . . . . .
    thy . . . . for Thou art truth and justice . . . . . .
V, 1–11 ·   The same theme is found here as in the preceding poem — God's
    greatness and man's unworthiness. Cf. *M.D.*, XI, 17–23. — *I Enoch*, XCIII,
    11 sq.
V, 1–2   The beginning is badly damaged, and has been reconstructed by
    Milik with the help of the few available characters and of *M.D.*, XI, 17–18.
    Cf. *I Enoch*, IX, 5.
V, 2–3   [*Thy deep secrets and Thy myster*]ies: Milik's reconstitution.

או. מתוך מגילת ההודיות

(Cliché American Schools of Oriental Research)

9. — The *Hymns* Scroll, *Hymn* IV.

and how may I understand without (that which) Thou hast created
⁷ for me?
What can I say if Thou openest not my mouth,
and how may I answer if Thou makest me not to understand?

⁸ Behold, Thou art the Prince of gods, the King of majesties,
The Lord of all spirits, the Ruler of all creatures.
⁹ Without Thee nothing is done and no man knows Thy good
pleasure.
Apart from Thee does nothing exist, ¹⁰ no man may pit his strength
against Thee,
In the presence of Thy glory does nothing exist, and Thy power
surpasses all measure.
Is there any, ¹¹ among Thy great and wondrous creatures
that might stand in the presence of Thy glory?
¹² And what is then that which returns unto dust in order that he
may (do) so?
Thou hast made them all, solely for the sake of Thy glory.

Hymn VI

(*The Sphere*, 2–18–1950, p. 223 – *Oṣar M.G.*, plate 37, 6–18)

⁵ . . . . . . thy mouth and thou hast commanded us . . . .
⁶ Now my soul . . . . they have [not] esteemed me.
They have set [my] soul like a ship upon the deep [seas;]
⁷ like a fenced city because of . . . .
For I am troubled as a woman in travail with her first-born child.
Anguish ⁸ and dreadful pain have seized her belly

V, 8   *King of majesties:* concerning probably some class of Angels. Cf.
Jude 8 (δόξας δε βλασημοῦσιν). — *II Peter*, II, 10 (wicked Angels). — *Ex.*, XI,
1 (LXX).
    Lord of all spirits: God's usual title in the *Parables of Enoch*, where it is
found over fifty times.
V, 11   Cf. *I Enoch*, XIV.
VI, 1–4   The first four lines are very badly damaged.
VI, 5   Note the first person plural: "Thou hast commanded *us*."
VI, 6–7   The anguish of the psalmist is compared to that of sailors in a
tempest, of men defending a besieged fortress, of a woman in labor with her
first child. The latter imagery is particularly stressed.
VI, 6   *Upon the deep seas* reading *bimeṣûlôth yam*.
VI, 7   *As a woman . . . :* cf. *Jer.*, XIII, 21.
VI, 7–10   We find here an anthology, as it were, of Biblical expressions, above
all from *Is.*, IX and LXVI and *II Sam.*, XXII. The labors of Messianic child-
birth are here described by the psalmist; the child about to be born is to be a
"wonderful Counselor," a Teacher.
    In lines 7 to 11 I have found a series of puns playing upon the words
mašber (womb) and *mišbar* (wave), and *ḥebhel* (pain) and *ḥebhel* (rope).
VI, 8   *Dreadful pain:* cf. *Mic.*, II, 10.
    Have seized: cf. *Dan.*, X, 16.
    For children . . . : cf. *Is.*, XXXVII, 3. — *II Kings*, XIX, 3.

filling with pain the crucible of her conceiving.

For children have come even to the womb of death

⁹ and the bearing of the Man has racked her with its anguish.

For from the womb of death has she brought forth a Man child

and in pains of Sheol shall spring forth from the ¹⁰ crucible of her
conceiving

The Wonderful Counselor in his might,

and the Man shall be delivered from the womb.

All wombs shall be shaken at the time of his conception;

¹¹ their delivery shall be in dreadful anguish,

and their conceiving in horror.

At the time of his delivery shall all pains seize ¹² the crucible of
conceiving.

To the bearing of nothingness is destined grievous suffering,

and to works of terror, the belly of the pit.

¹³ The foundations of the wall shall break up as a ship upon the
waters

and the clouds shall send forth a mighty cry.

They who sleep in the dust shall ¹⁴ be fearful

as those who cross the seas, because of the roaring of the waters.

Their wise men are to them as pilots upon the deep seas,

for ¹⁵ all their wisdom is destroyed in the roaring of the seas,

in the tumult of the oceans, in the waves of the seas.

They are fearful when the waves rise up ¹⁶ and the flowing waters,

because of the roaring of their voice and their tumult.

The gates [of Sheol shall open]

and in their turn shall all the arrows of the pit ¹⁷ make their voice
heard unto the ocean.

The gates [of Sheol] shall be opened [for all] the works of nothingness.

¹⁸ The doors of the pit shall close upon the conceiving of iniquity

and the eternal bars upon all the spirits of nothingness.

VI, 9   *The Man (gebher)*, cf. *M.D.*, IV, 20.
   Has she brought forth a Man child: Is., LXVI, 7.
   Spring forth: (yaghiah): cf. *Mic.*, IV, 10. – *Job*, XXXVIII, 8.
   The Crucible (kûr): euphemism. Cf. *Talm. bab.* – *Shabbath*, 140b.
VI, 10   *Wonderful Counselor in his might (pele' yôʿeṣ 'im gebhûrathô)*:
   cf. *Is.*, IX, 5: *pele' yôʿeṣ 'el gibbôr*.
VI, 11   *Their delivery (bemôladhêhem)*: cf. *Ex. Rabba*, I, 12.
VI, 12–18   An apocalyptic passage, describing a tempest very much like
   that of *Hymn*, II, and concluding with the eternal imprisonment of the
   wicked in Sheol.
VI, 14   *All their wisdom . . . : Ps.*, CVII, 27.

THE WAR OF THE SONS OF LIGHT

WITH THE SONS OF DARKNESS

THE WAR TRUMPETS

(*M.G.*, I, plate VIII — *Oṣar M.G.*, plate 23, 1–17)

[1] The trumpets shall sound until the slingers have thrown seven [2] times. Then shall the priests blow the trumpets of recall and the slingers return toward the first line [3] to take up their stations.

The priests shall sound the trumpets of assembly: from [4] the gates shall come forth the three detachments of the vanguard and they shall place themselves between the lines; the charioteers shall be at their sides [5] to the right and to the left.

The priests shall blow with the trumpets a long blast to marshal them for battle [6] and the leaders shall advance according to their sections each toward his station.

And when they shall stand in three sections, [7] the priests shall sound for them a second command, a calm and persistent sound, to march forward until they approach the [8] lines of the enemy.

VII, 1–2   *Seven times*: cf. *Jos.*, VI, 4 (seven priests, seven trumpets, seven days, compassing the city seven times of the seventh day).

VII, 2   Cf. VII, 16–17.

VII, 4   *The three detachments of the vanguard (šelôšah diglê bênayim):* *deghel* signifies the detachment grouped behind the banner: cf. the Septuagint, Vulgate and the Elephantine papyri (see A. COWLEY's index, *Aramaic Papyri of the Fifth Century B.C.*, Oxford, 1923, p. 282).

Bênayim (between the two), i.e., the two enemy lines. Cf. *I Sam.*, XVII, 4, 23 where Goliath is referred to as the man between the two (lines).

They shall seize their weapons, and the priests shall blow with the six trumpets [9] of massacre a shrill and persistent sound to direct the order of battle. The Levites and all the trumpeteers shall [10] blow, a mighty war-cry, to fill with terror the heart of the enemy. And with the mighty war-cry, [11] the spears of war shall fly out to over-throw the slain. The priests shall quicken the sound of the rams' horns [12] and shall blow a shrill and persistent sound to direct the order of battle until (the spears) have been thrown seven times toward [13] the enemy lines.

Then shall the priests blow with the trumpets to recall them [14] a calm, continued, persistent sound. According to this order shall the priests sound the command for the three detachments. At [15] the first throwing, the [priests] shall sound, [and shall blow] a sound of mighty noise [16] to direct the order of ba[ttle.] [Then shall the priests sound] for them [17] the trump[ets of recall, a calm continued and persistent sound, and they shall place] themselves in their stations . . . . .

AFTER THE VICTORY

(M.G., I, plate IX — Oṣar M.G., plate 29, 2–14)

[1] And after they have withdrawn from the slain to return to the camp, they shall all sing the canticle of return. In the morning, they shall wash their garments and shall cleanse them [2] of the blood of dead sinners. They shall return to the place where they stood; where they stood before the fall of their enemies. And they shall bless there, [3] all together, the God of Israel, and they shall glorify His Name and be glad. They shall speak and say: "Blessed be the God of Israel who keeps His mercy toward His Covenant and the testimonies [4] [of salvation toward the people which He has delivered.] He has gathered together the assembly of the nations for their destruction without remnant and in order to raise up in justice [5] . . . . [ho]rns to teach war and He gives strength unto those whose knees stagger, that they may stand firm.

[6] . . . . [He will take vengea]nce upon obdurate hearts and by the hand of those whose way is perfect, shall perish all the wicked nations.

[7] . . . . [to praise] Thy name, Lord of mercies, who keepest the Covenant of our fathers and with [8] . . . . by the might of Belial and by all the mysteries of his hostility; they have not washed [9] . . . . [the me]n (sub-

---

VII, 9–10   Cf. Jos., VI, 5, 16, 20.
VII, 14   Regulation (serekh): cf. M.D., I, 1; V, 1, etc.
XII, 6   Cf. H.C., V, 4–6.
XII, 8   The might of Belial: cf. M.D., I, 18, 23; II, 19.
              The mysteries of his hostility: cf. M.D., III, 23.
XII, 9   Thou hast kept. . . . . . cf. Hymn, III, 2–3.

mitted to) his power. Thou hast kept the soul of Thy redeemed and
Thou hast raised up [10] . . . . . [There is no salvation] for their valiant men, there is no deliverer for their swift men; there is no refuge
for their revered men. [11] . . . . And we, Thy holy
people, we praise Thy name for Thy deeds of truth [12] and we glorify
Thy mighty deeds . . . . the times and solemn eternal
assemblies; at the issu[ing] forth of the day and of the night
[13] . . . . Thy [glo]ry and Thy wondrous mysteries in the heaven[s] . . . . to Thee;
of dust . . . .

An Address by the Prince of Priests Before Battle

(M.G., I, plate IX — Oṣar M.G., plate 30, 1–10)

[1] For this is time of anguish for Israel . . . .
[2] and destruction upon all the wicked nations and for all . . . .
[3] Belial and all those who join him on the day . . . .
[4] The prince of priests shall stand and his brethren the [priests] . . .
. . . .
[5] The prayer of the time of battle . . . .
[6] all the lines in . . . .
[7] all his brethren and he shall comfort . . . .
[8] "Fear not and be not [disheartened, be not afraid because of them
and do not]
[9] go back and do not . . . . For theirs
is a wicked congregation; all their deeds are in darkness
[10] and toward them go their desires . . . .

A Canticle Before Battle

(M.G., II, plate XI — Oṣar M.G., plate 27, 9–15)

. . . .
[1] in a shower of rain to pour out justice upon all his offspring.
Arise, O Hero! Lead away Thy captives, O Glorious One!

XII, 10   [No salvation] for their valiant men . . . : cf. Jer., XLVI, 6 and
Am., II, 14.
XII, 12   The times and solemn assemblies: cf. M.D., I, 9, 15.
XIII, 1–10   This fragment is an imitation of Deut., XX. See also Mishna-
Sôṭah, VIII, 1.
XIII, 4   The Prince of priests: Deut., XX, 2 mentions merely the priest.
The Mishna (loc. cit.) specifies that it concerns a priest specially anointed
for battle (mešiah milḥamah).
XIII, 8   The passage is completed after Deut., XX, 3. According to the
Mishna, the exhortation was to be spoken in Hebrew.
1–3   The Prince of priests invokes God, imploring Him to destroy the
enemies of His people.
1   Hero (gibbôr), Glorious one ('îš kabhôdh) were appellations given to God,
Cf. Ps., XXIV, 8; XXIX, 1, etc.

Gather in ² Thy plunder, Author of mighty deeds!
Place Thy hand on the neck of Thine enemies
and Thy feet on the pile of the slain!
Strike the nations, Thine enemies,
and may Thy sword ³ devour the flesh of sinners!
Fill Thy land with glory
and Thine heritage with blessing!
A multitude of cattle in Thy lands,
silver, gold and precious ⁴ stones in Thy palaces.
Rejoice greatly O Sion!
Show thyself in the midst of jubilations, Jerusalem!
Cities of Judah, be joyful!
Keep ⁵ ever open [thy] gat[es]
that toward thee may be led the army of nations!
Their kings shall serve thee,
all thy oppressors shall revere thee
and the dust ⁶ [of thy feet shall they lick.
Daughters] of my people, utter cries of jubilation!
Adorn yourselves with magnificent attire!
Dominate over . . . .
. . . . ⁷ Israel to reign everlastingly.

---

2   *Thou that doest valiantly ('ôiš ḥayil):* cf. *Ps.,* CXVIII, 15–16.

3–7   Glory and prosperity were to follow upon victory; the pagans, led by their kings, would enter Jerusalem as prisoners, and Israel would reign for ever.

4–7   An eschatological description of the rejoicing of Jerusalem. Cf. *Is.,* LX and XLIX, 23.

A FRAGMENT FROM

AN UNKNOWN WORK

The Victory of Justice over Wickedness

(R.B., LVII, October, 1949, plate XVII)

1. . . . . revolt . . . . . .
2. they knew not the mystery of pa[st
and] the things of old they understood not.
They knew ³ not that which would come to them,
and they did not escape from the mystery of the past.
⁴ This is for you a sign:
For it will come to pass that when those who begot iniquity are
shut in,
wickedness will vanish before justice
as darkness vanishes ⁵ before the light;
as the smoke that passes away and is no more,
thus shall wickedness cease for ever
and justice shall be made manifest as the sun which governs ⁶ the
world.
All those who relied on the mysteries [of iniquity] will exist no more.
Knowledge will fill the world and there shall be no more folly.
⁷ The word which is to come is certain and the oracle is true;
know then that it will not turn back.

1–3   The wicked of antiquity, perhaps of the generation of the Flood (cf.
D.D., II, 14–21), knew nothing about the mystery of divine punishments,
and were annihilated. Cf. on the other hand, H.C., XI, 3–4.

4–7   The victory of light over darkness was to occur on the day of judgment,
after the imprisonment of the wicked Angels (cf. Hymn, VI, 17). Justice,
then, would be suddenly revealed (cf. M.D., IV, 19–20). The wicked would
vanish forever (cf. M.D., IV, 23) and the world filled with the knowledge
of God (cf. H.C., XI, 1).

Have not all [8] the peoples hated iniquity?
(Nevertheless), because of them it does continue.
Does not the proclamation of truth come forth from the mouth of
    all the nations?
[9] (Nevertheless) is there a lip, or a tongue that does hold fast to it?
What nation rejoiced because a stronger one oppressed it?
Who [10] will rejoice when its wealth will be wickedly stolen?
What nat[ion] . . . .
[11] . . . .

---

6   The mysteries of iniquity: *rezê [he'awel]*. Cf. *II Thes.*, II, 7.

7   Cf. *Is.*, LV, 11. — *I Tim.*, I, 15.

8–9   An interesting consideration: the pagans hated iniquity but did not
reject it; they knew truth, but did not follow it.

APPENDIX

TWO DOCUMENTS FROM MURABBA'AT

1. Two Chiefs of Bêth Mashkô to Yeshua' Ben Gilgôla'

[1] From the chiefs of Bêth Mashkô: from Yeshua' and from 'Eli'ezer [2] to Yeshua' ben Gilgôla', commander of the camp, greeting.

Let it be known unto thee [3] that the cow which Yehôseph ben 'Ariṣtôn takes from Ya'aqôbh [4] ben Yehûdah, who dwells in Bêth Mashkô, belongs to him (henceforth) by purchase.

[5] Moreover, if the Pagans had not been close to us, I would then have gone up (. . .) [6] and would have satisfied thee about that. Say not that it is out of contempt [7] that I did not go up to thee!

[1] Published by R. DE VAUX, Quelques textes hébreux de Murabba'at, R.B., April, 1953, pp. 269–273, and plate XIII.

From (min): a form of address; cf. *Gen. Rabba*, LXXV, 5 and the following document. Fr. de Vaux reads *ken* = thus; HABERMANN, *kan* = here.

Bêth Mashkô: an unknown locality. The termination in ô points to a Nabatean origin (DE VAUX).

[2] *Yeshua'* and *'Eli'ezer*: the two leaders of the community whose full names are given among the signatures.

Yeshua' ben Gilgôla', commander of the camp, i.e., the military chief of the Murabba'at district.

[4] *Ya'aqobh ben Yehûdah*, the owner of the cow, and the third to sign the document.

In Bêth Mashkô: 'abbêth Maškô for 'al bêth or bebhêth. Cf. H.C., XI, 6.

By purchase: mizzebhinûth, a Hebraicised form of the Aramaic zebhînta'.

[5] *If . . . not*: 'illulê še-.

The Pagans: goyîm, i.e., the Romans. — The last word is left unfinished for lack of room; it is resumed on next line.

[6] *I would have satisfied thee*: hiphṣêthîkha, from pṣh, a verb meaning "to satisfy, to content" in Talmudic Aramaic.

Out of contempt: min baśron (HABERMANN), from the Aramaic besar = to despise, and bûsran = "contempt, disdain."

[7] *Be in good health*: 'ehyeh šalûm. The correct form is heyeh.

Be in good health, as also the whole house of Israel!
8 Yeshua' ben 'Eli'ezer has written it
9 'Eli'ezer ben Yehôseph has written it
10 Ya'aqôbh ben Yehûdah by himself
11 Sha'ûl ben 'Eli'ezer, witness
12 Yehôseph ben Yehôseph, witness
13 Ya'aqôbh ben Yehôseph testifies

2. *Shim'ôn ben Kôsbah to Yeshua' ben Gilgôlah*

1 From Shim'ôn ben Kôsbah to Yeshua' 2 ben Gilgôlah and to the
men of the stronghold, 3 greeting.

I call Heaven to witness 4 that, unless thou breakest not away
from the Galileans whom thou hast protected, 5 all of them, I shall
fetter
6 thy feet as I have done 7 to Ben 'Aphlûl.
8 [Shi]m'ôn b[en Kôsbah, prince of Israel]

---

8 *Has written it: kethabha* (DE VAUX). HABERMANN reads *kothbah* = scribe.
10 *By himself: 'al naphšêh.* We find the same formula following the signature of
the sellers in the Aramaic contract published by J. T. MILIK, *R.B.*, April 1954,
pp. 182–190.
1 Published by J. T. MILIK, *Une lettre de Siméon Bar Kokheba, R.B.*, April,
1953, pp. 276–294.
   Shim'ôn ben Kôsbah: the leader of the second Revolt and the *Bar
Kokhebas* of Christian writers (Rabbi Aqiba, in *Talm.jer. — Ta'an.*, 68d,
recognised him as the Messiah: "there shall come forth a star (*kokhabh*)
out of Jacob"), and the *Bar Kozibha* (the son of falsehood) of Rabbinic
writers.
   J. T. MILIK thinks that the three names which appear in the letter may be
nicknames for underground fighters: Simeon the "Coriander," Yeshua' "of
the protuberant eyes," and "the famed negligent one" (Ben 'Aphlûl).
4 *Unless thou breakest not away from the Galileans: ûpheso[q] min hag-
gelîli'îm.* MILIK: "unless thou ceasest not (thy connections) with the Galileans." HABERMANN reads: *ûphesodh min*, "unless thou destroyest not the
sect" (*min* with a *scriptio defectiva*). The Galileans may be either rebels of
Galilean origin, or a Jewish sect mentioned in *Mishna-Yadaïm*, IV, 8 or
Judeo-Christians.

SUPPLEMENTARY NOTES

*The Doctrinal Traditions of Qumrân in the Light of
Recently Published Data*

During the years 1954 and 1955, two important collections of texts
were published: *The Treasure of the Hidden Scrolls in the Possession
of the Hebrew University*,[1] the posthumous work of Professor E. L.
Sukenik; and *Discoveries in the Judaean Desert — I, Qumrân Cave I*,
by D. Barthélemy and J. T. Milik.[2] The first work includes the complete edition of the fragmentary scroll of the *Book of Isaiah, The
War of the Sons of Light against the Sons of Darkness*, and the
Thanksgiving Hymns, or *Hôdhayôth;* and the second, manuscript
fragments collected in the first cave of Qumrân during the excavations of 1949. With the aid of these new documents, we shall try to
complete and define more exactly several of the doctrinal problems
evoked in the preceding chapters.[3]

The Eschatological War and the Kittim of Ashur

The War of the Sons of Light against the Sons of Darkness describes
the rules to be observed during the final combat. After a general description (Col. 1), the author writes of the program to be followed
during the forty years of war (Col. III). He gives details concerning
the trumpets and the insignia (Col. II), the weapons (Col. V),

---

[1] *Oṣar hammeghîllôth haggenûzôth shebbîdê ha-'Universiṭa' ha'ibhrîth*, Jerusalem, 1954.   [2] Oxford, 1955.
[3] For further details cf. my article *Quelques traditions de la Communauté de
Qumrân, C.S.*, 1955, pp. 25–58.

strategy (Col. VI), and conditions of admission into the army (Col. VII, 1–7). He also describes the role of the Priests and Levites (Col. VII, 9–15), the signals to be sounded at each stage of the fight (Cols. VIII-IX, 9), the war towers (Col. IX, 10–16), a long prayer to be said after victory (Cols. X-XIV, 1), and the ceremony for the following day (Col. XIV). The rest of the manuscript applies these same rules to the final combat against the king of the Kittim, and with a certain number of lacunae, finishes with an account of the ceremonies following victory.

What is one to think of this forty-years' war whose smallest details — even chronological details — are so carefully ordered in advance? The preamble to the document already gives a sufficiently clear idea:

[This is the order] of combat in view of the unleashing of the attack[4] of the Sons of Light against the party of the Sons of Darkness, the army of Belial, the band of Edom, Moab and the sons of Ammon, the ar[my of the sons of the East][5] and the Philistines, against the bands of the Kittim of Ashur, and their auxiliaries the ungodly of the Covenant.

The sons of Judah, the sons of Levi and the sons of Benjamin, the exiles of the desert, shall fight . . . according to all their bands, on the return of the exiles of the Sons of Light from the desert of the peoples[6] to camp in the desert of Jerusalem and after the combat they shall go up from there.[7]

[The king] of the Kittim [shall go] against Egypt[8] and, in his time, he shall leave in great wrath to fight against the kings of the north in order that his fury may destroy and cut off[9] the horn [of the multitude].[10]

[This] is the time of salvation for the people of God[11] and the age of dominion for all the members of its party. Eternal destruction for all the party of Belial. The confusion of the sons of Japheth shall be g[reat]; Ashur shall fall unsuccoured[12] and the reign of the Kittim shall cease. Iniquity shall be vanquished leaving no remnant and there shall be no escape for [the Sons] of Darkness.

[. . . of jus]tice shall illumine all the ends of the earth,[13] advancing and shining, until all the moments of darkness shall disappear and at the moment established by God His majestic eminence shall shine for all the duration [of eternity] for the peace and happiness, the glory, the joy and the long life of all the Sons of Light.

---

4 Cf. *Is.*, XI, 14.   5 Reconstruction after *Is.*, XI, 14.
6 Cf. *Ez.*, XX, 35.   7 To Jerusalem.   8 Cf. *Dan.*, XI, 41–42.
9 *Ibid.*, XI, 44.   10 An hypothetical reconstruction after *Dan.*, XI, 44.
11 *Dan.*, XII, 1.   12 *Ibid.*, XI, 45.   13 Cf. *Ps.*, XCVII, 4.

On the day when the Kittim shall fall, there shall be a battle and terrible carnage[14] before the God of Israel, for it is a day anciently predestined for the combat of destruction of the Sons of Darkness. Then shall fight, in a terrible carnage, the assembly of the "gods" and the company of men. The Sons of Light and the party of Darkness shall struggle together for the power of God, with the cry of a great crowd and the shout of the "gods" and of men, on the day of destruction. This is a time of great misery[15] for the people which shall be delivered by God; not one among all its sufferings was like unto it from the time of its hasty departure[16] until its end, in view of the eternal deliverance.

On the day of their combat against the Kittim [there shall be battle and] car[nage] in the combat. Three lots shall strengthen the Sons of Light to strike at iniquity and by three shall Belial encircle himself to thrust back the party [of God. The detach]-ments of the vanguard shall put fear into the heart and the power of God shall fortify the [heart]. In the seventh lot shall be the mighty hand of God Who shall strike down [the army of Belial and all] the angels of his kingdom . . . (I. 1–15)

This passage, which contains the key to the whole work, has, above all, a theological significance. It concerns the final struggle, at the end of which light and truth shall triumph over darkness and iniquity. It is a new expression of what is to be read in the *Manual of Discipline.*[17] Although a cosmic battle, the final combat will take place upon earth. Its general plan, as we have indicated in the notes, is borrowed from chapters XI and XII from the *Book of Daniel.* In both, the time of salvation and the triumph of God are preceded by wars, by defection among the members of the Covenant, and by "great tribulation," — an idea common to the apocalyptical writings of the Old and the New Testaments.

The description of "the party of God" reveals another Biblical source, — the *Book of Ezekiel.* "The exiles of the desert of the peoples" are, in fact, mentioned in *Ez.,* XX, 35; their return to the mountains of Israel precedes the war against Gog (*Ez.,* XXXVIII, 8); and

---

[14] The term *nahshîr,* of Persian origin, is well attested in Judeo-Aramaic. Cf. the Aramaic fragments of the *Testament of Levi* in the Bodleian Library, col. a, line 3 (*ûquerabha wenahshîrûta'* — battle and carnage) and the Targums on *Gen.,* XXV, 27 (*nahshirkan* — hunter).

[15] *Dan.,* XII, 1. Cf. *Joel* II, 2; *Matthew* XXIV, 21; *Apoc.,* VII, 14.

[16] *Mehishah 'ad tûmmah.* Cf. the eschatological use of the verb *hwsh* or *hysh* in the Bible (*Is.,* LX, 22), as well as in Rabbinic literature: "R. Aha said in the name of R. Joshua ben Levi: I, the Lord, in its time shall I hasten it (salvation), (*Is.,* LX, 22). If you have no merits, it will only come "in its time"; If you have merits, "I shall hasten it" (*S.S. Rabbah,* VIII, 14).

[17] *M.D.,* IV, 15–20.

this apocalyptic prince and his assembly are later – in a passage which unfortunately contains some lacunae – even mentioned by name:

> "to grow and become holy in the eyes of the rest of the nations in order to know. . . . when Thou shalt chastise Gog and all his assembly" [18]

The list of the enemies of the Sons of Light also comes to us directly from the Bible. The first two lines of the document state that the attack of the Sons of Light must be directed against Edom, Moab, Ammon and the Philistines; and in *Is.*, XI, 10–14, we read that after the great gathering together of the exiles of Israel, these

> "shall fly towards the coasts of the Philistines, towards the west; they shall spoil the sons of the east; they shall lay their hand upon Edom and Moab; and the children of Ammon shall obey them." [19]

But although the influence of *Is.*, XI is undoubted, the problem concerning the "Kittim of Ashur" reveals itself as being more complex. The theory put forward by Professor Sukenik,[20] who held that the Kittim of Ashur mentioned together with the Kittim of Egypt were the Seleucids in opposition to the Ptolomies, can no longer be considered tenable since the publication of the complete manuscript. The document does not mention the "Kittim of Egypt," [21] but only the "Kittim of Ashur" (I, 2), – the name "Kittim" being parallel with the "sons of Japheth" and "Ashur" (I, 6; XVIII, 2), – or else, as is mostly the case, the author writes of them simply as the "Kittim."

The expression "Kittim of Ashur" is not, to our knowledge, in any way authenticated; it was probably forged by the author of the manuscript. It was thought at first that the word "Ashur" joined to the word "Kittim," had some kind of geographical significance, and this hypothesis was easy to admit as long as there was equal question of the Kittim of Egypt. But without this parallel, the problem becomes less clear, especially since "Ashur" was not the habitual name employed in Hebrew for Syria, the land of the Seleucids.

It remains to be seen whether any other connection can be found in the Bible and in Jewish tradition, between "Kittim" and "Ashur." In the last prophecy of Balaam, *Numb.*, XXIV, 23–24, the Kittim appear in a mysterious context: [22]

---

18 *War*, XI, 15–16. Cf. *Ez.*, XXXVIII–XXXIX, and particularly XXXVIII, 16.
19 *Is.*, XI, 14.
20 See *Meghîllôth Genûzôth*, I, Jerusalem, 1948, p. 19. The same opinion is expressed in *'Osar* . . . , pp. 31–32, n. 14.
21 It refers instead to a war of the Kittim *against* Egypt.
22 The obscurity is partially due to textual difficulties which have led some critics to give free rein to their imagination.

"And he took up his parable and said:
Alas, who shall live when God doeth these things!
Ships shall come from the coast of Kittim.
They shall afflict Ashur, they shall afflict Eber.
They also shall perish for ever"

Jewish tradition, from the *Book of Daniel* (XI, 30) and the *Habakkuk Commentary,* until a mediaeval addition to the Palestinian Targum of Pseudo-Jonathan,[23] has interpreted this text eschatologically. The Kittim are a conquering nation of the end of time. They will bring down Ashur who, two verses earlier, were themselves the dreaded conqueror,[24] before being entirely destroyed for ever. It would follow that the words "of Ashur" lend an historico-eschatological definition to the term "Kittim." The term refers to the Kittim who are already masters of Ashur, the standard-bearers of the empire of Belial, the nation ready for the final combat at the end of which they will be struck down by the sword of God.

This initial picture leads us to conclude that we are being presented with a description of the eternal struggle between good and evil come to its final stage. This presentation has been effected by placing an eschatological event within an apparently historical framework, but which is, in reality, nothing other than a collection and re-utilisation of ancient Biblical texts. It would be extremely hazardous to try to pass on from this description to actual historical identification, and would lead to no established result. The only conclusion that we can draw, as far as the date of the work is concerned, is that it was written after the *Book of Daniel,* since it quotes from it. There must also have been a fairly long interval between the writing of these two documents for the *Book of Daniel* to have acquired the authority which the author of the *War Scroll* attributes to it.

Admission into the Army of Light

Only persons who fulfilled certain prescribed conditions were admitted into the camp of the Sons of Light. These conditions refer to age, physical and mental health, and to ritual purity.

The following details are set down concerning the age required for the combatants:

> The governors of the camps to be fifty or sixty years old;
> the officers and the overseers to be forty to fifty years old;
> the cavalry-men to be thirty to forty-five years old;
> the despoilers of the slain, the plunderers of booty, the cleansers of the land, the keepers of objects and the comptroller of provisions, to be twenty-five to thirty years old.[25]

---

[23] Concerning the Kittim, Pseudo-Jonathan mentions Byzantium, whereas the Vulgate, the Peshitta, and the Fragmentary Palestinian Targum identify them with the Romans.

[24] Cf. *Numb.,* XXIV, 22.   [25] *War,* VI, 14; VII, 1–3.

This division according to age is partially based on Biblical data, but more details are to be found in the *Rule of the Congregation* and in the *Damascus Document*.[26]

Having reached the required age, the combatants must be "all freely pledged to war,[27] perfect in spirit and in body, prepared for the day of vengeance." [28]

Concerning persons definitely excluded from the camp, we find the following prescriptions:

> "No man who is lame or blind or infirm in a permanent manner, nor any man affected by a bodily impurity, none of these shall go with them into combat.[29] . . . Whosoever shall not be pure because of his 'source' (of pollution) on the day of combat, shall not go down with them,[30] for the holy angels shall be with their armies [31] (VII, 4–6)."

It is interesting to note that the infirmities which prevent admission into the camp, are similar to those which prevented both priests and victims from participation in the sacrificial rites (*Lev.*, XXI, 18; *Deut.*, XV, 21). The general context which represents this war as a ritual act, and the mention of impurity, allows us, we think, to make this comparison, since the exclusion from the army of the lame and the blind would demand no special justification.

The rules of decency, strongly emphasised in the code of the Community,[32] remain in force during the campaign:

> "There shall be a place between all their camps at a distance of about two thousand cubits which shall serve as a latrine in order that no indecent nakedness shall be seen in the neighbourhood of their camps." [33]

Women and children are also forbidden entry into the camp:

> "No young boy and no woman shall go into their camps from the time of their leaving Jerusalem and their going into battle until their return." [34]

---

[26] The young men are inscribed in the army register from the age of twenty (*Numb.*, I, 3–4. — *Rule of the Congr.*, I, 8–9). The members of the Community can assume their various functions from the age of twenty-five (*Numb.*, VIII, 24 for the Levites; *Rule of the Congr.*, I, 12–13). Service must cease from the age of fifty (*Numb.*, VIII, 25). It should be remembered that according to *War*, II, 4–5, the liturgical duties of laymen were carried out by men who had passed the age of fifty. According to the *Damascus Document*, XIV, 6–7, a camp Overseer had to be between thirty and sixty years old, and the Overseer of all the camps, between thirty and fifty years old (*ibid.*, XIV, 8–9).

[27] *M.D.*, I, 7, 11; V, 1.   [28] *War*, VII, 5.

[29] Cf. *Lev.*, XXI, 17–21; *Deut.*, XV, 21. — *Rule of the Congr.*, II, 3–7.

[30] Cf. *Deut.*, XXIII, 11. For "source" see *Lev.*, XX, 18.

[31] The same motive is given in the *Rule of the Congr.*, II, 8–9.

[32] Cf. *M.D.*, VII, 12–13. See *Apoc.*, XVI, 15.

[33] *War*, VII, 6–7. Cf. *Deut.*, XXIII, 10, 13, 15.   [34] *War*, VII, 3–4.

This text brings information of the very greatest importance to bear on a problem until now unsolved: were the members of the Community celibate or married? Without mentioning all the texts which point to one conclusion or the other, it should be remembered that the community described by the *Damascus Document,* and by the *Rule of the Congregation,* is composed of married persons; that according to Philo and Pliny, the Essenes were celibate; that Josephus mentions the principal branch of this sect as practicing celibacy; and that the *Manual of Discipline,* although indirectly honouring the unmarried state, brings no positive argument to bear in its favor.

On the other hand, the *War Scroll* shows clearly that no woman may approach the camps of the Sons of Light during the final combat. The reason for this interdiction can be easily guessed: because of their association with the heavenly militia, and their consequent proximity to God, the Sons of Light are obliged to lead an "angelic" life. This practice is based upon the example of Moses as it is recounted in Rabbinic literature:

"It is because of his very special proximity to God that the Haggadah portrays Moses as having no knowledge of his wife after God had revealed Himself to him. The Haggadah is unanimous on this point."

. . . In the dialogue between God and the soul of Moses (in the midrash *Petirat Mosheh* in A. Jellinek's *Bet-ha-Midrasch,* p. 129), when the latter begs to be allowed to remain within the body of this just man, it reminds God that "the angels Ouza and Azael came down from Heaven and were corrupted, but this Moses of flesh and blood did separate himself from his wife on the day that Thou didst appear to him in the bush." This abstention is generally treated as though it were the direct and causal result of his intimacy with God, and the Rabbis, in their interpretation of *Numb.,* XII, 8, even see in it a direct commandment of God: '*With him do I speak mouth to mouth,* which is to say: it is from mouth to mouth that I told him to separate himself from his wife.' (*Siphre Numb.,* XII, 8, §103, Horovitz, p. 101, line 14). . . . The murmuring of Myriam and Aaron against Moses is interpreted as having taken place whilst they were discussing his strange behaviour, and it is in this manner, for example, that *Siphre* interprets *Numb.,* XII, 1:

'Myriam and Aaron talked against Moses concerning the Ethiopian woman': How could Myriam know that Moses was abstaining from 'fecundation and multiplication' (that is to say, from the commandment concerning procreation)? She saw that Sipporah did not adorn herself as did other women. Then said (Myriam) unto her: For what reason, then, do you not adorn yourself with jewels, as other women do? (Sipporah) answered: Your brother attaches no price to them! It is in this manner that Myriam learnt of it, that she told it to her brother (Aaron) and that the two of them spoke against him (Moses). — R. Nathan says: Myriam was at the side of Sipporah when that happened which is written (*Numb.*, XI, 27): 'And the boy ran (to announce it to Moses).' When Sipporah heard it (that the two elders had prophesied in the camp), she said: Woe to the wives of these men! (Probably because after this they separated themselves from their wives, as Moses had). It is in this manner that Myriam knew it; she told it to her brother and both of them began to speak against him (Moses).' (*Siphre Numb.*, §99, p. 98, lines 5–15).[35]

Although the text cited from the *War Scroll*, and the analogous passages from Rabbinic literature which I have so briefly mentioned, do not in any way solve the problem concerning the *practice* of celibacy, they do at least throw a vivid light upon the religious ideal which the Community set up for itself.[36] This ideal must have been common to all those circles in which the eschatological expectation was ardent. Saint Paul, for example, states quite clearly that the best preparation during the last days for the life of glory, is abstinence, even for the married. (I *Cor.*, VII; XV; II *Cor.*, VI). He takes care, however, not to pronounce it obligatory, conscious that he had no positive knowledge concerning the imminence of the Second Coming, and reacting also, perhaps, against the excesses which might have been practiced in the turbulent community of Corinth.

Sacrificial Worship

From the *War Scroll* we learn that the first sabbatical year of this forty-years war will mark the date of the resumption of the service of the Temple by the Sons of Light, and the reorganisation of worship. "They shall range the leaders of the Priests behind the Prince of the Priests and his second.[37] The twelve leaders shall be in office in perpetual worship before God, whereas the twenty-six leaders of the priestly classes shall be in service according to the turn of their class.[38] Behind these, shall they range the leaders of the Levites — who shall always be in service to the number of twelve,

---

35 RENEE BLOCH, *Quelques aspects de la figure de Moïse dans la littérature rabbinique*, in *Moïse, l'homme de l'Alliance*, pp. 1–8, note 84. — See also *Ex.*, XIX, 15.

36 This ideal might explain a strange omission in the *War Scroll*. Col. X, 2–6 reproduces almost textually the ceremony preceding the combat, during which the priest and the surveyors make an address according to the rule given in *Deut.*, XX, 2–8. On the other hand, the manuscript ignores verses 5–7, which order exemption from military service for all those who are engaged in build- a house, planting a vineyard, or *taking a wife*. Cf. also *Deut.*, XXIV, 5.

37 Cf. II *Kings*, XXV, 18; *Jer.*, LII, 24.

38 During the period of the Second Temple, the priests were divided into twenty-four classes (I *Chron.*, XXIV, 3–19; JOSEPHUS, *Ant. Jud.*, VII, XIV, 7; *Mishnah-Ta'an.*, IV, 2). Every priestly and Levitical class was obliged to officiate twice a week per year (*Talmud bab.-Ta'an.*, 17a; *Yôma*, 26a) whereas, during the week of the three principal feasts, all the classes were in office (*Mishnah-Suk.*, V, 6–7). Instead of twenty-four classes, the *War Scroll* mentions twenty-six. According to the Community calendar, the year consists of fifty-two weeks, — to which correspond the two turns of office per week of the twenty-six classes.

one from each tribe — and the heads of family from the assembly behind them, — who shall always stand at the gates of the Sanctuary, — whereas the leaders of their classes together with their numbered men shall be in office according to the feasts, the new moons, the Sabbaths and all the days of the year, their age being fifty years and more.[39] Such are they who shall officiate at the holocausts and sacrifices, preparing the incense of pleasant odour for the good pleasure of God, atoning for all His assembly [40] and satisfying themselves always before Him at the table of glory. (II, 1–7)

This passage will help to dissipate misunderstanding concerning the attitude of the Community toward sacrificial worship. Taking as their authority an equivocal phrase from the *Manual of Discipline* — "to obtain mercy on earth without the flesh of holocausts and the fat of sacrifice. The offering of the lips . . . shall be as the odour of righteousness and perfect conduct as the gift of an agreeable offering" (IX, 4–5) — certain authors have allowed it to be understood that the Community distinctly proclaimed the futility of sacrifice.[41] But as regards this interpretation, and taking into consideration that the author was a Jew living at the time when the Temple was still standing, it would seem very improbable that he would entertain such an attitude toward sacrifice. In addition, there is the testimony of the *Damascus Document,* according to which the Community had abandoned the Sanctuary on account of the irregularities committed by the Priests in the services of worship (VI, 11–20). Furthermore, the same document states that at the end of time the sons of Zadok will resume their sacerdotal functions (IV, 3–4). From these affirmations we have concluded that, in the interval between their secession and the end of time, sacrificial worship is not condemned by them, but relegated to second place.[42] That there may have developed, during this period, a certain spiritualisation of the idea of sacrifice, is incontestable, — as M. Delcor has clearly shown.[43] But this would not have diminished the longing for the Temple, nor, in consequence, the respect for the excellence and value of the sacrifices offered there.

The Angels, the Sword of God, and Final Victory

There is no doubt that the Community considered itself as the antechamber of Heaven, and its members part of the choir and of the celestial army.

---

[39] This passage refers to what rabbinic writings term the *ma'amadhôth,* i.e., lay groups associated for worship with the priestly and Levitical classes. Cf. *Mishnah-Ta'an.,* IV, 2; *Bikk.,* III, 2.   [40] Cf. *M.D.,* VIII, 3, 6.

[41] A. DUPONT-SOMMER, *Nouveaux aperçus* . . . , p. 178, note 13. — J. L. TEICHER, *Priest and Sacrifices in the Dead Sea Scrolls, J.J.S.,* 1954, pp. 93–99. — F.-M. BRAUN, *Essénisme et Hermétisme, Revue Thomiste,* 1954, pp. 535–536. — A. VINCENT, *Les manuscrits hébreux du désert de Juda,* Paris, 1955, p. 151, note 4.   [42] Cf. *supra,* p. 46.

[43] *Le sacerdoce, les lieux de culte, les rites et les fêtes dans les documents de Khirbet Qumrân, R.H.R.,* 1955, pp. 22–24.

Adherence to the Community implied an entry into communion
with the "Sons of Heaven":

"For Thou hast brought him into Thy assembly, among all the
    members of Thy council,
And into a common destiny with the angels of the Presence." [44]

The members will enjoy the Divine Presence for ever:

"All the children of Thy truth, Thou makest them to come before
    Thee for pardon,
Cleansing them of their sins by Thy great goodness
And establishing them before Thee, according to the multitude
    of Thy mercies throughout all eternity." [45]

As has been shown in the explanation of the first column of the
War Scroll, the influence of the angels on the progress of the war is
decisive.

The celestial hosts and the companies of the Sons of Light form
but one and the same army:

"To pass in review the arm[ies and Thy el]ect according to their
    thousands and their myriads, together with Thy saints [and all]
    Thy angels, in order that they may have the strength to prevail
    in the combat" (*War*, XII, 4–5).
"The Lord is holy and the King of glory is with us in company
    with the saints and the heroes of the army of the angels at the
    time of our visiting. The Hero of the combat is within our assem-
    bly and the army of his spirits is with us on our marches" (*War*,
    XII, 8–9).

The angels are the principal agents of victory, and above all, of the
final victory over the Kittim:

"When the mighty hand of God shall be lifted against Belial
    and against all [the army] of his kingdom, (striking him) an
    eternal blow, [so that the cry of the angels] and the shout of
    the saints (shall rise up) at the time of the pursuit of Ashur, the
    sons of Japheth shall fall down and shall not rise again and the
    Kittim shall be crushed without [remnant]. (*War*, XVIII, 1–3)
"Then, at the time of the judgement, the sword of God shall fall
    and all the children of his truth shall bestir themselves to [de-
    stroy] ungodliness and no son of wickedness shall remain. The
    Hero shall bind his bow and the (heavenly) fortress shall open
    [its gates] unto boundless space; the heavenly gates shall let out
    instruments of war and they shall be mighty from one end unto
    [the other]. . . ." [46]

The resurrected dead are invited to join forces with the combatants:

---

[44] *Hymn*, VI, 12–13. Cf. *ibid.*, XI, 11–14.
[45] *Hymn*, VII, 29–31. Cf. *M.D.*, XI, 15–17.   [46] *Hymn*, VI, 29–31.

"Ye who lie in the dust, lift up a sign!
Bodies gnawed by worms, give the signal for . . .
Cut off . . . the insolent in the combats." [47]

The angelic army is commanded by a Prince of Light:
"From the past Thou hast charged the Prince of Light to succour us. Within his hand are all the elect of righteousness and all the spirits of truth are under his dominion." [48]

Eternal aid will be brought "by the power of the mighty angel of the empire of Michael," [49] and it is this angel who, after the sword of God, is principally responsible for the final triumph. Of the Messiah there is no mention, as is also the case in Daniel and in chapters XXXVIII–XXXIX of Ezekiel. The leader of the army of the Sons of Light, the *Nasi* of the whole assembly, is as shadowy a personality as the Messiah of Israel in the *Rule of the Congregation*.[50] Nevertheless, in a collection of blessings from the same volume, there is a blessing of the Prince of the Congregation, in which the *Nasi* identifies himself quite clearly with the victorious Davidic Messiah.[51] This proves that within the Community, as also in official Judaism, diverse doctrinal tendencies co-existed concerning eschatology.

But this theological elasticity must not lead us to forget that in the last resort, victory over the Kittim and over the kingdom of darkness, lay exclusively with God:
"To Thee the combat and to Thee the power and not unto us! Neither our strength nor the energy of our hands have accomplished mighty deeds, but Thy strength and Thy great valor" (*War*, XI, 4–5).

"From the past Thou hast [predicted] unto us the moment when the power of Thy hand shall be turned against the Kittim in these words (*Is.*, XXXI, 8): 'Then shall Ashur fall with a sword which is not of man; a sword which is not of man shall devour him' (*War*, XI, 11–12).
"The God of Israel has called up the sword against all the nations, and by the saints of His people shall He accomplish acts of valor" (*War*, XVI, 1).

---

[47] *Hymn*, VI, 34–35. Cf. also *Hymn*, XI, 10–14.
[48] *War*, XIII, 10. Cf. *M.D.*, III, 20, 24–25.
[49] *War*, XVII, 6–7. Tradition attributes to Michael a capital role in the eschatological victory (*Dan.*, X, 13, 22; XII, 1; *Apoc.*, XII, 7). *Ex. Rabbah*, XVIII, 5, identifies the angel which destroyed the army of Sennacherib with Michael. The help of this same angel was implored of God by Judas Maccabee before the battle against the Nicanor (*I Macc.*, VII, 41; *II Macc.*, XV, 22–23).   [50] *Rule of the Congr.*, II, 11–21.
[51] Cf. BARTHÉLEMY-MILIK, *op. cit.*, pp. 127–129.

The Teacher in the Hymns' Scroll

Although for the most part forms of personal prayer, some of the Hymns contained in this manuscript seem to express the feelings of any member of the Community, whereas others appear to apply to the history and to the role of an unique individual, the founder and teacher of the group, — a personality most probably identical with the one referred to in other documents as the Teacher of Righteousness.

In one of the Hymns previously published (*Hymn* IV in our translation), a Teacher appears on the scene represented as the guardian of divine mysteries and surrounded by a group of zealous disciples, but opposed by the "prophets of falsehood," the "seers of deceit," the men of Belial. These themes return many times in the new texts, accompanied by other revealing traits.

"For the rebellious have I been a snare [52]
but for the repentant rebels an (instrument of) cure;
prudence for the simple
and firm conviction for the troubled of heart.[53]
Thou hast made of me an (object of) reproach and derision for
        traitors,
but the ground of truth and understanding for those (who follow) the straight path.
I have been (as a weight) upon the iniquity of the ungodly(?),
an object of calumny upon the lips of the violent,
the scoffers gnash their teeth.[54]
As for me, I have been a byword for the rebellious,
against me has raged the assembly of the ungodly . . .[55]
Thou hast made of me a sign for the elect of righteousness [56]
and a prophet versed in wondrous mysteries,
to try [those who practice] truth
and to put to the test them who love reproof.[57]
I have been the enemy of the prophets of falsehood. . . .
I have been a spirit of jealousy [58] toward all them that teach that
        which leads [astray].[59]
The doctrine of knowledge, Thou hast placed it in my heart
to unlock the source of understanding [60] unto the understanding.
But in exchange they have given them lips of uncircumcision
        and a foreign tongue [61]

---

[52] Cf. *Hos.*, V, 1.   [53] *Hymn*, I, 35; *M.D.*, X, 26.
[54] Cf. *Is.*, XXIX, 20; *Ps.*, XXXV, 16; *Lam.*, II, 16.   [55] Cf. *Ps.*, II, 1.
[56] Cf. *Numb.*, XXI, 8–9 (the bronze serpent). *M.D.*, VIII, 6.
[57] *Prov.*, XII, 1.   [58] *Numb.*, V, 14, 30.
[59] Cf. *Is.*, XXX, 10; *Hymn*, II, 32.
[60] Cf. *Prov.*, X, 11; XIII, 14; XVIII, 4.   [61] Cf. *Hymn*, IV, 16.

to the people without understanding that it may fall in its errors.[62] (*Hymn*, II, 8–19)

In the doctrinal struggle depicted in the lines just translated, the Teacher, a prophet versed in the mysteries, presents himself as a focus for all those who adhere to God, and also, like the bronze serpent lifted up by Moses, as a symbol of cure to the repentant sinner. But he is not only the center of conflicting argument and passion; he is the leader of a Covenant which is at the same time both God's Covenant and his own.

"I have been a subject of strife and contention [63] for my friends,
of jealousy and of wrath for the *members of my Covenant*. . . .
All those who bear the yoke of my foundation have spoken ill
    of me [64] with wicked lips
and the *members of my [Coven]ant* show themselves recalcitrant
    and murmur all about (me)" (*Hymn*, V, 22–24)

Elsewhere there is mention of the "bearers of the yoke of my instruction" (*Hymn*, VI, 19) and, perhaps, of "the aspersion of the Covenant" [65] entrusted to the Teacher (*Hymn*, V, 9). Like Moses, he is the mediator of a covenant with God, the revealer of divine doctrine which, without him, is inaccessible:
"For Thou, O my God, Thou hast hidden me from men [66]
and Thy Torah did disappear [with me
until] the time when Thou didst reveal Thy salvation unto me
    (Hymn, V, 11–12)
Like Moses again, he has charge of all his community:
"Thou hast made of me the father of the children of grace [67]
and as a foster-father [68] unto them that are wondered at [69]
They did open their mouth as a little child . . .
as a little child does play [70] upon the breast of its nurse (*Hymn*,
    VII, 20–22).

It seems clear that the Teacher is presented as a "new Moses," sent by God to renew the Covenant. The hypothesis which we have put forward on this subject finds, therefore, appreciable support in these

---

[62] Cf. *Hos.*, IV, 14; *Prov.*, X, 8, 16.   [63] Cf. *Hab.*, I, 3.
[64] Cf. *Talmud jer.* — *Dem.*, II, 22c.
[65] I do not follow Sukenik's transcription *wmyh bryt*, which appears to me to have no meaning, but propose *ûmazzeh berîth* instead. The latter expression signifies "he who asperges the Covenant" or, following the context, "the aspersion of the Covenant." Cf. *Ex.*, XXIV, 8; *Is.*, LII, 15. In *Tosephta-Parah*, XII, 12, *mazzeh* is the name given to the priest charged with the aspersion.   [66] Cf. *Ps.*, XVII, 8; XXVII, 5; LXIII, 3.
[67] Cf. *Gen.*, XVII, 45 (Abraham).   [68] Cf. *Numb.*, XI, 12 (Moses).
[69] Cf. *Zach.*, III, 8 (the priests).   [70] Cf. *Is.*, XI, 8.

new texts. This representation is in no way strange, since it is inscribed within the context of a general expectation of the coming of a new Moses; on the contrary, it can even, in a certain sense, be termed traditional.[71]

The Teacher carried out his ministry amidst a thousand perils; the passages which describe his tribulations are distinctly apocalyptic in tone:

"Thou hast protected my life against the pit and Thou hast given . . .
in the midst of the lions destined to the guilty,
of the lionesses which crush the bones of the mighty [72]
and which drink the blo[od] of the brave.[73]
Thou has made me to live among many fishers [74]
that spread their net upon the waters [75]
and with the hunters of the children of iniquity.[76]
It is there that Thou hast established me for judgment [77]
and Thou hast surely established in my heart the foundation of truth
and the aspersion (?) of the Covenant for them who seek it.
Thou hast closed the mouth of the young lions
whose teeth are as a sword
and whose great teeth are as a pointed spear.[78]
All their plans for violence are as the poison of dragons.[79]
They were many, but they have not opened their mouth against me . . .[80]
Thou hast protected the soul of the Poor One from the den of lions [81]
who have sharpened their tongue as a sword.[82]
But Thou, O my God, Thou hast closed up their teeth
Lest they should tear the soul of the afflicted and Poor One [83]
Thou hast made their tongue go back as a sword into its scabbard . . .[84]
To manifest Thyself mighty within me unto men [85]
Thou hast tried me [as gold] in the fire [86]
And as silver refined in the crucible of the blowers [87]
that I may be purified seven times.[88]
The violent and ungodly have fallen upon me to oppress me;
every day do they crush my soul.

---

[71] Cf. *La figure de Moïse au tournant des deux Testaments*, in *Moïse, l'homme de l'Alliance*, pp. 80–84.

[72] Cf. *Is.*, XXXVIII, 13.   [73] Cf. *Ez.*, XXXIX, 18.   [74] Cf. *Jer.*, XVI, 16.

[75] Cf. *Is.*, XIX, 8; *Hymn*, III, 26.   [76] *Jer.*, XVI, 16.   [77] Cf. *Hab.*, I, 12.

[78] Cf. *Ps.*, LVIII, 7.   [79] Cf. *Deut.*, XXXII, 33; *D.D.*, VIII, 9–10; XIX, 22.

[80] As Daniel in the lions' den.   [81] Cf. *Nah.*, II, 12; *S.S.*, IV, 8.

[82] Cf. *Ps.*, LXIV, 4.   [83] Cf. *Ps.*, VII, 3; *Job* XVIII, 4.

[84] Cf. *Jer.*, XLVII, 6.   [85] Cf. *Hymn*, I, 34; II, 24–25.

[86] Cf. *Is.*, XL, 19.

[87] *Mal.*, III, 3; *Eccli.*, XLIII, 4; *Hymn*, III, 10; *M.D.*, IV, 20.

[88] Cf. *Ps.*, XII, 7.

> But Thou, O my God, Thou shalt change the storm into a
> breeze.[89]
> Thou hast delivered the soul of the Poor One as a b[ird from
> the snare] [90]
> as a prey from the power of the lions." (*Hymn*, V, 6–19)

But in addition to the trials which he has to undergo at the hands
of his enemies, — trials permitted by God both for his purification,
and also to show, by greater contrast, the wonders which He has
worked in him, — the Teacher is the sad witness of the revolt of certain members of his Community. Here again, as in *Dan.*, XI and in
the *War Scroll*, the final triumph is preceded not only by the hostility of the ungodly, but also by the defection of many of the just.

> "Ev[en those who] eat my bread have lifted up their heel against
> me. . . .[91]
> The members of my [Coven]ant show themselves recalcitrant
> and murmur all about (me).
> Before the children of adversity do they speak ill [92] concerning
> the mystery which Thou hast hidden in me. . . .
> Because of their guilt, Thou hast hidden (from them) the fount
> of understanding [93] and the foundation of truth. . . .
> They have overtaken me on the narrow path [94]
> where there was no refuge . . .
> They have sounded my censure upon an harp
> and upon a cithern [95] their murmuring and shouting.[96]
> Anguish [has taken hold of me] [97] and sufferings
> as the pangs of a woman in travail.[98]
> My heart has roared against me.
> I have clothed myself in blackness [99] and my tongue has cleaved
> to the roof of my mouth . . .[100]
> For I eat the bread of distress [101]
> and unending tears are my drink.[102]
> My eyes are consumed because of grief [103]
> and my soul in the bitterness of every day (*Hymn*, V, 23–34).

Because of constant peril, the Teacher was hidden by God; and
with him the Torah, the fount of understanding, the foundation of
truth, the offshoot of the eternal plant, i.e. the whole of the nascent
Community, have disappeared from the eyes of men.[104] But after the
period of great tribulation, he will appear once more.[105]

The passages just quoted have already thrown some light on the
rôle of the Teacher concerning revelation and the safeguarding of

[89] Cf. *Ps.*, CVII, 29.   [90] Cf. *Ps.*, CXXIV, 7.   [91] Cf. *Ps.*, XLI, 10.
[92] Cf. *Lev.*, XIX, 6.   [93] Cf. *Is.*, XXIX, 14.   [94] Cf. *Lam.*, I, 3.
[95] Cf. *Is.*, XVI, 11.   [96] Cf. *Job*, XXX, 3; XXXVIII, 27; *Zeph.*, I, 15.
[97] Cf. *Ps.*, CXIX, 53.   [98] Cf. *Is.*, XIII, 8; XXI, 3.   [99] Cf. *Is.*, L, 3.
[100] Cf. *Ps.*, CXXXVII, 6.   [101] Cf. *Job*, III, 24.   [102] Cf. *Ps.*, CII, 10.
[103] Cf. *Ps.*, VI, 8; XXXI, 10.
[104] Cf. *Hymn*, V, 11–12, 26; VIII, 10–14; IX, 24.   [105] Cf. *Hymn*, V, 11–12.

divine truth. They have also shown that he was both father and guardian to his disciples. Some further texts, chosen from among many others, will explain his mission, and the place which he occupies in the history of salvation such as it is conceived in the theology of the Community.

Like Moses and the Servant of the Lord, he is an intimate friend of God:

> "For better than my father hast Thou known me . . .
> [from the entrails] of my mother hast Thou filled me up,
> and from the paps of her who conceived me has Thy mercy fallen
>   upon me. . . .
> From the time of my childhood Thou hast shown wisdom and
>   Thy judgment unto me
> and Thou hast supported me with certain truth.
> Thou hast delighted me with Thy holy spirit" [106] (*Hymn*, IX,
>   29–32).

By his teaching he feeds the eternal plant, of which the little group of his disciples forms the first offshoot:

> "Thou, O my God, Thou hast put into my mouth as a rain [107] for
>   all men . . .
> and as a fountain of living water which shall not lie (*Hymn*,
>   VIII, 16).
> By my hand hast Thou opened unto them a spring . . . (*Hymn*,
>   VIII, 21).
> If I take away my hand, it shall become as a des[ert] . . .
> its trunk as thorns in a salty land (*Hymn*, VIII, 24).

And although his splendor be changed into darkness [108] he will reappear seven times crowned with light, for the Lord is his eternal shining guide, and will finally establish his steps on the path of righteousness.[109]

The Expectation of a Messianic Prophet

The portrait of this Teacher is reminiscent of the messianic figure mentioned in the *Manual of Discipline*. At the end of time, God will send a messenger, the *Man*, whom He will have purified and sanctified, to

> "teach unto the just the knowledge of the Most High, and unto
> the perfect the wisdom of the sons of Heaven." [110]

---

[106] This passage recalls the "poems of the Servant of the Lord" in *Is.*, XLII and XLIX. More direct allusions or quotations may be found in three other passages: in *Hymn*, VII, 10 (*Is.*, L, 4); *Hymn*, VIII, 26–27 (*Is.*, LIII, 3–4); and in *Hymn*, VIII, 35–36 (*Is.*, L, 4).   [107] Cf. *Joel*, II, 3; *Hos.*, VI, 3.
[108] *Hymn*, V, 32.   [109] *Hymn*, VII, 24–25.
[110] *M.D.*, IV, 22. Cf. the whole passage IV, 18–22, whose meaning has been discussed by W. H. Brownlee in his article *The Servant of the Lord in the Qumrân Scrolls, II, B.A.S.O.R.*, 135, 1954, pp. 36–38.

The birth of this eschatological Man, at a time of general confusion and disorder, is described in one of the Hymns (*Hymn* VI, in our translation):

> "For I am troubled as a woman in travail with her first-born child.
> Anguish and dreadful pain have seized her belly
> filling with pain the crucible of her conceiving.
> For children have come even to the womb of death
> and the bearing of the Man has caused tortures by its pains.
> For from the womb of death has she brought forth a Man child
> and in pains of Sheol shall spring from the crucible of her con-
> ceiving
> The Wonderful Counsellor in his might
> and the Man shall be delivered from the womb."

Professor Brownlee believes "the Man" to be a messianic title, and he traces its origin to II *Sam.*, XXIII, 1 (David), and to *Zach.*, XIII, 7 (the Shepherd). This sense is even more evident in the Septuagint version of *Numb.*, XXIV, 17 (and also in XXIV, 7), and in two passages of the *Testaments of the Twelve Patriarchs* which depend on it (*The Test. of Juda*, XXIV, 1, and *The Test. of Napht.*, IV, 5).[111] It should be noted, however, that "the Man" of these texts refers to the Messiah-*King*. The biblical sources of the ideology of the suffering "*Man*," should perhaps rather be sought in *Zach.*, XII, 7, and more probable still, in *Lam.*, III, 1.

> "I am the Man that has seen affliction
> by the rod of his wrath."

It appears that at a certain stage in its doctrinal evolution, the theology of the Community began to identify the "Man," the eschatological Prophet, with the Teacher of Righteousness. This identification emerges from a fragment of the *Commentary of Psalm XXXVII*, verses 23–24.

> "By the Lord are the steps of the Man established and He de-
> lights in all his way.
> Even though he stumble, he shall not fall down,
> for the Lord holds his hand."

> Its interpretation concerns the Priest, the Teacher of [righteous-
> ness who] . . . (whom God) established in order that he might
> build for Him a Congregation of . . ." (Fragment II, 14–16).[112]

It is also probable that the Prophet mentioned in the *Manual of Discipline*, IX, 11, may be identified with this same "Man."

---

[111] *Art. cit.*, p. 37, note 30.
[112] Cf. J. M. ALLEGRO, *A newly discovered Fragment of a Commentary on Psalm XXXVII from Qumrân*, P.E.Q., 1954, pp. 69–75.

But what is his connection with the Messiahs of Aaron and Israel mentioned in the *Manual of Discipline* [113] and in the *Damascus Document*,[114] — that is to say, with the sacerdotal Messiah, and the Davidic Messiah? Although a priest, he does not appear to fit the rôle of the Messiah of Aaron, and certainly not that of the Messiah of Israel. Yet the question does not seem insoluble. Recently, we had occasion to remember that at the turn of the two Testaments the messianic expectation admitted of several qualities, — prophetic (Moses-Servant of the Lord), sacerdotal, and royal. These qualities, although divergent in their origin, eventually focused, according to both Jewish and Christian tradition, upon the conception of a unique Messiah. The theology of the Community, however, conserves the traditional elements, without appearing to develop from them any similar synthesis.

As the publication of the texts progresses, so do the beliefs of the Community become more clearly defined. Together with other sources of Palestinian tradition, they will help us to reconstruct the doctrinal framework of Judaism, out of which developed the Christian message, the Gospel of salvation.

---

[113] *M.D.*, IX, 11.

[114] *D.D.*, XII, 23 — XIII, 1; XIV, 19; XIX, 10–11; XX, 1. Concerning the problem of the two Messiahs, see *supra*, p. 116.

SELECTED BIBLIOGRAPHY

I. EDITIONS

(Those giving neither translation nor commentary are marked with an asterisk.)

J. M. Allegro. A newly discovered Fragment of a Commentary on Psalm 37 from Qumrân, *P.E.Q.*, 1954, pp. 69–75.

M. Baillet. Fragments araméens de Qumrân. Description de la Jérusalem Nouvelle, *R.B.*, 1955, pp. 222-245.

D. Barthélemy. Redécouverte d'un chaînon manquant de l'histoire de la Septante, *R.B.*, 1952, pp. 187-218.

D. Barthélemy, J. T. Milik. *Discoveries in the Judaean Desert I, Qumrân Cave I,* Oxford, 1955.

* M. Burrows, J. C. Trever, W. H. Brownlee. *The Dead Sea Scrolls of St. Mark's Monastery,* I. *The Isaiah Manuscript and the Habakkuk Commentary,* New Haven, 1950.—II. Fasc. 2: *Plates and Transcription of the Manual of Discipline,* New Haven, 1951.

F. M. Cross Jr. A new Qumran Biblical Fragment related to the original Hebrew underlying the Septuagint, *BASOR*, 132, 1953, pp. 15-26.

J. T. Milik. Fragments d'un midrash de Michée dans les manuscrits de Qumrân, *R.B.*, 1952, pp. 412-418.—Une lettre de Siméon Bar Kokheba, *R.B.*, 1953, pp. 276-294.—Une inscription et une lettre en araméen christo-palestinien, *R.B.*, 1953, pp. 526-539.—Un contrat juif de l'an 134 après J.-C., *R.B.*, 1954, pp. 182-190.—Le Testament de Lévi en araméen. Fragment de la grotte 4 de Qumrân, *R.B.*, 1955, pp. 398-406.

J. Muilenburg. A Qohelet Scroll from Qumrân, *BASOR*, 135, 1954, pp. 20-28.—Fragments of another Isaiah Scroll, *BASOR*, 135, 1954, pp. 28-32.

* L. Rost. *Die Damaskusschrift neu bearbeitet*, Berlin, 1933.

C. Rabin. *The Zadokite Documents*, Oxford, 1954.

S. Schechter. *Documents of Jewish Sectaries*, Vol. I: *Fragments of a Zadokite Work*, Cambridge, 1910.

P. W. Skehan. A Fragment of the "Song of Moses" (Deut. 32) from Qumrân, *BASOR*, 136, 1954, pp. 12–15.

J. Starcky. Un contrat nabatéen sur papyrus, *R.B.*, 1954, pp. 161-181.

E. L. Sukenik. *Meghîllôth genûzôth* I, Jerusalem, 1948; II, 1950.—**Oṣar hammeghîllôth haggenûzôth*, Jerusalem, 1954.

R. de Vaux. La grotte des manuscrits hébreux, *R.B.*, 1949, pp. 586-609.—Quelques textes hébreux de Murabba'at, *R.B.*, 1953, pp. 268-275.—Exploration de la région de Qumrân, *R.B.*, 1953, pp. 555-557.

Y. Yadin. *Meghillath Milḥemeth benê ôr bibhenê ḥôshekh*, Jerusalem, 1955.

* S. Zeitlin. *The Zadokite Fragments*, Philadelphia, 1952.

II.   BOOKS ON THE DEAD SEA SCROLLS

(with indication as to whether they give complete or partial translations of the documents)

H. Bardtke. *Die Handschriftenfunde am Toten Meer*, Berlin, 1952 (2d ed. 1954). [HC, MD, H (partial), W (partial)].

M. Burrows. *The Dead Sea Scrolls*, New York, 1955. [HC, MD, DD, H (partial), W (partial)].

M. Delcor. *Essai sur le Midrash d'Habacuc*, Paris, 1951. [HC].

G. R. Driver. *The Hebrew Scrolls from the Neighbourhood of Jericho and the Dead Sea*, London, 1951.

A. Dupont-Sommer. *Aperçus préliminaires sur les manuscrits de la Mer Morte*, Paris, 1950. [HC, DD (partial), H (partial), W (partial)]. (English translation *The Dead Sea Scrolls*, Oxford, 1952.)—*Nouveaux aperçus sur les manuscrits de la Mer Morte*, Paris, 1953. [MD].—(English translation, *The Jewish Sect of Qumrân and the Essenes, New Studies on the Dead Sea Scrolls*, London, 1954.)

K. Elliger. *Studien zum Habakuk-Kommentar vom Toten Meer*, Tübingen, 1953. [HC].

A. M. Habermann. *'Edah we-'Eduth*, Jerusalem, 1951. [HC, MD].

P. Kahle. *Die hebräischen Handschriften aus der Höhle*, Stuttgart, 1951.

H. E. del Medico. *Deux manuscrits hébreux de la Mer Morte*, Paris, 1951. [HC, MD].

A. Michel. *Le Maître de Justice d'après les documents de la Mer Morte, la littérature apocryphe et rabbinique*, Avignon, 1954. [HC].

G. Molin. *Die Söhne des Lichtes. Zeit und Stellung der Hand-*

schriften vom Toten Meer, Vienna, 1954. [HC, MD, DD, H (partial), W (partial)].

H. H. Rowley. *The Zadokite Fragments and the Dead Sea Scrolls,* Oxford, 1952.

A. Vincent. *Les manuscrits hébreux du désert de Juda,* Paris, 1955. [HC, MD, DD, H (partial), W (partial), some texts of Murabba'at].

E. Wilson. *The Scrolls from the Dead Sea,* New York, 1955.

III.   FURTHER TRANSLATIONS

1.   The Habakkuk Commentary

W. H. Brownlee. The Jerusalem Habakkuk Scroll, *BASOR,* 112, 1948, pp. 8-18.—Further Light on Habakkuk, *ibid.,* 114, 1949, pp. 9-10. —Further Corrections of the Translation of the Habakkuk Scroll, *ibid.,* 116, 1949, pp. 14-16.

A. Dupont-Sommer. Le "Commentaire d'Habacuc" découvert près de la Mer Morte, *R.H.R.,* t. 137, 1950, pp. 129-176.

G. Lambert. Traduction de quelques "psaumes" de Qumrân et du "pésher" d'Habacuc *N.R.Th.,* 1952, pp. 284-297.

J. van der Ploeg. Les rouleaux de la Mer Morte, *Bi. Or.,* 1951, pp. 1-13.

2.   The Manual of Discipline

W. H. Brownlee. The Dead Sea Manual of Discipline, *BASOR Supplementary Studies* 10-12, New Haven, 1951.

G. Lambert. Le Manuel de discipline du désert de Juda, *N.T.Th.,* 1951, pp. 938-975.

J. T. Milik. Manuale disciplinae, *Verb. Dom.,* 1951, pp. 129-158.

J. van der Ploeg. Le "Manuel de discipline" des rouleaux de la Mer Morte, *Bi. Or.,* 1951, pp. 113-126.

3.   The Damascus Document

R. H. Charles. Fragments of a Zadokite Work, in *The Apocrypha and Pseudepigrapha,* t. II, Oxford, 1912, pp. 785-834.

J. M. Lagrange. La Secte juive de la Nouvelle Alliance, *R.B.,* 1912, pp. 212-240.

I. Lévi. Un écrit sadducéen antérieur à la destruction du Temple, *R.E.J.,* t. 61, 1911, pp. 161-205.

4.   The Hymns

J. V. Chamberlain. Another Qumrân Thanksgiving Psalm, *Journal of Near Eastern Studies,* 1955, pp. 32-41.

A. Dupont-Sommer. La mère du Messie et la mère de l'Aspic dans un hymne de Qumrân, *R.H.R.,* t. 147, 1955, pp. 174-188.

G. Lambert. *Art. cit.* (cf. III, 1).

J. T. Milik. Duo cantica ex volumine Hymnorum nuper invento ad Mare Mortuum, *Verb. Dom.*, 1950, pp. 362-371.

R. Tournay. Les anciens manuscrits hébreux récemment découverts, *R.B.*, 1949, pp. 204-233. Cf. *ibid.*, 1950, pp. 621-626.

M. Wallenstein. *Hymns from the Judean Scrolls*, Manchester, 1950.— A striking Hymn from the Dead Sea Scrolls, *Bulletin of the John Rylands Library*, 1955, pp. 241-265.—A Hymn from the Scrolls, *V.T.*, 1955, pp. 277-283.

5. The War Scroll

M. Delcor. La guerre des fils de lumière contre les fils de ténèbres ou le Manuel du parfait combattant, *N.R.Th.*, 1955, pp. 372-399.

A. Dupont-Sommer. "Règlement de la guerre des fils de lumière," traduction et notes, *R.H.R.*, t. 148, 1955, pp. 25-43.

J. van der Ploeg. La Règle de la Guerre. Traduction et notes, *V.T.*, 1955, pp. 373-420.

6. The Copper Scrolls

K. G. Kuhn. Les rouleaux de cuivre de Qumrân, *R.B.*, 1954, pp. 193-205.—Die Kupferrollen von Qumrân und ihr Inhalt, *Th.L.Z.*, 1954, cols. 303-304.

7. The Documents from Murabba'at and its neighborhood

S. Abramson, H. L. Ginsberg. On the Aramaic deed of sale of the third year of the second Jewish Revolt, *BASOR*, 136, 1954, pp. 17-19.

H. Bardtke. Bemerkungen zu den beiden Texten aus dem Bar-Kochba Aufstand, *Th.L.Z.*, 1954, cols. 295-304.

S. A. Birnbaum. Bar Kokhba and Akiba, *P.E.Q.*, 1954, pp. 23-32.— The Beth Mashku Document, *P.E.Q.*, 1955, pp. 21-33.

H. L. Ginsberg. Notes on the two published Letters to Jeshua ben Galgola, *BASOR*, 131, 1953, pp. 25-27.

O. H. Lehmann, S. M. Stern. A legal Certificate from Bar Kochba's days, *V.T.*, 1953, pp. 391-396.

R. Marcus. A Note on the Bar Kokeba Letter from Murabba'at, *Journal of Near Eastern Studies*, 1954, p. 51.

J. T. Milik. Note additionnelle sur le contrat juif de l'an 134 après J.-C., *R.B.*, 1955, pp. 253-254.

I. Rabinowitz. A Hebrew Letter of the Second Century from Beth Mashko, *BASOR*, 131, 1953, pp. 21-24.

J. J. Rabinowitz. The legal Document from Murabba'at, *Biblica*, 1954, pp. 198-206.—Note sur la lettre de Bar Kokheba, *R.B.*, 1954, pp. 191-192.—A Clue to the Nabatean Contract from the Dead Sea region, *BASOR*, 139, 1955, pp. 11-14.

A. Rubinstein. The appellation "Galileans" in Ben Kosebha's letter to Ben Galgola, *J.J.S.*, 1955, pp. 26-34.

I. Sonne. The newly discovered Bar Kokeba letters, *Proceedings of the American Academy for Jewish Research*, 1954, pp. 75-108.

J. L. Teicher. Documents of the Bar-Kochba Period, *J.J.S.*, 1953, pp. 132-134.—Are the Bar Kokhba Documents genuine? *J.J.S.*, 1954, pp. 39-40.

IV.   INTRODUCTIONS

1.   General Introductions

E. P. Arbez. Notes on the New Hebrew Mss., *Catholic Biblical Quarterly*, 1950, pp. 173-189.

D. Barthélemy. Notes en marge de publications récentes sur les manuscrits de Qumrân, *R.B.*, 1952, pp. 187-218.

W. Baumgartner. Der palästinische Handschriftenfund, *Theologische Rundschau*, 1949, pp. 329-346; 1951, pp. 97-154.

A. Bea. De antiquis manuscriptis hebraicis prope Mare Mortuum inventis, *Verb. Dom.*, 1950, pp. 354-361.

M. Burrows. The Contents and Significance of the Manuscripts, *B.A.*, 1948, pp. 57-61.

F. M. Cross. The newly discovered Scrolls in the Hebrew University Museum in Jerusalem, *B.A.*, 1949, pp. 36-46.—The Manuscripts of the Dead Sea Caves, *B.A.*, 1954, pp. 2-21.

O. Eissfeldt. Der gegenwärtige Stand der Erforschung der in Palästina neu gefundenen hebräischen Handschriften, *Th.L.Z.*, 1949, cols. 95-98; 228; 595-600; 1950, 145-152.

F. V. Filson. Some recent Study of the Dead Sea Scrolls, *B.A.*, 1950, pp. 96-100.

H. L. Ginsberg. The Hebrew University Scrolls from the Sectarian Cache, *BASOR*, 112, 1948, pp. 19-23.

R. Goossens. L'état actuel des recherches sur les manuscrits de la Mer Morte et sur la secte de la Nouvelle Alliance, *Nouvelle Clio*, 1949-1950, pp. 634-671.

G. Graystone. The Dead Sea Scrolls, *Scripture*, V, 1953, pp. 112-122; VI, 1953, pp. 17-21; 131-143.

P. Kahle. The Age of the Scrolls, *V.T.*, 1951, pp. 38-48.

G. Lambert. Les manuscrits découverts dans le désert de Juda, *N.R.Th.*, 1949, pp. 286-304; pp. 414-416; 1950, pp. 53-65; pp. 199-202; pp. 493-515.

J. T. Milik. Note sui manoscritti di 'Ain Fešḫa, *Biblica*, 1950, pp. 73-94; pp. 204-220.—Ex discussione de manuscriptis Maris Mortui, *Verb. Dom.*, 1951, pp. 362-365.—Elenchus textuum ex caverna Maris Mortui, *Verb. Dom.*, 1952, pp. 34-45; pp. 101-109.

S. Moscati. *I manoscritti ebraici del deserto di Giuda*, Rome, 1955.

F. Nötscher. Der Handschriftenfund am Toten Meer, *Palästinahefte*, 1950, pp. 7-22.

F. Perez Castro. Los manuscritos del Mar Muerto, *Sefarad*, 1951, pp. 115-153; 1952, pp. 167-197.

J. van der Ploeg. Les manuscrits du Désert de Juda, Études et découvertes récentes, *Bi. Or.*, 1954, pp. 145-160.

J. Reider. The Dead Sea Scrolls, *J.Q.R.*, t. 41, 1950, pp. 59-70.

B. J. Roberts. *The Jerusalem Scrolls*, Z.A.W., 1950, pp. 224-245.

A. Y. Samuel. The Purchase of the Jerusalem Scrolls, *B.A.*, 1949, pp. 26-31.

I. L. Seeligmann. The Epoch-making Discovery of Hebrew Scrolls in the Judaean Desert, *Bi. Or.*, 1949, pp. 1-8.

J. Starcky, J. Milik. L'actuel état du déchiffrement des manuscrits du désert de Juda et le plan de leur publication, *Comptes rendus de l'Académie des Inscriptions et Belles-Lettres*, 1954, pp. 403-409.

J. C. Trever. The Discovery of the Scrolls, *B.A.*, 1948, pp. 46-57.—Preliminary Observations on the Jerusalem Scrolls, BASOR, 111, 1948, pp. 3-16.

G. Vermès. Où en est la question des manuscrits de la Mer Morte? *C.S.*, 1953, pp. 63-76.

G. E. Wright. A Phenomenal Discovery, *B.A.*, 1948, pp. 21-23.

2. Polemics concerning the authenticity and the antiquity of the Scrolls

W. F. Albright. Are the 'Ain Feshkha Scrolls a Hoax?, *J.Q.R.*, t. 40, 1949, pp. 41-49.

M. Burrows. A Note on the recently discovered Manuscripts, *J.Q.R.*, pp. 51-56.—Concerning the Dead Sea Scrolls—A Reply to Professor Zeitlin, *J.Q.R.*, t. 42, 1951, pp. 105-132.

G. R. Driver. The Hebrew Manuscripts, *J.Q.R.*, t. 40, 1949, pp. 127-134.—New Hebrew Manuscripts, *J.Q.R.*, t. 40, 1950, pp. 359-372.—Once again the Judaean Scrolls, *J.Q.R.*, t. 44, 1953, pp. 1-20.

I. Sonne. Final Verdict on the Scrolls?, *J.B.L.*, 1951, pp. 37-44.

J. C. Trever. The "suppressed" Scroll of the Haftarot, *J.Q.R.*, t. 41, 1950, pp. 71-81.

T. Wechsler. The "Hidden Geniza" once more or Mr Trever versus Mr Trever, *J.Q.R.*, 1951, pp. 247-250.—The Origin of the so-called Dead Sea Scrolls, *J.Q.R.*, t. 43, 1952, pp. 121-139.

S. Zeitlin. A Commentary on the Book of Habakkuk. Important Discovery or Hoax? *J.Q.R.*, t. 39, 1949, pp. 235-247.—Scholarship and the Hoax of the Recent Discoveries, *J.Q.R.*, pp. 337-363.—The alleged Antiquity of the Scrolls, *J.Q.R.*, t. 40, 1949, pp. 57-75.—Where is the Scroll of the Haftarot? *J.Q.R.*, t. 40, 1950, pp. 291-296.—When were the Hebrew Scrolls "discovered," in 1947 or in 1907? *J.Q.R.*, t. 40, pp. 373-378.—The Hebrew Scrolls: once more and finally, *J.Q.R.*, t. 41, 1950, pp. 1-58.—The Hebrew Scrolls: a Challenge to Scholarship, *J.Q.R.*, t. 41, 1951, pp. 251-275.—The Hebrew Scrolls and the Status of Biblical Scholarship, *J.Q.R.*, t. 42, 1951, pp. 133-192.—Bar Kokba and Bar Kozeba, *J.Q.R.*,

t. 43, 1952, pp. 77-82.—The Hebron Pogrom and the Hebrew Scrolls, *J.Q.R.*, t. 43, 1952, pp. 140-152.—The Fiction of the recent Discoveries near the Dead Sea, *J.Q.R.*, t. 44, 1953, pp. 85-115.—The Mishna in Yadaim IV.8, and "The Sectarians," *J.Q.R.*, t. 44, 1953, pp. 297-300.—The Antiquity of the Hebrew Scrolls and the Piltdown Hoax: A Parallel, *J.Q.R.*, t. 45, 1954, pp. 1-29.—The Essenes and the Messianic Expectations, *J.Q.R.*, t. 45, 1954, pp. 83-119.—A Note on the Fiction of the "Bar Kokba" Letter, *J.Q.R.*, t. 45, 1954, pp. 174-180.—The Propaganda of the Hebrew Scrolls and the Falsification of History, *J.Q.R.*, t. 46, 1955, pp. 1-39; pp. 116-180.

V. ARCHEOLOGY AND PALEOGRAPHY

W. F. Albright. On the Date of the Scrolls from 'Ain Feshka and the Nash Papyrus, *BASOR*, 115, 1949, pp. 10-19.—Comments on Dr. Lacheman's Reply and the Scrolls, *BASOR*, 116, 1949, pp. 17-18.

J. M. Allegro. Some archaeological sites and the Old Testament: Qumrân, *The Expository Times*, 1955, pp. 259-262.

S. A. Birnbaum. The Date of the Isaiah Scroll, *BASOR*, 113, 1949, pp. 33-35.—The Dates of the Cave Scrolls, *BASOR*, 115, 1949, pp. 20-22.—The Leviticus Fragments from the Cave, *BASOR*, 118, 1950, pp. 20–27.—The Qumrân (Dead Sea) Scrolls and Paleography, *BASOR Supplementary Studies* 13-14, New Haven, 1952. —The Date of the Covenant Scroll, *P.E.Q.*, 1949, pp. 140-147.—The Date of the Hymns Scroll, *P.E.Q.*, 1952, pp. 94-103.—An unknown Aramaic Cursive, *P.E.Q.*, 1953, pp. 23-41.—The Date of the Habakkuk Cave Scroll, *J.B.L.*, 1949, pp. 161-168.—Notes on the Internal and Archaeological Evidence concerning the Cave Scrolls, *J.B.L.*, 1951, pp. 227-232.—How old are the Cave Manuscripts? A Palaeographical Discussion, *V.T.*, 1951, pp. 91-109.

M. Burrows. The Dating of the Dead Sea Scrolls, *BASOR*, 122, 1951, pp. 4-6.—*Waw* and *Yodh* in the Isaiah Dead Scroll (DSIa), *BASOR*, 124, 1951, pp. 18-20.

D. Collier. Radiocarbon Method for Dating, *B.A.*, 1951, pp. 25-28.

B. Couroyer. A propos des dépôts de manuscrits dans des jarres, *R.B.*, 1955, pp. 76-81.

D. Diringer. The Early Hebrew Book-Hand, *P.E.Q.*, 1950, pp. 16-24. —Early Hebrew Writing, *B.A.*, 1950, pp. 74-95.

G. L. Harding. The Dead Sea Scrolls. *P.E.Q.*, 1949, pp. 112-116.— Khirbet Qumran and Wady Murabba'at, *P.E.Q.*, 1952, pp. 104-109.

P. Kahle. Zu dem Handschriftenfunde aus der Höhle, *Th.L.Z.*, 1951, cols. 161-166.

B. Kanael. Notes on the Ancient Hebrew Script in the Judaean Scrolls. *Bulletin of the Israel Exploration Society*, XVI, 1951, pp. 46-52.

J. L. Kelso. The Archeology of Qumran, *J.B.L.*, 1955, pp. 141-146.

E. R. Lacheman. A Matter of Method in Hebrew Palaeography,

J.Q.R., t. 40, 1949, pp. 15-39.—Reply to the Editor, *BASOR*, 116, 1949, pp. 16-17. Hebrew Palaeography again, *J.Q.R.*, t. 44, 1953, pp. 116-122.

O. H. Lehmann. Materials concerning the Dating of the Dead Sea Scrolls, I: Habakkuk, *P.E.Q.*, 1951, pp. 32-54.

J. T. Milik. Le giarre dei manoscritti della grotta del Mar Morto e dell 'Egitto tolemaico, *Biblica*, 1950, pp. 504-508.

R. North. Qumrân and its Archaeology, *Catholic Biblical Quarterly*, 1954, pp. 426-437.

A. Parrot. Les Manuscrits de la Mer Morte: le point de vue archéologique, *R.H.P.R.*, 1955, pp. 61-67.

Y. Ratzaby. Remarks concerning the distinction between *Waw* and *Yodh* in the Habakkuk Scroll, *J.Q.R.*, t. 41, 1950, pp. 155-157.

W. L. Reed. The Qumrân Caves Expedition of March 1952, *BASOR*, 135, 1954, pp. 8-13.

O. R. Sellers. Excavations of the "Manuscript" Cave at 'Ain Feshkha, *BASOR*, 114, 1949, pp. 5-9.—Radiocarbon Dating of Cloth from the 'Ain Feshkha Cave, *BASOR*, 123, 1951, pp. 24-26.

R. de Vaux. La cachette des manuscrits hébreux, *R.B.*, 1949, pp. 234-236. La grotte des manuscrits hébreux, *R.B.*, 1949, pp. 586-609.—Fouille au Khirbet Qumrân, *R.B.*, 1953, pp. 83-106.—Les grottes de Murabba'at et leurs documents, *R.B.*, 1953, pp. 245-267.—Explorations de la région de Qumrân, *R.B.*, 1953, pp. 540-561.—Fouilles au Khirbet Qumrân. Rapport préliminaire sur la deuxième campagne, *R.B.*, 1954, pp. 206-236.—Chronique archéologique, *R.B.*, 1954, pp. 567-568.

S. Yeivin. The Date and Attribution of the Leviticus Fragments from the Cache in the Judaean Desert, *BASOR*, 118, 1950, pp. 28-30.

VI.   PHILOLOGY AND TEXTUAL CRITICISM

W. F. Albright. New Light on Early Recensions of the Hebrew Bible, *BASOR*, 139, 1955, pp. 27-33.

W. H. Brownlee. Emendations of the Dead Sea Manual of Discipline and some Notes concerning the Habakkuk Midrash, *J.Q.R.*, t. 45, 1954, pp. 141-158; pp. 198-217.

M. Burrows. Orthography, Morphology and Syntax of the Saint Mark's Isaiah Manuscript, *J.B.L.*, 1949, pp. 195-214.

J. Carmignac. Précisions apportées au vocabulaire de l'hébreu biblique par la Guerre des fils de lumière contre les fils de ténèbres, *V.T.*, 1955, pp. 345-365.

M. H. Gottstein. Bible Quotations in the Sectarian Dead Sea Scrolls, *V.T.*, 1953, pp. 79-82.—A DSS Biblical Variant in a Medieval Treatise, *V.T.*, 1953, pp. 187-188.

P. Kahle. Zur Aussprache des Hebräischen bei den Samaritanern, *Festschrift A. Bertholet*, Tübingen, 1950, pp. 281-286.

R. Marcus. Textual Notes on the Dead Sea Manual of Discipline, *Journal of Near Eastern Studies*, 1952, pp. 205-211.

H. Michaud. A propos du nom de Qumrân, *R.H.P.R.*, 1955, pp. 68-74.

R. Meyer. Zur Sprache von 'Ain Feschcha, *Th.L.Z.*, 1950, cols. 721-726.

C. Rabin. The Dead Sea Scrolls and the History of the Old Testament Text, *Journal of Theological Studies*, 1955, pp. 174-182.

I. Rabinowitz. The Second and Third Columns of the Habakkuk Interpretation Scroll, *J.B.L.*, 1950, pp. 31-49.

E. Sjöberg. The Restoration of Col. II of the Habakkuk Commentary of the Dead Sea Scrolls, *Studia Theologica*, IV, 1952, pp. 120-128.

S. M. Stern. Notes on the new Manuscripts Find, *J.B.L.*, 1950, pp. 19-30.

S. Talmon. Notes on the Habakkuk Scroll, *V.T.*, 1951, pp. 33-37.—The Sectarian *Yḥd*—A Biblical Noun, *V.T.*, 1953, pp. 133-140.

M. Wallenstein. Some lexical Material on the Judean Scrolls, *V.T.*, 1954, pp. 211-214.

P. Wernberg-Møller. Observations on the interchange of ' and ḥ in the Manual of Discipline, (DSD), *V.T.*, 1953, pp. 104-107.—Notes on the Manual of Discipline, (DSD) I, 18; II, 9; III, 1-4, 9; VII, 10-12 and XI, 21-22, *V.T.*, 1953, pp. 195-202.—SDQ, ṢDYQ, and SDWQ in the Zadokite Fragments (CDC), the Manual of Discipline (DSD) and the Habakkuk Commentary, *V.T.*, 1953, pp. 310-315.—Some Reflections on the Biblical Material in the Manual of Discipline, *Studia Theologica*, IX, 1955, pp. 40-66.

VII.   HISTORICAL AND LITERARY STUDIES

M. Avi-Yonah. The "War of the Sons of Light and the Sons of Darkness" and Maccabaean Warfare, *Israel Exploration Journal*, 1952, pp. 1-5.

W. H. Brownlee. A Comparison of the Covenanters of the Dead Sea Scrolls with pre-Christian Jewish Sects, *B.A.*, 1950, pp. 50-72.—Biblical Interpretation among the Sectaries of the Dead Sea Scrolls, *B.A.*, 1951, pp. 54-76.—Light on the Manual of Discipline (DSD) from the Book of Jubilees, *BASOR*, 123, 1951, pp. 30-32.—The Historical Allusions of the Dead Sea Habakkuk Midrash, *BASOR*, 126, 1952, pp. 10-20.

M. Burrows. The Discipline Manual of the Judaean Covenanters, *Oudtestamentische Studiën*, VIII, 1950, pp. 156-192.—The Meaning of 'ŠR 'MR in DSH, *V.T.*, 1952, pp. 255-260.

J. Carmignac. Les Kittim dans la "Guerre des fils de lumière contre les fils de ténèbres," *N.R.Th.*, 1955, pp. 737-748.

E. Cavaignac. Quelques réflexions sur les documents d' 'Ain Fešḥa, *R.H.R.*, t. 138, 1950, pp. 152-159.

M. B. Dagut. The Habakkuk Scroll and Pompey's Capture of Jerusalem, *Biblica*, 1951, pp. 542-548.

M. Delcor. Le Midrash d'Habacuc, *R.B.*, 1951, pp. 521-549.—Où en est le problème du Midrash d'Habacuc? *R.H.R.*, t. 142, 1952, pp. 129-146.—Contribution à l'étude de la législation des sectaires de Damas et de Qumrân, *R.B.*, 1954, pp. 533-553; 1955, pp. 60-75.

C. Detaye. Le cadre historique du midrash d'Habacuc, *E.Th.L.*, 1954, pp. 323-343.

A. M. Dubarle. Une source du livre de la Sagesse?, *Revue des Sciences Philosophiques et Théologiques*, 1953, pp. 425-443.

A. Dupont-Sommer. *Observations sur le Commentaire d'Habacuc découvert près de la Mer Morte*, Paris, 1950.—*Observations sur le Manuel de discipline découvert près de la Mer Morte*, Paris, 1951. —Le Maître de Justice fut-il mis à mort? *V.T.*, 1951, pp. 200-215. —Contribution à l'exégèse du Manuel de discipline X, 1-8, *V.T.*, 1952, pp. 229-243.—La sainteté du signe "noun" dans le Manuel de discipline, *Bulletin de la Classe de Lettres de l'Académie Royale de Belgique*, 1952, pp. 184-193.—L'instruction sur les deux esprits dans le Manuel de discipline, *R.H.R.*, t. 142, 1952, pp. 5-35. —Le problème des influences étrangères sur la secte juive de Qumrân, *R.H.P.R.*, 1955, pp. 75-94.—Quelques remarques sur le "Commentaire d'Habacuc" à propos d'un livre récent, *V.T.*, 1955, pp. 113-129.—"Le chef des rois de Yâwân" dans l'Écrit de Damas, *Semitica*, 1955, pp. 41-57.

J. Février. La tactique hellénistique dans un texte de 'Ayin Fashkha, *Semitica*, 1950, pp. 53-59.

D. Flusser. Hassepher haḥisônî " 'Aliyyath Yeša'yahû" wehakkath šel Yam hammelaḥ, *Yedî'ôtph haḥebhrah laḥaqîratph Ereṣ Yiśra'el*, 1952, pp. 28-46.

D. N. Freedman. The "House of Absalom" in the Habakkuk Scroll, *BASOR*, 114, 1949, pp. 11-12.

C. T. Fritsch. Herod the Great and the Qumrân Community, *J.B.L.*, 1955, pp. 173-181.

R. Goossens. Les éléments messianiques des traditions sur Onias le Juste, chez Josèphe et dans le Talmud, *Bulletin de la Classe de Lettres de l'Académie Royale de Belgique*, 1950, pp. 440-469.— Onias le Juste, Messie de la Nouvelle Alliance, *Nouvelle Clio*, 1950, pp. 336-353.—Les Kittim du Commentaire d'Habacuc, *ibid.*, 1952, pp. 137-170.—L'énigme du signe "*nun*" dans le Manuel de Discipline, *ibid.*, 1954, pp. 5-39.

M. H. Gottstein. Anti-Essene traits in the Dead Sea Scrolls, *V.T.*, 1954, pp. 141-147.

H. Grégoire. Les gens de la caverne, les Qaraïtes et les Khazars, *Le Flambeau*, 1952, pp. 477-485.

I. M. Grintz. Anšê Hayyaḥad—Issiyîn—Beth (')Sin *Sinai*, 1952, pp. 11-43.

A. M. Habermann. 'Iyyûnîm bimegîllôth midbar Yehûdah, *Sinai*, 1953, pp. 141-167.

A. M. Honeyman. Notes on a Teacher and a Book, *J.J.S.*, 1953, pp. 131-132.

A. Jaubert. Le calendrier des Jubilés et de la secte de Qumrân. Ses origines bibliques, *V.T.*, 1953, pp. 250-264.

P. Kahle. Die Gemeinde des Neuen Bundes und die hebräischen Handschriften aus der Höhle, *Th.L.Z.*, 1952, cols. 401-412.—The Karaites and the Manuscripts from the Cave, *V.T.*, 1953, pp. 82-84. —Die im August 1952 entdeckte Lederrolle mit dem griechischen Text der kleinen Propheten und das Problem der Septuaginta, *Th.L.Z.*, 1954, cols. 81-94.

G. Lambert. Le Manuel de discipline de la grotte de Qumrân, *N.R.Th.*, 1951, pp. 938-956.—Le Maître de justice et la Communauté de l'Alliance, *N.R.Th.*, 1952, pp. 259-283.

S. Lieberman. Light on the Cave Scrolls from Rabbinic Sources, *Proceedings of the American Academy for Jewish Research*, 1951, pp. 395-404.—The Discipline in the so-called Dead Sea Manual of Discipline, *J.B.L.*, 1952, pp. 199-206.

R. Marcus. Philo, Josephus and the Dead Sea "Yaḥad," *J.B.L.*, 1952, pp. 207-209.

R. J. North. The Qumran "Sadducees," *Catholic Biblical Quarterly*, 1955, pp. 164-188.—The Damascus of Qumrân Geography, *P.E.Q.*, 1955, pp. 34-48.

B. Otzen. Die neugefundenen hebräischen Sektenschriften und die Testamente der zwölf Patriarchen, *Studia Theologica*, VII, 1953, pp. 125-157.

L. Parisius. Studie zur Form des 1. Abschnitts des DSD, *Z.A.W.*, 1955, pp. 103-106.

C. Rabin. The "Teacher of Righteousness" in the "Testaments of Twelve Patriarchs," *J.J.S.*, 1952, pp. 127-128.—Notes on the Habakkuk Scroll and the Zadokite Documents, *V.T.*, 1955, pp. 148-162.

C. Rabin, J. L. Teicher. On a puzzling passage in the Damascus Fragments., *J.J.S.*, 1955, pp. 53-55; p. 111.

I. Rabinowitz. The Authorship, Audience, and Date of the de Vaux Fragment of an unknown Work, *J.B.L.*, 1952, pp. 19-32.—Sequence and Dates of the extra-Biblical Dead Sea Scroll Texts and "Damascus" Fragments, *V.T.*, 1953, pp. 175-185.—A Reconsideration of "Damascus" and "390 Years" in the "Damascus" ("Zadokite") Fragments, *J.B.L.*, 1954, pp. 11-35.

B. Reicke. Die Taʿamire-Schriften und die Damaskus-Fragmente, *Studia Theologica*, 1949-1950, pp. 45-70.

B. J. Roberts. Some Observations on the Damascus Document and the Dead Sea Scrolls, *Bulletin of the John Rylands Library*, 1952, pp. 366-387.—The Dead Sea Scrolls and the Old Testament Scriptures, *ibid.*, 1953, pp. 75-96.

L. Rost. Die Sektenrolle, *Th.L.Z.*, 1950, cols. 341-344.—Bemerkungen zum neuen Habakkuktext, *Th.L.Z.*, 1950, cols. 477-482.—Der "Lehrer der Einung" und der "Lehrer der Gerechtigkeit," *Th.L.Z.*, 1953, cols. 143-148.—Zum "Buch der Kriege der Söhne des Lichts gegen die Söhne der Finsternis," *Th.L.Z.*, 1955, cols. 205-208.

H. H. Rowley. The Internal Dating of the Dead Sea Scrolls, *E.Th.L.*,

1952, pp. 257-276.—The Covenanters of Damascus and the Dead Sea Scrolls, *Bulletin of the John Rylands Library*, 1952, pp. 111-154.—The Historical Background of the Dead Sea Scrolls, *The Expository Times*, 1952, pp. 378-384.

A. Rubinstein. Urban Halakhah and Camp Rules in the "Cairo Fragments of a Damascene Covenant," *Sefarad*, 1952, pp. 283-296.

H. J. Schoeps. Handelt es sich wirklich um ebionitische Dokumente? *Zeitschrift für Religions- und Geistesgeschichte*, 1951, pp. 322-336.—Das gnostische Judentum in den Dead Sea Scrolls, *ibid.*, 1954, pp. 276-279.

K. Schubert. Die jüdischen und judenchristlichen Sekten im Lichte des Handschriftenfundes von 'En Fešcha, *Zeitschrift für katholische Theologie*, 1952, pp. 1-62.—Bemerkungen zum Verständnis einiger Termini in den Handschriften von 'En Fešḥa und im Damaskusdokument, *Th.L.Z.*, 1952, cols. 329-336.

M. H. Segal. The Habakkuk "Commentary" and the Damascus Fragments, *J.B.L.*, 1951, pp. 131-147.

S. Segert. Zur Habakuk-Rolle aus dem Funde vom Toten Meer, *Archiv Orientální*, 1953, pp. 218-239; 1954, pp. 99-113; pp. 444-459; 1955, pp. 178-183.

O. R. Sellers. A possible Old Testament reference to the Teacher of Righteousness, *Israel Exploration Journal*, 1955, pp. 93-95.

P. W. Skehan. Exodus in the Samaritan Recension from Qumrân, *J.B.L.*, 1955, pp. 182-187.

I. Sonne. A Hymn against Heretics in the newly discovered Scrolls, *Hebrew Union College Annual*, 1950-1951, pp. 275-313.

S. Talmon. Yom hakkippurim in the Habakkuk Scroll, *Biblica*, 1951, pp. 549-563.

J. L. Teicher. The Dead Sea Scrolls—Documents of the Jewish-Christian Sect of Ebionites, *J.J.S.*, 1951, pp. 67-99.—The Damascus Fragments and the Origin of the Jewish-Christian Sect, *J.J.S.*, 1951, pp. 115-143.—Jesus in the Habakkuk Scroll, *J.J.S.*, 1952, pp. 53-55.—The Habakkuk Scroll, *J.J.S.*, 1954, pp. 47-59.—Priests and Sacrifices in the Dead Sea Scrolls, *J.J.S.*, 1954, pp. 93-99.—Puzzling passages in the Damascus Fragments, *J.J.S.*, 1954, pp. 139-147.

J. Trinquet. Les liens "sadocites" de l'écrit de Damas, des manuscrits de la Mer Morte et de l'Ecclésiastique, *V.T.*, 1951, pp. 287-292.

R. de Vaux. A propos des manuscrits de la Mer Morte, *R.B.*, 1950, pp. 417-429.

G. Vermès. La Communauté de la Nouvelle Alliance d'après ses écrits récemment découverts, *E.Th.L.*, 1951, pp. 70-80.—A propos des "Aperçus préliminaires sur les manuscrits de la Mer Morte" de M. A. Dupont-Sommer, *C.S.*, 1951, pp. 58-69.—Le cadre historique des manuscrits de la Mer Morte, *R.Sc.R.*, 1953, pp. 5-29; pp. 203-230.—A propos des commentaires bibliques découverts à Qumrân, *R.H.P.R.*, 1954, pp. 95-103.

P. R. Weis. The Date of the Habakkuk Scroll, *J.Q.R.*, t. 41, 1950, pp. 125-154.

N. Wieder. The Habakkuk Scroll and the Targum, *J.J.S.*, 1953, pp. 14-18.—The "Law-Interpreter" of the Sect of the Dead Sea Scrolls: the second Moses, *J.J.S.*, 1953, pp. 158-175.—The term *QS* in the Dead Sea Scrolls and in Hebrew Liturgical Poetry, *J.J.S.*, 1954, pp. 22-31.

E. Wiesenberg. Chronological Data in the Zadokite Fragments, *V.T.*, 1955, pp. 284-308.

Y. Yadin. A Note on DSD IV 20, *J.B.L.*, 1955, pp. 40-43.

VIII.   DOCTRINAL PROBLEMS

J. P. Audet. Affinités littéraires et doctrinales du "Manuel de discipline," *R.B.*, 1952, pp. 219-238; 1953, pp. 41-82.

F. Baumgärtel. Zur Liturgie in der "Sektenrolle" vom Toten Meer, *Z.A.W.*, 1954, pp. 263-265.

J. M. Baumgarten. Sacrifice and Worship among the Jewish Sectarians of the Dead Sea (Qumrân) Scrolls, *Harvard Theological Review*, 1953, pp. 141-159.

M. Black. Theological Conceptions in the Dead Sea Scrolls, *Svensk Exegetisk Årsbok*, 1953-1954, pp. 72-97.

F. M. Braun. L'arrière-fond judaïque du quatrième Evangile et la communauté de l'Alliance, *R.B.*, 1955, pp. 5-44.

W. H. Brownlee. The Servant of the Lord in the Qumrân Scrolls, *BASOR*, 132, 1953, pp. 8-15; 135, 1954, pp. 33-38.

M. Burrows. The Messiahs of Aaron and Israel, *Anglican Theological Review*, 1952, pp. 203-206.

J. Coppens. La secte de Qumrân et son attente eschatologique, *Nouvelle Clio*, 1953, pp. 5-9.—Les documents du désert de Juda et les origines chrétiennes, *Cahiers du Libre Examen*, 1953, pp. 23-39.

O. Cullmann. Die neuentdeckten Qumrântexte und das Judenchristentum der Pseudoklementinen, *Beihefte zur Z.N.W. 21*, 1954, pp. 35-51.

J. Daniélou. Une source de la spiritualité chrétienne dans les manuscrits de la Mer Morte: la doctrine des deux esprits, *Dieu Vivant*, 25, 1953, pp. 127-136.—La communauté de Qumrân et l'organisation de l'Eglise ancienne, *R.H.P.R.*, 1955, pp. 104-116.

W. D. Davies. "Knowledge" in the Dead Sea Scrolls and Matthew 11, 25-30, *Harvard Theological Review*, 1953, pp. 113-139.

M. Delcor. L'eschatologie des documents de Khirbet Qumrân, *Revue des Sciences Religieuses*, 1952, pp. 363-386.—Le sacerdoce, les lieux de culte, les rites et les fêtes dans les documents de Khirbet Qumrân, *R.H.R.*, t. 154, 1953, pp. 5-41.—L'immortalité de l'âme dans le Livre de la Sagesse et dans les documents de Qumrân, *N.R.Th.*, 1955, pp. 614-630.

B. Gärtner. The Habakkuk Commentary (DSH) and the Gospel of Matthew, *Studia Theologica*, VIII, 1955, pp. 1-24.

R. Goossens. La secte juive de la Nouvelle Alliance et les origines chrétiennes, *Revue de l'Université de Bruxelles*, 1951, pp. 399-435.

W. Grossouw. The Dead Sea Scrolls and the New Testament, *Studia Catholica*, 1951, pp. 289-299; 1952, pp. 1-8.

S. A. Johnson. The Dead Sea Manual of Discipline and the Jerusalem Church of Acts, *Z.A.W.*, 1954, pp. 106-120.

K. G. Kuhn. Zur Bedeutung der neuen palästinischen Handschriftenfunde für die neutestamentliche Wissenschaft, *Th.L.Z.*, 1950, cols. 81-86.—Die in Palästina gefundenen hebräischen Texte und das Neue Testament, *Zeitschrift für Theologie und Kirche*, 1950, pp. 192-211.—Über den ursprünglichen Sinn des Abendmahls und sein Verhältnis zu den Gemeinschaftmahlen der Sektenschrift, *Evangelische Theologie*, 1951, pp. 508-527.—Πειρασμός—ἁμαρτία—σάρξ im Neuen Testament und die damit zusammenhängenden Vorstellungen, *Zeitschrift für Theologie und Kirche*, 1952, pp. 200-222.—Die Sektenschrift und die iranische Religion, *ibid.*, 1952, pp. 296-316.—Die beiden Messias Aarons und Israels, *New Testament Studies*, 1955, pp. 168-179.

A. Metzinger. Die Handschriftenfunde am Toten Meer und das Neue Testament, *Biblica*, 1955, pp. 457-481.

H. Michaud. Un mythe zervanite dans un des manuscrits de Qumrân, *V.T.*, 1955, pp. 137-147.

G. Molin. Die Rollen von 'En Feša und ihre Stellung in der jüdischen Religionsgeschichte, *Judaïca*, 1951, pp. 161-213.—Qumrân—Apokalyptik—Essenismus: eine Unterströmung im sogenannten Spätjudentum, *Saeculum*, 1955, pp. 244-281.

L. Mowry. The Dead Sea Scrolls and the Gospel of John, *B.A.*, 1954, pp. 78-97.

F. Nötscher. Jüdische Mönchsgemeinde und Ursprung des Christentums nach dem jüngst am Toten Meer aufgefundenen hebräischen Handschriften, *Bibel und Kirche*, 1952, pp. 21-38.

J. van der Ploeg. L'immortalité de l'homme d'après les textes de la Mer Morte, *V.T.*, 1952, pp. 171-175.

B. Reicke. Traces of Gnosticism in the Dead Sea Scrolls?, *New Testament Studies*, 1954, pp. 137-141.

J. Schmitt. Sacerdoce judaïque et hiérarchie ecclésiale dans les premières communautés palestiniennes, *Revue des Sciences Religieuses*, 1955, pp. 250-261.—Les écrits du Nouveau Testament et les textes de Qumrân. Bilan de cinq années de recherches, *ibid.*, 1955, pp. 381-401.

K. Schubert. Zwei Messiasse aus dem Regelbuch von Chirbet Qumran, *Judaïca*, 1955, pp. 216-235.

L. H. Silberman. The two "Messiahs" of the Manual of Discipline, *V.T.*, 1955, pp. 77-82.

J. L. Teicher. The Teaching of the pre-Pauline Church in the Dead Sea Scrolls, *J.J.S.*, 1952, pp. 111-118; pp. 139-150; 1953, pp. 1-13; pp. 49-58; pp. 93-103; pp. 139-153. Jesus' sayings in the Dead Sea

Scrolls, *J.J.S.*, 1954, p. 38.—The Christian Interpretation of the Sign X in the Isaiah Scroll, *V.T.*, 1955, pp. 189-198.

G. Vermès. Le "Commentaire d'Habacuc" et le Nouveau Testament, *C.S.*, 1951, pp. 337-349.—La figure de Moïse au tournant des deux Testaments, *Moïse, l'Homme de l'Alliance, C.S.*, Nos. 2-3-4, 1954, pp. 75-84.—Quelques traditions de la communauté de Qumrân, *C.S.*, 1955, pp. 25-58.

E. Vogt. Antiquum Kalendarium Sacerdotale, *Biblica*, 1955, pp. 403-413.

N. Wieder. The Doctrine of the two Messiahs among the Karaites, *J.J.S.*, 1955, pp. 14-25.

LIST OF ABBREVIATIONS

A.J.	Flavius Josèphe : *Antiquitates Judaicae*
B.A.	*Biblical Archaeologist*
B.A.S.O.R.	Bulletin of the American Schools of Oriental Research
B.J.	Flavius Josèphe : *Bellum Judaicum*
Bibl.	*Biblica*
Bi. Or.	*Bibliotheca Orientalis*
C.S.	*Cahiers Sioniens*
E. Th.L.	*Ephemerides Theologicae Lovanienses*
J.B.L.	*Journal of Biblical Literature*
J.J.S.	*Journal of Jewish Studies*
J.Q.R.	*Jewish Quarterly Review*
N.R.Th.	*Nouvelle Revue Théologique*
P.E.Q.	*Palestine Exploration Quarterly*
Q.o.p.l.s.	Philon : *Quod omnis probus liber sit*
R.B.	*Revue Biblique*
R.É.J.	*Revue des Études Juives*
R.H.R.	*Revue de l'Histoire des Religions*
R.Sc.R.	*Recherches de Science Religieuse*
T.M.	*Texte massorétique*
Th.L.Z.	*Theologische Literaturzeitung*
Verb. Dom.	*Verbum Domini*
V.T.	*Vetus Testamentum*
Z.A.W.	*Zeitschrift für die alttestamentliche Wissenschaft*